T0140597

Engineering the Transformation of the Enterprise

Stephan Aier • Peter Rohner • Joachim Schelp
Editors

Engineering the Transformation of the Enterprise

A Design Science Research Perspective

 Springer

Editors
Stephan Aier
Universität St. Gallen
St. Gallen, Switzerland

Peter Rohner
Universität St. Gallen
St. Gallen, Switzerland

Joachim Schelp
Universität St. Gallen
St. Gallen, Switzerland

ISBN 978-3-030-84657-2   ISBN 978-3-030-84655-8   (eBook)
https://doi.org/10.1007/978-3-030-84655-8

© The Editor(s) (if applicable) and The Author(s), under exclusive license to Springer Nature Switzerland AG 2021
This work is subject to copyright. All rights are solely and exclusively licensed by the Publisher, whether the whole or part of the material is concerned, specifically the rights of translation, reprinting, reuse of illustrations, recitation, broadcasting, reproduction on microfilms or in any other physical way, and transmission or information storage and retrieval, electronic adaptation, computer software, or by similar or dissimilar methodology now known or hereafter developed.
The use of general descriptive names, registered names, trademarks, service marks, etc. in this publication does not imply, even in the absence of a specific statement, that such names are exempt from the relevant protective laws and regulations and therefore free for general use.
The publisher, the authors, and the editors are safe to assume that the advice and information in this book are believed to be true and accurate at the date of publication. Neither the publisher nor the authors or the editors give a warranty, expressed or implied, with respect to the material contained herein or for any errors or omissions that may have been made. The publisher remains neutral with regard to jurisdictional claims in published maps and institutional affiliations.

This Springer imprint is published by the registered company Springer Nature Switzerland AG.
The registered company address is: Gewerbestrasse 11, 6330 Cham, Switzerland

Preface

Honoring Robert Winter

Robert Winter turned 60 in November 2020. To appreciate his work and to honor him as an esteemed personality, a broad range of professional colleagues and longtime companions both from the Institute of Information Management at the University of St. Gallen and from the international research community dedicated articles to this Festschrift.

The topics in this Festschrift reflect Robert's broad range of research interests: from business engineering and its application in corporate and business networking contexts to design science research as well as applied topics, where those research methods have been employed for modeling, data warehousing, IS management, enterprise architecture management, management of large and complex projects, and enterprise transformation.

At the University of St. Gallen's Institute of Information Management, the relevance of the research work for practice was in the foreground early on. Business engineering developed as a body of corresponding research methods. With the ongoing discussion about rigor and relevance of research, business engineering was also intensively scrutinized by Robert. At the same time, the discussion of design science research (DSR), which was about to be established in the international information systems (IS) research community, was taken up. In numerous projects with practitioners, the applied methods were refined, and contributions for and with practitioners were developed. The contributions of the Festschrift reflect Robert's ambition to uncompromisingly conduct high-class research that fuels the research community on the one hand and to pragmatically contribute to practice on the other hand. He has mentored a large number of young researchers, as evidenced by the many supervised habilitations and dissertations. At the same time, Robert has made his results available to established large organizations within the framework of project collaborations and competence centers, thus providing many valuable impulses for practice.

The Organization of the Festschrift

We organized the Festschrift into three parts. The first part is rooted in the perspective, where Robert's interest in research methodology took fire: business engineering, the methodology developed in St. Gallen with a strong focus on research being applied in corporate contexts. The second part dives deeper into design science research and spans from reflections on the practice of design science research, perspectives on design science research methodologies, up to considerations to teach design science research methodology. The third part finally comprises applications of design science research and related research methodologies to practical problems and future research topics.

Part 1: Business Engineering and Beyond

The opening chapters have been initiated by Robert's long-term colleagues at the Institute of Information Management: Walter Brenner and Hubert Österle.

Of course, the part on Business Engineering and Beyond begins with a contribution from Hubert Oesterle, who started the business engineering perspective in St. Gallen. And consequently, he develops a new perspective, live engineering, emanating from the business engineering perspective: *From business engineering to life engineering*. He focuses on the individual perspective of the quality of life in contrast to the established corporate value perspective established in business engineering.

In the second chapter, Walter Brenner discusses together with Benjamin van Giffen and Jana Koehler the *Management of artificial intelligence* and focuses on the feasibility, desirability, and viability of artificial intelligence.

Mateusz Dolata and Gerhard Schwabe extend the discussion on artificial intelligence in their chapter by asking *How fair is IS research?* They zoom into algorithmic fairness, corresponding discrimination risks in IS research, and resulting research opportunities for IS researchers.

Susanne Leist, Dimitris Karagiannis, Florian Johannsen, and Hans-Gert Penzel bring the business engineering perpective back and reflect on the role of metamodeling in their contribution *From business engineering to digital engineering – The role of metamodeling in digital transformation*.

Ulrike Baumöl and Reinhard Jung focus again by zooming into modeling with their contribution *Potentials and limits of modeling using the example of an artificial Real-World Model*.

Finally, Henderik A. Proper completes the first part with his contribution *On model-based coordination of change in organizations*, where he reflects on modeling and the resulting need to leave the "boxes-and-lines" metaphor being used in engineering and sets the stage for part two.

Part 2: Design Science Research

Shirley Gregor opens the sequence of contributions discussing design science research. In *Reflections on the practice of design science in information systems*, she shows existing issues in DSR and discusses them from both contributor and reviewer points of view.

Jan vom Brocke, Manuel Weber, and Thomas Grisold reflect the DSR contributions to the solution of real-world problems in *Design science research of high practical relevance – Dancing through Space and Time*. They discuss their experiences with applied research and develop quality criteria to demonstrate both practical relevance and societal value contributions of DSR.

Jan Marco Leimeister, Ernestine Dickhaut, and Andreas Janson reflect the pattern topic in their contribution *Design pattern as a bridge between problem-space and solution-space*. They delve into the codification of design knowledge and its application in both research and practical contexts.

Tuure Tuunanen and Jan Homström reflect another problem dimension between building and using design knowledge by limiting their contribution to and using the research results within a study and across research studies with their chapter *Incremental accumulation of information systems design theory*.

Jannis Beese adds to this perspective the time dimension and asks for *Assessing the temporal validity of design knowledge* in his contribution.

Finally, Alan R. Hevner contributes a scholarly perspective with *Pedagogy for doctoral seminars in design science research* and develops a curriculum for the doctoral level.

Part 3: Applied Fields

Stephan Aier, Barbara Dinter, and Joachim Schelp reflect in their contribution *Management of enterprise-wide information systems* the part of research work at Robert's chair that focuses on data warehousing, (enterprise) architecture, and transformation.

Lars Baake, René Fitterer, Anke Helmes, Tobias Mettler, and Peter Rohner discuss in their chapter *The competence center health network engineering—A retrospective* the research contributions at Robert's chair to the transformation of the Swiss health system.

Kazem Haki delves into platform ecosystems and develops *A research agenda for studying platform ecosystems*.

Hans-Ulrich Buhl, Björn Häckel, und Christian Ritter develop a management system for integrated risk and earnings management with a focus on increasing resilience in turbulent times in their contribution *A Concept for an IT-supported integrated earnings and risk management to strengthen the resilience of companies in times of crisis*.

Peter Gluchowski discusses using data vaults as a modeling approach for data warehouse systems in his contribution *Data Vault as a modeling concept for the data warehouse*.

Jörg H. Mayer, Christian Hebeler, Markus Esswein, Moritz Göbel, and Reiner Quick stay in the business intelligence context but focus on the usage perspective and are *Evaluating a forward-looking maturity model for enterprise performance management*.

Gunnar Auth reflects *The evolution of IT management standards in digital transformation – Current state and research implications*.

Antonio Fernandes and José Tribolet develop another perspective on enterprise-wide information systems with their contribution *Towards conscious enterprises: the role of enterprise engineering in realizing living sciences paradigms into management sciences*.

Paolo Spagnoletti and Stefano Za add a special perspective to organizations by discussing *Digital resilience to normal accidents in high-reliability organizations*.

Ralf Abraham, Stefan Bischoff, Johannes Epple, Nils Labusch, and Simon Weiss return to the research perspective and contrast it with the practitioners' one. They conclude that there is a gap to be surmounted and deliver some fresh thoughts on it in their contribution *Mind the gap: Why there is a gap between information systems research and practice, and how to manage it*.

Reima Suomi finally reflects humorously *The connection between Winter and information systems*.

St. Gallen, Switzerland

Stephan Aier
Peter Rohner
Joachim Schelp

Contents

List of Contributors

Ralf Abraham HSG Alumni, University of St. Gallen, St. Gallen, Switzerland

Stephan Aier Institute of Information Management, University of St. Gallen, St. Gallen, Switzerland

Gunnar Auth University of Applied Sciences, Meißen, Germany

Lars Baacke BEG Analytics AG, Schaffhausen, Switzerland

Ulrike Baumöl University of Liechtenstein, Vaduz, Liechtenstein

Jannis Beese Institute of Information Management, University of St. Gallen, St. Gallen, Switzerland

Stefan Bischoff HSG Alumni, University of St. Gallen, St. Gallen, Switzerland

Walter Brenner Institute of Information Management, University of St. Gallen, St. Gallen, Switzerland

Jan vom Brocke Institute of Information Systems, University of Liechtenstein, Vaduz, Liechtenstein

Hans-Ulrich Buhl Research Center Finance & Information Management, University of Augsburg, Project Group Business & Information Systems Engineering of Fraunhofer FIT, Augsburg, Germany

Ernestine Dickhaut Information Systems, Interdisciplinary Research Center for IS Design (ITeG), University of Kassel, Kassel, Germany

Barbara Dinter Chemnitz University of Technology, Chemnitz, Germany

Mateusz Dolata Faculty of Business, Economics and Informatics, University of Zurich, Zurich, Switzerland

Johannes Epple HSG Alumni, University of St. Gallen, St. Gallen, Switzerland

Markus Esswein Darmstadt University of Technology, Darmstadt, Germany

Antonio Fernandes Instituto Superior Technico, University of Lisbon, Lisbon, Portugal

René Fitterer SAP (Switzerland) AG, Regensdorf, Switzerland

Benjamin van Giffen Institute of Information Management, University of St. Gallen, St. Gallen, Switzerland

Peter Gluchowski Chemnitz University of Technology, Chemnitz, Germany

Moritz Göbel Darmstadt University of Technology, Darmstadt, Germany

Shirley Gregor Australian National University, Canberra, Australia

Thomas Grisold Institute of Information Systems, University of Liechtenstein, Vaduz, Liechtenstein

Björn Häckel Research Center Finance & Information Management, Augsburg University of Applied Sciences, Project Group Business & Information Systems Engineering of Fraunhofer FIT, Augsburg, Germany

Kazem Haki Institute of Information Management, University of St. Gallen, St. Gallen, Switzerland

Christian Hebeler Döhler GmbH, Darmstadt, Germany

Anke Helmes BOC Information Technologies Consulting GmbH, Berlin, Germany

Alan R. Hevner School of Information Systems and Management, Muma College of Business, University of South Florida, Tampa, FL, USA

Jan Holmström Aalto University, Otaniemi, Finland

Andreas Janson Institute of Information Management, University of St. Gallen, St. Gallen, Switzerland

Florian Johannsen University of Applied Sciences Schmalkalden, Schmalkalden, Germany

Reinhard Jung Institute of Information Management, University of St. Gallen, St. Gallen, Switzerland

Dimitris Karagiannis University of Vienna, Vienna, Austria

Jana Koehler Saarland University/DFKI, Saarbrücken, Germany

Nils Labusch HSG Alumni, University of St. Gallen, St. Gallen, Switzerland

Jan Marco Leimeister Institute of Information Management, University of St. Gallen, St. Gallen, Switzerland
Information Systems, Interdisciplinary Research Center for IS Design (ITeG), University of Kassel, Kassel, Germany

Susanne Leist University of Regensburg, Regensburg, Germany

Jörg H. Mayer Darmstadt University of Technology, Darmstadt, Germany

Tobias Mettler University of Lausanne, Lausanne, Switzerland

Hubert Oesterle Institute of Information Management, University of St. Gallen, St. Gallen, Switzerland

Hans-Gert Penzel ibi research, University of Regensburg, Regensburg, Germany

Henderik A. Proper Luxembourg Institute of Science and Technology, Belval, Luxembourg
University of Luxembourg, Belval, Luxembourg

Reiner Quick Darmstadt University of Technology, Darmstadt, Germany

Christian Ritter Research Center Finance & Information Management, University of Augsburg, Project Group Business & Information Systems Engineering of Fraunhofer FIT, Augsburg, Germany

Peter Rohner Institute of Information Management, University of St. Gallen, St. Gallen, Switzerland

Joachim Schelp Helsana Versicherungen, Zürich, Switzerland
University of St. Gallen, St. Gallen, Switzerland

Gerhard Schwabe Faculty of Business, Economics and Informatics, University of Zurich, Zurich, Switzerland

Paolo Spagnoletti Luiss University, Rome, Italy
University of Agder, Kristiansand, Norway

Reima Suomi University of Turku, Turku, Finland

José Tribolet INESC-ID Lisbon, Lisbon, Portugal

Tuure Tuunanen University of Jyväskylä, Jyväskylä, Finland

Manuel Weber Institute of Information Systems, University of Liechtenstein, Vaduz, Liechtenstein

Simon Weiss HSG Alumni, University of St. Gallen, St. Gallen, Switzerland

Stefano Za G. D'Annunzio University, Pescara, Italy

Part I
Business Engineering and Beyond

From Business Engineering to Life Engineering

Hubert Oesterle

Abstract Starting with a reflection of the business engineering discipline and its focus on the corporate value perspective, this contribution positions life engineering as a new discipline focusing on the individual perspective of the quality of life. Based on the example of a sleep coach it develops the different tasks a discipline life engineering has to address.

Keywords Business engineering · Life engineering · Quality of life · Life engineering discipline

1 Introduction

In the future, a *digital sleep coach* will help many people achieve healthy sleep and thus contribute significantly to their health and well-being. Today's sleep coach is data-minimal because it is mostly based on movement recordings from a smartwatch or subjective statements from personal entries. A future sleep coach is data-rich if he can access almost all digital personal data, from Internet usage to smartwatches to sensors in homes and vehicles, and even medical data. If he can actually help people with serious sleep problems, they will gladly give consent.

Such digital assistants will accompany us in all areas of life in a few years, in diabetes therapy, financial retirement planning, nutrition, entertainment, education, and so on. However, this raises some critical questions: How is the privacy of the individual to be safeguarded if personal and environmental data must be comprehensively collected and evaluated in order to model sleep behavior, and if the sleep coach needs the personal data of the specific user for individual coaching? Who develops such a sleep coach? A pharmaceutical company, an internet company, a health insurance company [1], the employer [2], the state? What interests do these

H. Oesterle (✉)
Institute of Information Management, University of St. Gallen, St. Gallen, Switzerland
e-mail: hubert.oesterle@unisg.ch

© The Author(s), under exclusive license to Springer Nature Switzerland AG 2021
S. Aier et al. (eds.), *Engineering the Transformation of the Enterprise*,
https://doi.org/10.1007/978-3-030-84655-8_1

3

pursue with the sleep coach? What else could a developer do with the data? How does a young company get hold of the data lying in the silos of the mega portals? Does a sleep coach endanger human autonomy? Who has the right or the duty to encourage people to sleep healthily?

Business engineering aims at business *value*. Sales of products and services, expansion of the customer base, customers' profitability (e.g. ARPU, Annual Revenue per User in the telecommunications industry), process costs in customer care, compliance and risk avoidance, return on sales, customer loyalty and need creation are just a few examples of business engineering concepts [3].

Life engineering aims at people's *quality of life*. Quality of life can mean pleasure and joy from food, sex or appreciation, but also avoidance of pain and suffering from illness, effort or humiliation. In the long run, people are concerned with meaning in life and satisfaction. But the path to quality of life is not as clear to science or the individual as it is in the case of sleep quality. That is why a whole happiness industry could develop, which is concerned with wellness, lifestyle, happiness training, self-discovery, ethics, philosophy and the like.

When the needs of self- and species-preservation, i.e., food, security, sex, and avoidance of effort become sufficiently satisfiable, the needs of selection come to the fore. We strive for status symbols, appearance, circle of friends, personal income, and wealth to improve our rank within our peer group. When we meet our own expectations, it boosts our self-esteem and thus conveys *satisfaction* [4].

Digital services, i.e. Tinder, Instagram and Amazon, influence our needs and accelerate the hamster wheel of consumption and money-making. Opinion forming, advertising and influencing use the entire toolkit of psychology, which derives knowledge more and more from personal data to influence our behavior (e.g. nudging).

Never before have people had such comprehensive, up-to-date, and automatically collected *behavioral data* (Quantified Self [5]). Never before have they had such powerful algorithms and machines to *recognize patterns* in this data. Never before has there been such close *collaboration between humans and machines* in all areas of life. So never before has it been possible to *control* people so effectively. Those mechanisms reveal themselves as manipulated information channels (e.g., filter bubbles), individualized communication of values, consumer offers, and even various forms of social scoring (e.g., credit reports and traffic offence registers).

Mankind is on the verge of a *socio-technical evolutionary leap*. Digitalization offers new mechanisms for social control, which companies, political parties and other organizations are already using intensively for their interests. Machine-based behavior control can be a unique opportunity to improve people's quality of life if development is driven by human interests, or an underestimated danger if interests other than those of the individual, guide development.

The Internet, sensor technology, and digital assistants from navigation to social media and online stores to automated insulin pumps illustrate this development. Data collection and machine learning are accelerating sociotechnical evolution [6]. It cannot be stopped; we can only try to guide it for the benefit of humans.

For this, we need a discipline of life engineering that brings together the findings of disciplines such as political science, psychology, neuroscience, machine learning, ethics and economics and derives concepts for living with a highly developed technology. Life Engineering is the further development of Business Engineering with the aim of improving quality of life.

2 Socio-cultural Evolution

Biological evolution is based primarily on mutation, recombination and selection and, apart from breeding experiments and, more recently, genetic manipulation, is hardly influenced by humans. Socio-cultural or socio-technical evolution obeys the same evolutional mechanisms, but partly follows a man-made, planned design of technology and organization.

2.1 Technological Evolution

Machine intelligence has been regarded as a central driver of social change ever since Daniel Bell's work on the "post-industrial society" in 1973 [7]. The Internet with its countless digital services, the digital assistants as apps on our end user devices, the mega portals from Facebook to Tencent, and finally the integration of these services in so-called superapps [8] have already massively changed our daily lives. *Sensor technology* together with powerful *wireless networks* (especially 5G) will add a dimension to the already gigantic data collections in the coming years [9]. Increasingly sophisticated machine learning algorithms and processors are taking knowledge about our lives to a new level. New forms of cooperation between humans and machines, especially *actuator technology*, integrate intelligent machines, for example autonomous navigation in cars, into our lives [10].

2.2 Homeostasis as a Driver of Evolution

Just as physiological homeostasis ensures the survival and further evolution of organisms, sociotechnical homeostasis allows technologies and forms of organization to emerge or disappear. Knowledge, power and capital are the dominant criteria of sociocultural selection [4].

2.3 Quality of Life

Evolution controls people through feelings (quality of life), through joy (happiness) and sorrow (harm) [11]. These feelings arise from the effect of perceptions on needs (see [4]). Greatly simplified, there are genetically determined, inherited needs such as food, safety, and sex, as well as avoidance of effort. With their cognitive abilities, humans derive patterns (secondary needs) from perceptions, for example by recognizing the effect of a high-calorie energy drink on their need for food, but at the same time learning that too much energy intake leads to fat formation and, in the longer term, health and attractiveness in selection suffer as a result. In many cases, humans have to weigh up between short-term satisfaction of needs (hedonia) and long-term satisfaction (eudaimonia).

Hedonia cannot be increased at will and, above all, it is not permanent due to accommodation. A long-term satisfaction is considered as the goal of humans in psychology and philosophy. Even if genes determine one third of satisfaction, individual life circumstances are responsible for two thirds and can be influenced by people and society for better or worse [11].

2.4 Options in Evolution

Companies act in the interests of *capital*, i.e. shareholders. Although they repeatedly profess their commitment to stakeholders and also fulfill this commitment if the pressure is great enough, the company's management is ultimately measured by its financial performance. Capital is the criterion for the development of new products and services, for the form of marketing, for pricing, etc., but above all for the performance assessment of employees. Capital is de facto the driver of sociotechnical evolution. This would not be a problem if people knew what was good for them and, more importantly, acted on it. Drug addiction, obesity, consumerism, environmental degradation, leisure stress, mental illness and indebtedness are indications that people do not always use technological opportunities for their own good.

Society needs to think about how it will incorporate machine intelligence and other technologies into reshaping its life. The technologization of society cannot be stopped. There are enough developers and companies in this world that can improve their situation through innovative business solutions. Those who opt out of the development race fall into the dependency of the technological leaders, as their solutions keep replacing conventional products and services, i.e. pushing them out of the market. If someone advocates quality of life, as we Europeans like to pretend to do, and believes that this sets them apart from allegedly primitive capital-driven societies, they have to realize that only those who lead the development can influence it in the sense of their values. Even well-intentioned regulation such as the GDPR can do little to change this. Sociotechnological evolution cannot be stopped, and it appears more threatening ex ante than ex post. Who today would want to return to a development level of 50 years ago?

We have the choice of leaving the control of development to capital alone or finding mechanisms to prioritize quality of life without lagging behind in development. This is not a call for an alternative economic system, but an encouragement to complement capitalist control with the possibilities of digitalization. Numerous initiatives by governmental and non-governmental organizations from consumer protection, education for digital independence, environmental protection, labor law, etc. recognize the need for action and advocate for people's goals from the perspective of humanism [12], ethics [13–15], Social Development Goals [16], etc. Although it may sound politically undesirable, it is precisely a social scoring system, such as China is testing in different variants, that has significant potential to ensure quality of life.

3 Sleepcoach Example

The call for a discipline of life engineering seems very academic. Therefore, let us illustrate with an example of how life engineering could have an effect. Today, there are numerous sleep apps that are supposed to bring people the sleep they urgently seek and that could noticeably improve their quality of life. Free access to all the data that determines sleep quality and that is available in many data silos from eMail, the social networks, medical findings and DNA analysis, as well as sleep trackers available on the market, could already lead to new and, above all, sound insights using machine learning techniques. The world of miniaturized, low-cost, and mobile sensors for skin resistance measurement, heart rate recording, blood pressure or blood glucose measurement, noise level measurement, air quality, exercise, etc., will open up a host of new indicators and, most importantly, enable real-time interventions (e.g., recommending a break from work). The sensor technology enables a *leap innovation* for a sleep coach and addresses a market with several millions of customers.

3.1 Target

A pharmaceutical company certainly wants to improve people's sleep, naturally thinking first of all of the sale of sleeping pills. So it will probably develop a sleep app that reminds the consumer to take the pill, at best making the dosage dependent on the consumer's (patient's) machine-measured state of arousal [17]. Business engineering optimizes the process from identifying potential customers, influencing them via medical portals, recommending them to their family doctor, reminding them to take the tablet, measuring the quality of their sleep and thus measuring the benefits, and finally automating the supply of the sleeping pills to the patient. The pharmaceutical company's metrics are the quantity sold and the price charged. It may accept the risk that the patient becomes addicted, i.e. can no longer sleep without the sleeping pill, possibly even that the dose has to be increased again and again.

Life Engineering seeks to improve the *quality of human life through healthy sleep*. It determines the connection between sleep and well-being as well as the possible influences on sleep, for example the food consumed, eMail usage in the evening and physical activity during the day. It is possible that a digital sleep coach does not recommend sleep medication and thus does not generate pharmaceutical sales.

At first glance, the goal of business and life engineering appears to be the same: healthy sleep. The implementation, on the other hand, is very different. Of course, the pharmaceutical company would also be willing to forego selling sleeping pills if customers used a digital sleep coach and paid for it. At least for now, this customer behavior is an illusion in the seemingly free world of the Internet, especially since taking a sleeping pill requires less personal behavior change than, say, taking a walk before bed. So one challenge for life engineering is to monetize a sleep coach that will eventually be available. One route might be through health insurance.

3.2   Data Access

Sleep apps have had very limited success so far. While there have been many attempts and start-ups, the benefits seem limited. For the most part, the apps are content with measuring sleep without surveying the influencing factors. The afore-mentioned *sensors and a wireless network like 5G* will fundamentally change the picture. Influencing factors such as the noise level, smartphone usage or heart rhythm will become usable together with the measured sleep quality.

However, this data is not yet available to the developer of a sleep app, but lies in the data silos of the mega portals. Article 20 of the GDPR (right to data portability) basically requires that all "data collectors" *transfer the data* to another digital service provider at the request of the consumer. This would theoretically enable the provider of a digital sleep coach to obtain all data relevant to sleep from various sources. However, what that might look like for real-time access to heart rhythm data, for example, is completely unclear. Life engineering should provide a technical and organizational answer.

3.3   Data Collection and Update

In conclusion, the first thing a start-up company with very limited resources has to do is requesting all the data from sources such as Google, Apple, Facebook, Netatmo, and Fitbit, clean it, and build a machine learning database from it. For the ongoing operation of the sleep coach, the sleep coach has to be able to use all these data sources in real time. This will overwhelm the technical and organizational capabilities of even the best-intentioned of all companies in the affected ecosystem.

Life engineering must therefore ensure that this data flow is possible and meets data protection requirements. It may be possible to achieve this with a Data Space (data marketplace) as conceived in GAIA-X [18] and IDS [19]. The European Public Spheres [20] of the German Federal Government and the European Union attempt to organize not only the Data Space, but the entire ecosystem for individual spheres of life [18, 21].

Regardless of whether government organizations or private-sector initiatives create the necessary data infrastructure, there is a need for *standards, procedures, mechanisms, and rules for collaboration* within such ecosystems. A life engineering discipline can act as a facilitator and contribute theoretical foundations.

3.4 Machine Learning

One challenge for life engineering is its extraordinarily broad interdisciplinarity. Being able to draw on the knowledge of disciplines such as psychology, sociology, ethics, philosophy, neuroscience, computer science, especially machine learning, business administration, and not least economics, is necessary.

Machine learning generates knowledge about the behavior of people and their environment. The Google Knowledge Graph is probably the best-known knowledge base, Google's Selfish Ledger a special further development for understanding human behavior. Knowledge bases documenting patterns for subdomains of human behavior are emerging in a variety of locations. Their goal is to predict and extract a particular behavior, such as buying behavior, but also political attitudes. The developers of a sleep coach need a comprehensive and detailed model of human behavior around sleeping. Ideally, they will have a structured access to existing knowledge that has been derived in various locations using analytical tools.

Life engineering thus needs access not only to the data of the digitized world, but also to the knowledge derived from it. This requires a *standardization of the knowledge representation*, an extremely demanding task, even if one disregards the legitimate interests of competitors in proprietary solutions. Here, too, a life engineering discipline can collect the existing approaches and propose further developments from them.

3.5 Market Access for a Digital Sleep Coach

Once sleep behavior and its influencing factors are sufficiently understood so that a digital sleep coach can help achieve sustainably better sleep, the knowledge to be translated into a digital service. There are several ways to achieve this:

- a new stand-alone app, i.e. an application on the smartphone, smartwatch, smartring and a server
- the redesign of an existing sleeping service already established on the market
- the integrated functionality of a mega portal like Apple, Google or Tencent
- a program that can be integrated into any app via API
- an open-source program and funding via the collected user data

If life engineering is to make a difference, it is crucial to understand market supply and market mechanisms to the extent that its concepts have a realistic chance of operating in an economically sustainable manner.

3.6 Funding for a Digital Sleep Coach

A sleep coach, as indicated above, requires considerable development effort. University research can at best provide basic concepts, building blocks and prototypes. A marketable sleep coach requires many times the resources of academic research projects.

Such financing is readily available if there is a compelling business model. Approaches that focus on quality of life rather than a capital objective alone call for novel mechanisms that leverage multiple revenue streams. Health insurers are increasingly coming up with applications to improve the health of their customers. Employers have an interest in rested employees with increased performance capabilities, and pharmaceutical companies can increase the effectiveness of their products. In some circumstances, even consumers of a sleep coach may be willing to pay a monthly subscription fee.

Life engineering faces the challenge of *adding the quality of life criterion to the capital criterion* in such a way that the necessary financial resources can be obtained for development and operation.

3.7 Public Regulation

The social market economy has produced a multitude of regulations designed to protect citizens from the harmful effects of an exclusively capital-driven economy. Examples include consumer protection, data privacy, drug laws and environmental standards. The possibilities of digitalization expand the question: can the state not only prevent negative developments, but even promote or require positive options. Chinese social scoring shows that digitized social governance can be used to encourage desirable behavior, for example, by awarding bonus points when a citizen engages in social goals. Corporate social scoring, i.e., the evaluation of corporate behavior, is even a realistic implementation opportunity for previously relatively ineffective standards such as ISO 26000 [22] on corporate social responsibility.

Such forms of intervention in social and economic life are very quickly labeled with terms such as paternalism, loss of freedom, and bureaucracy and are understood as the downfall of a liberal world order. Life engineering can develop proposals for replacing today's personnel-intensive and sometimes arbitrary control mechanisms with efficient, transparent, and objectifiable procedures [23]. Is a speed camera check carried out by police officers at considerable expense, with the subsequent bureaucratic processing and entry in a public traffic offender file, preferable to an automated speed check via the car's on-board electronics or via cameras on the roads with an automatic debiting of the penalty and a machine assessment of driving behavior? Insurance companies are already trying to assess the individual risk of insured persons with data from the on-board electronics and to calculate the insurance premium accordingly. That, too, is social scoring.

Life engineering offers the opportunity to make *societal governance mechanisms* more efficient, fairer and more consistent in many areas. It must address the extent to which government organizations have the *right* or even the *duty* to use digitization to implement democratically agreed rules.

3.8 Tasks of a Discipline Life Engineering

Before calling for a new scientific discipline, one should look very carefully to see if it does not already exist, under a different name. Psychology covers many aspects, but hardly makes use of the possibilities of a digitized world, apart from a few highly interesting approaches to recognizing personality traits from e-mails or social networks or subsuming the neurosciences. Statistics and computer science deal with the machine recognition of patterns in personal data, but do not connect them with psychology. Marketing science uses the findings of psychology and computer science but is primarily oriented to the sale of products and services and the short-term benefit for the buyer, if this is decisive for the purchase, but not towards the quality of life. Similar things can be said about the other disciplines mentioned, so that a separate discipline of life engineering is called for here. Although the interdisciplinarity required therein represents a difficult hurdle, the attempt must be dared, because what is at stake is too great: digitization for its own sake or for the sake of capital, or to safeguard people's quality of life.

A discipline Life Engineering has the following tasks:

- Quality of life model that allows evaluation of technological options.
- Access to anonymous personal and factual data so that research and companies can identify patterns in it
- Use of individual personal and factual data in the digital services
- Behavioral model that summarizes the findings of the various disciplines in a machine accessible form (e.g., in a neural network)
- Measurement of quality of life (Hedonia and Eudaimonia)
- Digitized control mechanisms

- Guidance for the construction of digital services
- Implementation of the findings in politics, companies and individuals

Years ago, it was my great pleasure to work with Robert Winter to establish the Business Engineering discipline and create a comprehensive range of research and education. Wouldn't it be a fascinating idea that Robert Winter could repeat his success story with the Executive MBA in Business Engineering with the goals of Life Engineering.

References

1. Techniker Krankenkasse: Online-Training gegen Schlafstörungen. (2020)
2. Olk, J.: shleep handelsblatt.pdf. Handelsblatt. https://www.handelsblatt.com/technik/it-internet/digitales-schlafcoaching-schlaf-tech-unternehmen-shleep-sammelt-1-4-millionen-euro-ein/v_detail_tab_print/25043662.html (2019)
3. Winter, R.: Business Engineering Navigator. Springer, Berlin (2011)
4. Österle, H.: Life Engineering. Mehr Lebensqualität dank maschineller Intelligenz? Springer Nature, Wiesbaden (2020)
5. Lupton, D.: The Quantified Self. A Sociology of Self-Tracking. Polity Press, Cambridge (2016)
6. Tegmark, M.: Life 3.0. Being Human in the Age of Artificial Intelligence. Knopf, New York (2018)
7. Bell, D.: The Coming of Post-industrial Society. (1973)
8. Eisenbrand, R.: Auf der Jagd nach der Super App: Wie die westlichen Tech-Konzerne Asien nacheifern wollen. https://omr.com/de/super-app-facebook-google/?utm_source=OMR+Daily+Newsletter&utm_campaign=97a31fe74d-EMAIL_CAMPAIGN_2020_01_28&utm_medium=email&utm_term=0_0eb6baef13-97a31fe74d-96451245&mc_cid=97a31fe74d&mc_eid=abcc4d87ca (2020). Accessed 29 Jan 2020
9. Zarnekow, R., Witte, A.-K.: Transforming personal healthcare through technology – a systematic literature review of wearable sensors for medical application. Proceedings of the 52nd Hawaii International Conference on System Sciences (HICSS), pp. 1–10. (2019)
10. Fleisch, E., Franz, Ch., Herrmann, A., Mönninghoff, A.: Die Digitale Pille. (2020)
11. Schröder, M.: Wann sind wir wirklich zufrieden? C. Bertelsmann Verlag, München (2020)
12. Portmann, E.: Fuzzy Humanist Trilogie Teil III: Von der Fuzzy-Logik zum Computing with Words. Springer Vieweg (2019)
13. Bendel, O.: Die Moral in der Maschine (Telepolis): Beiträge zu Roboter- und Maschinenethik. Heise Medien (2016)
14. IEEE: ETHICALLY ALIGNED DESIGN. A Vision for Prioritizing Human Well-being with Autonomous and Intelligent Systems. https://standards.ieee.org/content/dam/ieee-standards/standards/web/documents/other/ead_v2.pdf (2019)
15. Ethikrat, D.: Deutscher Ethikrat Big Data und Gesundheit. (n.d.)
16. How, J.P.: Ethically aligned design. IEEE Control Syst. (2018). https://doi.org/10.1109/MCS.2018.2810458
17. Alt, R., Puschmann, T.: Developing customer process orientation: the case of. Electr. Mark. **11** (4), 297–315 (2005). https://doi.org/10.1108/14637150510609372
18. BMWi: Project GAIA-X. A Federated Data Infrastructure as the Cradle of a Vibrant European Ecosystem. https://www.bmwi.de/Redaktion/DE/Publikationen/Digitale-Welt/das-projekt-gaia-x.pdf?__blob=publicationFile&v=22 (2019)
19. Otto, B., Lohmann, S., Steinbuß, S., Teuscher, A.: IDS Reference Architecture Model Version 2.0, (April), 92. https://www.fraunhofer.de/content/dam/zv/de/Forschungsfelder/industrial-data-space/IDS_Referenz_Architecture.pdf (2018)

20. Kagermann, H., Wilhelm, U.: European Public Sphere. Gestaltung der digitalen Souveränität Europas (acatech IMPULS). München (2020)
21. Datenethikkommission: Gutachten der Datenethikkommission. https://datenethikkommission. de/wp-content/uploads/191128_DEK_Gutachten_bf_b.pdf (2019)
22. Schmiedeknecht, M.H., Wieland, J.: ISO 26000, 7 Grundsätze, 6 Kernthemen. In Corporate Social Responsibility. Verantwortungsvolle Unternehmensführung in Theorie und Praxis. Berlin: Springer Gabler. https://link.springer.com/content/pdf/10.1007/978-3-662-43483-3.pdf (2015)
23. Síthigh, D.M., Siems, M.: THE CHINESE SOCIAL CREDIT SYSTEM: A MODEL FOR OTHER COUNTRIES? https://cadmus.eui.eu/bitstream/handle/1814/60424/LAW_2019_01. pdf?sequence=1&isAllowed=y (2019). Accessed 2 Jan 2020

Management of Artificial Intelligence: Feasibility, Desirability and Viability

Walter Brenner, Benjamin van Giffen, and Jana Koehler

Abstract Artificial Intelligence is evolving and being used in more and more products and applications in business and society. Research in artificial intelligence is dominated by computer science. The focus is on the development of innovative algorithms and the design of processors and storages required for different application scenarios. Numerous prototypes are developed for a wide variety of applications. Only a few of these prototypes make it into productive applications that create lasting business benefits. Discussions with numerous companies show that professional processes and structures are needed to develop and operate artificial intelligence applications. We refer to these processes and structures as management of informatics. This article describes our understanding of artificial intelligence, shows examples of concrete business benefits, lists exemplary challenges, and describes the basic processes of the management of artificial intelligence. This article is based on a comprehensive literature review as well as numerous structured and open discussions with people from applying companies and computer scientists from the academic environment who deal with artificial intelligence and its use. An extended version of the article has been published in the German Springer Essentials series titled "Bausteine eines Managements Künstlicher Intelligenz: Eine Standortbestimmung".

Keywords Artificial intelligence · Machine learning · Project management

W. Brenner (✉) · B. van Giffen
Institute of Information Management, University of St. Gallen, St. Gallen, Switzerland
e-mail: walter.brenner@unisg.ch; benjamin.vangiffen@unisg.ch

J. Koehler
Saarland University/DFKI, Saarbrücken, Germany
e-mail: jana.koehler@dfki.de

© The Author(s), under exclusive license to Springer Nature Switzerland AG 2021
S. Aier et al. (eds.), *Engineering the Transformation of the Enterprise*,
https://doi.org/10.1007/978-3-030-84655-8_2

1 Artificial Intelligence

Artificial intelligence (AI) addresses the question of whether intelligent behavior can be computed. The basis of modern AI is the metaphor of the intelligent agent [1, 2]. An intelligent agent can perceive its environment and, based on these perceptions, makes decisions that determine its further actions. If it is a rational agent, then its decisions must lead to the best possible action for it. We base our discussion on this definition, even though there are very different understandings of artificial intelligence in the literature. Since the 1950s, countless researchers in computer science and related fields have been engaged in the development of artificial intelligence methods and their use in business and society.

There are many different forms of artificial intelligence. Numerous authors give the impression that it is only a matter of time until there is artificial intelligence whose problem-solving power is equal to that of humans ("Strong AI" or "Artificial General Intelligence") or even surpasses it ("Super AI") [3]. Today, and in this paper, we are concerned with weak Artificial Intelligence, often referred to as "Narrow AI" or "Weak AI". This manifestation of Artificial Intelligence is capable of handling specific, constrained problems on its own. There are numerous algorithmic methods that are subsumed under the term Artificial Intelligence. A distinction is made between stochastic and deterministic methods. In deterministic methods, the output is completely determined by the parameter values and the initial state. Stochastic methods combine probability theory and statistics and are characterized by the fact that some parameters are described with random variables, so that for a given initial state the output is not necessarily always the same. Currently very successful AI methods such as machine learning or modern search algorithms that use Monte Carlo simulations belong to the stochastic methods. In particular, training neural networks for supervised machine learning employs stochastic methods. However, the application of a trained network to a given data set is deterministic, since the input values and the weights set in the network by training determine the output value. We understand machine learning as methods in which algorithms recognize patterns in data without being explicitly programmed [4].

Supervised machine learning uses annotated examples from input/output data to learn statistically significant patterns for the relationship between input and output, i.e., to approximate the underlying function that must be applied to the input to produce the output. Currently, Deep Learning, i.e., so-called deep neural networks that combine many layers of simple computational units, is particularly successful in performing such tasks [5]. Training data is of particular importance for managing artificial intelligence, which we will discuss later in this article. While in supervised learning training data is described, i.e., a picture of a dog is also labeled "dog", in unsupervised learning an algorithm searches for previously unknown patterns, distributions, or dependencies in the data [2] without any additional annotation. Even this rough description shows that the application areas of these two methods of artificial intelligence are very different.

In recent years, a kind of equation has become established in science and practice: "Artificial Intelligence = Machine Learning = Deep Learning". While we are convinced of the power of Deep Learning, we are of the opinion that it is part of the responsible and benefit-oriented handling of Artificial Intelligence to search for the appropriate method of Artificial Intelligence for an existing problem and not to proceed pragmatically according to the principle "If the only tool you have is a hammer, you tend to see every problem as a nail" and, accordingly, reduce Artificial Intelligence to Neural Networks and Deep Learning.

In 1943, McCulloch and Pitts [6] described elementary units that can represent logical functions in a linked manner and thus founded the beginnings of neural networks. Norbert Wiener founded cybernetics in the 1940s and investigated analogies between the actions of machines and living organisms [7]. McCarthy coined the term "artificial intelligence" in 1956, distinguishing himself from previous research activities to give more space to a logic-based approach to AI [2]. About 35 years ago, there was an initial hype about Artificial Intelligence in the context of expert systems. Data not available in sufficient volume, procedures for handling uncertain knowledge not yet developed, and limitations in storage and processing capabilities ended the euphoria. The next 15 years saw the so-called "winter" of artificial intelligence. The expectations raised in the hype were not fulfilled and, as a result, Artificial Intelligence was considered a very unattractive field in science and practice. About 10 years ago, Artificial Intelligence experienced a rebirth. The abundance of available data, massively increased storage and processing capabilities, and much more powerful algorithms led to an upswing that continues today. Anyone who has followed the development of speech recognition over the last few decades has seen how systems have improved. The future importance of artificial intelligence for solving numerous problems in business and society is undisputed.

2 Competitive Factor

Artificial intelligence is becoming a decisive competitive factor in more and more industries. Depending on the problem, both deterministic and stochastic methods are used. However, artificial intelligence, even if it is ultimately decisive for success, is only part of the overall solution. It is integrated into a software system that is connected to mechanical or electrical components in industrial applications, for example. The decisive factor is that the software system is used productively. Only then can it generate business benefits.

Increasing the productivity of elevators is a successful example of the use of artificial intelligence. In the 1990s, the elevator industry discussed the idea of so-called destination call control, in which passengers enter their destination floor via a terminal before starting their journey and are then assigned to one of the available elevator via a display. Figure 1 shows an input unit for a destination call control system.

Fig. 1 Destination call
control for an elevator (own
image)

Passengers specify the desired floor on the call control unit. For most passenger
requests, the destination call control system calculates the best possible distribution
of passengers to the available elevators. In the example from Fig. 1, the system tells
the passenger to use elevator D.

Various attempts to use artificial intelligence methods, such as genetic algorithms, neural networks or fuzzy logic, did not achieve the desired performance. If
one looks at the problem more closely, one finds that it is a combinatorial optimization problem in which a set of available passenger trips from different starting
floors to different destination floors must be optimally distributed among a set of
elevators so that the waiting and travel times of the passengers are minimized and
thus the transportation performance of the elevator system can be maximized. In the
1970s–1990s, so-called heuristic search algorithms were developed in the artificial
intelligence discipline, which were used, among other things, in Deep Blue's victory
over Gari Kasparov in 1997. These algorithms had matured to the point where they
could find the optimal travel sequence for an elevator out of the billions to trillions of
possible travel sequences in a few hundredths of a second on a standard industrial
PC. They were also able to further reduce the complexity of the optimization

problem by preempting an auction in which passengers are auctioned off to the elevator that offers the best ride sequence. In addition to the efficient implementation of the selected search algorithm—a backtracking search with branch and bound based on the A* search algorithm from AI—interfacing with the existing communication systems between the elevators, their drive and door controllers, and the terminals used to interact with passengers, was critical to the market viability of AI-based control [8, 9]. High-performance elevators in large buildings typically travel at a speed of 10–12 m/s. Thus, if an AI algorithm takes about 100 ms calculation time, an elevator has already advanced at least one floor in that time. Constant advance planning and rescheduling of the optimal travel sequences is necessary, since passengers also never behave as originally planned. With the up to 30% possible increase in transport performance achieved by artificial intelligence, especially in traffic peaks such as those that occur in large office buildings in the morning and at midday, the market breakthrough was possible, particularly in the high-rise segment with mixed use. Integration with access systems and the possibility of preferentially serving certain passenger groups within the same elevator system make this type of control very attractive to the market from a utilization and operational point of view, not only because of its improved efficiency but also because of its adaptability and flexibility. For passengers, the control system is interesting if it reduces waiting and travel times accordingly. In practice, the design of the passenger interface has proven to be very challenging and quite a few installations by some manufacturers had to be converted back to conventional systems in certain buildings with many visitors and low affinity for technology, as elderly people in particular could not understand the communicated assignment to an elevator [10].

Not only, but also because of advances in artificial intelligence, large Internet companies are successful even in times of crisis. Their websites illustrate how they learn from the behavior of their customers and thus, for example, create individualized offers. The high profits of these companies result from analyzing the search and shopping behavior of customers with deep learning to generate suggestions for products or services that might be of interest. But traditional companies also report success in using artificial intelligence. One large Swiss insurance company known to the authors owes an increase in profits in the high double-digit millions to its use.

3 Democratization

In the future, the use of artificial intelligence will no longer be the privilege of a few companies with very well-trained computer scientists who solve analytical problems in the sense of a mythical secret science with the help of complex algorithms incomprehensible to normal people. We believe that artificial intelligence will be democratized in the future.

On the one hand, this means that a large proportion of the workforce in companies will be enabled to use artificial intelligence as a tool. Companies are already working toward using artificial intelligence not only by computer scientists and mathematicians in operational processes, but also, for example, by using low-code environments to enable employees to gather their own experience and implement initial ideas for experiments and prototypes with their data. Afterwards, highly qualified specialists from different fields of knowledge, especially from computer science, can build and operate professional applications.

In addition to this capability-oriented perspective, we also understand democratization to mean that artificial intelligence will be used in companies in specialist domains and will be used in more and more digitized products and services. Artificial intelligence will thus become a "normal" component of many software systems. In the future, every company will use artificial intelligence in many domains in order to remain competitive. Statistical evaluations of customer preferences in marketing or the detection of errors in production are examples of applications in specialist domains. Consumers will increasingly use artificial intelligence in products and services. Suggestions for products in e-commerce applications, the recognition of dangerous situations in vehicles for the emergency braking assistant, voice recognition in Alexa or the translation system DeepL are examples of applications that are used today without the end customer knowing or being aware of which artificial intelligence methods are being used.

We assume that these developments will be essential for the roll-out of artificial intelligence. Against this backdrop, it is of crucial importance, especially for large companies, not only to see artificial intelligence as a task for individual specialists, but rather to involve a large part of the workforce in its development. Our assumption is that artificial intelligence must be broadly anchored in the company if it is to support products, services and business processes in the future. Finally, all employees must be enabled to contribute to artificial intelligence-enabled innovations, to participate in the corresponding developments and to ensure the operation of applications in the corporate environment.

We refer to these thrusts of the spread of artificial intelligence as the democratization of artificial intelligence. Vice versa, the democratization of artificial intelligence forces companies in more and more industries to deal with artificial intelligence productively to remain competitive in the future. Management of Artificial Intelligence, in our view, is the part of corporate governance and management of information technology that ensures the competitive use of Artificial intelligence.

4 Data

Data is the input and output for artificial intelligence applications. That is why many companies, when talking about the use of artificial intelligence, also talk about generating business value from internal data and external data, also made publicly available on the Internet. The amount of data that is already available today is almost unlimited, and large amounts of additional data are added every day. For example, approximately 500 h of video material are uploaded to YouTube every minute

[11]. The internal data stocks in companies have also grown rapidly in recent years due to image, audio and video files.

Artificial intelligence has become a crucial tool for analyzing large data sets and deriving business value from them. It does not take a lot to realize that even large companies are overwhelmed by having employees manually analyze such volumes of data. There is no alternative for companies, regardless of size and industry, to automating processes with artificial intelligence when it comes to evaluating data.

The quantity and quality of the data ultimately determine whether the use of artificial intelligence leads to useful results. Any form of manual and automatic information processing can only lead to good results if the input data is available in sufficient quantity and quality. Many companies currently realize that they are unable to use artificial intelligence in a beneficial way because the data required for the applications is not available at all or insufficient in quantity and quality. Companies that are leaders in the use of artificial intelligence in Switzerland report that between 80 and 90% of the effort required to build and operate artificial intelligence applications goes into data engineering, i.e., the provision of data of the required quality.

5 Tasks in the Management of AI

The professional examination of the sustainable and value-creating use of artificial intelligence is proving to be a very great challenge in business. It is becoming increasingly apparent that the focus is on management issues and less on technology issues if sustainable effects are to be achieved. We are aware of the controversial discussion that this statement will trigger.

The "Periodic Table of Artificial Intelligence" provides a good overview of available elements, which can also be combined to describe the constitutive elements of an artificial intelligence system [12]. There are various application scenarios for this: AI products can be compared with each other so that the organizational impact and the value potentials of an artificial intelligence system can be shown. The elements are each assigned to three groups, namely *assess*, *infer* and *respond* and thus also reflect the behavior and logic of an intelligent agent: assess—perceive information from the environment; infer—make a decision; respond—trigger an action. A use case is represented by selecting at least one element from each group. For example, a robot car assesses the current traffic situation (*assess*), calculates the probability of an accident for the next time step (*infer*), and possibly initiates a braking or evasive maneuver (*respond*). Each of these steps is specified in the form of an element.

If another artificial intelligence "winter" is to be avoided, the focus must be on the use of artificial intelligence. Against this background, in this section we only address the management challenges associated with artificial intelligence and not the technical and algorithmic challenges. We focus on selected challenges that can be attributed to the field of artificial intelligence management.

Paradigm shift The development of information systems has been characterized by two paradigms in the last decades: programming and parameterization. Information systems, regardless of the area of application, were and are usually programmed, i.e., ideas become code. In the context of software engineering and related fields, such as data modeling or project management, an enormous body of knowledge and experience has been built up on how software, even very complex software, can be successfully developed and operated. With the emergence of standard software in the 1970s and 1980s, parameterization became another way to develop information systems. Software is programmed to meet requirements. Information systems that use neural networks in the context of deep learning are primarily trained [13]. Parameterization takes place when, for example, the architecture of the network is determined. However, a great deal of programming must be done to prepare the data for training and testing.

The starting point of training is the acquisition of training data, which often needs to be labeled. If one wants to train a neural network to recognize dogs, a training data set with many images of dogs labeled as "dog" is needed, as well as images of other animals which are then labeled "not dog". With the help of training, a neural network detects existing patterns in the training data that are statistically significant for assigning an image to the term "dog". What patterns a deep neural network recognizes is generally not accessible to human analysis, which is why research on the transparency and explainability of deep learning is currently so extensive. It may be random collections of pixels in the background of dog images that the neural network uses as a basis for decision-making. If one wants to recognize not only dogs, but individual dog breeds, the images must additionally be labeled with the breeds, e.g., "Newfoundland" or "Saint Bernard".

Deployment scenarios Artificial intelligence will be used in a variety of scenarios. At least three different scenarios are emerging: (1) use of artificial intelligence for decision-making or support by specialists from a fixed or mobile workplace with full availability of the potential of the Internet and the capacities offered therein, (2) incorporation of artificial intelligence into fixed or mobile Internet applications without the user being aware that artificial intelligence is being used, and (3) use of artificial intelligence in microprocessors that are incorporated into physical products. Artificial Intelligence management must provide solutions for all deployment scenarios. When deep learning is used, training and use of the neural network can be separated. On very powerful computers the deep neural network is trained and on the less powerful microprocessors the deep neural network is used for making (deterministic) inferences.

Dealing with training data The training process results in numerous challenges for artificial intelligence management, such as obtaining the training data, labeling the training data, refining the training data, handling rights on the training data, as well as dealing with *bias* in training data. Undetected bias in training data has already led to numerous problems. For example, Amazon used artificial intelligence to support its recruiting process and systematically rejected female applicants through bias in training data [14]. Apple used a neural network to determine the limit of its credit card. The result, again through bias in training data, was that credit cards of female customers were systematically given lower credit limits than those of male customers [15]. The list of already published problems due to bias in training data could be continued at will.

Systematic recognition of value potentials   There are many discussions today about what artificial intelligence can do. The discussions that take place are often based on ideas from feature films, euphoric reports and untenable assumptions. There is a need for a systematic, comprehensible, and fact-based process that leads to ideas and prototypes, which are evaluated in a further step for their economic viability and potentials. A major challenge in recognizing the potential is envisioning the economic effects of using artificial intelligence when a prototype becomes a productive solution.

Data   Discussions with and reports from companies that are intensively involved in the use of artificial intelligence regularly lead to statements that more than 80% of the effort in projects in which artificial intelligence is used is attributable to the area of data. The spectrum of problems is very wide: insufficient quantity, insufficient quality, insufficient transparency about the origin of the data and legal problems. Artificial intelligence, as already stated, is based on data. If the data is not available, the use of artificial intelligence makes no sense. Even though we tend to get positive messages from companies again and again regarding the solution of the data problem, we remain skeptical. In particular, the lack of data quality has been a constant challenge for all people involved in operational information processing for decades. What is certain is that the growing importance of artificial intelligence is massively increasing the pressure on all parties involved to finally do their homework regarding data.

Competencies   There is still not enough knowledge about artificial intelligence in companies. On the one hand, there is a lack of very well-trained specialists who are able to solve complex problems with artificial intelligence. On the other hand, there is a lack of basic training for employees in the handling of data, i.e., data literacy, in the company departments and at the various hierarchical levels of a company. In our view, building up competence in artificial intelligence can only be achieved through a combination of training existing employees and recruiting specialists. Both approaches are very challenging for companies.

Architecture   The development or provision of environments for building prototypes and for professional operation requires further development of existing information system architectures in companies. When prototypes become productively deployable solutions, they must fit into the company's existing architecture or at least be compatible and compliant. This means that open-source software, as well as software that is only available as software-as-a-service from companies such as Google, Amazon, Microsoft or IBM must be integrated into the company's existing architecture. This task is made more difficult by the highly dynamic environment that exists in the further development of artificial intelligence at the moment. What seems good and right today may already be outdated or even wrong in 6 months.

Infrastructure Closely related to the "architecture" challenge is the procurement and provision of the hardware and software infrastructure required to build prototypes and run productive applications with artificial intelligence. Dealing with cloud solutions plays a decisive role. Make or buy decisions are very challenging when deploying infrastructure. Many ideas for using artificial intelligence can only be realized if large storage and processing capacity are available. Hardware requirements can be mitigated if pre-trained solutions or ready-made AI services are used, but here too it must be considered whether changes in the data do require regular retraining. As a rule, even for larger companies, building up the corresponding capacity can only be justified for particularly attractive business cases. Cloud-based applications can be a solution, provided that Internet connectivity is ensured throughout, but their pay-per-use costs should not be underestimated. The monopolistic position of companies such as Google, Amazon and Microsoft is an additional and aggravating factor, not only in this context.

Fears In numerous conversations and a survey that we were allowed to conduct for a large technology company, we see that fear of artificial intelligence is also widespread in the IT departments of companies. Job loss and inhumane dominance of artificial intelligence are just two themes that come up again and again. Even people who have a positive attitude towards rationalization and automation of processes in companies react skeptically and, in many cases, defensively when it comes to the use of artificial intelligence.

Ethics In many companies, and in some cases also in political and religious contexts, the fears of employees lead to the demand for ethical rules in dealing with artificial intelligence. In the context of our research on automated vehicles, we are repeatedly confronted with the question: Should an autonomous vehicle run over the two elderly gentlemen or the young woman with a baby carriage when there are only these two alternatives [16, 17]?

Security The use of artificial intelligence leads to new challenges, for example, through adversarial attacks, i.e., manipulation of the input interface. T-shirts that cripple automated vehicles have become known to a wider public [18]. The pattern printed on the T-shirts is interpreted by the artificial intelligence of an automated vehicle as a command to stop.

Law and regulation Artificial intelligence will also be used in products and services in regulated industries. Legal and regulatory requirements must be met. The traceability of decisions in stochastic AI systems has been a major challenge. Ethics has also made its way into law and regulation: The European Union, among others, has published guidelines for the development of trustworthy AI systems [19].

Roles Artificial intelligence, like many other developments in computer science, will lead to new roles in companies and to new job descriptions. In the environment of handling training data, for example, numerous roles will emerge. These must be defined in the context of artificial intelligence management.

Processes For dealing with artificial intelligence, documented and comprehensible processes are necessary that can be disseminated in the context of education and training, that lead to comprehensible solutions, and that are audit-proof. These processes must be embedded in the management of the company and the management of IT. How traceability and auditability on the one hand and intransparency and stochastically calculated decisions of an AI system on the other hand can be reconciled is an unresolved question.

Profitability Return on investment is a key business challenge. Investments in artificial intelligence must pay off in the end just like all other investments. It is of central importance to consider very early in the innovation process whether the realization of an innovative idea can pay off in the end. Euphoria and hype are not good advisors for sensible entrepreneurial decisions.

6 State of Research and Practice

In science, specifically in computer science and information systems, the study of managing artificial intelligence is just beginning. The development of even more powerful algorithms and the infrastructure required for artificial intelligence, e.g., processors or software modules, is in the foreground. Prototypes demonstrate in each case the progress that has been made.

We are not aware of any published process, document, or role models for artificial intelligence management. According to our research, professionalization is most advanced in the area of data science or data mining. The original model was a process for Knowledge Discovery in Databases (KDD) developed in the 1990s in the environment of Jet Propulsion Lab, Microsoft and GTE Laboratories [20]. In the late 1990s, the CRISP process [21] emerged, which is still the basis of numerous methods for analyzing data using artificial intelligence. CRISP-DM stands for CRoss-Industry Standard Process for Data Mining. This cross-industry process model was developed starting in 1996 as part of an EU-funded project by such well-known participants as DaimlerChrysler (then Daimler-Benz) and SPSS (then ISL). It divides the data analysis process into the steps "Business Understanding", "Data Understanding", "Modeling", "Evaluation" and "Deployment". It is not proprietary. CRISP-DM has been further developed by academia and practitioners. For example, it has been extended by Martínez-Plumed [22] to include additional components, such as "Data Source Exploration" or "Data Value Exploration". IBM has further developed the CRISP-DM method to the ASUM-DM method [23], SAS to the SEMMA method [24]. Microsoft has made a significant step towards an artificial intelligence management model with the TDSP method [25]. There are processes for training models, processes for handling data and a process that deals with "customer acceptance". While the TDSP method also focuses on technical aspects, it has also begun to incorporate some of the management building blocks. In this context, the "customer acceptance" process, which consists of a validation of the system and the project handover, is particularly worth mentioning. The TDSP model is widely used in science and especially in practice today.

When comparing the challenges we have described in this paper with the published models for data science, the deficits seem obvious. In projects and studies, we have looked more closely at the use of the published process models in applying companies. In leading companies, whose percentage share of the companies we estimate to be below 10%, management models are emerging. For example, intensive work is being done on combining agile software development, design thinking and the use of artificial intelligence. There are now also numerous companies that have adopted ethical rules for dealing with artificial intelligence. Awareness of specific threat scenarios posed by artificial intelligence is also emerging. However, if we summarily assess the state of science and practice, we conclude that the construction of prototypes, the content of which is often more or less random, dominates and that there are only fragments of artificial intelligence management visible. In view of the undisputed future importance of artificial intelligence, we believe there is a great need for action.

7 Approach

Based on numerous discussions with experts from business and academia, as well as our comprehensive analyses, we assert that artificial intelligence management must combine feasibility, viability and desirability, regardless of the specific processes involved. Figure 2 illustrates our approach. In the future, it will only be possible to achieve sustainable entrepreneurial success using artificial intelligence when the AI

Fig. 2 Basic approach to artificial intelligence management

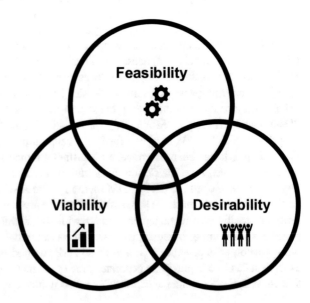

systems being developed are not only feasible, but also economically viable and desired, or at least accepted, from a user perspective.

Feasibility covers all aspects of artificial intelligence management that ensure that a technically feasible and scalable application is created that meets legal and regulatory requirements. Looking at the requirements we have described, *feasibility* covers all aspects that are necessary to first create prototypes and later a deployable solution. The process models we have described, and also many other approaches in business and practice, focus one-sidedly on the *feasibility* aspect. Satisfaction about the use of artificial intelligence already arises in many companies and among many business executives when a prototype somehow works and apparently achieves useful results. Questions about training data, scaling or legal issues are often pushed aside. This view is not surprising when dealing with a new development in computer science, such as neural networks and deep learning. First, it is a matter of taming the "beast". Today, only a few prototypes manage to be transferred into productive operation, because it has been forgotten to consider not only the technical feasibility but also the *feasibility* of economic viability and customer acceptance. This is shown by experiences from large companies as well as from leading scientific institutions that are at the interface between business and science.

Viability stands for the search for economic success. More specifically, the aim is either to generate more revenue or to save costs. Every decision in the context of the use of artificial intelligence must be consistently examined for its economic impact. This sounds trivial at first. However, when considering the complexity, the scope of the investments, and the expected dependencies, economic viability becomes a central issue. At least from today's perspective, it is enormously difficult to estimate based on prototypes how high additional revenues, cost reductions and the effort required to operate AI applications (e.g., applications that use AI in the form of neural networks) will be. From analyzing the costs of conventional applications, we know that only 10% of the costs are incurred in the innovation and development process and 90% of the costs during system operations. However, we see very successful approaches at individual companies where the benefits of using artificial intelligence can be demonstrated through a type of A/B testing [26]. From Amazon, it is circulated that more than 30% of the revenue comes from recommendations, which are probably made by using artificial intelligence. If a second "winter" of artificial intelligence is to be avoided, the consideration of business viability is of high importance.

Desirability ensures that the solutions developed with the help of artificial intelligence are accepted by the target groups and, more general, desired by society. Current media announces almost every week that artificial intelligence applications are rejected even among intended target groups. People react with rejection when they learn that artificial intelligence is involved in cancer diagnosis [27], in the brake assistant of a car [28], or in the calculation of school grades [29]. We are not sure whether this phenomenon is comparable to the negative reactions to advances in computer science that have been common for decades or whether it is a new phenomenon. However, we must concede that discussions around the use of artificial intelligence have already triggered controversial and broad social debates when it comes to the work of the future and the demand for an unconditional basic income. In any case, desirability includes that solutions using artificial intelligence are intensively discussed and tested with the intended target groups.

8 Processes

Based on existing approaches in science and practice for managing artificial intelligence, the challenges already described, our fundamental approach, i.e., feasibility, viability, and desirability, and our experience in constructing management models, we have developed a process model at a high level of abstraction (Fig. 3). Each process must consider the requirements for feasibility, viability, and desirability as part of its concretization and use.

   The process model consists of a core process that structures the development of artificial intelligence applications and divides it into the process steps *idea generation, building prototypes and testing, development and integration* and *operations and maintenance*. This core process is further subdivided into the supporting processes of *AI strategy development, data acquisition and provisioning, development of competencies and culture, development of technology infrastructure*, and *management of risk, regulation and compliance*. We recognize that these processes are not yet complete. Further research and collaboration will validate, develop and flesh out further elements in this process model.

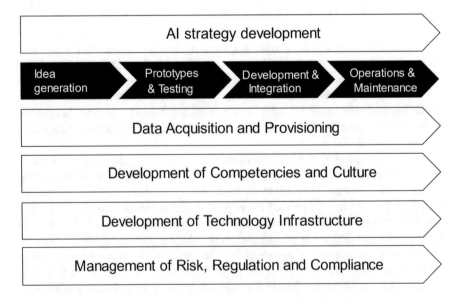

Fig. 3 Rudimentary processes of artificial intelligence management

8.1 Strategy Development

This process is responsible for ensuring that the deployment in a company is not random and only driven by opportunity but is geared to the long term and aligned with the corporate strategy and the future development of the company's business model. Depending on the strategy, resource decisions have to be made. In the next few years, we will see numerous companies completely aligning their business strategy and, as a consequence, their IT strategy with the use of artificial intelligence. The goal of these companies will be to combine maximum automation of processes with maximum individualization for customers. Pursuing such goals is not possible without a well-developed AI strategy. But even the selectively increased use of artificial intelligence in products and services requires strategic decisions. The list of management tasks in Sect. 5 of this article can serve as an initial checklist of which areas must be covered by an AI strategy.

8.2 Idea Generation

In the *idea generation* process, ideas are developed for the use of artificial intelligence in companies. The aim is to examine as systematically as possible all of a company's processes, products, services and business models to determine whether the use of artificial intelligence could be beneficial. The goal is to ideally develop business use cases and prototypes that are—technically feasible, humanly desirable and economically viable. Design thinking [30], for example, provides methods and tools that are suitable for meeting these requirements and—if applied correctly—for developing initial rudimentary prototypes and thus already laying the foundations for the work in the second process step *building prototypes and testing*. We propose to be guided by the three criteria *desirability, feasibility,* and *viability*. The criteria of desirability and viability ensure that the focus is not one-sidedly on technical feasibility. This is the case with many failed artificial intelligence projects. At the University of St. Gallen, we are testing the generation of ideas that meet the criteria of desirability, feasibility and viability in a course in which design thinking is combined with the use of artificial intelligence [31].

8.3 Building Prototypes and Testing

The goal of this process step is to further develop the idea evaluated as feasible in the previous *idea generation* process into prototypes. Technical feasibility in the construction of prototypes means that the required artificial intelligence method is available, can be used, and is at least fundamentally capable of contributing to the solution of the original task. The selection of the appropriate method from the artificial intelligence portfolio is of great importance in the context of building and testing prototypes. On the one hand, profound knowledge about artificial intelligence is necessary and on the other hand, one has to experiment with several artificial intelligence methods in order to make a good selection. Very often the available hardware is not able to handle the necessary artificial intelligence method. Comparing AI methods across different applications is even more difficult. An algorithm that performs better than all comparison candidates for one decision problem may prove very unreliable for another problem if the structure and distribution of the data differs, even if this is not obvious in the data.

In addition to technical feasibility, human desirability is a problem, if not the central problem, in the context of the second process step, *building prototypes and testing*. From many innovation projects with design thinking we have learned that so-called user tests with users or customers are a very promising way to find out the desirability of a solution. The prototypes must be implemented to the extent that they can be tested by humans. Only in this way is it possible to gain an impression of how desirable a solution is in later productive use. Design thinking, human-computer-interaction design and other fields of knowledge from science and practice provide methods and tools for user testing. The third step in the process step *building prototypes and testing* deals with economic viability. Based on the prototypes and the experience gained from user testing, it should be possible to make estimates of the economic benefit. In doing so, it is easier, but also not very easy, to estimate the costs. Often, especially in new areas, the effort is massively underestimated. We have learned from many innovative projects that a constructively sober view should be taken when evaluating prototypes. Especially with new hyped technology projects, there is a very euphoric mood where risks are underestimated and potential benefits are overestimated. For us, a solid risk analysis is another important part of the *building prototypes and testing* process. As part of this step, it is also important to think about the requirements for implementation. As with all information technology projects, the question of *make or buy* also arises for projects that focus on artificial intelligence. Dependence on technology giants such as Google, Amazon and IBM, which are very often used for prototyping, is apparently even more challenging in the medium and long term than working with traditional software companies such as SAP, Oracle or Salesforce. When prototyping in collaboration with technology giants, the rights to one's own data can be lost, which represents a novel challenge.

8.4 Development and Integration

The goal of the third process step is to convert the selected prototype into productive solutions. Depending on the method used, the right approach must be selected. There are two different paradigms for the part of an application that uses artificial intelligence methods: programming and training. Many Artificial Intelligence methods are implemented by developing a classical program code. When the solution using artificial intelligence is programmed, all the rules and all the experiences of software development apply. In the commercial internet world, especially when it comes to apps on mobile devices, the agile method is dominant today. When it comes to large complex software projects and software in embedded systems, the waterfall model still dominates in our view. The development of applications in which artificial intelligence is used can be used both in projects that are handled with agile methods and in projects that are handled with the waterfall model. Hence, it is important to make a clear decision in favor of one of the two approaches in software projects, although in our experience the agile approach has a clear advantage in terms of managing AI risks. As a rule, artificial intelligence is a part of an application or a software landscape. Accordingly, the part of the application that uses AI must be integrated into the application or application landscape. This means that all the rules and experiences from classic software development regarding architectures, inter-faces and integration challenges also apply to projects with artificial intelligence. Testing particularly these applications is a major challenge.

When machine learning methods are used in projects, training complements programming. The result of the training process in machine learning is a function that applies the learned pattern to new input data and thus calculates new outputs. This highly abbreviated description of the approach to machine learning projects provides only a very rudimentary basic understanding. Training models must be considered prominently in artificial intelligence management models. These new processes, which do not exist in traditional information management, include obtaining training and test data, labeling data, and measuring bias in data. For the management of artificial intelligence, it is important to identify the requirements that must be met when procuring training or test data, to measure whether any data that can be purchased meets the requirements, and to regularly re-survey the amount of data in order to adapt it to changes. If no suitable data is available, the data must be created by the company itself. There are established procedures for splitting the created data into training and test data, which ensure the independence of training and test data.

8.5 Operations and Maintenance

In IT, operation means running the fully developed applications and making them available to the users or, in the case of externally oriented systems, to the customers. The sub-processes assigned to the *operations* process include ongoing monitoring of the systems, for example with regard to response times (latency) and availability. In addition, the systems must be maintained, i.e., adapted to changes in the infrastruc-ture, e.g., further developments of the operating systems, and security and compli-ance with statutory regulations, e.g., data protection regulations, must be observed. In addition, detected errors in the applications must be eliminated as quickly as possible. If an error is in deep learning, it is probably due to the training data. However, identifying the exact cause there, cleaning the training data correctly and retraining the application is very time-consuming. To make matters worse, detecting errors in AI-based decisions can be delayed because they only become apparent when they occur in drastic form, since the input-output relationship is usually complex.

In addition, operating the infrastructure is one of the core tasks of the *operations* process. Many of the applications currently being developed are designed for operations in the cloud. This increases the complexity of the applications, but according to reliable statements tends to reduce the costs of operation. In principle, the operation of applications with artificial intelligence takes place in the same way as all applications. If machine learning methods are used, it must be checked whether a *concept drift* [32] or *out of range behavior* [33] could potentially exist in the application environment. In this case, it must be ensured that the models are regularly adapted through new training with current training data.

8.6   Data Acquisition and Data Provisioning

Data is the basis and *the material with* which artificial intelligence works. The procurement, quality assurance and provisioning of data are central processes within the framework of artificial intelligence management. Corporate reality shows that many good ideas for the use of artificial intelligence fail because of the availability or quality of the data. This insight is not new. Lack of data quality has been a major challenge for companies for decades. In the age of artificial intelligence, it has a devastating effect. Ownership and decision rights over data can also hinder innovative artificial intelligence applications. There are still many departments that, for various reasons, assume they are the sole owners of their data and can prevent it from being used by other areas of the company. Solving the old problems in dealing with data is a central prerequisite for the successful use of artificial intelligence. The importance of *data processes* is correspondingly great. If neural networks, for whose training, training data and test data are required, are to be used, further processes are needed that deal with the procurement, analysis and further development of the training data.

8.7   Development of Competencies and Culture

Like other technologies, artificial intelligence needs a *foundation* in companies in order to be used successfully. Building competencies for artificial intelligence is an indispensable prerequisite. Two paths must be taken: Further training of existing employees who have the necessary basic qualifications and acquisition of new employees. In many companies, especially in large enterprises, there are employees in the IT department and in research and development who are willing to undergo further training in artificial intelligence either because of their studies or because of their training or previous work experience.

A second important foundation for the successful use of artificial intelligence is the development of a positive attitude. From surveys of large companies, we know that many employees are afraid of the use or outcomes of artificial intelligence. Artificial intelligence is equated with a radical reduction in jobs and external control by robots. Triggered by these two arguments, there is a great deal of hidden fear in companies that is not openly communicated and forms a kind of silent resistance to artificial intelligence. Against this background, it is a central task of artificial intelligence management to ensure, as far as possible, a readiness for change in the use of artificial intelligence. Transparency about the projects, opportunities for information and further training can be useful measures to reduce fears.

8.8 Development of Technology Infrastructure

The use of artificial intelligence requires the establishment of special information technology infrastructures. This includes development and operating platforms, and the use of external infrastructures, for example from IBM, Microsoft, Google and Amazon. Depending on the intensity and degree of innovation of the use of artificial intelligence, it may be necessary to procure and operate special servers, for example from Nvidia, and storage. In addition, the necessary software must be procured and operated. Many companies use the infrastructures of Google, Amazon, IBM and Microsoft for the prototypes. In any case, it makes sense for a company that wants to use artificial intelligence competitively to build up enough competence to be able to create invitations to tender and check the offers received.

8.9 Management of Risk, Regulation and Compliance

The use of artificial intelligence in products, services and business models, and also in in-house applications, is associated with risks that should not be underestimated. We have already pointed out the risks posed by bias in the training data. Compliance quickly becomes more important here than the actual solution. Further risks arise, for example, from the use of artificial intelligence in products that are regulated, such as in banks, insurance companies or the automotive industry. Many applications used in these industries must be reviewed and permitted by the regulator. When artificial intelligence is used in these applications, permission must be obtained. In particular, the step from programming to training and the step from deterministic to stochastic decision models is sometimes very difficult when obtaining permits. We believe that comprehensive risk management, dealing with regulation, and establishing rules for compliance and adherence to them is a key task in managing artificial intelligence. If projects using artificial intelligence are developed along the three fields of action of feasibility, desirability, and viability, and if they are also taken into account in risk management, risk can be better controlled. All legal and compliance issues belong in the *feasibility* field of action, along with the availability and mastery of IT, because, if there are non-solvable compliance issues, we consider the solution as non-feasible.

9 Next Steps

The ideas and concepts for artificial intelligence management presented in this paper represent the beginning of application-oriented research in this field. We receive very positive reactions when discussing our ideas in academia and practice. It becomes clear that it is not enough to work on algorithms, software and hardware for the use of artificial intelligence. If the potential of artificial intelligence is to be leveraged for companies, artificial intelligence management is needed.

The next steps are to develop and test ideas on how to further refine this process model, to develop work products for each process step, and to address roles and the competencies needed to fulfill them. Artificial intelligence management will never be a standalone area of business management or information technology management. It must be integrated into existing management systems. This integration will be another next step.

However, it will be crucial to raise awareness, even among very technically oriented people, that technology alone is not enough to help artificial intelligence achieve a breakthrough. One example of this is how to deal with bias in artificial intelligence applications. Bias can be introduced into the application in various ways and the causes here can be of a technical or socio-technical nature. For this reason, a purely technical view is not sufficient for this topic. Some tools already exist for dealing with bias, for example from Google [34] and IBM [35], but some of them are still unsatisfactory because of their purely technical focus. In the future, these tools need to be made manageable. We are convinced that application-oriented computer science and information systems research can make a significant contribution to the establishment of artificial intelligence management. It is in this sense that the authors wish this contribution to be understood. It is based on an intensive and exciting collaboration between a computer scientist and two information systems experts.

References

1. Poole, D., Mackworth, A., Goebel, R.: Computational Intelligence: A Logical Approach. Oxford University Press. (1998)
2. Russell, S., Norvig, P.: Artificial Intelligence: A Modern Approach. Pearson Education Limited. (2013)
3. Kaplan, A., Haenlein, M.: Siri, Siri, in my hand: who's the fairest in the land? On the interpretations, illustrations, and implications of artificial intelligence. Bus. Horiz. **62**, 15–25 (2019)
4. Samuel, A.L.: Some studies in machine learning using the game of checkers. IBM J. Res. Dev. **3**, 210–229 (1959)

5. Deng, L., Yu, D.: Deep learning: methods and applications. Found. Trends Sig. Process. **7**, 197–387 (2014)
6. McCulloch, W.S., Pitts, W.: A Logical Calculus of the Ideas Immanent in Nervous Activity, (1943).
7. Wiener, N.: Cybernetics: Or Control and Communication in the Animal and the Machine. Technology Press (1948)
8. Koehler, J.: From Theory to Practice: AI Planning for High Performance Elevator Control. Springer, Berlin (2001)
9. Koehler, J., Ottiger, D.: An AI-based approach to destination control in elevators. AI Mag. **23**, 59–78 (2002)
10. Hillig, J.: Lift-Odyssee im Zürcher Stadtspital Triemli. https://www.blick.ch/news/schweiz/zuerich/lift-odyssee-im-zuercher-stadtspital-triemli-besucher-sind-mit-der-handhabung-nicht-klar-gekommen-id8088843.html (2018)
11. Hale, J.: More Than 500 Hours of Content Are Now Being Uploaded to YouTube Every Minute. https://www.tubefilter.com/2019/05/07/number-hours-video-uploaded-to-youtube-per-minute/
12. Bitkom: Digitalisierung gestalten mit dem Periodensystem der Künstlichen Intelligenz. Ein Navigationssystem Für Entscheider. Bundesverband Informationswirtschaft, Telekommunikation Und Neue Medien e.V. (2018)
13. van Giffen, B., Borth, D., Brenner, W.: Management von Künstlicher Intelligenz in Unternehmen. HMD Praxis der Wirtschaftsinformatik. **57**, 4–20 (2020)
14. Dastin, J.: Amazon scraps secret AI recruiting tool that showed bias against women. https://www.reuters.com/article/us-amazon-com-jobs-automation-insight/amazon-scraps-secret-ai-recruiting-tool-that-showed-bias-against-women-idUSKCN1MK08G (2018)
15. Myers West, S.: In the Outcry over the Apple Card, Bias is a Feature, Not a Bug. https://medium.com/@AINowInstitute/in-the-outcry-over-the-apple-card-bias-is-a-feature-not-a-bug-532a4c75cc9f
16. Awad, E., Dsouza, S., Kim, R., Schulz, J., Henrich, J., Shariff, A., Bonnefon, J.-F., Rahwan, I.: The Moral Machine experiment. Nature. **563**, 59–64 (2018)
17. Moral Machine. https://www.moralmachine.net/hl/de
18. Lossau, N.: Autonome Autos: Ein buntes Muster legt ihr Gehirn lahm. https://www.welt.de/wissenschaft/article202616258/Autonome-Autos-Ein-buntes-Muster-legt-ihr-Gehirn-lahm.html (2019)
19. Madaio, M.A., Stark, L., Wortman Vaughan, J., Wallach, H.: Co-designing checklists to understand organizational challenges and opportunities around fairness in AI. In: Proceedings of the 2020 CHI Conference on Human Factors in Computing Systems, pp. 1–14. Association for Computing Machinery, New York, NY (2020)
20. Fayyad, U., Piatetsky-Shapiro, G., Smyth, P.: The KDD process for extracting useful knowledge from volumes of data. Commun. ACM. **39** (1996)
21. Chapman, P., Clinton, J., Kerber, R., Khabaza, T., Reinartz, T., Shearer, C., Wirth, R.: Others: CRISP-DM 1.0: Step-by-step data mining guide. SPSS Inc. **9**, 13 (2000)
22. Martínez-Plumed, F., Contreras-Ochando, L., Ferri, C., Hernández Orallo, J., Kull, M., Lachiche, N., Ramírez Quintana, M.J., Flach, P.A.: CRISP-DM twenty years later: from data mining processes to data science trajectories. IEEE Trans. Knowl. Data Eng. 1–1 (2019)
23. IBM: Analytics Solutions Unified Method (2016)
24. Matignon, R.: Data Mining Using SAS@ Enterprise Miner. Wiley (2007)
25. Microsoft: What is the Team Data Science Process? https://docs.microsoft.com/en-us/azure/machine-learning/team-data-science-process/overview
26. Siroker, D., Koomen, P.: A / B Testing: The Most Powerful Way to Turn Clicks Into Customers. Wiley (2013)
27. May, A., Sagodi, A., Dremel, C., van Giffen, B.: Realizing digital innovation from artificial intelligence. In: Forty-First International Conference on Information Systems. (2020)

28. Herrmann, A., Brenner, W., Stadler, R.: Autonomous Driving: How the Driverless Revolution will Change the World. Emerald Group. (2018)
29. Evgeniou, T., Hardoon, D.R., Ovchinnikov, A.: What Happens When AI is Used to Set Grades? https://hbr.org/2020/08/what-happens-when-ai-is-used-to-set-grades (2020)
30. Brenner, W., Uebernickel, F.: Design Thinking: Das Handbuch. Frankfurter Allgemeine Buch (2015)
31. Design Thinking for AI. https://ai.iwi.unisg.ch/news/design-thinking-for-ai/
32. Schlimmer, J.C., Granger, R.: Beyond Incremental Processing: Tracking Concept Drift. (1986)
33. Amodei, D., Olah, C., Steinhardt, J., Christiano, P., Schulman, J., Mané, D.: Concrete problems in AI safety. arXiv preprint arXiv:1606.06565. (2016)
34. Wexler, J., Pushkarna, M., Bolukbasi, T., Wattenberg, M., Viegas, F., Wilson, J.: The What-If Tool: interactive probing of machine learning models. IEEE Trans. Vis. Comput. Graph. **26**, 56–65 (2020)
35. Bellamy, R.K.E., Dey, K., Hind, M., Hoffman, S.C., Houde, S., Kannan, K., Lohia, P., Martino, J., Mehta, S., Mojsilovic, A., Nagar, S., Ramamurthy, K.N., Richards, J., Saha, D., Sattigeri, P., Singh, M., Varshney, K.R., Zhang, Y.: AI fairness 360: an extensible toolkit for detecting, understanding, and mitigating unwanted algorithmic bias. IBM J. Res. Dev. **63** (2018)

How Fair Is IS Research?

Mateusz Dolata and Gerhard Schwabe

Abstract While both information systems and machine learning are not neutral, the identification of discrimination is more difficult if a system learns from data and discrimination can be introduced at several stages. Therefore, this article investigates if IS Research has taken up with this topic. A literature analysis is conducted and its discussion shows that technology, organization, and human aspects have to be considered, making it a topic not only for data scientist or computer scientist, but for information systems researchers as well.

Keywords Machine learning · Algorithmic fairness · Fairness in AI · Discrimination risks

1 Introduction

Advances in Machine Learning has brought to our attention that Information systems are not neutral: They can favour one group (e.g. white males) and disadvantage other groups (e.g. black females). While any system that makes or prepares decisions based on statistics may discriminate, machine learning adds intransparency to this issue: It is very difficult to determine whether and how a system that learns from data discriminates. These issues are discussed under the topic of "algorithmic fairness" [1–3]. Information systems research has a tradition of studying intended and unintended impacts of the application of information technologies. So we wanted to understand how IS research has taken up this topic and asked ourselves:

RQ 1. How much does current IS research address algorithmic fairness?

Large parts of Sects. 2 and 5 of this paper have been priorly published by us in collaboration with Stefan Feuerriegel [1].

M. Dolata · G. Schwabe (✉)
Faculty of Business, Economics and Informatics, University of Zurich, Zurich, Switzerland
e-mail: dolata@ifi.uzh.ch; schwabe@ifi.uzh.ch

© The Author(s), under exclusive license to Springer Nature Switzerland AG 2021
S. Aier et al. (eds.), *Engineering the Transformation of the Enterprise*,
https://doi.org/10.1007/978-3-030-84655-8_3

37

Assuming that there was at least some IS research on algorithmic fairness, we wanted to understand what issues were discussed and asked

RQ2. What are discrimination risks touched by IS research?

Critically looking at the current state of the art, we then asked

RQ3: What research opportunities does fairness in AI offer to IS researchers?

After introducing some background literature on algorithmic fairness and threats to it, we will present the methodology of the literature review. The results will be presented as use cases addressing algorithmic fairness and what discrimination risks are touched by them. We then discuss implications of those findings for IS research and close the paper with conclusions.

2   Related Work

The philosophical debates concerning fairness have been long dominated by the question of what distribution of what rights is fair. Today's understanding of fairness in democratic societies is based on the idea that all people with equal gifts have equal opportunities for advancement regardless of their initial position in society [4]. In short, the equal distributions of chances for self-advancement as a way to achieve equity in the distribution of goods (i.e., individuals' benefits are proportional to their input) dominates the current philosophical definition of fairness. Preventing individuals from improving their situation by limiting their chances—be it intentionally or otherwise—on the basis of their race, origin, or sex is therefore unfair.

The term "algorithmic fairness" (AF) refers to decision support whereby disparate harm (or benefit) to different subgroups is prevented [5]. In AF, the objective is to provide tools that both quantify bias and mitigate discrimination against subgroups.

Fairness is violated by biases. Biases can emerge at any point along the machine learning pipeline [5], namely (i) data, (ii) modeling, and (iii) an inadequate application, as discussed in the following and summarized in Fig. 1.

Data are used for making inferences; however, if data are subject to biases, inference replicates those biases. They are similar to biases from behavioral experiments and stem from data generation or data annotation [6]. Selection bias, i.e., fewer data for certain subgroups, results in less statistical power and thus a lower prediction performance. For instance, if people of color experience more policing, it is more likely to encounter data showing their recidivism. Measurement bias are errors in labels. Measurement bias can occur due to poor data quality and also originates from labels with prejudices (e.g., as entered by human annotators). Companies and organizations use legacy data when replacing human decision-making with automated decision-making. Since many legacy data lack proper documentation concerning their generation and annotation, there are used to train classifiers without sufficiently critical analysis.

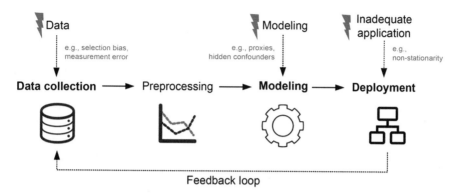

Fig. 1 Sources of algorithmic bias in a typical machine learning project

Modeling selects relevant features as input and combines them in a meaningful way, though often relying upon correlation rather than causation. Hence, modeling can also be a source of bias due to variables acting as proxies or confounders. The presence of proxies means that simply avoiding sensitive attributes is not sufficient, since machine learning uses other variables as proxies in order to implicitly learn relationships from sensitive attributes. For instance, even if race is blinded, ML can "guess" this value based on where a person lives; the ZIP code, then, can function as a proxy for race. A typical confounder is the socioeconomic status of an individual, which is likely to influence the choice of college as well as the neighborhood. Because the socioeconomic status is hidden, an algorithm might establish a direct link between the college education and neighborhood, although there is no real connection between the two. Algorithms used to learn a model can introduce bias, as well, by overweighting certain variables (e. g., ones with many different values).

An inadequate application of the model might occur in dynamic settings with drifts or non-stationarities in the underlying population. Here the data from the training population differ from those of the population after deployment. This causes a mismatch between the population at deployment and at training, where the lack of representativeness causes biased predictions. For instance, such situations occur—with or without intent—when a recidivism prediction system that was trained on data from certain states is applied outside of those states or when it remains in use without regular retraining on new data.

All in all, biases arise at various steps within the ML pipeline and can have multiple sources. The above shows that removing humans from decision support systems does not necessarily prevent biases but, on the contrary, might even reinforce them. Many of the sources of unfairness are not straightforward to identify and require thorough domain knowledge. This poses challenges to the ML developers, who often learn about a field from the data and calls for a more interdisciplinary approach towards fairness.

3   Procedure

In the first research question, we aim at identifying ways in which AF can contribute to information systems research. In particular, we explore how the state-of-the-art IS articles address the risks of unfairness in automated decision-making. This allows us to distinguish areas where such considerations would be necessary but might have been overlooked. This yields an overview of use cases of algorithmic fairness with particular relevance to the IS field. On the one hand, such an overview is necessary to make researchers aware of application areas in need of fairness-oriented research. On the other hand, it provides examples of algorithmic unfairness in state-of-the-art IS, which can be used to locate potentials of discrimination in related areas using analogy. Given the long history of decision support in IS, we decided to focus on use cases where discrimination is likely to emerge and remain unnoticed because of opaque data processing and reasoning, i.e., in the context of machine learning.

We employed the following procedure. First, we selected the sources to include the top IS journals ("basket of eight", that is, EJIS, ISJ, ISR, JAIS, JIT, JMIS, JSIS, MISQ), a leading IS engineering journal with strong focus on practical application areas (*Business & Information Systems Engineering*; BISE), and a prime journal from decision support (*Decision Support Systems*; DSS). Second, within the articles published in these 10 outlets between 2000 and January 2020, we selected those referring to "machine learning", "deep learning", or "learning systems" in their title, abstracts, keywords and other meta-data (search keywords "machine learn*", "deep learn*", "learn* system*" in the literature database Scopus). This yielded 197 articles out of 8768 overall. Third, in order to limit the scope to articles presenting ML-based solutions for one or several application areas, we reviewed titles and abstracts, as well as introduction sections, and employed further criteria: We discarded articles (i) without any reference to a specific application domain (conceptual papers, mathematical proofs, etc.), (ii) which focused on human learning and education, rather than machine learning, (iii) without a decision made by the system or based on the system's output (e.g., analyzing relationship-building in teams), (iv) where no individuals or organizations would be discriminated by the decision (e.g., predicting the lifetime of a machine in an on-board control unit). A subset of 67 relevant articles was identified for analysis.

To identify the most prominent application areas of ML in IS, we classified the articles according to multiple dimensions. First, we manually screened each article for any explicit or implicit references to the topics of fairness, justice, discrimination, or bias in the sense discussed in this article. Second, we identified the main application area(s) addressed in the article. Third, we reviewed the article for potential sources of bias or any risk of discrimination towards specific people or groups of people. In the following, we refer to the three dimensions of the analysis.

The 67 articles considered in this analysis are distributed across five journals: DSS (53 items), JMIS (6), ISR (4), MISQ (3), and ISJ (1 item). The prevalence of DSS coincides with the fact that its prime mission is to support decisions in application areas relevant to IS. Still, articles published in the other journals covered a wide selection of topics and, in most cases, address the same application areas found in DSS. This confirms the relevance of the presented application areas to IS discourse. There were no essential differences between the articles that could be explained by the outlet they were published in.

4 Use Cases of Algorithmic Fairness in IS

The structure of the summary reflects the intended audience, that is, IS researchers. We structure the results to present them with risks of discrimination for selected application areas. First, we summarize how the selected articles discuss biases and fairness issues. Second, we provide a systematic overview of the articles grouped by the application areas. For each area, we list typical use cases, i.e., information on what data is used for what purpose. This information describes the scope of the solutions presented in the papers. Furthermore, for each area, we list and discuss sources of algorithmic unfairness. This discussion relies on information provided in the papers (e.g., information concerning the origin of data or a description of the intended use), but we add an additional explanation as to how this might lead to discrimination once the system is deployed. We acknowledge that, in most cases, the articles do not state whether the system will be used in practice to support real decision-makers. Therefore, we can only refer to discrimination risk and potential biases, rather than to actual discrimination or bias. The discrimination risks listed below can be seen as exemplary instantiations of the biases described in the theoretical background. As such, they show that the danger of unfairness is nearly omnipresent.

Overall, 42 articles refer to a bias or an aspect of fairness; however, only 16 mention biases which might lead to discrimination. Out of those 16, 11 articles use data which they explicitly declare might generate bias: unbalanced data (e.g., [7, 8]), missing data (e.g., [9]), or data potentially perpetuating human bias (e.g., [6]). Two articles point to the risk of bias in natural language processing [10, 11]. Two articles declare that the algorithm they use might undervalue or overvalue specific predictors [12, 13]. One article focuses on minimizing unfairness in a specific application, that is, a call center. This article declares that the proposed application is intended to enhance fairness in a real application [14]. The remaining 27 articles refer primarily to bias as the motivation for the study but in a context in which human decision-makers are the ones who introduce bias and are subsequently replaced by automated decision-making, as in Jang [15]. In general, even if some articles mention bias issues, their focus is not on the actual risk of discrimination (who might suffer discrimination and under what circumstances). Yet, as presented in Table 1, each of the identified use cases bears the risk of discrimination.

Table 1 Example use cases for algorithmic fairness based on the literature review of ML applications in IS. For all reviewed papers and their classification, see [16]

Area	Example use cases	Discrimination risk
Education/student retention *Frequency:* 2 [17, 18]	This research stream draws upon past school records, environmental data (e.g., history of studying), and demographic data (e.g., residential code) regarding students in order to predict how likely the students are to drop the class or fail their exams. Based on results, this research claims to help the students make the right choice about the school or to help schools with the admission process and planning.	Feature selection, training, and testing done on data from specific countries (Belgium and the USA) might discriminate against students with school records from previously unseen countries. It might also perpetuate the race, gender, or age biases of the teachers who graded the exams in the past. There is also the risk of survivorship bias, whereby the model would be updated and tested on those who passed the admissions process, and ignore those who were not accepted because of the biased system.
Crime and fraud *Frequency:* 10 *Examples:* [19–22]	Nine papers use behavior and transaction data to detect patterns of criminal activity, e.g., cryptocurrency transactions that pertain to fraud and online profiles that are fake. In one case, economic, demographic, temporal, and past crime variables are used to predict locations at which offenses might occur.	First, these methods bear the risk of reinforcing feedback loops: policing in specific areas or in specific online communities turns up more crime, which in turn increases the efforts of policing in those circles. Second, systems are trained on data from past crimes, thus perpetuating the biases of police officers. Third, online analyses rely on textual data, which might discriminate against people with lower education levels, with reading or writing disorders, or those who are non-native users of a language.
Health information systems *Frequency:* 12 *Examples:* [23–26]	Seven papers use data from electronic health records to predict patient-specific risks (e.g., infections or kidney transplant failures). They improve diagnostics and the outcome of treatments (e.g., when only the most promising cases receive a kidney). Three papers use image recognition to classify tissues. Two papers use public data (news, online posts) to predict infection outbreaks.	If publicly available data are considered, the system might reinforce the selection biases of news and perform poorly on data written by non-native or disabled users of language. Risk-scoring applications in healthcare might suffer from sampling bias: they are trained predominantly for certain cohorts (e.g., white males are the most frequent test patients). They will perform poorly on other cohorts. Also, survivorship bias can emerge, because, e.g., nonrecipients of a treatment or transplant are not tracked anymore.
Individual risks in insurance and	A topic with a strong tradition in IS. Five papers use financial,	Apart from typical demographic data (age, gender, address), many

(continued)

Table 1 (continued)

Area	Example use cases	Discrimination risk
banking *Frequency:* 6 *Examples:* [27]	demographic, and professional career data of clients to compute a risk score of not paying off a loan. One paper uses demographics and driving behavior to predict risk scores and prices of automobile insurance.	variables used to train the systems referred to untypical data (e.g., "is a foreign worker", "applicant has a telephone", "years in the current residence"), which often (a) function as a proxy for ethnicity, individual preferences, or a specific individual situation (e.g., single mother) and (b) perpetuate biases from risk profiles manually created in the past.
Recommender systems *Frequency:* 6 *Examples:* [7, 28–30]	In such systems, data on a user's behavior on the web (links clicked, time spent on websites, time spent with specific contents, check-in behavior, IP address, etc.) is used to derive a profile of the user. Based on the similarity between the user profiles and/or similarity between the contents, users are offered recommendations for subsequent actions or personalized advertisement. Recommenders support the user by making them an adequate offering and to support the content providers and advertisers by matching content to an appropriate audience.	The discrimination might be two-fold and affect the user as well as the content provider. Popularity bias occurs, such that popular content gets even more popular (because more and more user profiles seem to like it), while niche content remains unpopular. Users can also experience discrimination: users from low-educated families or neighborhoods will be advertised worse schools and worse jobs than users from welloff neighborhoods, despite their individual potential. Furthermore, the recommenders are often linked to the emergence of the filter bubble, such that users identified as members of a specific sub-community are recommended content specific to this subcommunity, trapping them in a reinforcement loop.
Company or country performance *Frequency:* 9 *Examples:* [23, 24, 26]	Publicly available data from organizations (e.g., social media, product reviews, news, members' demographics) are used to predict an organization's value, revenue, innovation budget, creditworthiness, or even moral hazard that might occur in contacts with a company. These works help investors make the right investment or assist organizations in avoiding bankruptcy.	High likelihood of perpetuating selection bias from news and social media, where some organizations or economic sectors are featured more than others. Also, demographics of organizations (e.g., nationality or age of employees) function as proxies for location (ethnically diverse vs. nondiverse societies; urban areas vs. rural areas) and economic sector (sectors hiring migrants from the Southern Hemisphere vs. sectors hiring migrants from wealthier countries), such that whole sectors or regions can be discriminated against.

(continued)

Table 1 (continued)

Area	Example use cases	Discrimination risk
Market and stock exchange *Frequency:* 5 *Examples:* [31, 32]	Use historical data about stock exchange development to predict the future market. In addition, they use predefined scores to assess a proposed investment in terms of its social responsibility or its chance of producing the expected revenue.	Since the models use historical data, they might perform poorly on new companies or new, emerging sectors of the economy and discriminate against them. Also, the systems might perpetuate investors' biases from the past, and ignore environmental aspects (such as governmental infrastructure programs).
Retail and e-commerce *Frequency:* 7 *Examples:* [33–36]	One paper uses demographic, historic, and temporal-spatial data regarding clients for dynamic pricing in a supermarket. Others use online data (reviews, support dialogues between companies and clients, descriptions of products, descriptions of merchants, etc.) to prioritize and classify customer complaints. This should accelerate the handling of complaints or serve as a basis for product improvement.	Dynamic pricing should avoid predictors that act as proxies for sensitive features. The particular case of a dynamic pricing system in a supermarket is likely to discriminate against people with mobility issues due to their untypical temporal-spatial patterns. Using textual data for semiautomatic processing of customer complaints might discriminate against speakers of specific dialects, individuals with writing disorders or a low educational level, and non-native speakers if word choice is selected as the key attribute.
Social media *Frequency:* 9 *Examples:* [37–40]	Use primarily textual content from social networks (posts, tweets, comments), but also the structure of the network (friends, followers), (a) to derive further structural information about the network (four articles) or (b) to summarize opinions about an object (five articles). The structure oriented applications focus on the hotspots of a network: the top-persuader, the hotspot conversation, the topically or geographically most relevant conversations. The object-oriented articles focus on analyzing emotions towards an aspect or a person, e.g., to prevent hate-speech against an ethnic group.	The high dependency on textual content can introduce biases typical for natural language processing. These can include language bias, such that the application might work poorly on mixed-language content or content rendered in infrequently encountered languages, or bias against people with writing and reading disorders, those with a low educational level, dialect speakers, or non-native speakers, such that their contributions will not be considered because of grammatical or orthographical differences. In cases where the selection is based on word count, messages written for the purpose of branding and stigmatizing hate speech might also be blocked if they refer to the language they criticize. In addition, news themes that are prone to "fake news" vary over time and detection

(continued)

Table 1 (continued)

Area	Example use cases	Discrimination risk
		mechanisms should be adjusted regularly, so as not to stay biased against specific topics forever.
Human-computer interaction *Frequency:* 1 [41]	Uses eye-movement of the computer user to predict their task load and identify moments when, e.g., interruption by notifications would be acceptable. Claims to support the user.	In many human-computer interaction tools, physical behavior of the user is used to infer their cognitive state (emotions, stress, idle time) and adjust the operations of the system accordingly. Here, data collection should be conducted with an awareness of people with disabilities.

5 Discussion

IS employs machine learning in a range of application areas, yet rarely with consideration for aspects of fairness. As shown in Table 1, the discrimination might emerge not only through the use of unbalanced data or because of the mathematical attributes of specific algorithms, but also as a consequence of inadequate or unclear selection of data, implicit biases in the data, inappropriate application or interpretation of the outcome, biases inherent to natural language processing or usage of historic data, as well as insensitivity to proxies. Furthermore, it also shows that not only individuals or groups thereof are subject to potential discrimination. Companies and organizations [23, 24], and even countries [9], can suffer from algorithmic unfairness. In particular, their access to money on stock exchanges or from investors might be impacted by an absence of algorithmic fairness.

AF research has thus far been conducted almost exclusively by data science and ML researchers and has only recently attracted nascent interest in the field of IS (e.g., [42, 43]). However, automated decision-making is pre-sent in various disciplines, including, for instance, healthcare and credit rating. Given that legislation across the globe requires fair, accountable, and transparent decision-making, AF is likely to become a necessity in the design of decision support systems. Consequently, AF has profound social, technological, and organizational implications that require a holistic, scientific approach. As suggested above, IS is ideally suited to exploring the capabilities and implications of AF. The cover all the three classical IS dimensions 'people', 'technology' and 'organization'. People Extensive research is required to study user perceptions of fair AI. For instance, a better understanding is needed of which attributes are regarded as sensitive. In practice, sensitive attributes are likely to vary with the underlying use case. For instance, some attributes seem obvious (e.g., race), while other attributes are defined more vaguely (e.g., Christian or American), or are domain-specific (e.g., physically attractive).

Fair AI is related to the wider problem of value alignment: fairness is an important value for humans, one which needs to be taught to AI in decision support systems. IS has the chance to make a lasting impact in this area by specifying models for translating human values identified in philosophy or the social sciences to actionable design principles.

Trust represents the primary prerequisite for an IS ecosystem to succeed [44]. In traditional IS studies, users transfer trust from people or institutions to an IT artifact. Yet AI challenges the traditional conceptualization of trust, since the logic behind its reasoning can often be barely understood. To this end, future research should investigate how fair AI can help in building trust.

5.1 Technology

Several challenges exist when adapting fair AI to applications in practice. For instance, regulatory initiatives such as the GDPR enforce transparent algorithms, yet further research is required to reconcile transparent decision support with fair AI. Statistical approaches for modeling causality [45] are regarded by some as a way to implement fair AI that is tailored to specific uses cases. IS is equipped with the means to develop said casual models (e.g., structural equation models) and make a distinctive contribution to both practice and research in IS. However, this relies upon the premise that the philosophical concept of causality can be described in mathematical language.

IS practitioners demand design principles for implementing fair AI. Here IS as a discipline has the means to derive and test the design principles that guide the decision-making of practitioners (e.g., in choosing a definition of fair AI that is effective for the relevant domain application). Altogether, these efforts can result in information systems where the AI achieves "fairness by design".

Fair AI has direct implications for economics of IS. This is because fair AI is subject to a fairness-performance trade-off: fairness is achieved at the cost of lowering the prediction performance for certain subgroups [42]. However, the economic implications have been overlooked, despite the fact this this represents a key prerequisite for management decisions and thus industry adoption.

5.2 Organization

Fair AI is likely to have an impact on businesses and organizations. For instance, it can render new business models with regard to decision support systems feasible that would have been otherwise restricted by fairness laws. Building upon this, IS practitioners require a better understanding of how fair AI is linked to value propositions, value chains, and revenue models.

Organizational aspects of fair AI are strongly linked to governance. It has been argued that internal governance structures are failing at assuring the fairness of AI [46]. Hence, the effectiveness of different governance structures for the management of fair AI and their relation to other ethics-oriented processes should be investigated. IS, given its interest in governance of change and technology, has the potential to establish a new management framework with the goal of achieving fair AI.

Both governance and business models rely upon the legal frame offered by policy-makers. Given the increasing call for the regulation of AI applications in public and private spheres, various regulatory bodies have initiated discussions regarding the ethical and practical aspects of AI [47]. In this context, IS research, thanks to its real-world impact and expertise in industry, has the opportunity to shape policies.

6 Conclusions

Algorithmic fairness is not just a topic for data scientist or computer scientist; it is also a topic for information systems researchers. Only they are able to link the human, organizational and technical aspects. Up to now, we only see an emerging discourse on fair AI in the areas of decision support and related systems. However, the implications of algorithmic fairness go further and we thus call the IS research community to study the complete spectrum of its human, technological and organizational aspects.

References

1. Feuerriegel, S., Dolata, M., Schwabe, G.: Fair AI. Bus. Inf. Syst. Eng. **62**, 379–384 (2020). https://doi.org/10.1007/s12599-020-00650-3
2. Agarwal, A., Dudik, M., Wu, Z.S.: Fair regression: quantitative definitions and reduction-based algorithms. In: Chaudhuri, K., Salakhutdinov, R. (eds.) Proceedings of the 36th International Conference on Machine Learning, pp. 120–129. PMLR, Long Beach, CA (2019)
3. Pessach, D., Shmueli, E.: Algorithmic Fairness. arXiv:200109784 [cs, stat] (2020)
4. Rawls, J.: Justice as fairness: a restatement. Harvard University Press, Cambridge, MA (2001)
5. Barocas, S., Selbst, A.D.: Big data's disparate impact. Calif. L. Rev. **104**, 671 (2016)
6. Ahsen, M.E., Ayvaci, M.U.S., Raghunathan, S.: When algorithmic predictions use human-generated data: a bias-aware classification algorithm for breast cancer diagnosis. Inf. Syst. Res. **30**, 97–116 (2018). https://doi.org/10.1287/isre.2018.0789
7. Guo, J., Zhang, W., Fan, W., Li, W.: Combining geographical and social influences with deep learning for personalized point-of-interest recommendation. J. Manag. Inf. Syst. **35**, 1121–1153 (2018). https://doi.org/10.1080/07421222.2018.1523564
8. Wang, Q., Li, B., Singh, P.V.: Copycats vs. original mobile apps: a machine learning copycat-detection method and empirical analysis. Inf. Syst. Res. **29**, 273–291 (2018). https://doi.org/10.1287/isre.2017.0735
9. Van Gestel, T., Baesens, B., Van Dijcke, P., et al.: A process model to develop an internal rating system: sovereign credit ratings. Decis. Support Syst. **42**, 1131–1151 (2006). https://doi.org/10.1016/j.dss.2005.10.001

10. Galitsky, B.A., González, M.P., Chesñevar, C.I.: A novel approach for classifying customer complaints through graphs similarities in argumentative dialogues. Decis. Support Syst. **46**, 717–729 (2009). https://doi.org/10.1016/j.dss.2008.11.015

11. Kratzwald, B., Ilić, S., Kraus, M., et al.: Deep learning for affective computing: text-based emotion recognition in decision support. Decis. Support Syst. **115**, 24–35 (2018). https://doi.org/10.1016/j.dss.2018.09.002

12. Hsu, W.-Y.: A decision-making mechanism for assessing risk factor significance in cardiovascular diseases. Decis. Support Syst. **115**, 64–77 (2018). https://doi.org/10.1016/j.dss.2018.09.004

13. Li, X., Chen, H.: Recommendation as link prediction in bipartite graphs: a graph kernel-based machine learning approach. Decis. Support Syst. **54**, 880–890 (2013). https://doi.org/10.1016/j.dss.2012.09.019

14. Kim, J., Kang, P.: Late payment prediction models for fair allocation of customer contact lists to call center agents. Decis. Support Syst. **85**, 84–101 (2016). https://doi.org/10.1016/j.dss.2016.03.002

15. Jang, H.: A decision support framework for robust R&D budget allocation using machine learning and optimization. Decis. Support Syst. **121**, 1–12 (2019). https://doi.org/10.1016/j.dss.2019.03.010

16. Dolata, M., Feuerriegel, S., Schwabe, G.: A sociotechnical view of algorithmic fairness. Inf. Syst. J. (to appear)

17. Delen, D.: A comparative analysis of machine learning techniques for student retention management. Decis. Support Syst. **49**, 498–506 (2010). https://doi.org/10.1016/j.dss.2010.06.003

18. Hoffait, A.-S., Schyns, M.: Early detection of university students with potential difficulties. Decis. Support Syst. **101**, 1–11 (2017). https://doi.org/10.1016/j.dss.2017.05.003

19. Li, W., Chen, H., Nunamaker, J.F.: Identifying and profiling key sellers in cyber carding community: AZSecure text mining system. J. Manag. Inf. Syst. **33**, 1059–1086 (2016). https://doi.org/10.1080/07421222.2016.1267528

20. Kumar, N., Venugopal, D., Qiu, L., Kumar, S.: Detecting review manipulation on online platforms with hierarchical supervised learning. J. Manag. Inf. Syst. **35**, 350–380 (2018). https://doi.org/10.1080/07421222.2018.1440758

21. Sun Yin, H.H., Langenheldt, K., Harlev, M., et al.: Regulating cryptocurrencies: a supervised machine learning approach to de-anonymizing the bitcoin blockchain. J. Manag. Inf. Syst. **36**, 37–73 (2019). https://doi.org/10.1080/07421222.2018.1550550

22. Kadar, C., Maculan, R., Feuerriegel, S.: Public decision support for low population density areas: An imbalance-aware hyper-ensemble for spatio-temporal crime prediction. Decis. Support Syst. **119**, 107–117 (2019). https://doi.org/10.1016/j.dss.2019.03.001

23. Ma, Z., Sheng, O.R.L., Pant, G.: Discovering company revenue relations from news: a network approach. Decis. Support Syst. **47**, 408–414 (2009). https://doi.org/10.1016/j.dss.2009.04.007

24. Kuzey, C., Uyar, A., Delen, D.: The impact of multinationality on firm value: a comparative analysis of machine learning techniques. Decis. Support Syst. **59**, 127–142 (2014). https://doi.org/10.1016/j.dss.2013.11.001

25. Dong, W., Liao, S., Zhang, Z.: Leveraging financial social media data for corporate fraud detection. J. Manag. Inf. Syst. **35**, 461–487 (2018). https://doi.org/10.1080/07421222.2018.1451954

26. Nam, K., Seong, N.: Financial news-based stock movement prediction using causality analysis of influence in the Korean stock market. Decis. Support Syst. **117**, 100–112 (2019). https://doi.org/10.1016/j.dss.2018.11.004

27. Huang, Z., Chen, H., Hsu, C.-J., et al.: Credit rating analysis with support vector machines and neural networks: a market comparative study. Decis. Support Syst. **37**, 543–558 (2004). https://doi.org/10.1016/S0167-9236(03)00086-1

28. Li, X., Wang, M., Liang, T.-P.: A multi-theoretical kernel-based approach to social network-based recommendation. Decis. Support Syst. **65**, 95–104 (2014). https://doi.org/10.1016/j.dss.2014.05.006
29. Bauer, J., Nanopoulos, A.: Recommender systems based on quantitative implicit customer feedback. Decis. Support Syst. **68**, 77–88 (2014). https://doi.org/10.1016/j.dss.2014.09.005
30. He, J., Fang, X., Liu, H., Li, X.: Mobile app recommendation: an involvement-enhanced approach. MIS Quart. **43**, 827–849 (2019). https://doi.org/10.25300/MISQ/2019/15049
31. Tsang, E., Yung, P., Li, J.: EDDIE-Automation, a decision support tool for financial forecasting. Decis. Support Syst. **37**, 559–565 (2004). https://doi.org/10.1016/S0167-9236(03)00087-3
32. Vo, N.N.Y., He, X., Liu, S., Xu, G.: Deep learning for decision making and the optimization of socially responsible investments and portfolio. Decis. Support Syst. **124**, 113097 (2019). https://doi.org/10.1016/j.dss.2019.113097
33. Yuan, S.-T.: A personalized and integrative comparison-shopping engine and its applications. Decis. Support Syst. **34**, 139–156 (2003). https://doi.org/10.1016/S0167-9236(02)00077-5
34. Zhou, W., Tu, Y.-J., Piramuthu, S.: RFID-enabled item-level retail pricing. Decis. Support Syst. **48**, 169–179 (2009). https://doi.org/10.1016/j.dss.2009.07.008
35. Lycett, M., Radwan, O.: Developing a quality of experience (QoE) model for web applications. Inf. Syst. J. **29**, 175–199 (2019). https://doi.org/10.1111/isj.12192
36. Sun, X., Han, M., Feng, J.: Helpfulness of online reviews: examining review informativeness and classification thresholds by search products and experience products. Decis. Support Syst. **124**, 113099 (2019). https://doi.org/10.1016/j.dss.2019.113099
37. Duric, A., Song, F.: Feature selection for sentiment analysis based on content and syntax models. Decis. Support Syst. **53**, 704–711 (2012). https://doi.org/10.1016/j.dss.2012.05.023
38. Lane, P.C.R., Clarke, D., Hender, P.: On developing robust models for favourability analysis: model choice, feature sets and imbalanced data. Decis. Support Syst. **53**, 712–718 (2012). https://doi.org/10.1016/j.dss.2012.05.028
39. Fang, X., Hu, P.J.-H.: Top persuader prediction for social networks. MIS Quart. **42**, 63–82 (2018). https://doi.org/10.25300/MISQ/2018/13211
40. Dutta, H., Kwon, K.H., Rao, H.R.: A system for intergroup prejudice detection: the case of microblogging under terrorist attacks. Decis. Support Syst. **113**, 11–21 (2018). https://doi.org/10.1016/j.dss.2018.06.003
41. Shojaeizadeh, M., Djamasbi, S., Paffenroth, R.C., Trapp, A.C.: Detecting task demand via an eye tracking machine learning system. Decis. Support Syst. **116**, 91–101 (2019). https://doi.org/10.1016/j.dss.2018.10.012
42. Haas, C.: The price of fairness – a framework to explore trade-offs in algorithmic fairness. In: Proc. Intl. Conf. Information Systems. AIS, Munich (2019)
43. van den Broek, E., Sergeeva, A., Huysman, M.: Hiring algorithms: an ethnography of fairness in practice. In: Proc. Intl. Conf. Information Systems. AIS, Munich (2019)
44. Hurni, T., Huber, T.: The interplay of power and trust in platform ecosystems of the enterprise application software industry. Proc. European Conf. Information Systems. AIS, Tel Aviv (2014)
45. Pearl, J., Mackenzie, D.: The Book of Why: The New Science of Cause and Effect, 1st edn. Basic Books, New York (2018)
46. Crawford, K., Dobbe, R., Dryer, T., et al.: The AI now report (2019)
47. Smuha, N.A.: The EU Approach to Ethics Guidelines for Trustworthy Artificial Intelligence. Social Science Research Network, Rochester, NY (2019)

From Business Engineering to Digital Engineering: The Role of Metamodeling in Digital Transformation

Susanne Leist, Dimitris Karagiannis, Florian Johannsen, and Hans-Gert Penzel

Abstract Many of the digital technologies developed in recent years provide the foundation for digital innovations and through their value contributions also contribute to digital transformation. This transformation is imposing tremendous challenges for all enterprises since it allows for radical changes and an increasing pace of transformation. Against this backdrop the paper discusses the role of metamodeling in digital transformation processes as a systematic way to address digital innovation. We show how metamodeling supports the development and adaptation of business and technical systems in an efficient and effective manner. We discuss the benefits and challenges of metamodeling and highlight its contribution to digital transformation from a scientific and practical perspective. We derive the changing requirements for transformation projects and introduce the profile of a digital engineer. Finally, we evaluate metamodeling from a practical perspective and address its lack of dissemination in business practice.

Keywords Metamodeling · Digital innovation · Digital transformation · Business engineering · Digital engineering

S. Leist (✉)
University of Regensburg, Regensburg, Germany
e-mail: susanne.leist@wiwi.uni-regensburg.de

D. Karagiannis
University of Vienna, Vienna, Austria
e-mail: dimitris.karagiannis@univie.ac.at

F. Johannsen
University of Applied Sciences Schmalkalden, Schmalkalden, Germany
e-mail: f.johannsen@hs-sm.de

H.-G. Penzel
ibi research, University of Regensburg, Regensburg, Germany
e-mail: hans-gert.penzel@ibi.de

© The Author(s), under exclusive license to Springer Nature Switzerland AG 2021
S. Aier et al. (eds.), *Engineering the Transformation of the Enterprise*,
https://doi.org/10.1007/978-3-030-84655-8_4

1   Industrial Digital Environments

1.1   Observations of Digital Innovation Industry

Digital transformation refers to the fundamental change of how an organization offers added value to its customers.[1] Gartner distinguishes between the term "digitization" as "...anything from IT modernization to digital optimization" and the term "digital business transformation" as "the invention of new digital business models".[2] We consider the digital innovation as the introduction of either new digital offerings or new digital interactions to realize value for the consumer. Based on the survey of the world economic forum that analyzed 120 use cases[3] of digital innovation, we introduce some use cases to underpin our mindset with practical samples from industry.

Audi used digital technology to improve the customer experience during sales with the concept of Audi City[4] where so-called powerwalls enable the configuration of a personalized Audi virtually in full size. Smaller show rooms that only need four cars are now possible in more prominent locations in the city center. The stock of cars has been reduced and the user experience with multi-touch tables, tablets and powerwalls higher. In the shop in London, the sales went up to 60% compared to traditional showrooms. We consider this as a digitally improved customer interaction, hence an optimization of existing business.

The toy production company LEGO[5] opened their web-based 3D design tool for their development department for third party enthusiasts in order to create their own design of toy stones. A new business branch was established as the community also started to create movies and games using this design tool. The first LEGO movie achieved revenues of about $468 million. The resulting new business group evolved towards an open platform and became the incubator of the whole company. We consider this as new digital offerings, hence a digital transformation of new business.

The survey concludes with three major battle grounds for the digital customer: (i) From product and service to "experiences" as customers demand high-quality experiences and guaranteed outcomes like Disney's Magic Band[6] where visitors of Disney Land can manage the whole stay with a personalized wristband, (ii) Hyper-Personalization, customers expect personalized interactions like Ginger.io[7] that provide individual mental health care, (iii) From ownership to "access" as customer

---

[1] Translated: Boulton Clint (IDG), Lorbeer Klaus, Ab wann kann man von einer digitalen Transformation sprechen, Transform! 11/2018 magazine in conjunction with Computer Welt, computerwelt.at, CW Verlag, Wien.

[2] https://www.gartner.com/en/information-technology/glossary/digital-transformation

[3] http://reports.weforum.org/digital-transformation/

[4] http://reports.weforum.org/digital-transformation/audi/

[5] http://reports.weforum.org/digital-transformation/lego-group/

[6] http://reports.weforum.org/digital-transformation/disneys-magic-bands/

[7] http://reports.weforum.org/digital-transformation/ginger-io/

prefer to have access to available service rather than have ownership. The technology enterprise Cohealo[8] shares medical equipment with hospitals to reduce the need to buy their own.

Consequently the digital innovation demands new forms of organizations, like the concluded Digital Operating Models: (i) customer-centric that focuses on customer experience, (ii) extra frugal focusing on standardized organizations with a "less is more" culture, (iii) data powered building intelligence around an analytic and big data backbone, (iv) use of machines and automation for increased productivity and flexibility, (v) openness and agility as enabler for ecosystems around sharing customers.

We consider the aforementioned samples as the current start and continuation of the digital innovation. In the next chapter, we will observe the mega trend of digital innovation in science, where we assume an arrival in industry with a certain delay.

1.2 Digital Innovation as a Mega Trend in Academia

In order to analyze if the keywords of the title "industrial digital innovation environments" are relevant, we conducted a keyword-based survey over the last 10 years in the major publication platforms: (a) IEEE Xplore,[9] (b) ACM Digital Library,[10] (c) Springer Link,[11] (d) ScienceDirect.[12] For the assessment of the trend, we used different keyword combinations to retrieve publications in the years 2010–2019: (1) Industrial Digital Innovation Environment, (2) Industrial Innovation Environment, (3) Digital Innovation Environment, (4) Industrial Digital Environment, (5) Industrial Environment, (6) Digital Environment, (7) Innovation Environment, (8) Industrial Innovation, (9) Digital Innovation, (10) Industrial Digital Innovation. The search retrieves papers that mention the keyword in the text. The individual platforms have different trend curves. In order to indicate an overview of the total trend, we summarized the results according to the keywords (Fig. 1).

---

[8]http://reports.weforum.org/digital-transformation/cohealo/

[9]https://ieeexplore.ieee.org/Xplore/home.jsp

[10]https://dl.acm.org/

[11]https://link.springer.com/

[12]https://www.sciencedirect.com/

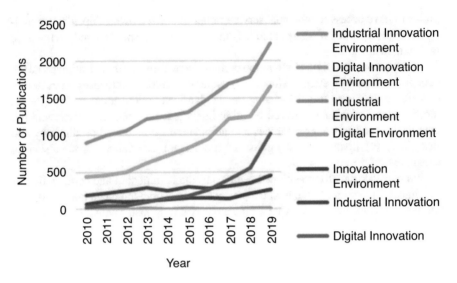

Fig. 1 Numbers of publications according to an exact search of terms in the IEEE, ACM, Springer and Science Direct publication repository without disciplines or meta data restrictions

1.3 Digital Technology as an Enabler for Digital Innovation

As digital innovation is the use of digital technology, this section introduces current and future digital technologies. Although the SONNET[13] initiative analyzed the digital technology focusing on the public administration domain, we consider most of the recommendations also applicable for industry. The list of digital technology in alphabetical order: (a) API—Economy: Turning a business or organization into a platform using and providing APIs. (b) Artificial Intelligence: Tasks requiring cognitive functions are performed by computers instead of humans. (c) Augmented Reality: Visualization of real-world objects that are integrated with virtual objects in real time. (d) Big Data and Data Analytics: Big Data deals with high volume, high velocity and high variety of information assets. Data Analytics is related to discover, interpret and communicate meaningful patterns. (e) Biometric: Automated recognition of measurable biological characteristics and behavior. (f) Block Chain: A peer-to-peer software technology that protects the integrity of a digital piece of information.[14] (g) Cloud Computing: Scalable and elastic IT-enabled capabilities are delivered as a service.[15] (h) Crowdsourcing: Combining the efforts

---

[13] EU Project SONNET: Analysis of Emerging Technologies, 2017; https://www.sonnets-project.eu/content/sonnets-roadmap-and-research-directions

[14] Gartner IT Glossary Blockchain. http://www.gartner.com/it-glossary/blockchain. Accessed 18 July 2017.

[15] Gartner IT Glossary Cloud Computing. http://www.gartner.com/it-glossary/cloud-computing/. Accessed 28 August 2017.

of numerous self-selected volunteers or part-time workers contributing to achieve a cumulative result.[16] (i) Digitalization: Conversion of analogue information into a digital form that can be understood by computers. (j) E-identities/signatures: Means for people to prove that they are who they say they are electronically.[17] (k) E-Participation: ICT supported participation of stakeholders prominently in political participation. (l) Gamification: Usage of game mechanisms—points, challenges, leader boards, rules and incentives in non-game business scenarios.[18] (m) Internet of Things: Internetworking and interconnection of physical devices through embedded electronics, sensors, actuators, software and network.[19] (n) Machine Learning: A subfield of computer science giving computers the ability to learn without being explicitly programmed.[20] (o) Mobile Devices: small computing device that can be held and operated by the hand to provide input and receive output.[21] (p) Natural Language Processing: Turning text or audio speech into encoded structured information.[22] (q) Open Data: Freely available data for everyone to use. (r) Personalization: Tailoring a service to the specific needs of an individual user or user group. (s) Participation/2.0: Open and bi-directional involvement of recipients of a solution. (t) Smart Workplace: Technology-enabled flexible, mobile and collaborative working environment that enables unconventional working patterns. (u) Social Media/Social Networking: Act of establishing online many-to-many human connections for the purpose of sharing information.[23] (v) Virtual Reality: Providing a computer-generated 3D surrounding enabling user actions like in the corresponding real-world nature.[24] (w) Wearables: Electronic miniature devices that are designed to be worn by humans.[25]

---

[16] Gartner IT Glossary Crowdsourcing. http://www.gartner.com/it-glossary/crowdsourcing/. Accessed 28 August 2017. Wikipedia Crowdsourcing. https://en.wikipedia.org/wiki/Crowdsourcing. Accessed 28 August 2017.

[17] European Commission Electronic Identities—a brief introduction. http://ec.europa.eu/information_society/activities/ict_psp/documents/eid_introduction.pdf. Accessed 15 August 2017.

[18] Gartner IT Glossary Gamification. http://www.gartner.com/it-glossary/gamification-2/. Accessed 17 August 2017.

[19] Gartner IT Glossary Internet of Things. http://www.gartner.com/it-glossary/internet-of-things/. Accessed 17 August 2017.

[20] Simon P (2013) Too Big to Ignore: The Business Case for Big Data: Wiley.

[21] Wikipedia Mobile device. https://en.wikipedia.org/wiki/Mobile_device. Accessed 28 August 2017.

[22] Gartner IT Glossary Natural Language Processing. http://www.gartner.com/it-glossary/natural-language-processing-nlp/. Accessed 17 August 2017.

[23] Gartner IT Glossary Social networking. http://www.gartner.com/it-glossary/social-networking/. Accessed 14 August 2017.

[24] Gartner IT Glossary Virtual Reality. http://www.gartner.com/it-glossary/vr-virtual-reality/. Accessed 17 August 2017.

[25] Gartner IT Glossary Wearable Computer. http://www.gartner.com/it-glossary/wearable-computer/. Accessed 17 August 2017.

1.4 Structure and Purpose of the Paper

All these examples demonstrate the value of digital innovations and their contribution to digital transformation. As long as digital innovations create business potentials, digital transformation will occur. Likewise, digital transformation is imposing tremendous challenges for all enterprises as it affects all of their areas. Additionally, since digital innovations allow radical changes, the pace of transformation increases. In view of this, we will discuss the role of metamodeling in digital transformation processes. Metamodeling is a very systematic way to address digital innovation. It supports further developments and maintenance over the full life cycle of business and technical systems in an efficient and effective manner. Thus, it provides long-term benefits. The aim is to discuss the benefits and challenges of metamodeling and to highlight its contribution to digital transformation from a scientific and practical perspective. We will first introduce the concept of metamodeling and identify its benefits and challenges for digital transformation. Using three examples, we will highlight the changing role of metamodeling in transformation projects and its (growing) contribution. At the same time, the changing requirements for transformation projects will be derived and the profile of a digital engineer will be introduced. Finally, metamodeling will be evaluated from a practical perspective and its lack of dissemination in business practice will be addressed.

2 Foundations About Metamodeling and Method Engineering

A metamodel is defined as a model of another model ("object model"). It is used for specifying the modeling language of the object model and determines the available modeling constructs (i.e. semantics), their structure and valid relations (i.e. syntax) and their graphical representations (i.e. notation) [1]. Since every metamodel needs a modeling language, which is also defined by a metamodel on a higher level, a level hierarchy of metamodels emerges. Furthermore, some definitions of a metamodel refer not only to the language of the object model but also to the modeling process (cf. [2, 3]). In these sources, models that graphically represent the modeling activities are also named as metamodels. Usually metamodeling languages are represented by data modeling techniques (e.g. ERM, UML class diagram). In the following analysis, we will primarily focus on metamodels which only define the syntactic and semantic aspects. The main contribution of metamodeling is to explicate the constructs of the used modeling technique and their relations to one another (i.e. semantic and syntax), which provides several benefits (cf. [4]):

- Increases the quality of modeling: All modeling constructs can be evaluated especially with regard to consistency, completeness and unambiguousness (cf. [5, 6]).

- Enables a systematic comparison, evaluation and development of models based on their ability to describe the artifact of interest and to verify whether the model fulfils its intended purpose.
- Enables the development of modeling tools: Metamodels are the essential basis for the development of modeling tools as they ensure the integrated and consistent implementation of different modeling techniques.
- Enables a systematic comparison and evaluation of software tools based on precise descriptions of their functions and data.
- Increases the understanding of the models: The metamodel provides a standardized documentation of all modeling constructs and their relation which helps to increase users' understanding.

Due to the far-reaching benefits, metamodeling is used in numerous domains (e.g., data processing, knowledge representation, requirements engineering, information systems, business process and workflow management) [7]. Despite the far-reaching benefits, the concept of metamodeling is especially used for three fundamental purposes in scientific literature: (1) design, (2) integration and (3) comparison (cf. [7]). For design purposes, metamodeling is applied for both the prescriptive definition of not yet existing and the descriptive modeling of already existing objects of interest. Additionally, metamodeling is applied to integrate different existing artifacts of (potentially) various kinds that have been created using different metamodels [7]. Finally, the concept of metamodeling is used to compare models, tools and various concepts, and thus, to initiate their evaluation and/or further development.

Method Engineering is a very prominent discipline in which the application of the concept of metamodeling is fundamental and in which metamodeling is used for all three purposes. The focus is to design, construct, and adapt methods, techniques and tools. It was initially a discipline inherent to the development of information systems [8–10]. The starting point of many publications in this application field is the variety of the existing software development methods. Despite the availability of a vast number of methods, researchers preferred to develop a new method for each occurring problem. The potential of already existing methods was not exploited [11] and by inventing new methods for every occurring problem, the (already) high number of methods was constantly growing. To counteract this tendency, approaches were developed in Method Engineering, which support the construction of new methods on the basis of already existing ones. In the meantime, a lot of such approaches have been developed and their fields of application have been widely extended.

The following core areas of Method Engineering can be outlined as follows (cf. [1, 9]):

- Specification and design of methods: Methods must be developed on the basis of the particular problem and specified in view of a later (partial) re-use. Thus, the prerequisite is a consistent and well-structured description based on metamodels of the method fragments.

- Comparison and evaluation of methods: Method Engineering offers a basis for the comparison of methods and their consistent evaluation. In this context, the concept of the metamodeling provides an important instrument for the comparative analysis not only of individual method fragments (e.g. modeling techniques, languages) and constructed methods, but also of Method Engineering approaches as such.
- Method integration and adaptation: In order to construct new methods, it is necessary to revert to existing methods and to adapt them to the respective (project) situation in a goal-oriented and contextual way. Thus, methods underlie continuous further development to suit different situations, e.g. by integrating selected method fragments with the help of metamodels.
- Management of method knowledge: The know-how derived from the process of development must be administrated and stored. This refers, above all, to the documentation of the influence of specific situations, contexts and goals on the suitability of individual method fragments. In addition, experience (positive as well as negative) made with the methods and the method construction used ought to be documented in a e-wide data base (cf. [9]).

3   Challenges of the Digital Transformation and Role of Metamodeling

In a recent study by CapGemini [12], 71.3% of the interviewed decision-makers stated that the conduction of digital transformation initiatives will be a central aspect for CIOs in the years to come. In contrast, only 36.5% rated their digital transformation efforts as successful [12]. A first challenge—that may hinder the success of digital transformation initiatives—concerns the strategic networking of companies in an increasingly dynamic market environment (cf. [13]). Hence, more and more enterprises set up cooperations with providers that primarily use digital sales channels and focus on product niches for being able to serve customer requirements [14, 15]. This deeply impacts the design of a company's business processes [14] since inter-organizational working procedures have to be designed across the collaborating partners [16]. At this point, the smooth interchange of information and deliverables between enterprises has to be assured, which poses major problems in practice [16, 17]. Hence, firms often tend to implement, execute and control their internal business processes in an autonomous way, neglecting the impact on the operational procedures at the partner companies [16].

A second challenge is the integration of digital technologies with the business processes [18]. While digital technologies (e.g. AI, cloud computing, enterprise social networks, etc.) can facilitate the above-mentioned inter-organizational collaborations (e.g. [19]) or the efficient design of touch points with customers and suppliers (e.g. [14]), they need to be embedded into the existing or newly developed process structures (e.g. [20, 21]). But due to pressure from the customer's side, such technologies are often introduced in an ad hoc fashion, and their influence on the process performance or the information flow is not thoroughly investigated (cf. [22]). It needs to be acknowledged that employees have to become acquainted with new technologies and existing working procedures need to be revised fundamentally [14, 23]. Therefore, a company must develop a digital vision or digital strategy [15], a topic many companies still lag behind [24].

A third challenge is represented by the decreasing information asymmetry between buyers and sellers (cf. [25]), which forces firms to continuously scrutinize consumers' current needs. Hence, using social media or online portals for price comparison, customers may easily get an overview of the market or product reviews (e.g. [14, 26]). In this respect, the analysis of data from both internal (e.g. CRM-systems) and external IT systems (e.g. social networks) may generate beneficial insights about topical customer requirements [27, 28]. Nevertheless, aspects like the volume, veracity, variety and velocity of the data have to be considered [29]. Many firms struggle to keep pace with continuously shifting consumer needs as the analysis of primary and secondary data to uncover customer requirements turns out to be time-consuming. In light of this, it is widely recognized that a "transformative vision" as well as complementing methods—which guide employees in turning the vision into reality—are needed to ensure the success of digital transformation initiatives [30]. While the development of digital transformation strategies is a lively discussed topic (cf. [31–33]), the creation of methods to systematically support the digital transformation is often neglected by firms.

In this respect, established methods from enterprise architecture management, business process management or change management can be referenced for instance. Such existing methods can then be adapted to new situations (e.g. [34]) that emerge in the course of a company's digital transformation efforts. Otherwise, new methods can be designed for a particular problem (cf. [35]). Thus, the design and adaption of methods is strongly supported with the help of metamodels (e.g. [36]). Hence, either new metamodels (for methods not yet existing) are "created" or existing ones "composed" to form a newly adapted method [36]. The next chapter provides various examples on how the metamodeling discipline has proven as helpful for different stages of the digital evolution.

4 From Past to Future

At first, we demonstrate our thoughts by referring to the Business Engineering approach. Then, an example for the field of Enterprise Engineering with the tool RUPERT is shown. Finally, an outlook on Digital Engineering and the emerging requirements is given.

4.1 Business Engineering

Business Engineering was established at the Institute of Information Management at the University of St. Gallen. The application of Business Engineering aims to support the transformation of companies with traditional business models to the information age. Driven by IT innovations and new business paradigms, the transformation means to fundamentally restructure existing companies or to create new ones. This is a circumstance, which poses tremendous challenges for the companies. To systematically exploit business potentials of those IT innovations, appropriate concepts, methods and tools as well as a systematic and collaborative approach for an interdisciplinary team are of utmost importance. Business Engineering is a design discipline and supports the collaborative, model-based conceptualization, design, and implementation of transformations in companies [37, 38].

Although the vision of the information age was first developed in the early 1990s by Hubert Österle and since then IT innovations with totally different potentials (e.g. Augmented and Virtual Reality) have emerged, it is still valid today. Accordingly, Business Engineering was continuously developed further based on the theoretical foundation of Method Engineering. Robert Winter has made major contributions to the continued developments of Business Engineering. His work and that of his students have greatly expanded the scope of the Business Engineering methods and established links to many related topics (e.g. Enterprise Architecture Management, Business-IT-Alignment, Business Innovation).

In the following section, we selected two models as examples, which evolved from "Robert Winter's school" and illustrate a first version of the Business Engineering metamodels. They were constructed as results of the Competence Center Banking Architecture of the Information Age (CC BAI) (cf. [39]). In this regard, the Business Engineering approach was also technically implemented as the so-called "Business Engineering Navigator" [40] (https://austria.omilab.org/psm/content/ben/info). In Fig. 2, both models focus the collaboration in a network organization including the customer as part of the network. The often-used relations "is-a" likewise "part-off" enable to modify or extend the modeling constructs in order to consider new customer contact channels (like social media platforms) within the customer process analysis for example.

Likewise, the business architecture metamodel can easily be modified e.g. in order to integrate customers in the innovation process (open innovation) within business architecture modeling. Furthermore, the definition of a metamodel on a higher level enables the consistent design of different (object) models (e.g. business architecture model, model for the customer process analysis).

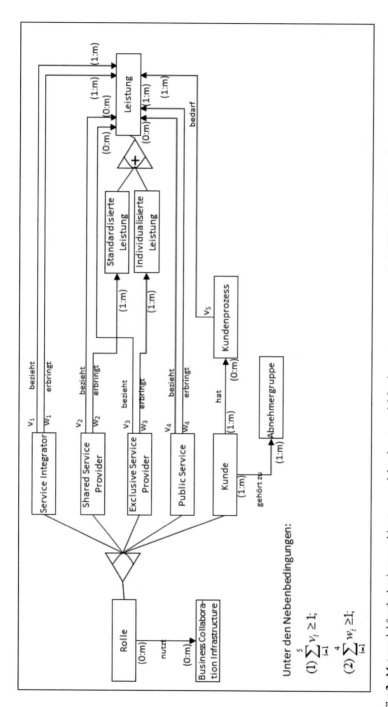

Fig. 2 Metamodel for the business architecture model and metamodel for the customer process analysis [39]—© 2004 Leist-Galanos; reprinted with permission

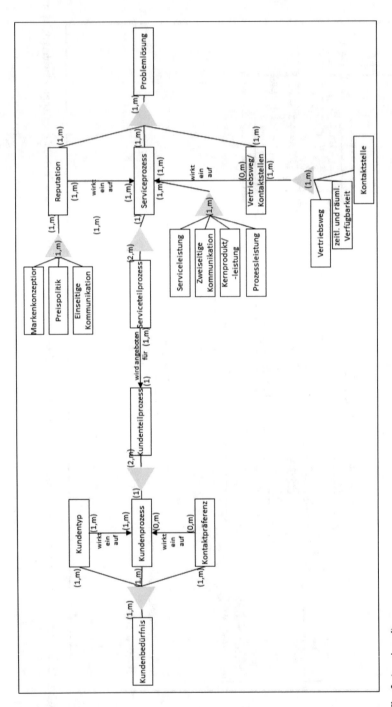

Fig. 2 (continued)

4.2   Enterprise Engineering

Enterprise Engineering "deals with the body of knowledge, principles, and practices" that aim at "the analysis, design, implementation and operation of an enterprise" ([41], p. 1). In this wide field, RUPERT (Regensburg University Process Excellence and Reengineering Toolkit) is an example for a modeling tool that supports firms in improving and redesigning their business processes [42]. The tool builds on established business process improvement (BPI) techniques (cf. [43]) that were transformed into conceptual model types with the help of metamodeling [44]. The model types are logically arranged—according to the DMAIC cycle of Six Sigma [45]—to form a modeling method, to support each stage of a BPI project and to elicit the conversion of employees' tacit process knowledge into suggestions for process improvement or redesign [46, 47]. Figure 3 provides an overview of the BPI techniques realized as model types in RUPERT.

In the Define stage, a rough overview of the process to be improved is given and customer and stakeholder requirements are gathered and specified as project goals. Then, key performance indicators are defined and the data collection is planned (Measure phase). In the Analyze phase, the data is analyzed and problem causes are searched for. Afterwards, solutions to improve the process performance are generated (Improve phase) and the effectiveness of the implemented suggestions is controlled (Control phase).

The model types realized via RUPERT allow to document, communicate and query the results generated by the project team in a BPI project [42]. In addition, the automated analysis of process data via descriptive statistics is enabled by a coupling with the freely available software "R" (https://www.r-project.org/) [44]. That way, knowledge captured in model instances is beneficially complemented by results from the data analyses [27]. RUPERT was realized with the help of the ADOxx metamodeling platform (https://www.adoxx.org/live/home), which has established in practice and research for more than 20 years now (cf. [48]).

Figure 4 gives an overview of the integrated metamodel of RUPERT. It is evident that nine model types were designed to realize the functionalities of above-mentioned BPI techniques. The classes and relations for each model type are highlighted. The statistical techniques (e.g. histograms, control charts, etc.) are covered by the Statistic Interface Model. Because the model types are logically arranged, there are interrelations between the metamodels, which are highlighted by the red arrows in Fig. 4. For instance, customer requirements (Critical-to-Quality factors) explicated in an instance of the CTQ/CTB Model can be automatically referenced later on to purposefully develop key performance indicators (using the Measurement Matrix Model) (see R1).

In summary, the metamodel as shown prepared the ground for the technical realization of the modeling tool RUPERT to support BPI projects.

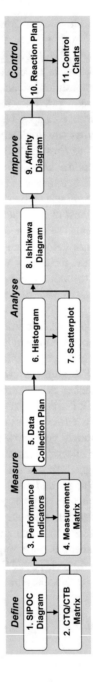

Fig. 3 Arrangement of techniques in RUPERT [44]—© 2016 Springer International Publishing; reprinted with permission

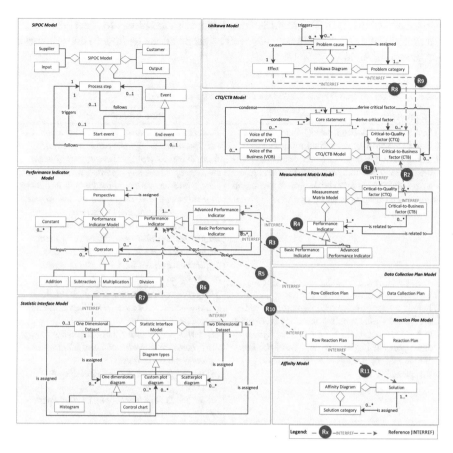

Fig. 4 Integrated metamodel of RUPERT showing the metamodels for each model type [42]— © 2017 Springer Fachmedien Wiesbaden GmbH; reprinted with permission

4.3 Digital Engineering

Due to the continuing evolution of the above-mentioned disciplines, the profile of a "Digital Engineer" in the "IoT/Digital Twin/Industry 4.0 era" has become increasingly important [49]. Thus, higher education institutions and universities need to teach the competencies required by the future labor market. This includes skills and knowledge in the fields of engineering and digital technologies, to put Digital Engineers in the position to increase performance "in both physical and business operations" and to enable "major process improvements" ([50], p. 16). For that purpose, a Smart Innovation Environment for Digital Engineers is needed, which is "an orchestration of software/hardware resources and workspace configurations articulated in an experimental setup to serve either as a didactic or a research laboratory" ([49], p. 1). At the moment, such environments are set up by OMiLAB "nodes" at universities or companies around the world [49] (https://www.omilab.

org/nodes/nodes.html). The requirements this environment has to meet—to enable the training of Digital Engineers—as well as propositions on how to address these, are shown in Table 1.

Table 1 Requirements for the Smart Innovation Environment [49]

Requirement	Smart Innovation Environment
The **Modeling Method Agility requirement.** There is a need for conceptual modeling methods that can be tailored for capturing multiple layers of abstraction, specificity and granularity—from high level business insights down to run-time constraints and properties.	*Building on the tradition of multi-perspective enterprise modeling, the proposed Smart Innovation Environment employs a generic concept of "modeling method" whose building blocks can be tailored through metamodeling in order to achieve alignment with a targeted domain, specificity and granularity. Integration and customisation of modeling languages are thus enabled, making them responsive to explicit "modeling method requirements". An initial toolkit of agile modeling environments is provided.*
The **Technology requirement.** There is a need for fast prototyping enablers—both for the agile modeling methods invoked in the previous point and for the cyber-physical counterparts of Digital Twins. Out-of-the box components must support evaluation and interoperability.	*The proposed environment is built on three pillars—each with its own toolkits and interoperability features:* *(a) toolkit for Digital Design Thinking to support facilitation workshops and ideation at business scenario level;* *(b) toolkit for Digital Twin modeling and integration;* *(c) toolkit for engineering of Digital Twin-based cyber-physical demonstrators.*
The **Openness requirement.** Open platforms and open interfaces are preferred in the choice of technology, to facilitate the reuse of prototypical building blocks and the accumulation of learned lessons.	*The proposed environment includes a Web integration platform and a set of out-of-the-box adaptors/services to facilitate interoperability between modeling environments and external artifacts/systems.* *A free metamodeling platform is employed to ensure that all modeling tools are open to further adaptation or reuse. Openness is the fundamental motivator for the OMiLAB ecosystem and its collaboration network.*
The **Digital Integration requirement**. Modeling environments must provide machine-readable semantic mediation from the business insights layer (where business model or product characteristics are co-created) down to the layer of cyber-physical demonstrators.	*The modeling method engineering technology builds on the notion of **Smart Models**—i.e. Conceptual Models that have three key qualities:* *(a) they decompose a socio-technical system across multiple perspectives and levels of detail while preserving semantic links across those perspectives/levels;* *(b) they make diagrammatic content available to both humans and machines, covering a semantic spectrum ranging from highly abstract business ideas/service designs down*

(continued)

Table 1 (continued)

Requirement	Smart Innovation Environment
	to the level of executable artifacts; *(c) they interact with other systems through a variety of connectivity options (pushing or querying model content).*
The **Knowledge Ecosystem requirement**. Co-creation requires shared knowledge assets to support knowledge transfer across adopters.	*The proposed environment benefits from being part of the OMiLAB digital ecosystem, whose on-line portal and community events facilitate both knowledge sharing and dissemination, while also enabling a social dimension, thus boosting its value as a collaboration network.*

5 Benefits and Challenges of Metamodeling in Digital Transformation

The aforementioned examples demonstrate the value of metamodeling for the construction of methods that support the transformation of a business and also highlight the relevance of metamodeling as a basis for Business Engineering, Enterprise Engineering and Digital Engineering.

The most obvious benefit appears to be the advantage to be able to first create a method, which is then tailored to the situational requirements (domain-specific, goal-oriented and user-specific) by combining suitable method fragments that already exist. In the simplest case, this can be the adaptation of the metamodel by means of modifying the modeling language or by extending its modeling constructs. Likewise, the completion of new method fragments and their consistent integration into the method base, requires the application of metamodeling. By this means, new views onto the problem can be taken and eventually it allows the execution of a method, which is perfectly adapted to the situation. Therefore, a higher flexibility is achieved by means of combining existing method fragments or integrating new or modified method fragments.

Since it is possible to revert to existing results—that do not have to be manually collected, entered again or manually implemented as programme code—metamodeling enables to reduce project execution times. A good example that illustrates this advantage is the challenge of digital transformation to define processes from and end-to-end perspective and across company boundaries. Although many companies have generally modelled their processes, they use individual languages. Metamodeling facilitates the merging of the individual languages and thus enables consistent modeling for the company network.

Ultimately the quality of the projects will increase too, if relevant results and experiences from previous projects find their way into new ones. Reducing information losses (because of the discontinuity of different formats) through metamodel-based transformations increases the project quality as well. This can also be shown in concrete terms by the example of the second challenge the integration of digital technologies. The integration of new digital technologies and the development of their full potential has always been the primary concern of Business Engineering's methods. The further development of the Business Engineering's methods and the continuous adaptation to the requirements of new digital technologies have a large share in improving the quality of the transformation projects.

The said benefit potentials can basically be achieved irrespective of whether a software tool e.g. metamodeling platform is available or not. However, the full potential of metamodeling resp. method engineering is only realized with the support of such a platform. Since the generation of a method base supports not only to modify or integrate method fragments but also documents the experience in applying the method fragments. At the same time quality management processes are to be established when modifying or integrating the method fragments and implementing the platform.

Admittedly, the examples and explanations have pointed at the beneficial potentials of metamodeling, which enable a very systematic way to address innovation, provide long-term benefits, allow for effective further developments, and efficient maintenance over the full life cycle of business and technical systems. This is even more valid when we think about long end to end processes with complex data structures that reach across company boundaries. However, it shows, that metamodeling and method construction is mainly performed by research institutes and is rarely incorporated into practical projects. Assuming that companies act rationally, there must be reasons for rejecting metamodeling, not least because of the required efforts for creating metamodels to systematically construct methods. We see three major causes why it is so difficult to bring metamodels to practice these days.

First, enterprises (and not only startups!) tend to think in much shorter term than in the past. The classical strategic approach was to understand today's starting point, to define a desired end state 4 or 5 years from now, and to find means and resources to get from here to there. Contemporary strategic approaches are much more process oriented: Take the next step, understand from the market where it leads you to, adapt and change direction as needed, and do this in an iterative way. This is the concept of agile strategies. The original concept of agile programming as formulated by [51] in the Utah "Manifesto for Agile Software Development" in 2001 has now been widely extended to agile business strategies.

Second, it is much easier these days to follow such an iterative approach in practice. In a world where networked enterprises are the new normal, modular solutions have been developed not only for business process interfaces and logical data interfaces (this is why we have so many business standardization boards!) but also for linking software by providing their technical correlates, i.e. application programming interfaces (APIs). Therefore, a valid business model in itself may be just to provide a new front end with superior UX and to link it to an existing API. Or there may be a new business consisting of a new product or service, linked via one API to the front end and via another API to transaction processing in the back. Or an innovative transaction processing machine is created in the background that can be linked to the rest of the world via existing APIs. A strategic differentiation for those companies does not result from creating own methods or software tools but from applying solutions that are available on the market straigt away to build a new business service.

Third, in the daily business, most pracitioners do not have the time and ressources to become acquainted with the skills required for constructing adapted methods to solve a particular problem. The same holds true for establishing competencies in realizing the constructed methods in form of software tools, e.g., with the help of metamodeling platforms.

Against this background, we conclude: Metamodeling may not be needed by those smaller companies that just provide a narrow range of services or products based on existing APIs. But yes, metamodeling is urgently needed by the majority of companies that shape more complex business models. It is a fundamental discipline to create, adapt and formally specify methods that are required to enable the successful conduction of digital transformation projects (see Sect. 3). In this respect, the job profile of a "Digital Engineer" will be of utmost importance in the near future. Hence, more and more companies will search for employees that have the ability to perform digital design and engineering activities in light of the challenges mentioned above (e.g., agile strategies, modular software solutions, etc.) (cf. [49]). Considering this, the establishment of Smart Innovation Environments, like the one of OMILab [49], is essential to put young professionals in the position to develop and technically realize methods for diverse project constellations occuring in a highly dynamic market.

References

1. Strahringer, S.: Metamodellierung als Instrument des Methodenvergleichs: Eine Evaluierung am Beispiel objektorientierter Analysemethoden. Shaker (1996)
2. Henderson-Sellers, B., Bulthuis, A.: Object-Oriented Metamethods. Springer Science & Business Media (2012)
3. Rosemann, M., zur Mühlen, M.: Der Lösungsbeitrag von Metadatenmodellen beim Vergleich von Workflowmanagementsystemen. Arbeitsberichte des Instituts für Wirtschaftsinformatik (1996)
4. Fettke, P., Loos, P., Pastor, K.: Ein UML-basiertes Metamodell des Memorandums zur vereinheitlichten Spezifikation von Fachkomponenten. Architekturen, Komponenten, Anwendungen, Proceedings zur 1 Verbundtagung Architekturen, Komponenten, Anwendungen (AKA 2004) (2004)
5. Schütte, R.: Grundsätze ordnungsmäßiger Referenzmodellierung - Konstruktion konfigurations- und anpassungsorientierter Modelle. Gabler, Wiesbaden (1998)
6. Sinz, E.J.: Ansätze zur fachlichen Modellierung betrieblicher Informationssysteme: Entwicklung, aktueller Stand und Trends. Otto-Friedrich-Universität (1995)
7. Karagiannis, D., Höfferer, P.: Metamodels in action: an overview. ICSOFT. 1, 11–14 (2006)
8. Brinkkemper, S.: Method engineering: engineering of information systems development methods and tools. Inf. Softw. Technol. 38(4), 275–280 (1996)
9. Heym, M.: Methoden-Engineering: Spezifikation und Integration von Entwicklungsmethoden für Informationssysteme (1993)

10. Tolvanen, J.-P., Rossi, M., Liu, H.: Method engineering: current research directions and implications for future research. In: Working Conference on Method Engineering, pp. 296–317. Springer (1996)
11. Tolvanen, J.-P.: Incremental method engineering with modeling tools: theoretical principles and empirical evidence. PhD Thesis, University of Jyvaskyla (1998)
12. CapGemini: Studie It-Trends 2019 (2019)
13. Hayes: Von Starren Prozessen Zu Agilen Projekten - Unternehmen in Der Digitalen Transformation (2015)
14. Henriette, E., Feki, M., Boughzala, I.: Digital Transformation Challenges. In: MCIS, p. 33 (2016)
15. Jahn, B., Pfeiffer, M.: Die digitale Revolution—Neue Geschäftsmodelle statt (nur) neue Kommunikation. Market. Rev. St Gallen. **31**(1), 79–93 (2014)
16. Bouchbout, K., Akoka, J., Alimazighi, Z.: Proposition of a generic metamodel for interorganizational business processes. Paper presented at the Proceedings of the 6th International Workshop on Enterprise & Organizational Modeling and Simulation, Hammamet, Tunisia (2010)
17. Telang, P.R., Singh, M.P.: Specifying and verifying cross-organizational business models: an agent-oriented approach. IEEE Trans. Serv. Comput. **5**(3), 305–318 (2011)
18. CapGemini: Studie It-Trends 2020 (2020)
19. Richter, A., Ott, F., Kneifel, D., Koch, M.: Social Networking in einem Beratungsunternehmen. Mensch & Computer 2009: Grenzenlos frei!? (2009)
20. Fuchs-Kittowski, F., Klassen, N., Faust, D., Einhaus, J.: A comparative study on the use of Web 2.0 in enterprises. Fraunhofer-Publica - Publication Database of the Fraunhofer-Gesellschaft (2009)
21. Kane, G.C., Alavi, M., Labianca, G., Borgatti, S.P.: What's different about social media networks? A framework and research agenda. MIS Quart. **38**(1), 275–304 (2014)
22. Tajudeen, F.P., Jaafar, N.I., Sulaiman, A.: Role of social media on information accessibility. Pac. Asia J. Assoc. Inf. Syst. **8**(4), 3 (2016)
23. Gimpel, H., Röglinger, M.: Digital transformation: changes and chances–insights based on an empirical study (2015)
24. Ried: Digital-Strategie: 4 Große It-Trends Bestimmen 2019 (2019)
25. Laudon, K.C., Laudon, J.P., Schoder, D.: Wirtschaftsinformatik: eine Einführung, 3rd edn. Pearson Deutschland, Hallbergmoos (2016)
26. Wirtz, B.W., Mory, L., Piehler, R.: Web 2.0 and digital business models. In: Handbook of Strategic e-Business Management, pp. 751–766. Springer (2014)
27. Fill, H.-G., Johannsen, F.: A knowledge perspective on big data by joining enterprise modeling and data analyses. In: 2016 49th Hawaii International Conference on System Sciences (HICSS), pp. 4052–4061. IEEE (2016)
28. Kirchgeorg, M., Beyer, C.: Herausforderungen der digitalen Transformation für die marktorientierte Unternehmensführung. In: Digitale Transformation oder digitale Disruption im Handel, pp. 399–422. Springer (2016)
29. Buhl, H.U., Röglinger, M., Moser, F., Heidemann, J.: Big Data. Springer (2013)
30. Westerman, G., Bonnet, D., McAfee, A.: Leading Digital: Turning Technology into Business Transformation. Harvard Business Press (2014)
31. Chanias, S.: Mastering digital transformation: the path of a financial services provider towards a digital transformation strategy (2017)
32. Chanias, S., Myers, M.D., Hess, T.: Digital transformation strategy making in pre-digital organizations: the case of a financial services provider. J. Strat. Inf. Syst. **28**(1), 17–33 (2019)
33. Matt, C., Hess, T., Benlian, A.: Digital transformation strategies. Bus. Inf. Syst. Eng. **57**(5), 339–343 (2015)
34. Ralyté, J., Rolland, C.: An approach for method reengineering. In: International Conference on Conceptual Modeling, pp. 471–484. Springer (2001)

35. Ralyté, J., Deneckère, R., Rolland, C.: Towards a generic model for situational method engineering. In: International Conference on Advanced Information Systems Engineering, 2003, pp. 95–110. Springer (2003)
36. Karagiannis, D., Fill, H.-G., Höfferer, P., Nemetz, M.: Metamodeling: Some application areas in information systems. In: International United Information Systems Conference, pp. 175–188. Springer (2008)
37. Winter, R., Österle, H.: Business Engineering-Auf dem Weg zum Unternehmen des Informationszeitalters. Springer, Berlin (2000)
38. Österle, H.: Business Engineering. Prozeß-und Systementwicklung: Band 1: Entwurfstechniken. Springer (2013)
39. Leist-Galanos, S.: Methoden zur Unternehmensmodellierung – Vergleich, Anwendungen und Diskussion der Integrationspotenziale. Habilitation, Universität St. Gallen (2004)
40. Winter, R.: Business engineering navigator: Gestaltung und Analyse von Geschäftslösungen "Business-to-IT". Springer (2010)
41. Liles, D.H., Johnson, M.E., Meade, L., Underdown, D.R.: Enterprise engineering: a discipline? In: Society for Enterprise Engineering Conference Proceedings, vol. 1195. Citeseer (1995)
42. Johannsen, F., Fill, H.-G.: Metamodeling for business process improvement. Bus. Inf. Syst. Eng. **59**(4), 251–275 (2017)
43. Meran, R., John, A., Staudter, C., Roenpage, O.: Six Sigma+ Lean Toolset: Mindset zur erfolgreichen Umsetzung von Verbesserungsprojekten. Springer (2014)
44. Johannsen, F., Fill, H.-G.: Supporting business process improvement through a modeling tool. In: Karagiannis, D., Mayr, C.H., Mylopoulos, J. (eds.) Domain-Specific Conceptual Modeling, pp. 217–237. Springer, Berlin (2016)
45. Snee, R.D., Hoerl, R.W.: Leading Six Sigma: A Step-by-Step Guide Based on Experience with GE and Other Six Sigma Companies. Ft Press (2003)
46. Johannsen, F., Fill, H.-G.: Codification of knowledge in business process improvement projects (2014)
47. Johannsen, F., Fill, H.-G.: Supporting knowledge elicitation and analysis for business process improvement through a modeling tool (2015)
48. Fill, H.-G., Karagiannis, D.: On the conceptualisation of modelling methods using the ADOxx metamodelling platform. Enterprise Modell. Inf. Syst. Architect. (EMISAJ). **8**(1), 4–25 (2013)
49. Karagiannis, D., Buchmann, R.A., Boucher, X., Cavalieri, S., Florea, A., Kiritsis, D., Lee, M.: OMiLAB: a smart innovation environment for digital engineers. Paper presented at the PRO-VE 2020 – the 21st IFIP/SOCOLNET Working Conference on Virtual Enterprises (2020)
50. Holland, D., Crompton, J.: The Future Belongs to the Digital Engineer. Xlibris Corporation (2013)
51. Beck, K., Beedle, M., Van Bennekum, A., Cockburn, A., Cunningham, W., Fowler, M., Grenning, J., Highsmith, J., Hunt, A., Jeffries, R.: Manifesto for agile software development (2001)

Potentials and Limits of Modeling Using the Example of an Artificial Real-World Model

Ulrike Baumöl and Reinhard Jung

Abstract Models and modeling play key roles for understanding the world and how it works including artificially created real worlds, and for representing and transferring knowledge about the world. Based on an example the paper aims to show the possibilities, but also the limitations of models. Particularly we discuss what knowledge can and cannot be transferred by model abstractions on type level and how they contribute to understanding the functioning of the world.

Keywords Modeling · Artificial real-world models · Knowledge representation · Limitations of modeling

1 In Search of the Way the World Works

Perhaps as long as curiosity has existed in humans, we have been trying to understand the world and how it works. Even early artifacts, such as cave drawings or the Nebra disk, represent an attempt to capture the world in a model in order to better understand it. At least as important is the process of modeling, which on the one hand serves to analyze the real world, it is on the other hand the basis for understanding the objects and their interrelationships. In other words, it serves the acquisition of knowledge. This knowledge is passed on by the modeler in the model. However, this is always done from their perspective and thus every model is also a subjective representation of reality. Thus, for the specific interpretation of a model, appropriate contextual information is required. At the same time, the concept of reality has to be discussed. The central question here is whether (a) reality is to be

U. Baumöl
University of Liechtenstein, Vaduz, Liechtenstein
e-mail: ulrike.baumoel@unisg.ch

R. Jung (✉)
Institute of Information Management, University of St. Gallen, St. Gallen, Switzerland
e-mail: reinhard.jung@unisg.ch

© The Author(s), under exclusive license to Springer Nature Switzerland AG 2021
S. Aier et al. (eds.), *Engineering the Transformation of the Enterprise*,
https://doi.org/10.1007/978-3-030-84655-8_5

understood in the narrow sense or (b) reality can also be understood as an artificially created world. This paper chooses the more open interpretation (b) and refers to an artificially created real world (AR), which, however, could also very well exist in the natural real world in the sense of the insight "it's a small world afterall".

However, the goal of all models is basically the same: answers to a wide variety of questions are to be generated. The questions are based on different objectives and ranges; sometimes the answer is already known, e.g., 42, and must be specified by the question.

The aim of this paper is to show the possibilities, but also the limitations of models. It is to be argued that a model with its abstraction on type level can be factually completely correct, but some essential facts and thus the functioning of the AR are not revealed. So the question remains whether with a factual, data-oriented representation in a model the functioning of the world can be understood.

To address this question, an AR is modeled in the following chapter. The resulting model is to be assumed to be factually correct. The process of modeling has the goal of making the model interpretable for certain, knowledgeable experts (here: experts of the AR) and thus enabling the derivation of knowledge about the AR. The modeler, who wishes to remain unnamed for reasons of scientific reputation, has incorporated into the model a subjective interpretation driven by knowledge of instances in the AR. The consequences of the modeling process and the interpretability of how the AR works are also discussed in the chapter. The paper concludes with a brief conclusion and outlook.

2   The Way the World Works Using the Example

2.1   Model Description

In the following, a conceptual data model is presented according to the entity-relationship approach, which goes back to Chen [1]. Entity types in the form of rectangles ("boxes") with identifiers for the type itself and attributes as well as relationship types in the form of edges ("arms") with an identifier for the reading direction from top to bottom or from left to right were used as model elements.

The object area and thus the section of the AR shown here concerns something with which the jubilarian is very familiar. The authors will also "move" exclusively on the type level when commenting on the model and will not make any reference to the level of the instances in order to maintain a certain tension and a surprise effect as long as possible. A review of the model will therefore only be possible for people who know the jubilarian sufficiently well or who are themselves well acquainted with the mapped AR.

The following preliminary remarks are required regarding the conceptual data model:

- The authors are aware that some principles of proper modeling [2] were violated during the model development. Especially students with ambitions for a respectable degree are therefore strongly advised not to refer to the present paper in their scientific work.
- For modeling-economic reasons, the focus was not on the real system—this term alone is actually not correct due to the properties of the AR—but already the observed object system was a model in the form of a textual description on Wikipedia, which is not to be quoted here both due to its dubious scientific quality and for the reason already mentioned above (preservation of suspense and the surprise effect).

The conceptual data model presented (Fig. 1) describes a situation that can basically occur in any small town. Thus, the authors aim at a model with a claim to general validity, but of course they cannot efficiently prove the general validity and even have to fear that a falsification is possible for some model components.

In the aforementioned small town in what is actually a great country, lives, among others, a rather well-known family. Probably the most famous member of the family, and thus the main protagonist of AR, is the male head of the family, although his wife, the three children, and even the pet (in this case a dog) are also prominent actors. Even his parents, especially his mother, achieve notoriety. Apparently, she is responsible for the destruction of a computer system that the head of the family previously used for the presumably illegal disposal of potentially radioactive waste from his company.

2.2 Model Discussion

When looking at the model, it is noticeable that a certain generality is definitely given. The model can certainly be used to represent various (small) cities and the inhabitants living in them. It is questionable, of course, whether the destroyed-computer-system-waste complex occurs in a sufficiently large number of cities; but it would be possible. Further, it should be noted that the interactions between instances occurring in the AR can only be represented very inadequately. This could be due to one of the following three reasons:

1. The model is incomplete with respect to the underlying AR, so entity and relationship types would need to be added.
2. The model cannot represent the complete semantics due to the limitation to the data view; in this case, a more holistic modeling approach with additional views would be more purposeful.
3. Due to their abstraction, models hide some phenomena of the real world and thus "anonymize" them.

The authors assume that the (subjectively!) perceived insufficient mapping of the AR into a conceptual data model is due to the last two reasons. Ultimately, the model

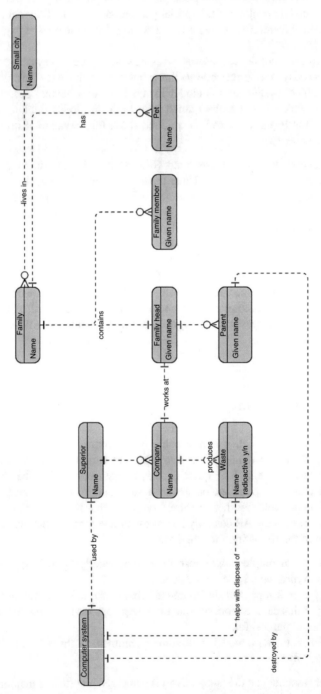

Fig. 1 Mapping of the AR into a conceptual data model

represents static structures that are very generally valid, especially in the right part of Fig. 1. It is noticeable that the left part of the model, on the other hand, represents more specific facts (not generally applicable to every small city) that facilitate inference to the AR. Thus, although type-level modeling was done correctly, the model contains two sections with different levels of abstraction. To be specific, not every small town will have people who work in an enterprise with potentially radioactive waste.

3   Conclusion and Outlook

In the beginning there was the question of the analysis of the functioning of the world and the role of modeling and models for the cognitive process. The usefulness of creating a model of the natural or artificial real world is undisputed. The proof is given by many well-known models: Architectural models are two examples: the large model of St. Peter's Basilica developed by Sangallo around 1547 [3], and the representation of the real world in model railroads [4].

These models clearly show the external structure of the depicted real worlds and the relationships of the elements to each other. For example, without the model of St. Peter's Basilica, it would not have been possible to make assumptions about and map its structural integrity. However, even this model cannot be fully interpreted correctly without a knowledge of the historical context of the time it was created, the knowledge available at the time, the materials, and the profile of the modeler. A model enriched with this information and knowledge of the modeler's mental model enables constructions of the real world that sufficiently explain its functioning. The potentials of modeling and the resulting model are therefore obvious.

The limits become apparent where there is "unmodelability". Relationships that can be materialized directly, e.g., the affiliation of a person to a family, can be mapped and also interpreted in the instance. However, relationships that are not directly materializable, such as the emotional relationship of a family member to the boss and the resulting manifestations of the instances, can neither be mapped nor interpreted in the model or explained in the instance from the model.

This finding gives rise to the need for further research. The question can be pursued how classically developed models can be extended by the described "unmodelability".

The way modeling is supported today offers potential at this point. Today, complicated models are usually created on the basis of a technical platform, so that, for example, digital twins of buildings are created in the context of Building Information Modeling (BIM), which enable classification and implementation in the real context. If such models are now created with their object and relationship types and supplemented by possible interactions on the non-materializable level with interaction types, it may also be possible to analyze the expressions on the instance level. The variety of expressions in a system that can almost be categorized as chaotic, i.e., as complex, can at best be captured here with the help of the potentials of artificial intelligence.

With these remarks we close the article—may the jubilarian spend many more productive and creative hours developing such and similar research ideas.

References

1. Chen, P.P.-S.: The entity-relationship model – toward a unified view of data. ACM Trans. Database Syst. **1**(1), 9–36 (1976)
2. Becker, J., Rosemann, M., Schütte, R.: Grundsätze ordnungsmässiger Modellierung; Wirtschafts informatik. **37**(5), 435–445 (1995)
3. Thoenes, C.: Der Neubau. In: Brandenburg, H., Ballardini, A., Thoenes, C. (eds.) Der Petersdom in Rom: die Baugeschichte von der Antike bis heute, pp. 165–303. Michael Imhoff Verlag, Petersberg (2015)
4. Lechner, U.: Modellbahn Träume – Die schönsten Anlagen aus dem "Modelleisenbahner", 3rd edn. Transpress Verlag, Stuttgart (2002)

On Model-Based Coordination of Change in Organizations

Henderik A. Proper

Abstract Change seems to be an inherent property of organizations and the enterprises they undertake. During such changes, *coordination* among the different actors involved is key, in particular when there is a need to consider the longer term impact of change.

When the complexity of an organizations, and/or the context in which it operates, is high, the need emerges to use "represented abstractions" of the organization and its context to support coordinated change. These "represented abstractions", taking the form of e.g. sketches, narrative descriptions, diagrams, spreadsheets, or formal specifications, are used for informed decision making about changes, as well as to coordinate changes among the different actors that may be involved. We take the stance that these "represented abstractions" are all forms of *models*. Doing so, does requires us to look beyond the "boxes-and-lines" metaphor that seems to be the traditional way of looking at models in our field.

Meanwhile, the transition to the digital age has resulted in organizations to be (and operate in) a complex and hybrid mix of human and digital actors, while the pace of change has increased as well. This also puts more pressure on the *coordination* of the changes, and as a direct consequence also puts more pressure on the use of *model-based instruments*.

The goal of this paper is to explore some of the challenges that these model-based instruments will need to meet (while indeed looking beyond the "boxes-and-lines" metaphor). To this end, we will start with a discussion of our current understanding of the notion of model. We then zoom in on the use of models in the coordination of change. Using this as a base, we finalize with a discussion of some of the main challenges we see in improving the use of model-based instruments for the coordination of change in organizations.

Keywords Coordination of change · Enterprise modeling · Conceptual modeling

H. A. Proper (✉)
Luxembourg Institute of Science and Technology, Belval, Luxembourg

University of Luxembourg, Belval, Luxembourg
e-mail: e.proper@acm.org

© The Author(s), under exclusive license to Springer Nature Switzerland AG 2021
S. Aier et al. (eds.), *Engineering the Transformation of the Enterprise*,
https://doi.org/10.1007/978-3-030-84655-8_6

1 Introduction

Change seems to be an inherent property of organizations and the enterprises they undertake. These changes may be related to internal factors, such as the constellation of human actors involved in an organization, the build-up of experience/organizational knowledge, etc. Most changes, however, will find their ultimate cause in external factors, such as changes in the socio-economical context, changes in the environment, as well as technological developments.

When the complexity of an organizations, and/or the context in which it operates, is high, the need emerges to use "represented abstractions" of the organization and its context to support coordinated change. These "represented abstractions", taking the form of e.g. sketches, narrative descriptions, diagrams, spreadsheets, or formal specifications, are used for informed decision making about changes, as well as coordinate changes among the different actors that may be involved. As we will discuss in more detail in Sect. 2, we take the stance that these "represented abstractions" are essentially models. This does, indeed, require us to look beyond the "boxes-and-lines" metaphor that seem to have become the traditional way of looking at models in our engineering-oriented field.[1] Organizational scientists may argue that there are more design related artifacts used in organizations than may meet the engineer's eyes [1]. Or as Junginger [2] puts it: "*Naturally, they [engineers] are looking for forms and practices of design they are familiar with.*" Junginger [2] also states: "*Design literally shapes organizational reality.*", which resonates well with concepts such as "*organizational design*" [3], "*sensemaking*" [4] and the "*authoring of organizations*" [5]. In line with this, we argue that, depending on the situation at hand, texts, sketches on the back of napkins, spreadsheets, formal specifications, etc, or even animations and simulations, can all act as models.

Periods of great change in human society have often been driven by the emergence of disruptive technologies, such as the introduction of the printing press, the steam engine, the car or the telephone [1]. Such technology-driven impacts tend to start slowly, but as soon as the technology matures, the pace and depth of their impact on society and organizations increases rapidly. Our society is now, driven by the development of information technologies (IT), transitioning from the industrial age to the "digital age".

The role of IT in organizations started by mainly being a "mere" supportive tool for administrative purposes, resulting in the "automation of information processing activities". The emergence of e-commerce (indeed, also powered by the emergence of the world-wide-web) resulted in a stronger role of IT as a key actor in business processes, sometimes even fully replacing human activities. The increased use of artificial intelligence (AI) also enables a further "automation" of (business) processes, while "big data" fuels this with the necessary data. Finally, the further maturation of IT in terms of e.g. increased interoperability across organizational

---

[1] Business Informatics, including organizational engineering, enterprise engineering, and enterprise architecture.

boundaries, the usage of standardized platforms, and the adoption mobile device in society, has now even resulted in the emergence of IT-based business models. Companies such as Amazon, AirBnB, Uber, Netflix, Spotify, and Bitcoin, provide examples of the latter. The CEO of a major traditional bank can even be quoted as stating "We want to be a tech company with a banking license" [6].

The transition to the digital age now drives organizations to change faster and more fundamentally. These changes impact the complete "design" of organizations and the enterprises they engage in; from their business model, the definitions of the actual products and services offered to their clients, via the business processes that deliver these products and services, and the information systems that support these processes, to the underlying IT infrastructure.

In general, change in organizations goes by different names, including *business transformation, enterprise transformation, business innovation, digital transformation*, etc. These latter forms of organizational change, generally pertain to top-down initiated forms of change. In other words, change that is initiated explicitly under the auspice of senior management. At the same time, change in organizations may also occur in terms of emergent/bottom-up change. This includes minor changes to processes and rules to "make things work" [7], organizational drift [8], as well as the creation of Shadow-IT [9].

For an organization, in particular in relation to the enterprises it may pursue, it is important to ensure alignment/coherence of its key aspects [10, 11], including e.g. business strategy, IT, organization, culture, marketing, etc. To improve, and maintain, such coherence it is important to ensure there is coordination of change among the involved actors [12]. Both in the case of bottom-up and in the case of top-down initiated change.

As mentioned above, when the complexity of the organization itself, and/or the contexts in which it operates, is high, the need emerges to use "represented abstractions" (i.e. models) to enable enable informed decision making about, as well as the coordination of change. The transition to the digital age puts more pressure on the *coordination* of change, and as a direct consequence also puts more pressure on the use of *model-based instruments*.

The goal of this paper is to explore some of the challenges that these *model-based instruments* will need to meet, while indeed looking beyond the "boxes-and-lines" metaphor. To this end, we will start (in Sect. 2) with a discussion of our current understanding of the notion of model. In Sect. 3, we then zoom in on the use of models for the coordination of change. Using this as a base, Sect. 4 finalizes the paper with a discussion of some of the main challenges we see in improving the use of model-based instruments for the coordination of change in organizations.

2 Domain Models

In the context of software engineering, information systems engineering, business process management, and enterprise engineering & architecting in general, many different kinds of models are used. We consider each of these kinds of models as being valued members of a larger family of domain models. As the words model, and modeling, have different connotations in daily discourse, we prefer to use the term domain model instead.

2.1 The Notion of Domain Model

Based on general foundational work by e.g. Apostel [13], and Stachowiak [14], more recent work on the same by different authors (e.g. [15–20] as well as our own work (e.g. [21–24]), we consider a domain model to be:

> An *artifact* that is *acknowledged* by an *observer* to *represent* an *abstraction* of some *domain* for a particular *purpose*.

With *domain*, we refer to "anything" that one can speak/reflect about explicitly. It could be "something" that already exists in the "real world", something desired towards the future, or something imagined. The *observer* observes the domain by way of their senses and/or by way of (self) reflection. What results in the mind of the observer is, what is termed a *conceptualization* in [16], and what is called *conception* in [25].

Models are created to serve a purpose. In other words, the model is to be used for some goal, by some actors, in some context. The purpose of a model, ultimately paves the way for its **Return on Modelling Effort** (RoME, see Chap. 4 of [52]).

We consider a model to be an *artifact*. It is something that exists outside of our minds; i.e. a "represented abstractions". In our fields of application, one tends to limit such an artifact to the "boxes-and-lines" metaphor, while within the field of e.g. software engineering in particular, one has developed the implicit assumption that models are artifacts with a highly controlled structure (syntax) and mathematically defined semantics [17]. However, as mentioned above, models can take other forms as well, such as texts, sketches on the back of a napkin, spreadsheets, formal specifications, animations, physical objects, etc [1, 26]. Which form is the most effective, depends on the purpose for which the model is created.

At an overall level, we suggest to distinguish between two main (mixable) flavors for the *form* of a model:

1. Models can be of a *lingual* nature, involving e.g. text, graphical symbols, or a mathematical formalism.
2. Models can be of an *experiential* nature, involving e.g. the use of physical elements, animations, simulations, or tactile sensation.

Fig. 1 Ogden and Richard's semiotic triangle [28]

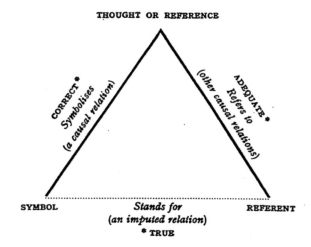

A model is the representation of an *abstraction* of an observed domain. This implies that, in line with the *purpose* of the model, some (if not most) "details" of the domain are consciously filtered out by the observer. For domain modeling [23], important abstraction flavors are [27]: (1) *selection*, where we decide to only consider certain elements and/or aspects of the domain; (2) *classification* (including typing); (3) *generalization*; and (4) *aggregation*.

2.2 Semiotic Roots

The semiotic triangle by Ogden and Richard [28], as depicted in Fig. 1, is often used as a base to theorize about meaning in the context of (natural) language [29–32]. Several authors, including ourselves, use it to reason about the foundations of (information) systems modeling (see e.g. [33–36]).

As shown in Fig. 1, the semiotic triangle expresses how an actor (in using a language to communicate) assigns meaning (a *thought or reference*) to the *combination* of a *symbol* and a *referent*, where the former is some language utterance, and the latter is something that the actor can refer to. The *referent* can be anything, in an existing world, or in a desired/imagined world. It can involve physical phenomena (e.g., tree, car, bike, atom, document, picture, etc), mental phenomena (e.g., thoughts, feelings, etc), as well as social phenomena (e.g., marriage, mortgage, trust, value, etc).

It is important to keep in mind that [28 , pp. 11–12]: "*Symbol and Referent, that is to say, are not connected directly (and when, for grammatical reasons, we imply such a relation, it will merely be an imputed as opposed to a real, relation) but only indirectly round the two sides of the triangle.*" The latter implies that the connection between the symbol and the referent always goes by way of a thought in the mind of some actor.

2.3   It Takes Two to Communicate

Even though it was created from a communication oriented perspective, the semiotic triangle on its own is "single sided" in the sense that it only refers to one actor. In the context of communication, specifically including the coordination of change in organizations, it is important to acknowledge the fact that there are at least two actors involved. Any language utterance (such as domain models) has both a *writer* and a *reader* [31]. In terms of the semantic triangle, this implies that both the author and writer have their own thoughts about the symbol, in the context of possibly the same referent.

If the referent is a physical thing in the existing world, reader and writer have a chance of indeed looking at the same referent. When the referent is a physical thing in a possible/desired future world, it already becomes more challenging to ensure that they are considering the same referent. When the referent is not a physical thing, but rather a social thing, or even a mental thing, matters become even more challenging. The latter kind of situations might be mitigated by more meta-communication [37] between reader and writer, e.g., involving the description of their focus, paraphrasing, or using a domain-independent system of ontological categories to calculate the relations between their individual conceptualizations [38].

2.4   Generalization to Models

In applying the semiotic triangle in the context of modeling, one should be careful as it was originally intended to be used in the context of natural language communication via written symbols. Some of the resulting concerns are discussed in e.g. [23, 33, 39, 40].

One concern we would like to raise explicitly is related to the fact that models can, based on the definition given above, be of a *lingual* as well as an *experiential* nature. As such, this would require the postulation of a generalized version of the semiotic triangle, where *symbol* is replaced by the more generic notion of a (meaning carrying) *artifact* (or sign). The suggested adaption is shown in Fig. 2.

In Fig. 2, we specifically use the word *artifact* and not model. Not every artifact that on observer may see as "standing for" the referent necessarily has to be model

Fig. 2 Generalized
semiotic triangle

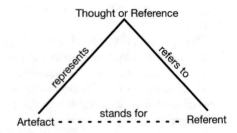

(see Sect. 2.6). Conversely, following our definition, every model is indeed required to be an artifact.

2.5 Conceptual Models vs. Utilization Design Models

In line with the above discussion, a domain model should be (the representation of) the abstraction of (the conceptualization of) a domain. At the same time, for different (1) computational purposes, such as the ability to use the model as a base for simulation, computer-based reasoning, execution, or database design, and/or (2) *experiential* purposes, such as the ability to touch, interact with, or feel the model, it may be necessary to include "features" in the domain model that are not "true" to the original domain.

These "features" result in a model that does *not* correspond to (an abstraction of) the original domain. One could even say that it has been "compromised" in order to provide some computational and/or experiential *utility*.

This is where we suggest to make a distinction between *conceptual models* and *utilization design models* in the sense that (in line with [23]) a *conceptual model* is defined as:

> A model of a domain, where the purpose of the model is dominated by the ambition to remain as-true-as-possible to the original domain conception

while a *utilization design model* includes "compromises" to enable some computational and/or experiential *utility*.

Note the use of the word ambition in the definition of conceptual model. As discussed in [23], we are not suggesting there to be a crisp border between conceptual models and utilization design models. However, the word *ambition* also suggest that a modeler/observer, as their insight in a domain increases, should be driven to reflect on the conceptual purity of their conceptualization and of the resulting model.

Utilization design models certainly have an important role to play. However, it is important to be aware of the "compromises" that had to be "designed into" the original domain conceptualization, to obtain the desired computational/experiential utility of the model.

As such, it is also possible that one conceptual model has different associated utilization design models, each meeting different purposes.

2.6 Instantiations of Models

As a consequence of the fact that a domain model is an abstraction of the domain, it must be possible (for an observer) to identify multiple "situations" that provide different (more specific) instantiations of the model [23].

This enables us to introduce a qualifier on the relationship between a model and a set of possible instantiations. For instance, the relation might have an epistemic intentions in the sense that the set of instantiations corresponds to the set of observable situations in "reality", which mean that the model represents knowledge about the existing world. An example of such a model, would be a domain model pertaining to a "law of nature".

The relationship between the model and the possible instantiations might also have a deontic intention in the sense that the set of instantiations corresponds to the desired, obliged, or required situations. This is where we find models in the role of guidelines, protocols, rules, designs, etc.

In the context of designing and engineering parts of organizations and their enterprises, this distinction also allows us to move from analysis to design.

2.7 Modeling Happens Naturally

Whenever we study, or reflect about, complex phenomena such as constructions, processes we observe in nature, information systems, business models, organizations, etc, we tend to use an abstraction (in our mind) of the actual phenomenon. When we externalize this abstraction in terms of some artifact, then this artifact is a model (to us, as an individual) of the observed phenomenon. As such, modeling happens naturally.

Of course, when the requirements regarding different qualities of the model [35, 41] increase, more cognitive effort will be needed to create (and understand) the domain abstraction and the model. The (extra) effort should, of course, be in line with the (expected) earlier mentioned RoME (Return on Modeling Effort).

This has also triggered studies into the competences needed from modelers in order to produce models [42–44]. It also formed the base of work towards more natural forms of modeling [45, 46], as also echoed in more recent ideas on grassroots modeling [19].

3 The Role of Models in Coordinating Change

In this section, we explore the use of models in the coordination of change in organizations and the enterprises they engage in. We start from the perspective of *informed decision making* regarding the directions of change. We then shift the focus towards the use of models for *informed coordination* of change.

3.1 Informed Decision Making

Different aspects of an organization, including its structures, purpose, value proposition, value propositions, business processes, stakeholder goals, information systems, etc, can be captured in terms of (interconnected) models. Just as senior management uses financial modeling to *enable* decision making from a financial perspective, models of the other aspects of an organization can be used to enable informed decision-making regarding the other aspects as well [26, 47, 48]. The informative value (indeed, RoME) of such models comes even more to the fore when the models are interlinked, thus providing a coherent perspective on all relevant aspects, also enabling "cross-cutting" analysis [49, 50].

In [51], it is suggested that, in the context of organizations and their enterprises, there are (at least) seven high-level purposes for the creation of models of systems/ organizations:

1. *Understand*—Understand the working of the current affairs of an organization and/or its environment.
2. *Assess*—Assess (a part/aspect of) the current affairs of an organization in relation to a e.g. benchmark or a reference model.
3. *Diagnose*—Diagnose the causes of an identified problem in the current affairs of an organization and/or its environment.
4. *Design*—Express different design alternatives, and analyze properties of the (desired) future affairs of the organization.
5. *Realize*—Guidance, specification, or explanation during the realization of the desired affairs of an organization.
6. *Operate*—Guidance, specification, or explanation for the socio-cyber-physical actors involved in the day-to-day operations of an organization.
7. *Regulate*—Externally formulated regulation on the operational behavior of (an) organization.

In specific situations, these high-level purposes can be made more specific in terms of, e.g., the need for different stakeholders to *understand*, *agree*, or *commit* to the content of the model [52], or for a computer to be able to interpret the model in order to e.g. automatically analyze it, use it as the base of a simulation/animation, or even execute it. Furthermore, depending on additional factors, such as the abilities of the actors involved in the creation and utilization of the model, the intended usage of the model, the need for understanding/agreement/commitment to the model from different stakeholders, etc, these overall purposes can be refined even further [53].

The specific purpose of a model that is to be used in a specific context, also provides us with possible requirements on a model as an artifact, including the required level of precision, completeness, format, etc. As argued before, a sketch, of e.g. a new business process, on the back of a napkin can already be regarded as a model; assuming that for the purpose at hand a sketch suffices. If, however, there is a need to simulate the new business process, the sketch will not suffice. As such (see Sect. 2.7), the purpose of a model also has a direct relationship to its RoME.

Orthogonal to the above discussed high-level purposes two other classes of high-level purposes we would like to mention are:

8. Design knowledge—Reference models (as also mentioned above in the assess purpose) can be used to capture (opinion or evidence-based) design knowledge.
9. Harmonization—Meta-models and/or (foundational) ontologies [16] can be used to "harmonize" or even "standardize" the way we observe, abstract from, and create models of, the world/organizations around us.

3.2 Informed Coordination of Change

Changes in organizations are ultimately the result of the decisions taken by the actors involved in/with the organization, as well as the actions that follow from these decisions. This may pertain to top-down initiated changes, as well as bottom-up up initiated changes, where *governance mechanisms* may be in place to define the "rules of the game" [12, 54]. This may involve both formal rules defining how decisions are made, their authority, needed compliance, etc, as well as informal rules about the way changes are made.

For an organization, in particular in relation to the enterprises it may pursue, it is important to ensure alignment/coherence of its key aspects [10, 11], including e.g. business strategy, IT, organization, culture, marketing, etc. To improve, and maintain, such coherence it is important to ensure there is *coordination* of change among the involved actors [12]. Both in the case of bottom-up and in the case of top-down initiated change. As argued in [11, 12], such coordination requires (different levels of) shared understanding of, agreement on, and commitment to: (1) what the overall strategy of the organization and its enterprise(s) is, (2) its current affairs, i.e. the current situation, as well as the relevant history leading up to it, and possible trends towards the future, (3) the current affairs of the context of the organization, and (4) what (given the latter) the ideal future affairs of the organization and its enterprise(s) are.

When combining (1) the need for coordination between the actors involved in change, (2) the need for informed decision making (see Sect. 3.2), (3) the notion of design conversations [2], and (4) the notion of *authoring of organizations* [55], we arrive at what one might call *informed coordination*, where models are the information carrier enabling informed decision making and coordination among the actors involved.

When considering the role of models in the context of *informed coordination*, it is also important to acknowledge their potential role of models as boundary objects [56, 57] in the communication among the different actors involved. The concept of boundary objects originated from organizational sciences [58]. An early approximation of this concept in the "world of engineering" can be found in terms of *views* and *viewpoints* [59] that enable the communication on the design of an organization (and its different aspects) with different groups of stakeholders [52].

Here, we should also re-iterate the role of models (in terms of meta-models and ontologies) with the purpose of *harmonizing* the way we capture, and speak about, changes to the organization.

4 Challenges on the Use of Models

It is important to reiterate the fact that in this paper we take the view that whenever we start using "represented abstractions" to support us in informed coordination, we start using models. The driving challenge then becomes how to make the use of these models more effective and efficient, and improve the RoME in particular. So, the question is not whether to use models or not, but rather how to make their use more effective and efficient. In this section we will discuss some of the main challenges we see in making the use of models for the coordination of change more effective and efficient.

In earlier work we also identified challenges for domain modeling in general [40], as well as challenges on the use of an existing enterprise modeling language (i.e. ArchiMate [60]) in the context of digital transformations [61]. In this section, we draw on these earlier discussed (research) challenges, while also focusing more specifically on challenges in relation to informed coordination.

4.1 *Semantic Grounding of Models*

Models used in the context of informed coordination should be understandable to the actors who are involved in their creation and use, in particular in situations where the model needs to act as a boundary *object* [56]. We therefore posit that a domain model should be grounded in the terminology as it is actually *used* (naturally) by these latter actors.

Most existing enterprise modeling languages (e.g. process models, goal models, value models, architectural models, etc.), only offer a "boxes and lines" based representation, which, by its very nature only provide a limited linkage to the (natural) language as used by a model's broader audience.

While these notational styles enable a more compact representation of models, they generally offer no means to provide a "drill down", or "mouse over", to an underlying grounding in terms of e.g. natural language verbalizations. As such, they leave no room for situation specific nuance that is especially needed when models are used as boundary objects [56]. A first challenge is therefore more specifically:

- *How to ground enterprise models in terms of natural language like verbalizations, without loosing the advantages of having compact notations (as well).*

4.2 Creating Shared Understanding

Coordination of change involves multiple actors. Therefore, for coordination to be effective, these actors should have a (good enough) shared understanding the models they use to coordinate changes. Based on Ogden and Richard's semiotic triangle [28], we can identify two main challenges related to achievement of a shared understanding:

- *How to ensure that different creators/readers of a model relate it to the same domain/referent?*
- *How to ensure that different creators/readers of a model have the same understanding (thought) of the model, assuming they relate it to the same domain/referent?*

The first of these two challenges is an important topic in the context of collaborative modeling, where groups of people are expected to e.g. jointly create an model [62–64].

The second challenge relates directly to the question of model understanding. For instance, empirical studies have shown that diagrams can easily be misunderstood [65–67], which is likely to lead to problems of understanding and use [68–70].

To improve the understanding of models, several authors have already been able to elaborate evaluation criteria to obtain a better quality in the design of these languages and the diagrams that accompany them. The most recognized, and the most successful to date, are the nine Moody criteria [71], based on the concept of *cognitive effectiveness*. These criteria have been applied in many projects [72, 73].

A final challenge pertaining to shared understanding, which is related to RoME, is:

- *How to measure the "depth" of shared understanding, and how much shared understanding is necessary?*

Using techniques like paraphrasing, one may indeed be able to obtain some insight into the "depth" of shared understanding one has reached. At the same time, this adds to the effort of modeling, so this has to be weighed against the expected returns. Collaborative modeling approaches tend to integrate the assessment of a shared understanding, in relation to the modeling goals, into the actual modeling process [62–64].

4.3 Aligning Normative Frames

As discussed in [40], when modeling (in particular when creating our abstractions of a domain), we are influenced by our normative frames. More specifically, these normative frames influence what we consider to be observable, thinkable, and changeable, about (the design of) an organization.

Examples (see [40]) of such normative frames are: (1) the *philosophical stance* (e.g. objectivist, subjectivist, etc.) of the actors involved, (2) *cognitive biases* which the actors involved in modeling may have developed during their professional, educational, and private lives, (3) *self interests* which the actors may have regarding the domain being modeled, (4) the *design frameworks* we use in the context e.g. enterprise architecture, and (5) the conceptual structures that are "hard-wired" into the modeling language(s) and conventions one may use.

When coordinating change, it will be necessary to ensure that the normative frames of the actors involved are "aligned enough". Without such alignment, achieving a shared understanding will likely to be very difficult. The need for alignment should also be seen in relation to the purpose of the coordination, and the purpose of the model that is being created. The general challenge can be summarized as:

- *Which normative frames exist?*
- *How to ensure that all actors involved are aware of the role of the normative frame(s)?*
- *How to ensure that the normative frames used by the actors involved are aligned (enough), among them, and in relation to the coordination and modeling purposes?*

4.4 Agility vs. Coordinated Change

Organizations in the digital age need to thrive and operate in a highly complex and dynamic environment. As a result, modern-day organizations need to be agile in order to survive. In the context of IT, the need for more agility has triggered the emergence of software development approaches, such as Agile, DevOps, etc. One of the key messages from these approaches is to avoid a big-design up front (BDUF), which could be at odds with the need to ensure enterprise-wide alignment of key concerns.

If the sketch on the back of a napkin of a new business process and its underlying IT support, suffices as a design document for an agile project, then this might be fine for the immediate sponsor of the agile project. At the same time, however, one might wonder if a pile of such "sketches" would suffice to conduct an organization-wide cyber-risk analysis, or to conduct a compliance check to e.g. the EU's GDPR.[2] As such, while a "sketch" might suffice the project goals of an agile project, it might not meet the overall goals of the enterprise, and its ongoing transformations, as a whole (such as coherence management, risk management and compliance).

---

[2] http://eur-lex.europa.eu/legal-content/EN/TXT/PDF/?uri=CELEX:32016R0679

Whatever the outcome of such a debate, it leads to the need to define situational factor, which define the purpose, the available resources for modeling efforts, and the potential return on modeling effort. The resulting challenge is therefore:

- *To provide the means to identify what kind of modeling is needed in specific situations, including the ability to make a conscious trade-offs between local project needs and more organization-wide needs to coordinate across changes.*

4.5   Orientation of Models

The tension between the (agile) needs of projects, and the need to manage a portfolio of projects as part of a larger (portfolio) of transformations, also result in a need to reflect on the modeling concepts to be used in the different situations.

For example, at an organization-wide level, it might be better to use so-called architecture principles [74] to express the overall *direction of change*, rather than the more detailed boxes-and-lines diagrams such as used in ArchiMate [75] models. At the same time, the latter type of models are a prerequisite to conduct a detailed impact analysis, or a thorough GDPR compliance check.

As such, we observe (for now) there to be two overall strategies a model may exhibit with regards to its (intended) relation to its instantiations (e.g. an epistemic or a deontic intention; see Sect. 2.6):

10. Models following an *extensional* style in the sense of containing explicit representations of domain concepts, such as, in the case of organizational design: actors, roles, processes, resources, etc.
11. Models following an *intensional* style such as design constraints or architecture principles, stating more general rules/properties.

The terms *extensional* and *intensional* are borrowed from set theory. For instance, an extensional definition of the even numbers, would require one to list all numbers individually:

$$\{2, 4, 6, 8, 10, \ldots\}$$

while an intensional definition would be:

$$\{n \times 2 \mid n \in \mathbb{N} \wedge n > 0\}$$

We would argue that modeling languages such as ArchiMate and UML are more geared towards the *extensional* strategy, while architecture principles are more geared towards an *intensional* strategy. As such, further challenges are:

- *When is an intensional or an extensional strategy most effective, in relation to the speed of change in an organization, as well as the considered scope of change (e.g. organization-wide, or business-unit specific).*

- *What are good modeling languages to express models following an intensional or an extensional strategy respectively.*

4.6 Model Management

When limiting one's definition of model to "boxes-and-lines" only, most organizations will already have to deal with the need to manage a large collection of models that describes parts of the as-is and to-be situation. Some authors even suggest to use the term *enterprise cartography* to (a.o.) manage such a collection of models [76].

When taking a broader perspective on the notion of a model, then the set of models to be managed becomes even larger, including, e.g. a traceable path from informal/textual models to more formal models. Examples of this can be found in the context of requirements engineering [77], as well as regulations [78–80].

Managing the resulting set of models as a whole seems akin to a mission impossible. As a result, some RoME-based triage needs to be made. At the same time, IT-based approaches [51, 76] can be used to support the management of the resulting models at differentiated levels of integration and traceability.

The resulting challenge is therefore:

- *How to manage the portfolio of models created when coordinating change in an effective way, possibly using modern-day IT-based solutions.*

5 Conclusion

The goal of this paper was to explore some of the challenges that model-based instruments will need to meet to support the informed coordination of change, in particular now that we have entered the digital age, resulting in an even higher pace of change.

We started with a review of our current understanding of model, which also took us beyond the "boxes-and-lines" metaphor. Based on this, we explored the role of models towards *informed decision* making regarding change, as well as *informed coordination* of change. We then discussed six (clusters of) challenges for the practice of modeling: semantic grounding, shared understanding, aligning normative frames, agility vs. coordinated change, orientation of models, and model management. Each providing ample opportunities for future research.

With regards to the latter challenges, we also explicitly made the point that (since modeling happens naturally) it is not the question whether to use models or not, but rather how to make their use more effective and efficient.

References

1. Magalhaes, R., Proper, H.A.: Model-enabled design and engineering of organisations. Organ. Design Enterprise Eng. **1**(1), 1–12 (2017)
2. Junginger, S.: Organizational design legacies & service design. Design J. (2015), special Issue: Emerging Issues in Service Design
3. Magalhaes, R. (ed.): Organization Design and Engineering: Coexistence, Cooperation or Integration? Palgrave-Macmillan, London (2014)
4. Weick, K.E.: Sense making in Organizations. Sage, Beverly Hills, CA (1995)
5. Taylor, J.R.: The communicational basis of organization: between the conversation and the text. Commun. Theory. **6**(1), 1–39 (1996)
6. Hamers, R.: We want to be a tech company with a banking license (2017)
7. Alter, S.: Theory of workarounds. Commun. Assoc. Inf. Syst. **34**, 55 (2014)
8. Mandis, S.G.: What Happened to Goldman Sachs: An Insider's Story of Organizational Drift and Its Unintended Consequences. Harvard Business Review Press, Boston, MA (2013)
9. Handel, M.J., Poltrock, S.: Working around official applications: experiences from a large engineering project. In: Proceedings of the ACM 2011 Conference on Computer Supported Cooperative Work. pp. 309–312. CSCW '11, Association for Computing Machinery, New York, NY (2011). https://doi.org/10.1145/1958824.1958870
10. Henderson, J.C., Venkatraman, N.: Strategic alignment: leveraging information technology for transforming organizations. IBM Syst. J. **32**(1), 4–16 (1993)
11. Wagter, R., Proper, H.A., Witte, D.: A theory for enterprise coherence governance. In: Saha, P. (ed.) A Systematic Perspective to Managing Complexity with EA. IGI Publishing, Hershey, PA (2013)
12. Proper, H.A., Winter, R., Aier, S., de Kinderen, S. (eds.): Architectural Coordination of Enterprise Transformation. The Enterprise Engineering Series. Springer (2018)
13. Apostel, L.: Towards the formal study of models in the non-formal sciences. Synthese. **12**, 125–161 (1960)
14. Stachowiak, H.: Allgemeine Modell theorie. Springer (1973)
15. Guarino, B., Guizzardi, G., Mylopoulos, J.: On the philosophical foundations of conceptual models. Inf. Modell. Knowl. Bases XXXI. **321**, 1 (2020)
16. Guizzardi, G.: On ontology, ontologies, conceptualizations, modeling languages, and (meta)-models. In: Vasilecas, O., Eder, J., Caplinskas, A. (eds.) Databases and Information Systems IV – Selected Papers from the Seventh International Baltic Conference, DB&IS 2006, July 3–6, 2006, Vilnius, Lithuania. Frontiers in Artificial Intelligence and Applications, vol. 155, pp. 18–39. IOS Press (2006)
17. Harel, D., Rumpe, B.: Meaningful modeling: what's the semantics of "semantics"? IEEE Comput. **37**(10), 64–72 (2004)
18. Rothenberg, J.: The nature of modeling. In: Artificial Intelligence, Simulation & Modeling, pp. 75–92. Wiley, New York, NY (1989)
19. Sandkuhl, K., Fill, H.G., Hoppenbrouwers, S.J.B.A., Krogstie, J., Matthes, F., Opdahl, A.L., Schwabe, G., Uludag, O., Winter, R.: From expert discipline to common practice: a vision and research agenda for extending the reach of enterprise modeling. Bus. Inf. Syst. Eng. **60**(1), 69–80 (2018)
20. Thalheim, B.: The theory of conceptual models, the theory of conceptual modelling and foundations of conceptual modelling. In: Handbook of Conceptual Modeling, pp. 543–577. Springer (2011)
21. Bjekovic, M., Proper, H.A., Sottet, J.S.: Embracing pragmatics. In: Yu, E.S.K., Dobbie, G., Jarke, M., Purao, S. (eds.) Conceptual Modeling – 33rd International Conference, ER 2014, Atlanta, GA, USA, October 27–29, 2014. Proceedings. LNCS, vol. 8824, pp. 431–444. Springer (2014)
22. Hoppenbrouwers, S.J.B.A., Proper, H.A., Weide, T.P.v.d.: A fundamental view on the process of conceptual modeling. In: Delcambre, L., Kop, C., Mayr, H.C., Mylopoulos, J., Pastor,

O. (eds.) Conceptual Modeling – ER 2005, 24th International Conference on Conceptual Modeling, Klagenfurt, Austria, October 24–28, 2005, Proceedings. LNCS, vol. 3716, pp. 128–143. Springer (2005)

23. Proper, H.A., Guizzardi, G.: On domain modelling and requisite variety – current state of an ongoing journey. In: Practice of Enterprise Modelling (PoEM) 2020. Springer (2020), Forthcoming

24. Proper, H.A., Verrijn–Stuart, A.A., Hoppenbrouwers, S.J.B.A.: Onutility-based selection of architecture-modelling concepts. In: Hartmann, S., Stumptner, M. (eds.) Conceptual Modelling 2005, Second Asia-Pacific Conference on Conceptual Modelling (APCCM2005), Newcastle, NSW, Australia, January/February 2005. Conferences in Research and Practice in Information Technology Series, vol. 43, pp. 25–34. Australian Computer Society, Sydney (2005)

25. Falkenberg, E.D., Verrijn-Stuart, A.A., Voss, K., Hesse, W., Lindgreen, P., Nilsson, B.E., Oei, J.L.H., Rolland, C., Stamper, R.K. (eds.): A Framework of Information Systems Concepts. IFIP WG 8.1 Task Group FRISCO, IFIP, Laxenburg, Austria (1998)

26. Proper, H.A.: Enterprise architecture: informed steering of enterprises in motion. In: Hammoudi, S., Cordeiro, J., Maciaszek, L.A., Filipe, J. (eds.) Enterprise Information Systems – 15th International Conference, ICEIS 2013, Angers, France, July 4–7, 2013, Revised Selected Papers. LNBIP, vol. 190, pp. 16–34. Springer (2014)

27. Batini, C., Mylopoulos, J.: Abstraction in conceptual models, maps and graphs. In: Tutorial presented at the 37th Intl. Conf. on Conceptual Modeling, ER 2018, Xi'an, China (2018)

28. Ogden, C.K., Richards, I.A.: The Meaning of Meaning – A Study of the Influence of Language upon Thought and of the Science of Symbolism. Oxford, Magdalene College, University of Cambridge (1923)

29. Cruse, A.: Meaning in language, an introduction to semantics and pragmatics. Oxford University Press, Oxford (2000)

30. Morris, C.: Signs, Language and Behaviour. Prentice Hall, Englewood Cliffs, NJ (1946)

31. Searle, J.R.: A taxonomy of illocutionary acts. In: Expression and Meaning: Studies in the Theory of Speech Acts. Cambridge University Press, Cambridge (1979)

32. Ullmann, S.: Semantics: An Introduction to the Science of Meaning. Basil Blackwell, Oxford (1967)

33. Henderson-Sellers, B., Gonzalez-Perez, C., Walkerden, G.: An application of philosophy in software modelling and future information systems development. In: Franch, X., Soffer, P. (eds.) Advanced Information Systems Engineering Workshops, pp. 329–340. Springer (2013)

34. Kecheng, L., Clarke, R.J., Andersen, P.B., Stamper, R.K., Abou-Zeid, E.S. (eds.): IFIP TC8/WG8.1 Working Conference on Organizational Semiotics – Evolving a Science of Information Systems. Kluwer, Deventer, the Netherlands (2002)

35. Krogstie, J.: A semiotic approach to quality in requirements specifications. In: Kecheng, L., Clarke, R.J., Andersen, P.B., Stamper, R.K., Abou-Zeid, E.S. (eds.) Proceedings of the IFIP TC8 / WG8.1 Working Conference on Organizational Semiotics: Evolving a Science of Information Systems, pp. 231–250. Kluwer, Deventer, the Netherlands (2002)

36. Lankhorst, M.M., Torre, L.v.d., Proper, H.A., Arbab, F., Boer, F.S.d., Bonsangue, M.: Foundations. In: Enterprise Architecture at Work – Modelling, Communication and Analysis. The Enterprise Engineering Series, 4th edn, pp. 41–58. Springer (2017)

37. Hoppenbrouwers, S.J.B.A.: Freezing Language; Conceptualisation Processes in ICT Supported Organisations. Ph.D. thesis, University of Nijmegen, Nijmegen, the Netherlands (2003)

38. Guizzardi, G.: Ontology, ontologies and the "i" of fair. Data Intell. 2(1–2), 181–191 (2020)

39. Partridge, C., Gonzalez-Perez, C., Henderson-Sellers, B.: Are conceptual models concept models? In: Ng, W., Storey, V., Trujillo, J. (eds.) Conceptual Modeling. ER 2013. LNCS, vol. 8217, pp. 96–105. Springer (2013)

40. Proper, H.A., Bjekovic, M.: Fundamental challenges in systems modelling. In: Mayr, H.C., Rinderle-Ma, S., Strecker, S. (eds.) 40 Years EMISA 2019, pp. 13–28. Gesellschaft fur Informatik e.V., Bonn (2020)

41. Bommel, P.v., Hoppenbrouwers, S.J.B.A., Proper, H.A., Weide, T.P.v.d.: QoMo: A modelling process quality framework based on SEQUAL. In: Proper, H.A., Halpin, T.A., Krogstie, J. (eds.): Proceedings of the 12th Workshop on Exploring Modeling Methods for Systems Analysis and Design (EMMSAD 2007), held in conjunction with the 19th Conference on Advanced Information Systems (CAiSE 2007), Trondheim, Norway, pp. 118–127. CEUR-WS.org (2007)

42. Frederiks, P.J.M., Weide, T.P.v.d.: Information Modeling: the process and the required competencies of its participants. Data Knowl. Eng. 58(1), 4–20 (2006), best paper award in NLDB 2004 conference

43. van der Linden, D.J.T., Hadar, I.: Cognitive effectiveness of conceptual modeling languages: examining professional modelers. In: Proceedings of the 5th IEEE International Workshop on Empirical Requirements Engineering (EmpiRE) (2015)

44. Wilmont, I., Barendsen, E., Hoppenbrouwers, S.J.B.A., Hengeveld, S.: Abstract reasoning in collaborative modeling. In: Hoppenbrouwers, S.J.B.A., Rouwette, E.A.J.A., Rittgen, P. (eds.) Proceedings of the 45th Hawaiian International Conference on the System Sciences, HICSS-45; Collaborative Systems Track, Collaborative Modeling Minitrack. IEEE Explore, Los Alamitos, CA (2012)

45. Bjekovic, M., Sottet, J.S., Favre, J.M., Proper, H.A.: A framework for natural enterprise modelling. In: IEEE 15th Conference on Business Informatics, CBI 2013, Vienna, Austria, July 15–18, 2013, pp. 79–84. IEEE Computer Society Press, Los Alamitos, CA (2013)

46. Zarwin, Z., Bjekovic, M., Favre, J.M., Sottet, J.S., Proper, H.A.: Natural modelling. J. Object Technol. 13(3), 1–36 (2014)

47. Harmsen, A.F., Proper, H.A., Kok, N.: Informed governance of enterprise transformations. In: Proper, H.A., Harmsen, A.F., Dietz, J.L.G. (eds.) Advances in Enterprise Engineering II – First NAF Academy Working Conference on Practice-Driven Research on Enterprise Transformation, PRET 2009, held at CAiSE 2009, Amsterdam, The Netherlands, June 11, 2009. Proceedings. LNBIP, vol. 28, pp. 155–180. Springer, Amsterdam (2009)

48. Proper, H.A., Lankhorst, M.M.: Enterprise architecture – towards essential sensemaking. Enterprise Modell. Inf. Syst. Architect. 9(1), 5–21 (June 2014)

49. Jonkers, H., Lankhorst, M.M., Quartel, D.A.C., Proper, H.A., Iacob, M.E.: ArchiMate for integrated modelling throughout the architecture development and implementation cycle. In: Hofreiter, B., Dubois, E., Lin, K.J., Setzer, T., Godart, C., Proper, H.A., Bodenstaff, L. (eds.) 13th IEEE Conference on Commerce and Enterprise Computing, CEC 2011, Luxembourg-Kirchberg, Luxembourg, September 5–7, 2011, pp. 294–301. IEEE Computer Society Press, Los Alamitos, CA (2011)

50. Op't Land, M., Proper, H.A., Waage, M., Cloo, J., Steghuis, C.: Enterprise Architecture – Creating Value by Informed Governance. . The Enterprise Engineering Series. Springer (2008)

51. Proper, H.A.: Digital Enterprise Modelling – Opportunities and Challenges. In: Roelens, B., Laurier, W., Poels, G., Weigand, H. (eds.) Proceedings of 14th International Workshop on Value Modelling and Business Ontologies, Brussels, Belgium, January 16–17, 2020. CEUR Workshop Proceedings, vol. 2574, pp. 33–40. CEUR-WS.org, http://ceur-ws. org/Vol2574/short3.pdf (2020)

52. Proper, H.A., Hoppenbrouwers, S.J.B.A., Veldhuijzen van Zanten, G.E.: Communication of enterprise architectures. In: Enterprise Architecture at Work – Modelling, Communication and Analysis. The Enterprise Engineering Series, 4th edn, pp. 59–72. Springer (2017)

53. Proper, H.A., Bjekovic, M., Gils, B.v., de Kinderen, S.: Enterprise architecture modelling – purpose, requirements and language. In: Proceedings of the 13th Workshop on Trends in Enterprise Architecture (TEAR 2018). IEEE, Stockholm (2018)

54. Hoogervorst, J.A.P.: Enterprise Governance and Enterprise Engineering. The Enterprise Engineering Series. Springer, Berlin (2009)

55. Taylor, J.R., Van Every, E.J.: When Organization Fails: Why Authority Matters. Routledge, London (2004)

56. Abraham, R., Niemietz, H., de Kinderen, S., Aier, S.: Can boundary objects mitigate communication defects in enterprise transformation? Findings from expert interviews. In: Jung, R., Reichert, M. (eds.) Proceedings of the 5th International Workshop on Enterprise Modelling and Information Systems Architectures, EMISA 2013, St. Gallen, Switzerland, September 5–6, 2013. LNI, vol. 222, pp. 27–40. Gesellschaft fur Informatik, Bonn, Germany (2013)

57. Levina, N., Vaast, E.: The emergence of boundary spanning competence in practice: implications for implementation and use of information systems. MIS Q. **29**(2), 335–363 (2005)

58. Star, S.L., Griesemer, J.R.: Institutional Ecology, 'Translations' and Boundary Objects: Amateurs and Professionals in Berkeley's Museum of Vertebrate Zoology 1907-39. Soc. Stud. Sci. **19**(4), 387–420 (1989)

59. Lankhorst, M.M., Torre, L.v.d., Proper, H.A., Arbab, F., Steen, M.W.A.: Viewpoints and visualisation. In: Enterprise Architecture at Work – Modelling, Communication and Analysis. The Enterprise Engineering Series, 4th edn, pp. 171–214. Springer (2017)

60. Band, I., Ellefsen, T., Estrem, B., Iacob, M.E., Jonkers, H., Lankhorst, M.M., Nilsen, D., Proper, H.A., Quartel, D.A.C., Thorn, S.: ArchiMate 3.0 Specification. The Open Group (2016)

61. Gils, B.v., Proper, H.A.: Enterprise modelling in the age of digital transformation. In: Buchmann, R.A., Karagiannis, D., Kirikova, M. (eds.) The Practice of Enterprise Modeling – 11th IFIP WG 8.1. Working Conference, PoEM 2018, Vienna, Austria, October 31–November 2, 2018, Proceedings. LNBIP, vol. 335, pp. 257–273. Springer (2018)

62. Barjis, J.: Collaborative, participative and interactive enterprise modeling. In: Filipe, J., Cordeiro, J. (eds.) Enterprise Information Systems, 11th International Conference, ICEIS 2009, Milan, Italy, May 6-10, 2009. Proceedings. LNBIP, vol. 24, pp. 651–662. Springer (2009)

63. Sandkuhl, K., Stirna, J., Persson, A., Wißotzki, M.: Enterprise Modeling: Tackling Business Challenges with the 4EM Method. Springer (2014)

64. Stirna, J., Persson, A.: Ten Years Plus with EKD: Reflections from Using an Enterprise Modeling Method in Practice. In: Proper, H.A., Halpin, T.A., Krogstie, J. (eds.): Proceedings of the 12th Workshop on Exploring Modeling Methods for Systems Analysis and Design (EMMSAD 2007), held in conjunction with the 19th Conference on Advanced Information Systems (CAiSE 2007), Trondheim, Norway, pp. 97–106. CEUR-WS.org (2007)

65. Hitchman, S.: Practitioner perceptions on the use of some semantic concepts in the entity relationship model. Eur. J. Inf. Syst. **4**, 31–40 (1995)

66. Hitchman, S.: The details of conceptual modelling notations are important – a comparison of relationship normative language. Commun. AIS **9**(10), (2002)

67. Nordbotten, J.C., Crosby, M.E.: The effect of graphic style on data model interpretation. Inf. Syst. J. **9**(2), 139–155 (1999)

68. Caire, P., Genon, N., Heymans, P., Moody, D.L.: Visual notation design 2.0: Towards user comprehensible requirements engineering notations. In: 21st IEEE International Requirements Engineering Conference (RE2013), pp. 115–124 (2013)

69. Masri, K., Parker, D., Gemino, A.: Using iconic graphics in entity relationship diagrams: the impact on understanding. J. Database Manag. **19**(3), 22–41 (2008)

70. Purchase, H.C., Carrington, D., Allder, J.A.: Empirical evaluation of aesthetics-based graph layout. Empir. Softw. Eng. **7**(3), 233–255 (2002)

71. Moody, D.L.: The "physics" of notations: toward a scientific basis for constructing visual notations in software engineering. IEEE Trans. Softw. Eng. **35**(6), 756–779 (2009)

72. Granada, D., Vara, J.M., Bollati, V.A., Marcos, E.: Enabling the development of cognitive effective visual DSLs. In: Dingel, J., Schulte, W., Ramos, I., Abrahao, S., Insfran, E. (eds.) Model-Driven Engineering Languages and Systems: 17th International Conference, MODELS 2014, Valencia, Spain, September 28–October 3, 2014. Proceedings, pp. 535–551. Springer (2014)

73. Moody, D.L., Heymans, P., Matulevicius, R.: Visual syntax does matter: improving the cognitive effectiveness of the i* visual notation. Requir. Eng. **15**(2), 141–175 (Jun 2010)

74. Greefhorst, D., Proper, H.A.: Architecture Principles – The Cornerstones of Enterprise Architecture The Enterprise Engineering Series. Springer (2011)
75. Lankhorst, M.M., Hoppenbrouwers, S.J.B.A., Jonkers, H., Proper, H.A.,Torre, L.v.d., Arbab, F., Boer, F.S.d., Bonsangue, M., Iacob, M.E., Stam, A.W., Groenewegen, L., Buuren, R.v., Slagter, R.J., Campschroer, J., Steen, M.W.A., Bekius, S.F., Bosma, H., Cuvelier, M.J., ter Doest, H.W.L., van Eck, P.A.T., Fennema, P., Jacob, J., Janssen, W.P.M., Jonkers, H., Krukkert, D., van Leeuwen, D., Penders, P.G.M., Veldhuijzen van Zanten, G.E., Wieringa, R.J.: Enterprise Architecture at Work – Modelling, Communication and Analysis. The Enterprise Engineering Series, 4th edn. Springer (2017)
76. Tribolet, J.M., Sousa, P., Caetano, A.: The role of enterprise governance and cartography in enterprise engineering. Enterprise Modell. Inf. Syst. Architect. **9**(1), 38–49 (2014)
77. Pohl, K.: The three dimensions of requirements engineering: a framework and its applications. Inf. Syst. **19**(3), 243–258 (1994)
78. Engers, T., Nijssen, S.: Connecting people: semantic-conceptual modeling for laws and regulations. In: Janssen, M., Scholl, H.J., Wimmer, M.A., Bannister, F. (eds.) Electronic Government, pp. 133–146. Springer, Berlin (2014)
79. Ghanavati, S., Amyot, D., Peyton, L.: Compliance analysis based on a goal-oriented requirement language evaluation methodology. In: Proceedings of the 7th IEEE International Requirements Engineering Conference (RE 2009), pp. 133–142. IEEE Computer Society, Los Alamitos, CA (2009)
80. Miller, L.W., Katz, N.: A model management system to support policy analysis. Decis. Support. Syst. **2**(1), 55–63 (1986)

Part II
Design Science Research

Reflections on the Practice of Design Science in Information Systems

Shirley Gregor

Abstract Design science research (DSR) now enjoys a degree of recognition in information systems, with special issues in journals, dedicated tracks in conferences and well-recognized guidelines for the conduct of DSR. A number of issues regarding DSR, however, are still the subject of debate. This essay addresses these issues, drawing on prior analytic work and personal experience and reviews of DSR in practice. Variation in the incidence of DSR publications amongst leading journals is shown. Other conclusions are that the need for inductive and abductive thinking in addition to deductive methods for knowledge generation is not as well accepted as it could be, that further work could be done on gathering evidence for the impact of DSR and that there is reason to think that work on the epistemology of DSR has value.

Keywords Design science research · Design knowledge · Methodology

1 Introduction

Design science is concerned with the development of design knowledge with scientific legitimacy of how things (artifacts) can or should be constructed or arranged (i.e. designed), usually by human agency, to achieve desired goals [1]. Design knowledge in the information systems (IS) discipline concerns artifacts such as systems development methods, organizational databases, platform architectures, data analytics algorithms and organizational strategies. The development of novel, sound and reliable design knowledge and the ways in which this knowledge is used have important consequences for organizations, economies, societies and individuals.

S. Gregor (✉)
Australian National University, Canberra, Australia
e-mail: shirley.gregor@anu.edu.au

© The Author(s), under exclusive license to Springer Nature Switzerland AG 2021
S. Aier et al. (eds.), *Engineering the Transformation of the Enterprise*,
https://doi.org/10.1007/978-3-030-84655-8_7

Research approaches classed under the broad umbrella of design science have been given various labels, including the early depiction of the *systems development* or *engineering research* approach by Nunamaker et al. [2]. In this essay the term *design science research* (DSR) is used to encompass the various approaches, including variants such as action design research.

DSR is now generally well recognized in IS, with special issues in journals (e.g. [3]), dedicated tracks in conferences and well-recognized guidelines for the conduct of DSR (e.g. [4]). A number of well-regarded research centers successfully focus on DSR. For instance, Jay Nunamaker's work with colleagues at the University of Arizona is ongoing [5]. Amongst a number of instances in Europe, the Institute of Information Management at the University of St Gallen emphasizes that it is "dedicated to applied and design-oriented research at the interface between business and IT" [6 , p. 75].

A number of issues regarding DSR, however, are still the subject of debate. These issues include a perception that it is difficult to publish DSR in the best journals [7], the need for design theory [8], the ways in which design knowledge is developed [9] and the usability of design principles [10]. This essay reflects on some of the questions that remain of interest: 1) How well accepted is DSR in IS? 2) What is design knowledge? 3) How is design knowledge generated? 4) How is design knowledge utilized? and 5) Is work on the epistemology of DSR useful?

Personal reflections are presented for each of these questions, drawing on arguments made in my own prior work and that of others. In addition, in order to compare these perspectives with what DSR scholars actually do when practicing DSR, evidence is drawn from a number of published reviews of DSR studies. Within the scope of the essay only an outline of responses to each of the questions addressed can be given. However the comparison with evidence from reviews does yield some insights and also points to areas in which further reviews might be of interest.

2 Approach

An individual's views on DSR and how it is conducted will in part reflect their own background and experiences, in journal review cycles, in editorial roles and in interactions with other researchers. In this essay I build on my prior work on DSR epistemology, so my own background has some relevance. This background includes an undergraduate science degree in mathematics and psychology and then a period working as a software engineer, systems analyst and project leader, during which time I undertook employer-sponsored postgraduate study in what was then termed "computing". I also took some classes in philosophy from interest. Subsequently I moved to academia and completed a Master's degree in computer science and then a PhD in IS. This background means I am comfortable with and enjoy both behavioral research and DSR. However, when I moved to IS for my PhD, I could see that there was little recognition of or guidance for undertaking DSR in IS. I was familiar with the DSR type approach in computer science and some areas of mathematics, but in these fields there is not a great deal written on scientific methodology—an understanding of how research is performed and knowledge generated is somewhat implicit in disciplinary culture.

Thus, in 1999 I joined with Frada Burstein to author an article on "the systems development or engineering approach" to research in IS [11]. Further work has followed on epistemological issues in IS, much of it in response to problems encountered by myself and students. Along with many others who write on DSR, I continue to be inspired by the work of Herbert Simon who believed that in the sciences of the artificial what was needed was:

> A science of design, a body of intellectually tough, analytic, partly formalizable, partly empirical, teachable doctrine about the design process. [12 , p. 113]

The "partly formalizable" wording is important, as Simon recognized that there was room in the sciences of the artificial for human creativity and inventiveness, as in other sciences.

A further concern is the link between the creation and dissemination of credible design knowledge and professional ethics. This link was highlighted in a period I spent as Director of the Professional Standards Board of the Australian Computer Society. Failure to pay attention to well-established design knowledge can lead to flawed or failed IS, sometimes with considerable harm done to individuals.

In this essay I discuss the questions raised in the introduction by calling on some of my prior work, much of which depends on arguments based in the philosophy of science and technology. However, as a check, my views can be compared with evidence from surveys of empirical DSR studies: that is, studies that build and evaluate IS artifacts. A number of prior review articles present and analyze patterns of interest across various samples of empirical DSR studies. There appears to have been little work, however, that reflects on the finding from more than one of these reviews in combination. Even though prior reviews have been carried out against different frameworks and with different foci of interest, some overlaps can be found that allow comparisons to be made.

A sample of reviews for the current essay was selected by searching the AIS eLibrary separately for both AIS journals and conferences, using the search strings "design science" "literature review" and also "design science" "systematic review". In addition, the review by Samuel-Ojo et al. [13] was included as it was referred to in one of the initial reviews found and is relevant to the research questions. The review by Morrison and George [14] was also included, as although it uses concepts in ways that differ from current usage it gives some historical perspective. Reviews were selected that focused on the practice of DSR, with work where design knowledge was generated, rather than solely theoretical work about DSR methods or epistemology. Reviews that focused on specific aspects of DSR that are out of scope in terms of the research questions were also omitted. Table 1 shows the five reviews in the primary sample, in order of year of publication. Hereafter these studies are referred to by the authors' names alone.

Table 1 Reviews of design science practice in information systems

Study	Publication year	Sample characteristics	Focus
Morrison and George [14]	1995	1986–1991; CACM, MS, MISQ; n=180	Software engineering type research
Samuel-Ojo et al. [13]	2010	2006–2009; DESRIST conferences; n = 92	DSR trends and outcomes
Gregor and Hevner [15]	2013	2006–2011; MISQ; n = 13	Types of knowledge contribution
Leukel, Mueller and Sugumaran [16]	2014	2009–2013; volumes 1–5 of BISE journal, n = 48; 2011–2013 BISE proceedings; n = 97	Artifacts, foundations, evaluation methods
Engel, Leicht and Ebel [17]	2019	2004–2019; journals in Senior Scholar Basket (MISQ, JMIS, JAIS, ISR, EJIS, ISJ, JSIS, JIT); n = 97	Build, evaluate, outcome framework

Notes: *BISE* Business & Information Systems Engineering [18], *CACM* Communications of the ACM, *DESRIST* Design Science Research in Information Systems and Technology, *EJIS* European Journal of Information Systems, *ISR* Information Systems Research, *JAIS* Journal of the Association of Information Systems, *JMIS* Journal of Management Information Systems, *MISQ* Management Information Systems Quarterly, *MS* Management Science

3   Discussion

3.1   *How Well Accepted Is DSR in IS?*

DSR now appears to have at least a reasonable level of acceptance in IS, given the special issues on the topic, specialized tracks at conferences and the availability of accepted guidelines for conducting DSR. Nevertheless, Peffers et al. [7] in their introduction to a special issue on DSR note a perception that it is difficult to publish DSR in the best journals.

What do reviews of patterns in publishing DSR tell us?

As far back as 1995 Morrison and George [14] performed a review of what they termed "software engineering research" in Management Information Systems (MIS/SE), which was research concerned with the development of IS in organizations, congruent with Nunamaker et al.'s [2] depiction of "systems development" as a research methodology. These depictions are amongst the earliest of what is now termed DSR in IS. The Morrison and George review was of publications from 1986 to 1991 in *Communications of the ACM, Management Science* and *MIS Quarterly*. The review found that the percentages of articles that were MIS/SE in these journals over the 6 year period were respectively: 31% in CACM, 2% in MS and 27% in MISQ. The number of DSR articles published in MISQ had stayed between 5 and 10 per year over the sample timeframe.

The Leukel at al review found in the *BISE* journal from 2009 to 2013 that 48 of 80 (60%) of articles were DSR. BISE in 2020 reported an impact factor of 5.837 and a Scopus CiteScore of 7.6 [19], meaning that it ranks very well amongst IS journals.

Table 2 DSR publications in AIS Senior Scholar's basket journal 2004–2019 (source [17])

Journal	Number of articles	%
European Journal of Information Systems	21	21.6
Information Systems Journal	5	5.2
Information Systems Research	4	4.1
Journal of the Association for Information Systems	24	24.7
Journal of Information Technology	2	2.1
Journal of Management Information Systems	23	23.7
Journal of Strategic Information Systems	3	3.1
Management Information Systems Quarterly	15	15.5
Total	97	100.0

One could conclude that having a relatively large percentage of DSR articles is not a drawback for a journal (assuming the proportion of DSR articles in BISE has not dropped markedly between 2013 and 2019).

The Engel et al. review of journals in the AIS Senior Scholar's basket from 2004 to 2019 reported for DSR "an increasing trend in publications, which seems to happen in waves over time" [17 , p. 8], possibly corresponding to special issues in journals. Table 2 shows the number of DSR articles found in each journal in this study. The figures suggest that some of the journals are more open to DSR work than others are.

The case of MISQ is interesting. The Gregor and Hevner review showed an average of close to two DSR articles per year for 2006–2011. The Engel et al. review shows 15 articles from MISQ across 16 years, 2004–2019, an average of just under 1 per year. This average is considerably below the 5–10 per year noted in the Morrison and George review for 1986–1991. Again, the figures may not be directly comparable as the two reviews used different conceptualizations of DSR. However, it raises the question as to whether the number of DSR articles in some journals is decreasing.

3.2 What Is Design Knowledge?

Design knowledge is "how-to" prescriptive knowledge, rather than the "what-is" descriptive knowledge common in the behavioral and natural sciences. The artifacts that the design knowledge concerns in DSR have a physical form, in that they occur in space and time in the real world. Thus, an IS/IT artifact is different from knowledge, an abstraction. The software that is at the heart of IS cannot readily be observed, as it exists in electronic circuits, so some level of abstraction is always required to represent a software artifact, e.g. as pseudcode.

The distinction between descriptive and prescriptive forms of knowledge is discussed in terms of different forms of logic in work on knowledge representation (e.g., see [20]). Descriptive knowledge can be represented in propositional logic

Table 3 Incidence of publications at different knowledge levels

Knowledge level	Samuel-Ojo et al. [13 , p. 130]	Engel et al. [17 , p. 9][a]
1. Implementation of an Artifact	13 (14.1%)	7 (5.8%)
2. Constructs, models, methods	70 (76.1%)	100 (84%)
3. Design theories	9 (9.85%)	12 (10.1%)
Total	92 (100%)	119 (100%)

Note: [a]Some of the 97 articles contributed to knowledge at more than one level

forms such as: IF X THEN Y. Prescriptive knowledge can be considered in terms of "the logic of action" [21]. In design science research a general form for expressing prescriptive knowledge is a design principle. Gregor, Chandra Kruse and Seidel [1] synthesize existing definitions of design principles to give a general form: "For Implementer I to achieve or allow Aim A for User U in Context C employ Mechanisms M1, M2, M3.... involving Enactors E1, E2, E3, ... because of Rationale R". The mechanisms employed to achieve aims can be described by representation tools such as flowcharts, pseudocode, algorithms, architectural dia-grams, modelling tools, narrative descriptions of methods and screen layouts, or a combination of these.

Gregor and Hevner [15] recognize a continuum from the knowledge recognized in an instantiation of an artifact (Level 1), through nascent design theory in the form of design principles, schemas and methods (Level 2) through to full design theory—a mature body of knowledge (Level 3). Some have questioned whether there is a need for design theory, instead stressing the primacy of knowledge at the artifact level, see [19].

What do the reviews tell us? Both the Samuel-Ojo et al. and the Engel et al. reviews examined the types of knowledge produced in terms similar to the Gregor and Hevner levels (Table 3). Both reviews show publications across all three levels, with the majority at the intermediate second level. Both found approximately 10% of publications produced design theory, an indication that it is perceived to have value.

3.3 How Is Design Knowledge Generated?

In prior work I have argued, with colleagues, that design knowledge is produced through a combination of reasoning processes of induction, deduction and abduction [9, 22–24]. Mature design theory can result from a synthesis of work across a number of studies [9]. Österle et al. [25] propose that DSR includes both deductive and inductive reasoning. Similar views can be found in work on design theorizing in management research in general. van Aken et al. say there is no straightforward process for identifying knowledge about how outcomes and performance of generic design come about. They suggest a process of "combining one's social and technical expertise, logic, generic explanatory theory on the phenomena in play and consci-entious cross-case analysis of design instantiations" [26, p. 6].

Table 4 Knowledge creation strategies (Engel et al. [17, p. 11])

Strategy	Frequency
Deductive	41 (42.2%)
Inductive	23 (23.7%)
Mix	33 (34.0%)
Total	97 (100%)

Some authors have emphasized the development of DSR knowledge from the descriptive sciences through a deductive process. Walls et al. [27] proposed that design theory be developed through a process in which supporting kernel theory is selected from theories in the natural science database and "combined with characteristics of existing artifacts in the environment to create new design theories" (p. 48). Kuechler and Vaishnavi [28] proposed "design-relevant explanatory/predictive theory (DREPT)" that formally links general theory constructs from outside IS to the design realm.

Strictly speaking, in logic the move from descriptive to prescriptive forms of knowledge is problematic. From a statement in propositional logic, X causes Y, one cannot deduce that in order to achieve Y one should necessarily undertake X as there may be other ways of achieving Y. Further, the link between propositional logic and the representation of action sequences, such as Do X1, then Do X2, then Do X3, to achieve Y is even more problematic.

Niinluoto [29] says that the "top down" (deductive) method is the first of two ways in which design knowledge can be derived. In a second way, when there is insufficent knowledge in the descriptive basic sciences to deduce a technological rule, then knowledge is obtained "from below", by building artifacts with trial-and-error and experimentation (induction and abduction). Hevner (in [30]) also recognizes both approaches. He sees the first, where there is a reliance on kernel theory to predict the design of artifacts, as being appropriate when there is a relatively stable environment. He also sees a second approach, where there is a need to "move away from the limitations of kernel theory prediction" (p. vi) in complex and fast changing environments and instead use adaptive learning and incremental search processes.

What do the reviews tell us? Engel et al. analysed their sample in terms of whether they judged a knowledge creation strategy to be deductive, inductive or a mix of these (Table 4). The deductive approach represents a relatively large proportion of the total. This finding may in part be due to a tendency in IS research in general to focus more on the context of justification (theory testing) rather than the context of discovery (theory building) [22]. It may also be due to the influence of early writers on DSR who emphasized deduction from kernel theory.

Engel at al. also analysed the proportion the pattern of publications across the four types of knowledge contribution in [15]: invention, exaptation (re-purposing), improvement and routine design. Table 5 shows the proportion they found in comparison with the original Gregor and Hevner analysis. Both analyses show no publications in routine design, as expected. The majority of publications are in the improvement category with relatively few in invention and exaptation. These latter two categories are those that require more inventiveness and creativity and may be

Table 5 Knowledge contribution types

Contribution type	Gregor and Hevner [15 , p. 348]	Engel et al. [17 , p. 14]
Invention	0 (0%)	3 (3.1%)
Exaptation	3 (23.1%)	12 (12.2%)
Improvement	10 (76.9%)	83 (84.7%)
Routine design	0 (0%)	0 (0%)
Total	13 (100%)	98 (100%)

more difficult to produce, as well as managing publication. Smith and Hitt [31] note in their study of eminent management theorists the difficulties these researchers had in getting their novel work published.

3.4 How Is Design Knowledge Utilized?

The question of the utilization and impact of DSR has two aspects: impact in academia and impact in practice.

The impact of DSR studies in academia can be studied with citation analyses. However, there appears to be comparatively little work in this respect. An exception is the review by Samuel-Ojo et al. who found that citations varied with type of contribution: half of the papers that featured better design theory had a citation count that was more than average but skewed with a wider variability (p. 132). This finding can be compared with the study by Colquitt and Zapata-Phelan [32] who reviewed the theoretical contributions made in articles in the 50 years from 1958 to 2007 in the *Academy of Management Journal.* Their study found that articles that are rated moderate to high in terms of both theory building and theory testing enjoyed the highest citation rates.

It is expected in DSR also that papers that present very novel findings are highly cited (e.g. the first data mining algorithm article [33]). It would also be expected that theory and review articles in DSR that present a mature body of knowledge, also enjoy high citation rates, as they do in other forms of research. One example is the theory of visual notations by Moody [34], which synthesizes theory and empirical work to develop a full design theory. Google Scholar show over 1200 citations for this work.

More work could be done analyzing the research impact of DSR.

The impact of DSR on practice is difficult to gauge, an issue recognized in science policy for research in general. Findings from DSR are likely to flow to practice via many channels, including collaborative projects with industry, industry-based PhDs, industry-oriented publications and books, textbooks and teaching.

It is not expected that design knowledge should be applied uncritically in practice. Much design knowledge is probabilistic in nature, rather than having the nature of universal laws. Thus, design knowledge can be suggested for consideration as an option for achieving a goal, rather than being a definitive prescription. Van Aken

[35] captures this idea well in saying that some "technological rules" (design principles) are algorithmic in nature and can be followed directly, while others are more heuristic in nature. In any case, one would expect that practitioners apply design knowledge in the context of well-accepted professional practice, as in software engineering and user-centred design, so that applications of knowledge are appropriately tested during application development.

Lukyanenko and Parsons [10] discuss design theory indeterminacy and the problems that can occur when practitioners attempt to implement design principles. They offer useful advice on how the specification of design principles can be improved so they are more accessible to practitioners.

A further thought is that it should not be expected that DSR knowledge as published in journals should necessarily be directly accessible by practitioners. Additional work can be needed to explain DSR theory in industry outlets, particularly with illustrative case studies, and with the fuller coverage that is possible in books.

3.5   Is Work on the Epistemology of DSR Useful?

There is now considerable work on how DSR can or should be performed: that is, the epistemology of DSR. Engel et al. noted that about half the papers they found concerning DSR in their original sample were "methodological" papers, rather than showing engagement in the production of DSR knowledge. This finding can be viewed in different ways. A positive view is that there is ongoing effort devoted to establishing DSR and improving its practice. An alternate view is that it would be preferable to have more people actually doing DSR than writing about it. Further, Peffers et al. [7 , p. 130] note that:

> over time, with the great number of guidelines, rules and frameworks, DSR researchers found themselves faced with a difficult challenge, namely an excess of advice and expectations for how to carry out DSR. The many guidelines and objectives published in journals and conferences make it difficult and costly to carry out DSR projects. This problem remains unsolved to the present day and it remains difficult to present DSR outcomes without running a foul of some of these rules.

Personal experience provides an illustration. With one action design research study, a reviewer was insistent that we had to use the word "ensemble" to describe our artifacts, as the person felt the word was needed to match the canonical description of action DSR. However, the review process is rarely straightforward, and reviewers' idiosyncrasies are likely to be regularly encountered with any type of research, not just DSR.

Personal experience also shows that other researchers, particularly junior researchers appreciate having some guidance on how to undertake and communicate DSR, judging by comments received at conferences and in email communications. I have been asked by junior researchers, even in computer science, to help them present DSR work so it is acceptable in articles and theses.

Table 6 Methodological approach (Engel et al. [17, p. 11])

Approach	Frequency[a]
Hevner et al. [38]	60 (46.9%)
Peffers et al. [4]	21 (16.4%)
Others (none over 6 each)	48 (37.5%)
Total	128 (100%)

Note: [a]Some of the 97 articles referred to more than one approach

Another interesting example of the application of epistemological work has arisen. In Australia organizations can claim tax write-offs for expenditure on research and development (R&D). Many millions of dollars can be involved when the claim is for a large information systems development. The legislation governing whether write-offs are allowable is cast very much in the form of the traditional scientific method. The applicant needs to show that the outcome (solution) was not known in advance on the basis of current knowledge, a hypothesis for a solution has to be advanced, experimentation tests the hypothesis and then logical conclusions are drawn and new knowledge generated. I have been employed as an expert witness by a law company to provide advice in court cases on how the methods of DSR equate to the traditional scientific method, relying largely on [7, 36]. In DSR, the hypothesis is equivalent to the testable propositions in Gregor and Jones [36]. That is, the hypothesis is advanced that an artifact designed as described (e.g. with pseudocode, architectural descriptions and so on), can achieve certain stated aims. The hypotheses can then be tested and the results reported. Organizations, including multi-nationals doing business in Australia, need to take care that they present their claims in such a way that it conforms to the DSR equivalent of the scientific method, so that their work can be distinguished from routine design (see [37]).

The review article by Engel et al. has some relevant data. They found that two approaches to DSR were the most cited (Table 6). Engel et al. see the levels of application as disproportionate. However, a positive take on the data is that it shows there are some well recognized guidelines available that have a high level of acceptability.

4 Conclusions

This essay has discussed some open questions regarding DSR. It draws on prior analytic work on DSR and also reviews of DSR in practice. Some conclusions follow.

1. DSR does appear to be reasonably well accepted in IS, although there are differences in the level of publishing DSR across journals. DSR authors can consider these patterns when looking for outlets for their work.
2. The knowledge generated in DSR is prescriptive "how-to" knowledge, rather than descriptive "what-is" knowledge. Analysis of publishing patterns shows a predominance of "nascent theory" work, with a reasonable amount of work

classed as "design theory", while "artifact implementation" has the lowest incidence. In terms of knowledge contribution type, the majority of publications are in the improvement category with relatively few classed as invention and exaptation. The analyses taken together suggest that it is more difficult to undertake and publish genuinely innovative and novel work (perhaps relying on creativity and inductive reasoning) rather than incremental improvement work that may be more deductive in nature.

3. There are still differences in views on how DSR should be generated. Some authors make good arguments for a plurality of modes of reasoning approaches: inductive, deductive and abductive. Others have tended more towards supporting deductive approaches from kernel theory. Analyses of publishing patterns show that the deductive approach is the most widely used, while mixed approaches are also popular and the inductive approach has reasonable representation.

4. There is not a great deal of evidence from reviews to show how design knowledge is utilized, either in academia or practice. Evidence for its use comes from observation of teaching curriculum, book and industry publications, industry collaborations and so on.

5. Concern has been expressed about the proportion of effort devoted to the epistemology of DSR and the plethora of guidelines available for DSR researchers. However, there are methodologies that enjoy a large degree of support and acceptability in journal publications. Interestingly, epistemological work also has application in government policy areas such as taxation.

In conclusion, DSR is now accepted in IS although there are still some open issues. Reviews of IS practice can shed light on some of these issues. The Engel et al. review was particularly helpful in preparing this essay as it was built on a carefully constructed analytic framework. Further work of this nature is advocated.

Acknowledgements Thank you to Christian Engel and Phillip Ebel for their comments.

References

1. Gregor, S., Chandra Kruse, L., Seidel, S.: The anatomy of a design principle. J. Assoc. Inf. Syst. (2020, to appear)
2. Nunamaker Jr., J.F., Chen, M., Purdin, T.D.: Systems development in information systems research. J. Manag. Inf. Syst. **7**(3), 89–106 (1990)
3. Winter, R.: Design science research in Europe. Eur. J. Inf. Syst. **17**(5), 470–475 (2008)
4. Peffers, K., Tuunanen, T., Rothenberger, M.A., Chatterjee, S.: A design science research methodology for information systems research. J. Manag. Inf. Syst. **24**(3), 45–77 (2007)
5. Nunamaker, J.F., Twyman, N.W., Giboney, J.S., Briggs, R.O. Creating high-value real-world impact through systematic programs of research. MIS Q. **41**(2) (2017)
6. European Research Center for Information Systems (ERCIS). Annual Report 2019. https://www.ercis.org/sites/ercis/files/structure/downloads/ercis_annual_report.pdf

7. Peffers, K., Tuunanen, T., Niehaves, B.: Design science research genres: introduction to the special issue on exemplars and criteria for applicable design science research. Eur. J. Inf. Syst. **27**(2), 129–139 (2018)
8. Iivari, J.: A critical look at theories in design science research. J. Assoc. Inf. Syst. **21**(3), 10 (2020)
9. Gregor, S.: On theory. In: Galliers, R., Stein, M.-K. (eds.) The Routledge Companion to Management Information Systems. Routledge, pp. 57–72 (2017)
10. Lukyanenko, R., Parsons, J.: Research perspectives: design theory indeterminacy: what is it, how can it be reduced, and why did the polar bear drown? J. Assoc. Inf. Syst. **21**(5), 1 (2020) https://doi.org/10.17705/1jais.00639
11. Burstein, F., Gregor, S.: The systems development or engineering approach to research in information systems: an action research perspective. In: Proceedings of the 10th Australasian Conference on Information Systems, pp. 122–134. Victoria University of Wellington, New Zealand (1999)
12. Simon, H.A.: The Sciences of the Artificial, 3rd edn. MIT Press, Cambridge, MA (1996)
13. Samuel-Ojo, O., Shimabukuro, D., Chatterjee, S., Muthui, M., Babineau, T., Prasertsilp, P., et al.: Meta-analysis of design science research within the IS community: trends, patterns, and outcomes. In: International Conference on Design Science Research in Information Systems, pp. 124–138. Springer, Berlin (2010)
14. Morrison, J., George, J.F.: Exploring the software engineering component in MIS research. Commun. ACM. **38**(7), 80–91 (1995)
15. Gregor, S., Hevner, A.R.: Positioning and presenting design science research for maximum impact. Manag. Inf. Syst. Q. **37**(2), 337–355 (2013)
16. Leukel, J., Mueller, M., Sugumaran, V.: The state of design science research within the BISE community: an empirical investigation. In: International Conference on Information Systems Proceedings (2014)
17. Engel, C., Leicht, N., Ebel, P.: The imprint of design science in information systems research: an empirical analysis of the AIS senior scholars' basket. International Conference on Information Systems Proceedings, vol. 7 (2019)
18. BISE. www.bise-journal.com/
19. Baskerville, R., Baiyere, A., Gregor, S., Hevner, A., Rossi, M.: Design science research contributions: finding a balance between artifact and theory. J. Assoc. Inf. Syst. **19**(5), 3 (2018)
20. Russell, S.J., Norvig, P., Davis, E., Edwards, D.: Artificial Intelligence: A Modern Approach. Pearson, Boston (2016)
21. Segerberg, K., Meyer, J.J., Kracht, M.: The logic of action. In: Zalta, E.N., Nodelman, U., Allen, C., Anderson, R.L. (eds.) Stanford Encyclopedia of Philosophy. Stanford, CA, The Metaphysics Research Lab (2016)
22. Fischer, C., Gregor, S., Aier, S.: Forms of Discovery for Design Knowledge, ECIS 2012 Proceedings. Paper 64. http://aisel.aisnet.org/ecis2012/64 (2012)
23. Gregor, S.: Building Theory in the Sciences of the Artificial. DESRIST'09, May 7–8, Malvern, PA (2009)
24. Gregor, S., Müller, O., Seidel, S.: Reflection, Abstraction, and Theorizing in Design and Development Research. Proceedings of European Conference on Information Systems, University of Utrecht, Utrecht, Netherlands, 5–8 June (2013)
25. Österle, H., Becker, J., Frank, U., Hess, T., Karagiannis, D., Krcmar, H., et al.: Memorandum on design-oriented information systems research. Eur. J. Inf. Syst. **20**(1), 7–10 (2011)
26. Van Aken, J., Chandrasekaran, A., Halman, J.: Conducting and publishing design science research: inaugural essay of the design science department of the Journal of Operations Management. J. Oper. Manag. **47**, 1–8 (2016)
27. Walls, J.G., Widmeyer, G.R., El Sawy, O.A.: Assessing information system design theory in perspective: how useful was our 1992 initial rendition. J. Inf. Technol. Theory App. **6**(2), 43–58 (2004)

28. Kuechler, W.L., Vaishnavi, V.: A framework for theory development in design science research: multiple perspectives. J. Assoc. Inf. Syst. **13**(6), 395–423 (2012)
29. Niiniluoto, I.: The aim and structure of applied research. Erkenntnis. **38**(1), 1–21 (1993)
30. Rai, A., Burton-Jones, A., Chen, H., Gupta, A., Hevner, A.R., Ketter, W., Parsons, J., Rao, R., Sarker, S., Yoo, Y.: Editor's Comments: Diversity of design science research. MIS Q. **41**, 1, iii–xviii (2017)
31. Smith, K.G., Hitt, M.A. (eds.): Great Minds in Management: The Process of Theory Development. Oxford University Press on Demand (2005)
32. Colquitt, J.A., Zapata-Phelan, C.P.: Trends in theory building and theory testing: a five-decade study of the Academy of Management Journal. Acad. Manag. J. **50**(6), 1281–1303 (2007)
33. Agrawal, R., Imieliński, T., Swami, A.: Mining association rules between sets of items in large databases. In: Proceedings of the 1993 ACM SIGMOD International Conference on Management of Data, pp. 207–216 (1993).
34. Moody, D.: The "physics" of notations: toward a scientific basis for constructing visual notations in software engineering. IEEE Trans. Softw. Eng. **35**(6), 756–779 (2009)
35. Van Aken, J.E.: Management research as a design science: articulating the research products of mode 2 knowledge production in management. Br. J. Manag. **16**(1), 19–36 (2005)
36. Gregor, S., Jones, D.: The anatomy of a design theory. J. Assoc. Inf. Syst. **8**(5), Article 19, 312–335 (2007)
37. Gregor, S.: R&D Tax Incentives and Software Development, Department of Industry, Innovation and Science, Canberra, Australia. Commissioned report (2020)
38. Hevner, A.R., March, S.T., Park, J., Ram, S.: Design science in information systems research. MIS Q. 75–105 (2004)

Design Science Research of High Practical Relevance

Dancing Through Space and Time

Jan vom Brocke, Manuel Weber, and Thomas Grisold

Abstract Design science research (DSR) is an established research paradigm aiming to create design knowledge on innovative solutions for real-world problems. As such, DSR has the potential to contribute to the solution of real-world problems of great societal value. In this article, we discuss how DSR can maximize such practical impact. Reflecting on our long-standing collaboration with the globally operating Hilti company, we report on a rich empirical case and derive principles in order to increase the practical relevance and societal contribution of DSR projects. We also derive quality criteria through which DSR articles can demonstrate practical relevance and societal value contribution.

Keywords Design science research (DSR) · Practical impact · Clinical research · Practice research · Societal impact · University–business collaboration · Business process management · Digital innovation

1 Introduction

Over the past years, DSR has matured as a research paradigm, aiming for innovative solutions to real-world problems [1, 2]. Important milestones have been accomplished. These range from guidance on how to *design* DSR projects [3], *evaluate* DSR artifacts [4–6], *manage* DSR projects [7], *identify* and *mitigate* risks in DSR projects [8], as well as *building theory* from DSR projects and *publishing* DSR results [9, 10]. In this article, we aim to advance the current state of the field by sharing experience and providing guidance to further advance the practical relevance and societal value that DSR can make.

Despite the undisputed potential of DSR to make important contributions to real-world problems, we argue that there is a lot more potential to be unleashed. Central

J. vom Brocke (✉) · M. Weber · T. Grisold
Institute of Information Systems, University of Liechtenstein, Vaduz, Liechtenstein
e-mail: jan.vom.brocke@uni.li; manuel.weber@uni.li; thomas.grisold@uni.li

© The Author(s), under exclusive license to Springer Nature Switzerland AG 2021   115
S. Aier et al. (eds.), *Engineering the Transformation of the Enterprise*,
https://doi.org/10.1007/978-3-030-84655-8_8

to our argument is that DSR cannot only address economical but also societal challenges [2]. We ground this position in two motivations. On the one hand, we observe that DSR—as it has been published in the premier outlets of our field, such as the International Conference on Design Science Research in Information Systems and Technology (DSRIST)—still has demonstrated somewhat limited practical impact and societal value, as e.g. measured by the number of patents, products, and services, or start-ups stemming out of this research. On the other hand, we observe that much of the practical work that has led to innovations, such as Airbnb, Uber or Zoom, has rarely been based on DSR, nor has it been discussed in the DSR discourse to generate design knowledge that can potentially advance innovative information systems design. This a missed opportunity. We, as a research community, should move forward and increase the real-world-orientation of DRS.

We argue that the practical impact and societal contribution of DSR can be fostered by a stronger collaboration between the academic and practice world. We argue that this collaboration can be achieved through two movements: (a) academics should move more towards real-world contexts, while (b) practitioners should have the opportunity to contribute to the DSR academic body of knowledge. In the DSR discourse, both movements have been articulated more recently. On the one hand, there is the discourse advocating for research to move more into practice, as outlined, for example, by the call to "fail early and often" [11] and other seminal contributions in our field, such as the call for action design research (ADR) [12]. On the other hand, there is a discourse circling around the question of how we can involve practice in research projects. This is outlined e.g. by the emerging field of Clinical Information Systems Research [13], studying the results of theory-based interventions in organizations as an element of professional practice while prioritizing the achievement of practical outcomes as the primary goal.

In this article, we argue that DSR should be conducted within a continuous dialogue of research and practice. Put a bit provocatively, we argue that DSR needs to overcome thinking in two worlds, practice and academia, and to further embrace research in *one* overarching world. We envision this as a continuously evolving process at the intersection of problem and solution knowledge. Along these lines, we introduce the metaphor of a *dance* between academics and practitioners. Imagine two dancers: an academic and a practitioner. Now imagine that the dance floor is divided along two types of knowledge; problem knowledge and solution knowledge. And now think of a dance that unfolds on this dance floor. There is a joint rhythm and sometimes, dancing happens more in the problem sphere, sometimes more in the solution sphere. Sometimes it is somewhere in between. Sometimes practitioners and academics move together, sometimes they detach and perform solos to reconnect shortly after. It's a dynamic process and at each point, someone contributes something to the joint accomplishment of the DSR performance. In our long-standing cooperation with the Hilti Corporation, such "dancing" has led to several artifacts and a wealth of design knowledge, which have been studied and applied in *one* world, and which have created very meaningful impact in practice.

In this article we derive principles for DSR that take place as a mutually unfolding collaboration between research and practice. We first draw on the DSR literature to emphasize the need for aligning academia and practice in DSR. We then present the Hilti case, reflect on our experiences and show exemplary artifact's that have been developed in this case. We, then, conceptualize essential moves of DSR as a mutually unfolding collaboration and derive principles to maximize the impact of DSR.

2 Research Background

2.1 Bridging Academic and Practice in Design Science Research

The discourse on DSR has repeatably articulated ideas on how to further align academia and practice. These ideas provide the grounds for our discussion on how to foster the impact of DSR. We see suggestions to move from academia towards practice, and we also see suggestions to move from practice towards academia. The following positions illustrate these attempts.

In their work on feedback loops in design science, Abraham et al. [11] argue to "fail early and often". They suggest incorporating feedback on the problem understanding and potential solution development as soon and often as possible during the DSR process. They build on the idea of concurrent evaluation of intermediate artifacts, as it has been suggested by Sonnenberg and vom Brocke [5]. They differentiate four types of evaluation: the problem evaluation (eval 1), the design evaluation (eval 2), the implementation evaluation (eval 3) and the use evaluation (eval 4).

Sein et al. [12] have introduced the concept of *action design research* (ADR), following the idea of involving the researcher throughout the research (design) process. They argue that the development of IT-based artifacts is often detached from the organizational setting. Therefore, they propose ADR as a new research method, aiming to both build and implement innovative IT artifacts within an organizational context and learn from such interventions. Their proposed ADR method consists of four stages, each backed up with principles to grasp the underlying beliefs, values, and assumptions: i) formulation of the problem, ii) building, intervention, and evaluation, iii) reflection and learning, iv) formalization of learning.

As an innovative move to engage practice more in research, Baskerville et al. [13] have started to develop the genre of clinical research in Information Systems (IS) Research, which appears promising to foster impact of DSR, too. This practice-based research approach aims to advance IS impact in organizations. Clinical research shares some commonalities with action research (AR), and therewith also ADR, where the primary goal is to generate and develop practical outcomes. However, clinical research differs from action research by prioritizing the achievement of practical outcomes as the primary goal. Thus, clinical research seeks to make contributions to and impact on practical problems, which makes it very suitable for DSR aiming to generate design knowledge, specifically by means of two types of design entities (solutions to problems) and design theories (knowledge about solutions to problems).

As an innovative way to generate design knowledge, Kruse et al. [14] suggest to investigate real-world design projects, which the authors have not necessarily conducted themselves, such as the development of smartphones, web conferencing tools, and others. Building on research methods from archeology, they suggest an approach on how to empirically analyze such artifacts, projects and processes in order to generate design knowledge. They emphasize the role and strong involvement of the (design science) researcher throughout the design process to reconstruct the design context. Also, they argue that DSR and the community's contributions or even researchers from other disciplines can fuel the discussion to solve real-world problems and thus provide solutions to address societal challenges.

Winter and Albani [15] build on the argument that organizational design issues and engineering problems are often complex and they point to limitations of Hevner's [16] "three-cycle view of DSR" in addressing this complexity. Referring to ADR [12] as well as the Spiral Model, which is commonly used in software development [17], they develop a *one-cycle view* of DSR, where every single iteration of the cycle allows for reshaping the DSR Knowledge Base (KB). Along this spiral cycle, there exist alternating design and evaluation activities. The iteration will be executed as long as a solution has been developed that is sufficient to address the problem. Finally, when the iteration ends, the newly developed artifact and its characteristics is meant to be added to the DSR KB to advance our knowledge on the design of information systems.

To summarize, research has been calling to strengthen the collaboration between practice and academia in a number of ways. In this line of thinking, it has been stressed that such an alignment would positively affect the impact of DSR because both problem understanding and solution design would intrinsically reflect both the practice and the academic view. Still, we see that the notion of two worlds, namely the academic world and the practice world, is still predominant in most of the approaches. The one-cycle approach [15] makes an attempt to overcome this thinking. This is inspirational to us and central to the approach we develop. Still, in this model, the notion is one of a structured and linear process, which evolves in a spiral shape towards a solution. To our experience, how-ever, impactful DSR needs to be even more sensitive towards its situational context—which itself is constantly evolving over time [18].

2.2 Towards Understanding DSR as a Dance Between Academics and Practitioners

The experience from our own research shows that impactful practice-academia cooperation in DSR is rarely a straight-forward process. Rather, it is evolving, driven by unexpected events and emerging opportunities. There can be unanticipated moves into different directions, which path the way for new ideas. Then, there are intermediate solutions, which have not planned for in advance but occur along the way. As we progress and move forward, we find new means to develop solutions. Simultaneously, we find new ends-in-view that emerge often unexpectedly but seem important in the course of the research process [19].

To emphasize these dynamics, we introduce a new metaphor to describe DSR. More specifically, we use the concept of "dance" as a metaphor to explore the dynamic and evolving relationship between practitioners and academics during DSR projects.[1] Metaphors play an important role for theorizing. They are formed by conjoining unrelated knowledge domains and thus point to new opportunities for the understanding and enquiry of a certain phenomenon [20]. This resonates with theories in the cognitive sciences stressing that metaphors do not carry meaning themselves. Rather, meaning is constructed and pursued by cognizing agents as they aim to explore and direct their attention to new aspects of the environment [21]. On this view, metaphors are at the center of thinking and the creation of novelty. When using metaphors as theorizing devices, researchers can recognize and construct similarities between two (unrelated) knowledge domains such that new meanings emerge altogether [22]. On this account, metaphors offer a new vocabulary for looking at complex and abstract phenomena in order to make sense about the phenomenon, define new constructs and identify new avenues for future research [23].

For the purpose of this article, we stress that the dance-metaphor points our theorizing about DSR research to three central points:

1. We acknowledge that impactful DSR projects are dynamic evolvements where the competences and needs of one dance partner (e.g. the practitioner) preponderate at some point and thus, "guide" the dance. At a later point, however, the other partner (e.g. the academic) may take over. The other partner exerts more influence on the progress of the project, then, because she/he has a clear idea about the direction in which the knowledge creation activities should move to.
2. The dance metaphor points to other concepts that are involved. The dance floor, for example, metaphorically constitutes the space through which academics and practitioners move. We imagine this space as being multi-dimensional. Certain areas on the dancefloor are more familiar to the academic and some others are

---

[1] For the sake of our argument, we deliberately refrain from referring to a specific kind of dance. In honor of Robert Winter, the recipient of this commemorative publication, and his Brasilian origin, the inclined reader may imagine the dance of Samba whenever we use the metaphor.

more familiar to the practitioner. Dancing moves lead to different areas so that both dance partners can explore the world through the eyes of their counterpart.
3. A good dance implies a joint activity. It is not about opposing viewpoints. When dancers engage in a performance, each dancer focuses on the accomplishment of his/her own part *while* contributing to the larger whole, that is, the accomplishment of the performance. As we shall argue, our own experiences show that effective as well as joyful design science research projects are characterized by an open, vivid and trustful atmosphere where everyone can bring in and actualize his strengths and interests—while contributing to the larger purpose of the project.

In what follows, we will share our experience by reporting on the past decades of a collaboration with the Hilti Corporation. We will illustrate how this work has evolved and we will exemplify some of the artifacts that have been built along the way and have realized considerable impact in the organization. Based on this report, we will then provide a new conceptualization of DSR as a "joint dance" of both academia and practice, rather than as a planned process moving from one side to the other. We will characterize the "dance floor" and introduce elementary dance moves, which can change spontaneously in response to changing rhythms in order to deliver a performance and choreography at the end.

3   The Journey of Hilti and Its Adoption of BPM

The Hilti Corporation is a global leader in the construction industry that provides products, software, and services to customers worldwide. The family-owned company employs around 30,000 employees, is headquartered in Liechtenstein, and deals with about 250,000 individual customer contacts each day. Its founder, Martin Hilti, has envisioned an integrated enterprise resource planning system very early after founding the company in 1941. A few decades later, this vision has been realized and Hilti has become one of the very few companies worldwide to operate globally on a one single instance ERP system.

Hilti`s commitment towards ambitious and innovative solutions has been reflected in a strong cooperation with academia. Martin Hilti has been one of the founders of the University of Liechtenstein in 1961. In 2006, Hilti has generously founded the Inaugural Hilti Endowed Chair for Business Process Management, and in 2007 the chairholder, one of the co-authors, has started his work at the University of Liechtenstein where he initiated innovative forms of alignment with the Hilti Corporation in a number of DSR activities accompanying the company in its ambitious endeavors in business process management and digitalization.

In the same year, the Hilti Chair also started to teach DSR courses together with his colleague Robert Winter from the University of St. Gallen. Robert Winter was of the pioneers in Information Systems Design Research [24] who later published the one cycle view in DSR [15] and also advocated to "fail often and early" [11]. The joint teaching led to many innovative ideas, including the framing of DSR as a journey through space and time [25].

Reflecting on the past years, it is interesting to see that it has been a great journey, albeit not one with well-defined starting and ending points or a well-developed travel plan. Another way to look at this trajectory is that of a floating, or "dance" through space and time—many dances, actually—which have shown quite remarkable performances.

The full Hilti story has been described in a number of articles [26–35]. In the following, we highlight a few developments which we deem characteristic and relevant for the dynamics of our "dance"-metaphor as we have experienced it and find it insightful to increase the practical relevance of DSR. In the following, we focus on six selected "performances" which evolved over time and in context.

In 2000, Hilti launched one of their biggest transformation projects in the company's history, called "Global Process and Data (GPD)". The main objective was to introduce global standards on data and processes as well as a global system solution to overcome local silos. By the end of 2010, eight production plants had to be operated and more than 18,000 users were working with SAP as their Enterprise Resource Planning (ERP) system. 6000 employees used the mobile application. The idea of this project was to pursue a global path, since Hilti was faced with non-standardized processes, data structures and system landscapes. The overarching goal of this GPD transformation project was to realize and capitalize on new business opportunities by achieving globally integrated processes, data structures and system applications.

The global transformation project posed several challenges. Overcoming silo thinking, integrating the existing processes into one single SAP solution, and standardizing heterogeneous systems were some of the key obstacles that needed to be managed. Further challenges included keeping the big picture in mind and taking a holistic BPM perspective that considers aspects such as strategic alignment, governance, people, and culture [36]. Hilti works across a range of regions, cultures, and operating environments. Every market organization or location has different needs. Therefore, a total standardization of all processes was not feasible. Hilti searched for a solution to find a balance between global consistency and local relevancy. Local process variations are key for a successfully performing BPM organization. Each location should be able to fulfill their specific needs to a certain degree.

As a solution, Hilti decided to work according to a model called "solid core and flexible boundary" [30], a model that evolved from practical problem solving rather than from the academic literature, yet it is very projectable and perceived useful by many other organizations. The essence of this model is to reflect the demands of a changing business environment while maintaining the high stability of the global core systems and processes. The solid core represents a foundation for Hilti's core systems and processes whereas the flexible boundary component implies agility to experiment with new technologies for specific needs. These two strategic components ensured business modularity with flexible control [26, 37].

The solid core comprises of standard software which covers the standard business processes and handles the most critical data. The goals of the solid core include business value creation and reliability. The flexible boundary covers specific needs that cannot be addressed in the solid core. They undergo frequent change or put too much risk on the core systems. If a market organization wants to make use of the flexible boundary, it is free to do so. Yet the location or business unit is not forced to include the flexible boundary in their strategy. The business modularity offers substantial benefits for Hilti today. With a combination of a solid core and flexible boundaries, Hilti standardized its processes depending on the current business situation or location. This approach enabled Hilti to better fulfill customer and employee needs based on efficiency gains through a solid core and, where required, specific solutions through a flexible boundary [26].

Over the course of the GPD project, Hilti as been able to leverage many innovative technologies and new business opportunities, such as a global contact center [38]. The project has been initiated due to a local IT need but finally resulted in a global transformation of Hilti´s customer service processes and the required infrastructures. Until 2006, different processes were in place and operated in Hilti customer centers worldwide. Likewise, different systems, such as communications systems, were in use. This has led to different capabilities and possibilities depending on the location in terms of reporting, evaluation and comparability of customer service performance. In the 45 largest markets, Hilti managed to transform its customer services departments in 2015. Activities included the implementation of a unified communications system solution, the transformation of customer service processes to the redesign of organizational structures, uniform global standards and employee training. To illustrate the impact of this successful project, 1500 agents have been deployed and more than 6500 telephones and several hundred fax devices are now administered and managed from a central location. 200,000 daily customer contacts are being processed through this center [38].

The vast amount of customer contact data gave inspiration to another innovative project. The goal was to analyze all customer care notes in order to further learn about customers` needs. A million customer care notes are registered annually in the CRM system. The researchers proposed to analyze these customer care notes using "topic modeling", and they have developed a prototype to apply such text analytics algorithms in practice [39]. The solution was tested in two countries (Germany and France) on the basis of approx. 25–30,000 customer care notes. Figure 1 shows how topics have been analyzed.

With the help of a dashboard, the incoming service requests were visualized based on their topics and subtopics. These topics could also be displayed over time and subdivided according to customer segments and their location. The biggest challenge arose in relation to the accuracy and visualization of the topic modeling method. The collaborative setting and the development of this solution along several iterative cycles has finally resulted in significant time savings and improved accuracy in the classification of customer queries. Based on these results, the work and quality of customer service and, above all, customer satisfaction could also be increased. Here, too, it has been shown how the use of modern technologies enables

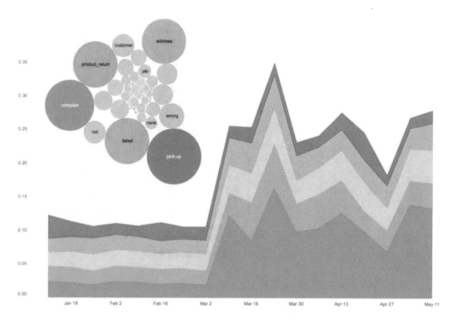

Fig. 1 Text analytics on customer care notes using MineMyText.com [40]—© 2016 Association for Information Systems; reprinted with permission

Hilti to further develop customer processes and facilitate work in organizations [41]. The project has also led to a better understanding of applying text analytics as a strategy of inquiry in information systems research [39, 40] and organizational research [42]. Also, a prototype, MineMyText.com, is used both in organizations and universities.

In 2017, Hilti and the University of Liechtenstein have been awarded the Global Award for Excellence in BPM & Workflow of the Workflow Management Coalition (WfMC) for their exceptional achievements in establishing global processes and data. At about the same time, Hilti has set off an initiative to challenge the existing paradigm of process management. It has launched a project to envision the next generation of BPM, investigating the potential of innovative technology, such as process mining and robotic process automation.

The project was inspired by the ten principles of good BPM which have been identified in research [43, 44]. Four principles have been put into focus to shape the next generation BPM approach for Hilti: (1) Purpose, (2) Context-awareness, (3) Technology-appropriation, and (4) simplicity [43]. In what follows, we exemplify how context-awareness has been addressed by means of an innovative artifact developed in our joint DSR activities.

Analyzing the usage of the existing Global Process Management System (GPMS) we found that the majority of stored documents have not been accessed of modified within the last 2 years. Hilti also experienced that operational staff is seeking for additional process information. Users access this system to search for answers

Fig. 2 Process context
matrix (own illustration)

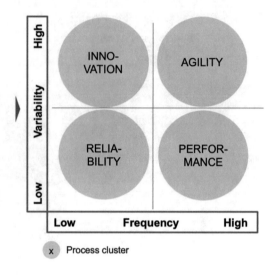

x Process cluster

frequently even though approximately more than 17,000 documents are considered outdated. Additional valuable information to be considered while conducting a process step is no longer presented in a user-friendly way. Also, the current GPMS is set up as a stand-alone repository and not connected to surrounding applications.

Building on the BPM Context Framework, which had been developed in research prior to the project [18], a survey was conducted at Hilti to assess the contextual diversity of existing processes. The results have been discussed in two workshops involving researchers from the University of Liechtenstein and all global process owners. Two dimensions have been identified most relevant: variability and frequency. The resulting 2×2 matrix is shown in Fig. 2.

The new generation GPMS considers key success factors for managing each of the four context types. It provides prescriptions regarding all six core elements of BPM for managing processes accordingly: IT, Methods, Strategic Alignment, Governance, People and Culture [36].

In all of the exemplary projects and initiatives, DSR has played an important role. It has been applied in different modes, specifically involving different stakeholder groups including Hilti employees, who actively participated in the research. In each project, we went through several cycles in order to reshape our common understanding regarding problem and solution knowledge [2]. Although these initiatives differed in their conception, planning, and implementation, there was an overarching mission, namely to make corporate activities more effective and efficient across functional units. This mission was achieved through collaboration between both practitioners and academics.

4 DSR as a Dance Through Time and Space

Based on these observations, we build on the previously articulated idea of DSR as a "journey through time and space" [2], and we extend this notion by the "dance" metaphor. We argue that DSR is a journey, with a starting point, an ending point and a path in-between. The way it unfolds resembles a dance.

We make the following observations in terms of the dance-metaphor:

4. Academia and practice have been moving together according to a joint "rhythm"; sometimes closer together, sometimes more on their own; sometimes more active, sometimes more passive; but in any given situation, there was a mutual commitment towards a joint performance and the accomplishment of the project.
5. Academia and practice moved to different parts of the dance floor, sometimes focusing more on knowledge about problems, sometimes more on knowledge about solutions. Sometimes it was drawn on knowledge from practice and at other times, on knowledge from academia.
6. Academia and practice engage in different yet coupled and complementary performances, e.g. sometimes more related to problem understanding and sometimes more to solution development and evaluation.

Drawing on our dance metaphor, we now conceptualize the dance floor as the space in which this collaboration happens. Analyzing the joint academia-practice activities in more detail, we can observe four types of joint action. We also identify different roles which are associated with academia and practice at different stages of the projects. Also, we identify the moves from one type to the other, again with different roles for both academia and practice. The dance floor is depicted in Fig. 3.

The dance floor depicts the space in which DSR projects occur as a 2×2 matrix. Central to the dancefloor metaphor is the observation that practitioners and academics draw on different knowledge sources [45]. This is depicted through the horizontal axis. Practitioners primarily draw on "know-how" knowledge [46] as they experience phenomena in their everyday activities and develop knowledge that lies "in the action" [47]. They can report on how phenomena evolve and thereby clarify their underlying characteristics [48]. In the context of DSR, they can provide rich descriptions about problems or solutions.

Academics, in turn, develop knowledge that is oriented towards an explicit and fact-based reasoning about the world. Their approaches are more systematic and analytical. Academics aim to establish "knowing that" about the world. This pertains both to problems as well as solutions [46].

Both epistemologies can benefit from each other [49, 50]. For example, academics can enrich their theories through the viewpoints of practitioners—simply because they can come to recognize aspects of a phenomenon that cannot be seen by means of certain methods or are treated in the current discourse [51]. Similarly, practitioners can benefit from analytic approaches as espoused in the academic discourse [45]. We have pointed to several of such examples in the preceding sections of this manuscript.

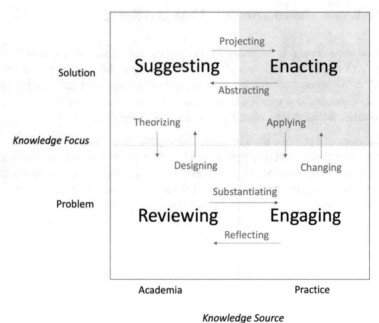

Fig. 3 The DSR dancefloor and its elementary moves (own illustration)

The vertical axis refers to the focus of a DSR project at a given point in time. The model suggests that the focus tends to be on the problem or on the solution side. This does not mean to be static, of course. On the contrary, the focus can change. For example, after knowledge has been built up about a given problem, the focus can shift to the solution.

Accordingly, the dancefloor represents a 2×2 matrix with four possible areas in which a DSR project can be located at a specific point in time. Further, we identify eight essential transitions from one quadrant to the other, resulting in 12 "dance moves" either within one quadrant or across quadrants. In Table 1, we have defined each dance move and we shed light on two aspects. First, we label each quadrant to emphasize the core activity. Second, we outline the main interest from the academic as well as practitioner point of view.

The individual moves show that there is always one partner who takes the lead—similar to when two people dance together. This means that depending on the initiative or project and whether we are concerned with problems or solutions, researchers' or practitioners' needs are dominant.

We therefore see the on-going dialogue between researchers and practitioners as a joint effort. We have illustrated this with the Hilti initiatives and projects described above. The purpose of this dance is always to achieve a joint performance, whereby the ultimate goal is to generate impact (at the end of the dance, we ideally end up in the upper right quadrant).

Table 1 Elementary moves and the role of practice and academia

Activities	Description	Role of practice	Role of academia
Enacting	Putting a solution to use in practice.	Applying a solution in context.	Testing the effects of a solution in use.
Suggesting	Providing normative statements about solutions projectable to contexts.	Relating statements to practice context.	Developing normative statements.
Engaging	Establishing a dialogue about problems in practice.	Articulating problems.	Understanding a problem.
Reviewing	Reviewing and locating the problem context in the literature.	Guiding the search process regarding applicability.	Mapping problems to problem descriptions.
Theorizing	Relating the solution knowledge to the problem knowledge.	Guide theorizing e.g. regarding level of abstraction and specify.	Contextualize solution in the literature.
Designing	Developing a potential solution to be applied to a problem.	Informing the development of a solution.	Derived from literature, developing a solution knowledge.
Substantiating	Adding empirical evidence for a theoretically specified problem.	Reporting on a problem.	Framing a problem understanding.
Reflecting	Contextualizing a practical problem against the background of the literature.	Guiding the search process regarding applicability.	Relating a problem to existing literature.
Applying	Enacting a solution for a practical problem.	Applying a solution in practice.	Observing and interpreting the change process.
Changing	Changing practice in order to solve a problem.	Detecting a problem and develop a solution.	Observing and interpreting the change process.
Projecting	Projecting academically developed solution to practical context.	Contextualizing the solution.	Implementing the solution.
Abstracting	Considering a theoretical solution, based on a practical one.	Observing and developing explanations of the practical solution.	Sharing information about the solution in practice.

5   Discussion and Implications

We have set out to reflect on our long-years' experience conducting DSR in cooperation with the Hilti Corporation, and based on this empirical context, we introduced the "dance" metaphor to capture some of our essential observations. We have further conceptualized our observations by means of introducing the so-called DSR "dancefloor" and we have also introduced 12 essential moves both academics and practitioners jointly make on this dancefloor performing DSR. In the following, we reflect on the implications of our argument, and we derive four specific guidelines to maximize practical relevance of DSR.

5.1 Establishing a Continuing Relation of Mutual Trust and Respect

Our experience shows that key to a successful collaboration between research and practice is continuous and strong engagement. Specifically, it is important to learn how to communicate in the same language and understand each other's needs, experiences, and challenges, as well as to establish shared values. It must be ensured that academics know what practitioners are concerned with, and vice versa, practitioners should be open and sensitive to the way academics think about problems and solutions. It is important to be aware of and leverage the different perspectives which practitioners and academics can bring to joint projects and processes. It is also essential to create an open and honest communication culture and establish transparent communication channels. We learnt that when academics and practitioners both know about the mutual relevance of a DSR project, matters can be discussed quickly and informally. This is particularly important when adjustments to processes need to be made and change can be pre-empted [52].

In this vein, we stress that continuous engagement proved to be an important enabler for DSR projects. Effective ideas emerge most efficiently when there is a successful relationship management in place and both dance partners have a mutual understanding about their respective contexts. This, however, takes time, patience and a common orientation towards a goal.

Based on our experience, these observations hold across projects of different types. Regardless of whether projects take a few weeks or several years, it is important to account for both theory and practice. In the words of Kurt Lewin, there is nothing as practical as a good theory [53]. In this sense, we validate, adjust and sharpen our academic perspectives with respect to insights from practice. If, for example, a new model or theoretical concept is formed, we invite our practice partners to share their views in terms of when and under what circumstances it is useful. We found that in an atmosphere where these interactions are possible, we can continuously gain inspiration to develop and apply new solution knowledge.

As a quality criterion for DSR, we advise to *include an explicit section regarding the quality of the relationship between researchers and practitioners in DSR articles (Criterion 1).* Thereby, researchers can share how relevant knowledge was developed, and future studies can explicitly draw on these insights. Thereby, such a description can provide as a hallmark to prove the effectiveness of the study. Former research has already alluded to the importance of adding descriptions on the situational context of DSR projects [2]. Such section may be a good place to outline the quality of the academia-practice relationship in the context of a study.

5.2 Studying Design Where It Happens

We found that a central factor for making DSR practically relevant is to *study design where it happens*. Our dancefloor metaphor specifies different loci or stages where design might happen and where knowledge about practice can be gained. In line with Kruse et al. [14], we specifically challenge the logic of DSR according to which, researchers study apparent problems, develop solutions and, then, eventually evaluate how practice would reflect on the solution or problem. As the design of innovative solutions to real-world problems happens around the world, by millions of people, day to day, we see great potential to go out there and to study such design processes. According to the dancefloor conceptualizations, this would mean to start more in the engaging and enacting quadrant and to take design science studies from there. As the dance unfolds, it will also move over to the academic side (a number of times), e.g. by reflecting on and abstracting from observations in practice.

From a theoretical point of view, close attention to context is important to develop theories that are more faithful to how IT is actually being used. Following recent claims, research practices in IS tend to be "de-worlded" [54], that is, there is a disengagement between research and practice. This observation points to a stronger need to account for actual organizational practices in theorizing [55]. Therefore, it appears crucial to develop contextualized insights to understand why, how and when people use IT artifacts [56]. We believe that our dancefloor metaphor is a suitable means to sustain our attention towards practical context, and it also points to different research moves to transfer between context and abstract theoretical knowledge.

To capture context, we see the need for documenting DSR projects with a strong eye to details. We advise both practitioners and academics to communicate as well document the progress of the joint efforts, and especially, which insights were gained at what points in the process and why. With the help of the dancefloor metaphor, we hope to create coordinates to locate the process, describe the knowledge types that are important at specific stages, and bring in both worlds' perspectives. This dissemination of design knowledge can be in form of scientific articles, panel discussions with practitioners and academics, or, for example, student workshops at universities and colleges.

As a quality criterion for DSR, we advise to **explicitly review both problem and solution knowledge from a practice perspective in a DSR article (Criterion 2).** Similar to a literature review [57–59], we need a review covering both the problem and solution knowledge developed in practice. Further, in the implication section, we advise to **include a discussion as to how the design knowledge generated in a DSR project has advanced and what has been found in the reviews of extant problem and solution knowledge in practice (Criterion 3).** That said, we see the need for further research in developing guidelines on how to conduct such reviews and impact analysis.

5.3   Seeking and Embracing Opportunities to Make an Impact

Our framework emphasizes a strong exchange between research and practice. So far, we have mainly discussed this from the perspective of theorizing. It must be noted, however, that the position we have been advocating for implies that we should seek and embrace opportunities to develop impact of practical relevance and societal value. In this regard, we want to stress two points.

On the one hand, in order to generate value for society, solutions should address real-world problems. This may seem trivial but it has strong implications for practice. Oftentimes, we observe that research does not depart from actual real-world problems. Instead, it builds on points that are primarily considered important in the research discourse. Over the years, therefore, we have been increasingly motivated to put theoretical research and projects into practice. We have also taken on practical problems as expressed by various industry partners, in order to conceptualize them and work out solutions as well as recommendations for action in practice.

On the other hand, we learnt that we should be much more confident about our capabilities to contribute to solving problems of greater importance. To this end, we should look for problems that extend the traditional arena of IS research. For ex-ample, there have been calls for management and organization scholars to tackle grand challenges [60], and also information systems research has started to identify grand challenges [61]. Given the increasing prevalence of digital technologies, we see IS design research at the forefront to contribute here. We as DSR scholars, are in a prime position to develop and evaluate IT artifacts aiming for innovative solutions that make a sustainable impact. The question is, how do we find such opportunities? All the more we stress that academics should move towards the real-world context. Together with relevant stakeholders and policy-makers, they should develop IT solutions that can make an impact in addressing grand challenges, e.g. by designing solutions that consider the contextual needs of user groups.

As a quality criterion for DSR, we advise to *include a section in DSR articles arguing in how far the design knowledge generated would relate to real-world problems of practical relevance and societal value (Criterion 4).* Given that DSR is an accumulative and evolving endeavor [2], we understand that most DSR projects would not solve a practically relevant problem of great societal importance. This is why it is particularly important for each article to argue and explain how the developed contribution may lead to solutions of societal relevance. Such an illustra-tion can also provide the grounds to outline important and meaningful avenues for future research.

5.4   Perform the DSR Dance "On the Flight"

In our own work, we have learnt that the way how academics and practitioners work together can take on different forms. Using the Hilti collaboration as an example, we were able to show how the collaboration has evolved over the years. In this example, the foundation of the Hilti Endowed Chair for Business Process Management contributed strongly to establishing a rich and long-lasting relationship and this setting also served to provide many occasions for joint work. Most of them were not framed in terms of conventional DSR projects, as described e.g. by Peffers et al. [3]. In our case, the cooperation evolved around different occasions, such as joint seminars, innovation labs and global competitions, which took us on specific "dances", of very different rhythms.

What we find striking, and which might be insightful for fellow researchers, too, is that useful DSR often derives from straight forward design projects. These projects may have their idiosyncratic trajectories but two aspects are important: (1) the design process is transparent and (2) the design process supports the research objective and context. This is what we like to refer to as DSR "on the flight", meaning to conduct DSR as it happens, document it and use principles assuring rigor and relevance. But in our experience, in order to support maximum practical relevance, DSR should be led by the specific case and context rather than by prescribed methodologies.

As a quality criterion for DSR, we advise to **include a section in DSR articles describing the very specific design process as it has been conducted in the research at hand (Criterion 5).** The research design section is the most appropriate section to include this description and, in addition to a high-level conceptualization of the design process, high quality DSR shall also provide a log file of very specific activities which have been conducted. Such a log file can, for instance, be provided in the appendix of an article. Also, appropriate tools have been developed by the DSR community [62, 63] to document and communicate the design process along the way. The tool MyDesignProcess.com (www.mydesignprocess.com), for instance, allows authors to declare which process steps should be included into a report for readers and reviewers, which can then be accessed via a URL.

6   Conclusion

To illuminate the role of academics and practitioners in impactful DSR projects, we have introduced and used the metaphor of a dance. An important implication is to conceptualize the collaboration to occur on a dancefloor, that is, a metaphorical space where different knowledge foci as well as knowledge sources are dominant. First and foremost, DSR should generate design knowledge on solutions for real-world problems, and we need to ask: How can we measure and evaluate practical impact of DSR? What are methods and appropriate measures? Addressing these questions will further unleash the strong potentials we have developed within the DSR community—and help addressing the challenges of our time.

This article sets the pathway for further research projects where practitioners and researchers are closely working together. Both can use our design science dancefloor to position their projects and navigate themselves to generate practical and societal impact. They can also use our dancefloor to guide the evolution and management of any DSR project. Based on our report, we also encourage to report on similar "dances" and share best practices and pitfalls both in BPM [64] and DSR endeavors [25].

Building on the conceptualization of the DSR dancefloor and the DSR dance moves, we have derived guidelines for fellow researcher to increase the practical relevance of their work as well as to demonstrate such relevance in their paper. For the latter, we have derived specific quality criteria to consider when writing up and revising manuscripts, making specific recommendations on sections to include to a DSR article to foster its practical impact and societal value contribution.

References

1. Hevner, A.R., March, S.T., Park, J., Ram, S.: Design science in information systems research. MIS Q. **28**(1), 75 (2004)
2. vom Brocke, J., Winter, R., Hevner, A., Maedche, A.: Accumulation and evolution of design knowledge in design science research—a journey through time and space. J. Assoc. Inf. Syst. **21**(3), 520–544 (2020)
3. Peffers, K., Tuunanen, T., Rothenberger, M.A., Chatterjee, S.: A design science research methodology for information systems research. J. Manag. Inf. Syst. **24**(3), 45–77 (2007)
4. Sonnenberg, C., vom Brocke, J.: Evaluation patterns for design science research artefacts. In: Helfert, M., Donnellan, B. (eds.) Proceedings of the European Design Science Symposium (EDSS) 2011, vol. 286, pp. 71–83. Springer, Berlin (2012a)
5. Sonnenberg, C., vom Brocke, J.: Evaluations in the science of the artificial – reconsidering the build-evaluate pattern in design science research. In: Peffers, K., Rothenberger, M., Kuechler, B. (eds.) Design Science Research in Information Systems. Advances in Theory and Practice, pp. 381–397. Springer, Berlin (2012b)
6. Venable, J., Pries-Heje, J., Baskerville, R.: FEDS: a framework for evaluation in design science research. Eur. J. Inf. Syst. **25**(1), 77–89 (2016)
7. vom Brocke, J., Lippe, S.: Taking a project management perspective on design science research. In: Winter, R., Zhao, J.L., Aier, S. (eds.) Global Perspectives on Design Science Research, pp. 31–44. Springer, Berlin (2010)
8. Venable, J., Baskerville, R., Pries-Heje, J.: Designing TRiDS: treatments for risks in design science. Australas. J. Inf. Syst. **23** (2019)
9. Gregor, S., Hevner, A.R.: Positioning and presenting design science research for maximum impact. MIS Q. **37**(2), 337–355 (2013)
10. Gregor, S., Jones, D.: The anatomy of a design theory. J. Assoc. Inf. Syst. **8**(5), 312–335 (2007)
11. Abraham, R., Aier, S., Winter, R.: Fail early, fail often: towards coherent feed-back loops in design science research evaluation. Proceedings of the International Conference on Information Systems – Building a Better World through Information Systems. 35th International Conference on Information Systems (ICIS 2014), Auckland, New Zealand (2014)
12. Sein, M.K., Henfridsson, O., Purao, S., Rossi, M., Lindgren, R.: Action design research. MIS Q. **35**(1), 37–56 (2011)

13. Baskerville, R., vom Brocke, J., Mathiassen, L., Scheepers, H.: Special issue call for papers: Clinical research from information systems practice. Eur. J. Inf. Syst. (2020)
14. Kruse, L.C., Seidel, S., vom Brocke, J.: Design archaeology: generating design knowledge from real-world artifact design. 32–45 (2019)
15. Winter, R., Albani, A.: Restructuring the design science research knowledge base. In: Baskerville, R., De Marco, M., Spagnoletti, P. (eds.) Designing Organizational Systems, pp. 63–81. Springer, Berlin (2013)
16. Hevner, A.R.: A three cycle view of design science research. Scand. J. Inf. Syst. **19**(2), 87–92 (2007)
17. Boehm, B.W.: A spiral model of software development and enhancement. Computer. **21**(5), 61–72 (1988)
18. vom Brocke, J., Zelt, S., Schmiedel, T.: On the role of context in business process management. Int. J. Inf. Manag. **36**(3), 486–495 (2016)
19. Joas, H.: The Creativity of Action. University of Chicago Press (1996)
20. Cornelissen, J.P., Oswick, C., Thøger Christensen, L., Phillips, N.: Metaphor in organizational research: context, modalities and implications for research—Introduction. Organ. Stud. **29**(1), 7–22 (2008)
21. Lakoff, G., Johnson, M.: Metaphors We Live by. University of Chicago Press (2008)
22. Cornelissen, J.P.: What are we playing at? Theatre, organization, and the use of metaphor. Organ. Stud. **25**(5), 705–726 (2004)
23. Örtenblad, A., Putnam, L.L., Trehan, K.: Beyond Morgan's eight metaphors: adding to and developing organization theory. Hum. Relat. **69**(4), 875–889 (2016)
24. Winter, R.: Design science research in Europe. Eur. J. Inf. Syst. **17**(5), 470–475 (2008)
25. vom Brocke, J., Hevner, A., Maedche, A. (eds.): Design Science Research. Cases. Springer International Publishing (2020)
26. Schmiedel, T., vom Brocke, J., Uhl, A.: Operational excellence. In: Uhl, A., Gollenia, L.A. (eds.) Digital Enterprise Transformation: A Business-Driven Approach to Leveraging Innovative IT, pp. 207–230. Gower Publishing (2014)
27. vom Brocke, J.: Interview with Martin Petry on "Digital Innovation for the Net-worked Society". Bus. Inf. Syst. Eng. **58**(3), 239–241 (2016)
28. vom Brocke, J., Braccini, A.M., Sonnenberg, C., Spagnoletti, P.: Living IT infra-structures—an ontology-based approach to aligning IT infrastructure capacity and business needs. Int. J. Account. Inf. Syst. **15**(3), 246–274 (2014)
29. vom Brocke, J., Debortoli, S., Müller, O., Reuter, N.: How in-memory technology can create business value: insights from the Hilti case. Commun. Assoc. Inf. Syst. **34**(1), 151–167 (2014)
30. vom Brocke, J., Fay, M., Schmiedel, T., Petry, M., Krause, F., Teinzer, T.: A journey of digital innovation and transformation: the case of Hilti. In: Oswald, G., Kleinemeier, M. (eds.) Shaping the Digital Enterprise, pp. 237–251. Springer International Publishing (2017)
31. vom Brocke, J., Petry, M., Schmiedel, T.: How Hilti masters transformation. 360° – Bus. Transform. J. **1**, 38–47 (2011)
32. vom Brocke, J., Petry, M., Schmiedel, T., Sonnenberg, C.: How organizational culture facilitates a global BPM project: the case of Hilti. In: vom Brocke, J., Rosemann, M. (eds.) Handbook on Business Process Management 2: Strategic Alignment, Governance, People and Culture, pp. 693–713. Springer, Berlin (2015)
33. vom Brocke, J., Petry, M., Sinnl, T., Kristensen, B.Ø., Sonnenberg, C.: Global processes and data: the culture journey at Hilti Corporation. In: vom Brocke, J., Rosemann, M. (eds.) Handbook on Business Process Management 2: Strategic Alignment, Governance, People and Culture, pp. 539–558. Springer, Berlin (2010)
34. vom Brocke, J., Simons, A., Schenk, B.: Transforming design science research into practical application: Experiences from two ECM teaching cases. ACIS 2008 Proceedings, pp. 1049–1058 (2008)
35. vom Brocke, J., Sinnl, T.: Applying the BPM-Culture-Model–The Hilti Case. 21st Australasian Conference on Information Systems (ACIS), Brisbane, Australia (2010)

36. Rosemann, M., vom Brocke, J.: The six core elements of business process management. In: vom Brocke, J., Rosemann, M. (eds.) Handbook on Business Process Management 1, pp. 107–122. Springer, Berlin (2010)
37. Petry, M., Nemetz, M., Wagner, A., Maschler, M., Goeth, C.: IT mega-trends at Hilti: mobility, cloud computing and in-memory technology (SAP HANA). 5th IT Academy, Locarno, Switzerland (2013)
38. vom Brocke, J., Schmiedel, T., Simons, A., Schmid, A., Petry, M., Baeck, C.: From local IT needs to global process transformation: Hilti's customer service program. Bus. Process. Manag. J. **22**(3), 594–613 (2016)
39. Debortoli, S., Müller, O., Junglas, I., vom Brocke, J.: Text mining for information systems researchers: an annotated topic modeling tutorial. Commun. Assoc. Inf. Syst. **39**, 110–135 (2016)
40. Müller, O., Junglas, I., vom Brocke, J., Debortoli, S.: Utilizing big data analytics for information systems research: challenges, promises and guidelines. Eur. J. Inf. Syst. **25**(4), 289–302 (2016)
41. Müller, O., Junglas, I., Debortoli, S., vom Brocke, J.: Using text analytics to derive customer service management benefits from unstructured data. MIS Q. Exec. **15**(4), 243–258 (2016)
42. Schmiedel, T., Müller, O., vom Brocke, J.: Topic modeling as a strategy of inquiry in organizational research: a tutorial with an application example on organizational culture. Organ. Res. Methods. **22**(4), 941–968 (2019)
43. vom Brocke, J., Grisold, T.: Erfolgreich Digitalisieren – Ansätze für ein modernes Prozessmanagement. Controlling. **32**(S), 102–107 (2020)
44. vom Brocke, J., Schmiedel, T., Recker, J., Trkman, P., Mertens, W., Viaene, S.: Ten principles of good business process management. Bus. Process. Manag. J. **20** (2014)
45. Van de Ven, A.H., Johnson, P.E.: Knowledge for theory and practice. Acad. Manag. Rev. **31**(4), 802–821 (2006)
46. Bartunek, J.M., Rynes, S.L.: Academics and practitioners are alike and unlike: the paradoxes of academic–practitioner relationships. J. Manag. **40**(5), 1181–1201 (2014)
47. Grisold, T., Klammer, A., Kragulj, F.: Two forms of organizational unlearning: insights from engaged scholarship research with change consultants. Manag. Learn. **51**(5), 598–619 (2020)
48. Schön, D.A.: The Reflective Practitioner: How Professionals Think in Action. Basic Books (1983)
49. McKelvey, B.: Van De Ven and Johnson's "engaged scholarship": Nice try, but…. Acad. Manag. Rev. **31**(4), 822–829 (2006)
50. Van de Ven, A.H.: Engaged Scholarship: A Guide for Organizational and Social Research. Oxford University Press (2007)
51. Grisold, T., Mendling, J., Otto, M., vom Brocke, J.: Adoption, use and management of process mining in practice. Bus. Process. Manag. J. **25**(6) (2020)
52. Badakhshan, P., Conboy, K., Grisold, T., vom Brocke, J.: Agile business process management. Bus. Process. Manag. J. **26**(6), 1505–1523 (2019)
53. Greenwood, D.J., Levin, M.: Introduction to Action Research: Social Research for Social Change. SAGE (1998)
54. Hovorka, D.S., Johnston, R., Riemer, K.: Reclaiming meaning in IS theory: theory for why, not what. Proceedings of the Information Systems Foundations Work-shop (ISF 2014 Workshop), 18 (2014)
55. Grover, V., Lyytinen, K.: New state of play in information systems research: the push to the edges. MIS Q. **39**(2), 271–296 (2015)
56. Avgerou, C.: Contextual explanation: alternative approaches and persistent challenges. MIS Q. **43**(3), 977–1006 (2019)
57. vom Brocke, J., Simons, A., Niehaves, B., Riemer, K., Plattfaut, R., Cleven, A.: Reconstructing the Giant: On the Importance of Rigour in Documenting the Literature Search Process. 17th European Conference on Information Systems (ECIS), Verona, Italy (2009)

58. vom Brocke, J., Simons, A., Riemer, K., Niehaves, B., Plattfaut, R., Cleven, A.: Standing on the shoulders of giants: challenges and recommendations of literature search in information systems research. Commun. Assoc. Inf. Syst. **37**(Article 9), 205–224 (2015)
59. Webster, J., Watson, R.T.: Analyzing the past to prepare for the future: writing a literature review. MIS Q. **26**(2), 8–13 (2002)
60. George, G., Howard-Grenville, J., Joshi, A., Tihanyi, L.: Understanding and tackling societal grand challenges through management research. Acad. Manag. J. **59**(6), 1880–1895 (2016)
61. Becker, J., vom Brocke, J., Heddier, M., Seidel, S.: In search of information systems (grand) challenges. Bus. Inf. Syst. Eng. **57**(6), 377–390 (2015)
62. Morana, S., vom Brocke, J., Maedche, A., Seidel, S., Adam, M.T.P., Bub, U., Fettke, P., Gau, M., Herwix, A., Mullarkey, M.T., Nguyen, H.D., Sjöström, J., Toreini, P., Wessel, L., Winter, R.: Tool support for design science research—towards a software ecosystem: a report from a DESRIST 2017 Workshop. Commun. Assoc. Inf. Syst., 237–256 (2018)
63. vom Brocke, J., Fettke, P., Gau, M., Houy, C., Maedche, A., Morana, S., Seidel, S.: Tool-support for design science research: design principles and instantiation. SSRN Electr. J. (2017)
64. vom Brocke, J., Mendling, J., Rosemann, M. (eds.): Business Process Management Cases. Digital Innovation and Business Transformation in Practice, vol. 2. Springer (2021)

Design Pattern as a Bridge Between Problem-Space and Solution-Space

Jan Marco Leimeister, Ernestine Dickhaut, and Andreas Janson

Abstract Designing novel technologies provide challenges to developers. To support developers in designing these technologies, design knowledge must be codified and made applicable for the future. In systems development, design patterns provide proven solutions to solving recurring problems. They contain templates for describing design information, often in tabular form, and are established tools for making complex knowledge accessible and applicable. Design patterns play a critical role in both practice and research in finding potential solutions. For researchers, patterns can provide a method for codifying design knowledge for future research. For practitioners, design patterns provide established solutions to recurring problems. By applying them in a particular context, the pattern represents elements of both the problem-space and the solution-space, providing an opportunity to bridge the gap between the two spaces. Due to the abstraction of design patterns, they can be used for different application scenarios. The preparation of the design knowledge in the design pattern is a critical step to support the user in the best possible way, that determines the usefulness of the pattern.

Keywords Design pattern · Design knowledge · Design science research

J. M. Leimeister (✉)
Institute of Information Management, University of St. Gallen, St. Gallen, Switzerland

Information Systems, Interdisciplinary Research Center for IS Design (ITeG), University of Kassel, Kassel, Germany
e-mail: janmarco.leimeister@unisg.ch

E. Dickhaut
Information Systems, Interdisciplinary Research Center for IS Design (ITeG), University of Kassel, Kassel, Germany
e-mail: ernestine.dickhaut@uni-kassel.de

A. Janson
Institute of Information Management, University of St. Gallen, St. Gallen, Switzerland
e-mail: andreas.janson@unisg.ch

© The Author(s), under exclusive license to Springer Nature Switzerland AG 2021
S. Aier et al. (eds.), *Engineering the Transformation of the Enterprise*,
https://doi.org/10.1007/978-3-030-84655-8_9

137

1 Introduction

In information systems (IS) research, the accumulation of design knowledge is becoming increasingly important for research and practice [1]. In particular, the Design Science Research (DSR) paradigm, which is widely used to design and develop technologies [2], focuses on the development and evaluation of new technologies, applying rules and concepts such as design theories and principles that can be used to map and support design processes [3]. However, at first, it is necessary to take a closer look at what design knowledge is and how it is generated in DSR projects. The ability to generate and use knowledge has become an important quality characteristic for design-oriented research [4]. When we study the understanding and use of design knowledge in IS research, the focus is on harnessing design knowledge for the future. Vom Brocke et al. [5, p.6] emphasize "the goal of DSR is to generate knowledge about how to effectively build innovative solutions to important problems". Good design should not be used only for a "single success story" [6]. Reusability and learning from design knowledge are critical to the success of DSR projects and beyond. This raises the problem of how acquired (design) knowledge should be codified so that others can use the knowledge to solve design problems in depth.

Contextual knowledge is often necessary to better classify the problem and thus identify and develop the right solution approach to solve a problem. To achieve this, the problem context must initially be understood, the problem identified and classified, and then the appropriate solution developed. To be able to solve problems in development, support is needed that codifies extensive design knowledge in a practical manner and helps the user to find a suitable solution for the problem at hand. For this purpose, design knowledge must be codified in a practical one.

This paper introduces the approach of design patterns for the codification of design knowledge. The peculiarity of design patterns is that they combine content that provides a solution direction with information from the problem context [6]. Thus, design patterns provide elements from both the problem-space and the solution-space, allowing the user to find creative solutions suitable for the problem at hand with the help of codified design knowledge. To this end, design patterns differ from other approaches to codify design knowledge, such as design principles, and the distinctive features of design patterns in unifying elements from problem-space and solution-space are elaborated.

2 The Concept of Knowledge in the Background of Design-Oriented Research

Before we can consider the specificity of codifying design knowledge in design patterns, we first have to take a closer look at what knowledge is generally and how design knowledge is distinguished from knowledge.

Knowledge comprises information that is gathered through the interpretation of experiences. Therefore, knowledge is built up through interaction with the world and is organized and stored in the mind of an individual. Two forms of knowledge can be distinguished:

1. *Tacit knowledge exists* unconsciously in a person's mind without the need to put it into words.
2. *Explicit knowledge* can be communicated to others and recorded in written documents and procedures.

While explicit knowledge can be easily transferred, other types of knowledge, such as tacit knowledge, are difficult to transfer [7]. Knowledge is created by individuals and becomes valuable by being passed on to other individuals [8]. However, to make the knowledge usable for the future and accessible to others, it must be captured and codified [9]. Challenges arise particularly from the application of theoretical knowledge in a practical context [10]. To ensure that this knowledge has added value in practice, it must be individually adapted to the respective context.

In addition to the distinction between tacit and explicit knowledge, knowledge can be divided into know-how, know-why, and know-what [11]. Know-how knowledge is acquired through "learning-by-doing", i.e. in the execution of the activity. Second, know-why is based on rules and techniques learned through training. Third, know-what is an important way in which knowledge is generated [11]. To acquire know-what knowledge, information about the problem context and the need to implement the solution must be provided.

Knowledge generation is a process in which individuals cross the boundary of the old into a new self by acquiring new knowledge [8]. In the process, new conceptual artifacts and structures for interactions emerge that offer possibility. Knowledge influences how reality is viewed. The same reality can be viewed differently depending on the knowledge one has. The context of the situation is important to generate knowledge because the context helps to relate and classify the information.

Knowledge generation starts with socialization, which is the process of transforming new tacit knowledge through shared experiences in daily social interaction. Tacit knowledge is difficult to formalize, thus, it is often time and space specific. The knowledge can only be acquired through shared experience [1].

Design knowledge is a special form of knowledge, namely knowledge about the design of a system including the associated methods and constructs [2]. A person acquires this knowledge, for example, through experience in designing systems or through education. Design knowledge is gained from creative insights as well as trial-and-error processes and therefore does not usually have a close deductive relationship to existing scientific knowledge [12]. It exists initially only as tacit knowledge in the person's mind. The experiential space, and thus the existing design knowledge of a person, varies depending on the person's level of experience. By actively applying the tacit knowledge, an individual solution can be found. Design knowledge should ideally be reusable for similar problems. However, challenges arise in an application when problems at hand are very general and the design knowledge must be abstract yet actionable enough [13].

Design knowledge is characterized by vagueness, hierarchy, and links to other knowledge-bits, which makes it difficult to share [14]. In system development, the sharing of design knowledge is an important step towards developing high-quality systems with high user acceptance. In large software projects, knowledge does not exist in the head of a single person [14] but is based on the shared knowledge of several people. Thus, implicit design knowledge should be transferred into explicit knowledge and made accessible to other people [15]. In practice, internal company wikis are often used to organize knowledge transfer and design patterns for this purpose. We will look at these challenges in the next chapter, where processes of codifying design knowledge will be addressed.

3   Sharing Design Knowledge

3.1   Externalization of Design Knowledge

The SECI model (socialization—externalization—combination—internalization) by Nonaka and Takeuchi is a concept that describes the emergence of organizational knowledge [2]. As a standard model for knowledge generation, transfer, and development of knowledge, the SECI model forms a basis for describing the explication of tacit knowledge into explicit knowledge (see Fig. 1).

The model classifies knowledge into explicit knowledge, which is objective, codified, transferable, and formal, and tacit experiential knowledge, which is difficult or impossible to convey and is only very inadequately codified. Tacit knowledge

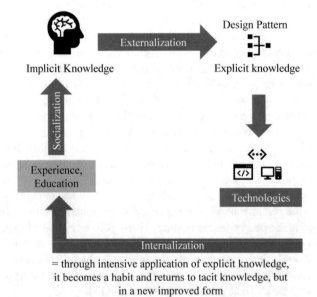

Fig. 1 Externalization of design knowledge (based on the SECI model) [8]

is based on experiences, culture, emotions, and values and is manifested in methodological and social competencies more than in qualifications, i.e. also in action routines and procedures, but also convictions, beliefs, and culturally codified schemata. The explication of an implicit context is an essential prerequisite for the creation of new knowledge.

Socialization is the exchange of experience through both horizontal and vertical communication. In the exchange of experience, knowledge is developed through conversation, at a conference, or through imitation. According to the SECI model, the transformation from unconscious to conscious knowledge is called externalization. By including images, metaphors, or models, implicit knowledge is externalized in such a way that it can be understood by others. In combination (combination = explicit-to-explicit), existing explicit knowledge is combined with other knowledge content to form new, explicit knowledge. Different contents can be transformed by media, from analog to digital, and expanded by adding other contexts.

The reverse process from conscious to unconscious knowledge is called internalization. In this process, explicit knowledge is transformed into tacit knowledge, which means that experiences and knowledge gained through previous socialization, externalization, or combination are integrated into individual mental models.

The SECI model can be applied to the process of codifying design knowledge through design patterns. Design knowledge is initially tacit and difficult for other people to grasp in its form. By codifying design knowledge in design patterns, it is codified and recorded in a communicable form of representation. Now the knowledge can be picked up by other people and be used as a set of rules. Design knowledge can exist in many disciplines. For example, legal design knowledge differs from design knowledge in DSR. The legal expert brings knowledge about legal requirements to design novel technologies [16]. Nevertheless, legal design knowledge can also be codified into design patterns (externalization) [17]. The codified legal design knowledge can be used by others. However, there is special caution required in the way the design knowledge is represented if people outside the domain are to use the externalized design knowledge. A developer may have a large repertoire of solutions to design software, but usually little legal knowledge.

3.2 Codification Approaches of Design Knowledge

Since knowledge is often vaguely formulated, the codification of design knowledge requires special methods. There are already various approaches that deal with methods for codifying design knowledge to be able to capture it for the future and to share it with others (see Table 1).

Cheat sheets are a common method for capturing design knowledge, especially in system development. A large amount of knowledge is stored in a small space, usually on a "one-pager" [25]. This allows the user to obtain a large amount of information briefly and thus find a solution to any problem as quickly as possible

Table 1 Overview of various methods for codifying design knowledge

Categorization of knowledge (according to [3])	Method for codifying design knowledge	Source
Know-how	Knowledge maps	[18]
	Mind maps	[19]
	Conceptual maps	[18]
	Wikis	[20]
	Prototypes	[21]
	Design principles	[22]
	Design patterns	[23]
Know-why	Cheat sheets	[24]
	Prototypes	[21]
	Design patterns	[23]
Know-what	Wikis	[20]
	Design principles	[22]
	Design Patterns	[23]

[26]. In particular, the development of cheat sheets is a crucial way to retrieve knowledge and bring it to the point from a learning perspective [24].

Knowledge maps or similar approaches such as mind maps or conceptual maps are based on the idea of representing knowledge as it is stored in memory. In comparison to cheat sheets, they use a graphical representation and visualize relationships between individual elements using connections and arrows [18]. Knowledge maps have proven useful in identifying areas where are gaps in knowledge, resources, and knowledge flow. These approaches are especially used when knowledge is to be captured but not shared. Wikis are created for knowledge transfer, especially in teams and organizations. They focus on the transfer of individual knowledge [20].

Wikis have the advantage of an overview page that allows users to find exactly the information they need. In practice, wikis often replace exchanges between individuals within an organization. The way knowledge is codified within the wiki varies depending on the author of the contribution. Knowledge transfer between IT professionals often occurs through information systems. This often includes additional information found in system documentation and user training materials [27].

Prototypes are often used for communication between developers and other disciplines. They allow both sides to demonstrate requirements and possible functionalities in a practical way [21]. They provide a cost-effective demonstration of the system and offer the opportunity to contribute to expertise [28]. These approaches do not provide a solution to the challenge of codifying design knowledge in such a way that it can be understood by disciplines outside the domain. Facts such as lack of structure, use of technical terms, and incompleteness lead to low use of these tools. It must be ensured that design knowledge is formulated in a clear, unambiguous, and accessible language and is free of inconsistencies and contradictions [10].

In system development, design patterns are a solution to solve recurring problems and challenges [23]. Design patterns are established tools for making complex knowledge accessible to system developers. The advantage of patterns in comparison to design principles, for example, is that they cover all three forms of knowledge while providing an established approach to development practice. In the literature, patterns are often referred to as "templates" of established solutions for frequently recurring problems in system development.

4 Design Science Research and Design Patterns

Although the IS discipline has extensive experience in digitizing and designing sociotechnical artifacts, the underlying design knowledge is not systematically accumulated across different settings and projects and therefore cannot be transferred and reused in new contexts [29].

Design patterns originally come from the field of architecture and were established by the work around Alexander et al. [30], in which architects are supported in the design of houses and the planning of cities by design patterns. In design, architects regularly face recurring problems in which proven solutions can be applied. Proven solutions do not add value to others until they are shared on a sufficient scale. Thus, design patterns are used to capture proven solutions to recurring problems and make them usable for the future.

After design patterns have revealed themselves to be useful in architecture, many different disciplines adopt the idea of design patterns and transferred it to various disciplines. In system development, design patterns have become established primarily through the work of the so-called "Gang of Four (GoF)" around Gamma et al. [31].

Design patterns represent abstract and thus generally applicable and reusable solutions for recurring problems. "Best practices" are codified in design patterns and are made usable for the future. For this purpose, a design pattern offers a kind of "template", which is structured in the same way for all patterns. They do not present innovative solutions and do not "reinvent the wheel" but build on proven solutions. At the same time, a design pattern offers approaches to solutions for many problems. Thus, design patterns address one of the problems identified by Brocke et al. [5] in the reuse of design knowledge by codifying design knowledge in design patterns in an abstract way.

Petter et al. [32] see four crucial phases in the life cycle of design patterns (see Fig. 2). In the first phase, the development of the pattern, both domain knowledge from the corresponding domain and theories from the literature together with existing "best practice" solutions flow into the development. Thereupon, the pattern is used in the second phase and comes to a practical use in the third one, the use, in order to solve recurring problems. In all three phases described so far, the design pattern can be continuously evaluated.

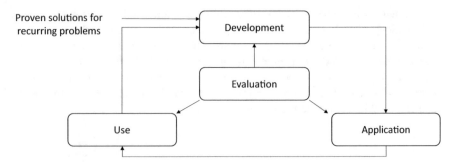

Fig. 2 Design pattern life cycle (based on [32])

5 Problem-Space and Solution-Space in System Development

DSR projects aim to solve problems in application domains. In doing so, a detailed understanding and description of the problem, as well as the positioning of those within the problem-space, are essential. Two key components describe the problem-space: the application context and the quality criteria for solution acceptance [5].

The application context describes the problem in its context. The problem-space, the main stakeholders of the problem-space, the mutual influence of those with the design solution are discussed. In addition, problem-spaces are closely tied to time and place. The relevance of today's problem may not be tomorrow [5]. Therefore, it is essential to record the time in which the problem was perceived. Contextual aspects of location include relevant geographic indications such as rural vs. urban environments or already developed vs. developing countries. Overall, the context of the application of a DSR project defines an ideographic basis for the dissemination of design knowledge.

The second key component deals with how well the design solves the problem. In describing the quality criteria for the problem, the sociotechnical aspects of the design solution must be recognized. Therefore, design requirements include mixed objectives from technology, quality information, human interaction, and societal needs. This is accompanied by acceptance criteria for evaluating potential design solutions and guides designing both formative and summative evaluation methods.

Thus, positioning a DSR project in the problem-space establishes the situational context and research goals of the project (i.e., quality criteria for design innovation) [33]. The effective reuse of design knowledge for future research depends on how well this problem-space can be transferred to the new research projects. The transferability of design knowledge provides information on how well new research contexts and objectives adapt to the knowledge base. This context can be described in terms of several dimensions, including domain, stakeholder, time, and place. Low transferability of design knowledge in a project indicates a very specific context with restrictive goals. In contrast, high transferability of design knowledge and more general applications of it to problem domains would support—even within and/or between different application domains. Legner et al. [29] found that knowledge accumulation occurred incrementally as a result of maturing abstract and situational domain knowledge (solution-space) and in response to evolving roles of data (problem-space).

The design knowledge in solution-space comprises the knowledge for solving related problems. It includes not only results but also activities of the DSR. Results of DSR can take different forms, such as artifacts as well as design patterns or theories. Artifacts should support replication and reuse by future research projects. Design theories and principles help understand how and why artifacts meet the goals of the problem-space.

However, knowledge in the solution-space may also relate to design processes and the evaluation of activities to design, evaluate, and refine DSR results in iterative cycles. Design activities include a search process to identify the best design candidates from the solution-space. Information about goodness criteria from the problem-space is used for value maximization while constrained by resource availability and applicability. For the reusability of design knowledge in the future, it is important to refer to the fundamentals of design. This can be done through kernel theories as well as by recording creative insights that have led to innovative design improvements.

In the solution-space, the suitability of solutions varies depending on the selected target problem. Design activities within a project can cover a larger part of the problem-space than solutions from research. The more suitable a solution is, the more operational it is for the users in the application. The degree of suitability refers to the normative solution power. More unsuitable solutions may have a lower normative force to guide problem-solving behavior. This makes the solution less prescriptive compared to a manual. Thus, the lower the fitness of the solution, the greater the effort required to apply the design knowledge to a new problem.

There is a trade-off between transferability and suitability of design knowledge. Often, higher suitability implies more restriction to a particular context. In turn, a less fit representation of design knowledge may support higher transferability. Techniques for representing design knowledge that enables reusability need to be developed. Exemplary of this is configurational configuration models or methods that allow the tradeoff between the transferability and suitability of design knowledge to be managed [5]. Using such techniques, design knowledge is represented for alternative solution variants that fit in different contexts of the problem-space.

6 Design Patterns to Close Knowledge Gaps

Developers of novel technologies, such as AI-based smart personal assistants [34], acquire design knowledge through experience, the training they have received, and problems they have already solved, which they can use to solve problems that arise in the future. Here, the amount of existing design knowledge in the person's problem/solution-space differs depending on the person's wealth of experience and the training they have received so far. According to Nonaka [8], the existing design knowledge of a developer can be called tacit knowledge. This must be made available to others via externalization first and can be done either orally or in writing through codification.

Design patterns externalize tacit design knowledge by codifying it for other people and recording it in written form. With the help of the externalized design knowledge, (design) problems can now be solved. While experienced developers have access to a wealth of experience, inexperienced developers usually have significantly fewer "best practices". As a result, the solution-space also differs depending on the level of experience. Due to their abstract representation, design patterns do not offer a so-called recipe for problems to be solved but support the user to find a suitable solution for the problem at hand by pointing out possible solution approaches. Thus, a design pattern can be the solution for many problems.

The user of the design pattern is in the problem-space with the problem at hand and searches for a suitable solution in the solution-space. It should be noted that for numerous problems there is no single correct solution, but several solutions can solve the problem satisfactorily. The design pattern provides the user with food for thought about possible solutions, which expands the user's solution-space and allows him to search individually for a suitable solution.

According to vom Brocke et al. [5], patterns are a component of the design knowledge base. They help to find suitable solutions for existing problems. By providing information about the problem context, it helps to understand the problem to be solved in detail and thus to find the truly appropriate solution. In addition to the description of the problem, a core component of a pattern is the solution and an associated description of the procedure for solving the problem. The elements described so far contain information directly from the problem or solution-space. However, the user is missing information that describes statements about effects of the implementation of the design pattern on the technology or helps him to select the right pattern. These elements are located between the problem-space and the solution-space and can be categorized as evaluation according to vom Brocke [5]. The user receives knowledge from the design pattern, which describes why the practical implementation of the pattern is necessary. A description of the target state after the successful implementation of the pattern supports the user to select and understand the pattern.

A design pattern not only presents the solution, it also describes the problem to be solved. Depending on the domain and application context, the pattern refers to the requirements to be solved or the problem to be solved. As a result, a pattern encompasses aspects of both the problem-space and the solution-space and links the two domains into each other. This allows the user to draw a bridge between the problem to be solved and the possible solution. While other approaches to knowledge codification, such as wikis, cheat sheets, and design principles focus primarily on the solution to the problem, design patterns bridge the two spaces. Additional information such as user stories, consequences, or use cases supports users to generate knowledge around the problem domain and thus changes the way they search for solutions.

Processing Emotional Data	Current Period of Development Process	
	☐ Patterns of interaction ☐ Architectural patterns	
	☐ Learning patterns ☒ Data processing pattern	

Goal

Users should receive dialogues that are adapted to their emotions. However, data that allows conclusions to be drawn about the user's emotionality should neither be processed nor stored or used for profiling.

Law	Requirements	Service quality
• Non-chain-ability • Processing of sensitive data only with consent • No discriminatory decisions	• No processing of intimate data • No complete user profile • Setting options for users	• Complaisant dialogues • Human dialogues	• Interpreting and responding to emotions • Avoiding sensitive topics

Consequences		Influences
Law	**Service quality**	
• Protection of personal data • Protection of intimacy and privacy • No profiling possible	• Personal configuration • Dialogues appropriate to the current emotional situations	• Empathy • Data minimization • Appropriation • Protection of privacy and intimacy • Non-discrimination

Solution

- Emotion recognition on the device through an emotion anthology
  Three steps to recognize user emotions:
  1. Signal processing: Digitization of the acoustic/visual signal
  2. Feature calculation: A feature selection algorithm selects the most important features of emotions from the signal
  3. Comparison of the feature with the database, assignment of the feature to a specific emotion
- Linking with typical signal words: Based on frequency and probability, categorisation is performed.
- Additional factors can be done through speech recognition.
- Generation of an emotionally appropriate response takes place on the user's end device.

Important Data Protection Regulations

- Art. 5 Para. 1 lit. b (Purpose limitation), lit. c (Data minimization) (Here, opening clauses such as Art. 6 para. 3 of the GDPR and member state regulations based on this in the BDSG, HDSIG and HHG may also have to be observed, particularly for data processing by public bodies).
- Art. 9 of the GDPR (processing of special categories of personal data) (here, the opening clauses in Art. 9 para. (4) of the GDPR and the Member State regulations based on it in the BDSG, HDSIG and HHG may also have to be taken into account, especially for data processing by public bodies).
- Art. 22 of the GDPR (automated decisions in individual cases, including profiling), (where applicable, Member State regulations based on the opening clause of Art. 22 para.(2) lit.(b) of the GDPR must be observed).

Confirmation of implementation of contents of design pattern   Date   Signature

Fig. 3 Design pattern "Processing Emotional Data"

7 Design Patterns and Their Relationship to Design Principles

In IS research, design principles have been established in recent years as a proven means of codifying design knowledge [35, 36]. Design principles provide users with necessary information about the design of technologies in the shortest possible time. In the DSR paradigm, design principles are often formulated together with design requirements and represent concrete specifications for the design of the technology.

The work from Kruse et al. [36] classified design principles into three categories: a) action-oriented, b) materiality-oriented, and c) action and materiality-oriented. Design patterns can also be classified into these categories [6], but they contain further information that goes beyond these categories. This is because design knowledge is generated and tested through the application and use of design patterns. The codified design knowledge in design patterns goes beyond a mere instruction to do something and offers an explanation of how to implement it. Design patterns act as a bridge between design knowledge and the developed technology. Compared to design principles, design patterns additionally present action-oriented and material information. And exactly this content differs design patterns from design principles. The purpose of design principles can be described as a rule or behavioral standard [37] that gives precise instructions on how an artifact must be built [38]. Design patterns, on the other hand, contain information that conveys to the user the intention of why something must be implemented.

Figure 3 shows the exemplary design pattern "Processing Emotional Data". The design pattern contains elements such as target state, problem, effects, and solution, which provide the user with extensive information. With the help of the abstract solution approach in the pattern, a solution is searched for in the user's solution space for the problem that exists in practice. Another crucial feature is that design patterns gain added value with increasing time and application. By repeatedly establishing the solution presented, it is sharpened and must prove itself in a large number of projects. Design principles, on the other hand, are usually developed with a strong technology focus and are not updated over time.

8 Conclusion

In this paper, we show the specifics of design knowledge and the benefits of codifying design knowledge. Especially, in case of practical useabal design solutions approaches to codifing the knowledge may be needed. Thus, we demonstrate how design knowledge is externalized through design patterns by using the SECI model and Nonaka's thoughts [1]. Our contribution is intended to contrast design patterns with other approaches for codifying knowledge and work out its practical applicability. Thus, we propose that design patterns may close knowledge gaps and provide fruitful interactions between the problem-space and the solution-space.

References

1. Gregor, S., Jones, D.: The anatomy of a design theory. Assoc. Inf. Syst. (2007)
2. Österle, H., Becker, J., Frank, U., Hess, T., Karagiannis, D., Krcmar, H., Loos, P., Mertens, P., Oberweis, A., Sinz, E.J.: Memorandum on design-oriented information systems research. Eur. J. Inf. Syst. **20**, 7–10 (2011)

3. Peffers, K., Tuunanen, T., Niehaves, B.: Design science research genres: introduction to the special issue on exemplars and criteria for applicable design science research. Eur. J. Inf. Syst. **27**, 129–139 (2018)
4. Nonaka, I., Toyama, R.: The knowledge-creating theory revisited: knowledge creation as a synthesizing process. Knowl. Manag. Res. Pract. **1**, 2–10 (2003)
5. vom Brocke, J., Winter, R., Hevner, A., Maedche, A.: Accumulation and evolution of design knowledge in design science research–A journey through time and space. JAIS. (2019)
6. Dickhaut, E., Li, M.M., Janson, A.: Developing lawful technologies – a revelatory case study on design patterns. HICSS. 54 (2021 in Erscheinung)
7. Müller, R.M., Thoring, K.: A typology of design knowledge: a theoretical framework. AMCIS. (2010)
8. Nonaka, I., Takeuchi, H.: The Knowledge-Creating Company. How Japanese Companies Create the Dynamics of Innovation. Oxford University Press (1995)
9. Faraj, S., Sproull, L.: Coordinating expertise in software development teams. Manag. Sci. 1554–1568 (2000)
10. Lukyanenko, R., Jeffrey, P.: Design Theory Indeterminacy: What is it, how can it be reduced, and why did the polar bear drown? JAIS. 1–59 (2020)
11. Garud, R.: On the distinction between know-how, know-what, and know-why. Adv. Strat. Manag. 81–102 (1997)
12. Baskerville, R., Baiyere, A., Gergor, S., Hevner, A., Rossi, M.: Design science research contributions: finding a balance between artifact and theory. JAIS. **19**, 358–376 (2018)
13. Baxter, G., Sommerville, I.: Socio-technical systems: from design methods to systems engineering. Interact. Comput. **23**, 4–17 (2011)
14. Zhang, G., Su, X., Zhou, G.: Blog-based dynamic organization and management for multi-discipline knowledge. 515–517 (2010)
15. Morse, W.C., Nielsen-Pincus, M., Force, J.E., Wulfhorst, J.D.: Bridges and barriers to developing and conducting interdisciplinary graduate-student team research. Ecol. Soc. **12**(2), 8 (2007)
16. Dickhaut, E., Janson, A., Roßnagel, A., Leimeister, J.M.: Interdisziplinäre Anforderungsmuster für smarte persönliche Assistenten. Mittel zu Erfassung divergenter Anforderungen aus Informatik und Recht. Datenschutz und Datensicherheit (DuD) (2020)
17. Dickhaut, E., Thies, L.F., Janson, A.: Die Kodifizierung von Gestaltungswissen in interdisziplinären Entwurfsmustern. Lösungen im Spannungsfeld zwischen Rechtsverträglichkeit und Dienstleistungsqualität. Datenschutz und Datensicherheit (DuD) (2020)
18. Zenkert, J., Holland, A., Fathi, M.: Discovering contextual knowledge with associated information in dimensional structured knowledge bases. International Conference on Systems, Man, and Cybernetics, pp. 923–928 (2016)
19. Wheeldon, J., Faubert, J.: Framing experience: concept maps, mind maps, and data collection in qualitative research. Int J Qual Methods. **8**, 68–83 (2009)
20. Phuwanartnurak, A.J.: Interdisciplinary Collaboration through Wikis in Software Development. IEEE, Piscataway, NJ (2009)
21. Winkler, M., Huber, T., Dibbern, J.: The Software Prototype as Digital Boundary Object: A Revelatory Longitudinal Innovation Case. (2014)
22. Seidel, S., Chandra Kruse, L., Székely, N., Gau, M., Stieger, D.: Design principles for sensemaking support systems in environmental sustainability transformations. Eur. J. Inf. Syst. **27**, 221–247 (2018)
23. Alexander, C.: The timeless way of building. Oxford University Press, New York (1979)
24. Song, Y., Guo, Y., Thuente, D.: A quantitative case study on students' strategy for using authorized cheat-sheets. IEEE Frontiers in Education, pp. 1–9 (2016)
25. Hsiao, I.-H., Lopez, C.: Lessons learned from students' cheat sheets: generic models for designing programming study guides. IEEE 16th International Conference on Advanced Learning Technologies (ICALT), pp. 209–211 (2016)

26. Kaindl, H., Falb, J., Melbinger, S., Bruckmayer, T.: An approach to method-tool coupling for software development. Fifth International Conference on Software Engineering Advances, pp. 101–106 (2010)
27. Pawlowski, R.: Bridging user organizations: knowledge brokering and the work of information technology professionals. MIS Q. **28**, 645 (2004)
28. Winkler, M., Brown, C., Huber, T.L.: Recurrent knowledge boundaries in outsourced software projects: a longitudinal study. ECIS. (2015)
29. Legner, C., Pentek, T., Otto, B.: Accumulating design knowledge with reference models: insights from 12 years' research into data management. J. Assoc. Inf. Syst. (JAIS). (2020)
30. Alexander, C.: A Pattern Language: Towns, Buildings, Construction. Oxford University Press (1977)
31. Gamma, E., Helm, R., Johnson, R., Vlissides, J.: Design Patterns: Elements of Reusable Object Oriented Software. Addison Wesley Professional (1994)
32. Petter, S., Khazanchi, D., Murphy, J.D.: A design science based evaluation framework for patterns. DESRIST (2008)
33. Gregor, S., Hevner, A.R.: Positioning and presenting design science research for maximum impact. MIS Q. 337–355 (2013)
34. Knote, R., Janson, A., Söllner, M., Leimeister, J.M.: Value co-creation in smart services: a functional affordances perspective on smart personal assistants. J. Assoc. Inf. Syst. (JAIS). (2020)
35. Chandra Kruse, L., Nickerson, J.V.: Portraying Design Essence. 51st Hawaii International Conference (2018)
36. Seidel, S., Chandra Kruse, L., Székely, N., Gau, M., Stieger, D.: Design principles for sensemaking support systems in environmental sustainability transformations. EJIS. **27**, 221–247 (2018)
37. Bellucci, E., Zeleznikow, J.: Managing Negotiation Knowledge with the goal of developing Negotiation Decision Support Systems. ACIS 2005 Proceedings (2005)
38. Chandra, L., Seidel, S., Gregor, S.: Prescriptive knowledge in IS research: conceptualizing design principles in terms of materiality, action, and boundary conditions. HICSS. 4039–4048 (2014)

Incremental Accumulation of Information Systems Design Theory

Tuure Tuunanen and Jan Holmström

Abstract This paper proposes an organizing device for accumulation of information systems (IS) design theory components within a study but also across research
studies. The proposed framework enables actors to understand the relationship over
time between search spaces of information systems design science theory (ISDT)
development by one and the same or different actors. The proposition rests on the
notion that ISDT development is an iterative and incremental process that often
happens across different research studies. Finally, we argue that with the proposed
framework, ISDT knowledge is more easily transferred and combined with the
search processes.

Keywords Information systems · Design science · Theory development ·
Incremental accumulation

1 Introduction

Theory development has become a focal point of information systems (IS) research.
Many of our highly ranked journals use theory development, or a lack of it, when
considering the publication potential of a manuscript. Gregor [1] responded to this
debate and emphasized the IS research community's need to understand what a
theory is in relation to the nature of the IS discipline. For this purpose, Gregor [1]
argued that there are actually different types of theories with which our discipline
works. Our paper focuses on the development of design and action-type IS theory or

T. Tuunanen (✉)
University of Jyväskylä, Jyväskylä, Finland
e-mail: tuure@tuunanen.fi

J. Holmström
Aalto University, Otaniemi, Finland
e-mail: jan.holmstrom@aalto.fi

© The Author(s), under exclusive license to Springer Nature Switzerland AG 2021
S. Aier et al. (eds.), *Engineering the Transformation of the Enterprise*,
https://doi.org/10.1007/978-3-030-84655-8_10

information systems design theory (ISDT) [2]. ISDT development has been a focus of design science research since the early 1990s [3, 4].

However, the IS literature, particularly that pertaining to design science research (DSR), has not provided ways to understand how ISDT is accrued through an incremental accumulation process, especially across different studies [4]. Only recently, the IS literature has recognized this as a problem for advancing DSR [5]. We see that there are issues related to the transfer and combination of ISDT components that should be solved. We note that some attention in the literature has been placed on the accumulation process [6, 7]. For example, Feldman et al. [8] have posited that new theoretical knowledge combinations are a result of individual interaction with different symbolic domains and fields of expertise. Different symbolic languages, which are developed in parallel search spaces, restrict and slow down combinations, as those that are successful are an outcome of individuals overcoming the bounds of rationality [9].

Simon and Klahr's [10] search space model explicates the interaction between individual, field, and multiple symbolic domains as a process of a search in different spaces. Furthermore, Simon [9] has argued that search processes are simultaneously separated and connected. They are separated because the different actors [11] conducting the searches are boundedly rational so that different individuals or groups may, in parallel, develop partly contradictory designs or even opposing paradigms [12]. The search spaces are also connected because the theoretical knowledge, like ISDTs, that has been accumulated by such searches can be combined later to produce something that exceeds the sum of its parts [13]. Hence, in order to facilitate the accumulation of ISDTs across studies, there needs to be an organizing device that enables search activities to be compatible with each other [13, 14].

The problem that we discuss is how to conceptually link the accumulation of ISDT components with the search spaces in DSR. Consequently, we argue that more research is needed to improve understanding of problems related to ISDT development; more specifically, the challenges related to the incremental accumulation of ISDTs across studies. Therefore, the objective of this paper is to provide an organizing device for accumulation of ISDTs within a DSR study, but also across DSR studies.

In the paper, we first review literature on design science theory and ISDT development and elaborate upon our argument for the need to understand the ISDT component accumulation process [4, 5]. Thereafter, we show the means for accomplishing this and discuss the implications for research and conclude.

2   Design Science Research and Theory Development

This paper builds on the general notion that the importance of induction and abduction should be recognized in theory development [15]. Similarly, we see in the argument presented by Colquitt and Zapata-Phelan [16] that theories accumulate incrementally and iteratively, which is the foundation of the work presented here. That means although we discuss theory development within the DSR domain, we do not see that ISDT development radically differs from theory development using other research approaches in IS, such as empirical positivistic or qualitative interpretive approaches. The notion of theory accumulation is, therefore, not new to science or IS as a discipline.

Gregor and Hevner [17] highlighted this by proposing three varying levels of theory. The most mature theory is labeled as level 3, "well-developed design theory about embedded phenomena." The mid-level theory is level 2, "nascent design theory—knowledge as operational principles/architecture." Level 1, the most basic form of ISDT, is "situated implementation of artifact." More recently, Baskerville and Vaishnavi [18] have elaborated on this idea by proposing that at level 1, the researchers should look at solutions (i.e., artifacts), but also pre-theory design frameworks, which they argue to precede level 2 nascent design theories. Baskerville and Vaishnavi [18] also note that the transition from a solution to a pre-theory to a nascent and well-developed design theory is usually not a smooth refinement process but one marked by radical conceptual jumps carried out by one or more researchers over a period of time.

This paper attempts to propose an organizing device that supports the evolution of ISDT from level 1 to level 3. We argue that although the incremental and iterative nature of theory accumulation has been recognized when applying other research approaches (see, e.g., [15, 16]), the DSR literature does not yet provide organizing devices to support such ISDT accumulation processes across studies. Here, we follow the original proposition made by Walls et al. [4] of how ISDT forms over a length of time and through different studies, see, e.g. [5].

Theory development or building, as labeled by Nunamaker et al. [3], has been a focus of design science research since the early 1990s. Although many of the early papers focused more on artifact development than theory development, Walls et al. [4] already discussed the need for theory development. Walls et al. [4] saw design as a form of knowledge accumulation. Hevner et al. [19] similarly noted the importance of theory development.

However, the debate didn't really bloom until Gregor and Jones' paper [2] described the anatomy of an ISDT, or a design theory as they called it. This work builds on the earlier effort by Gregor [1] that proposed five types of theories: analysis, explanation, prediction, explanation and prediction, and design and action. Gregor [1] further suggested that theory types have four common components: a means of representation, constructs, statement of relationships, and scope. In addition to these, Gregor [1] suggested that there are three elements contingent to the purpose of the theory. These are causal explanations, testable propositions or hypotheses, and prescriptive statements. Consequently, Gregor and Jones [2] argued that an ISDT is composed of eight constructs, which are divided into core and additional constructs. The core constructs are purpose and scope, constructs, principle of form and function, artifact mutability, testable propositions, and justificatory knowledge. The additional constructs are principles of implementation and expository instantiations. Here onwards, we refer to these eight constructs as the ISDT constructs.

This description of an ISDT in combination with the earlier paper about the five types of theory initiated a discussion about the need to further understand how an ISDT forms over a length of time. Kuechler and Vaishnavi [20] promoted the idea of dividing ISDTs into different maturity levels, namely kernel theories, mid-level theories, and design theories, with the notion being that the theory matures over the length of time as more theoretical knowledge is accumulated. Similarly, Pries-Heje and Baskerville [21] suggested the concept of theory nexus, which is a set of constructs and methods that enable the construction of models that connect design science research theories with alternative solutions. This is rather close to the mid-range theory concept promoted by Kuechler and Vaishnavi [22], who adapted the definition of Merton [23] to this: "Theories that lie between the minor but necessary working hypotheses that evolve in abundance during day-to-day research and the all-inclusive systematic efforts to develop a unified theory."

However, although the literature evidently sees this aspect of ISDT development as important, it does not clearly manifest how this is accomplished across studies. Moreover, the literature is more focused on theory development efforts within a particular DSR study. For example, Nunamaker et al. [3], Peffers et al. [24], and Sein et al. [25] all incorporated theory development into their individually proposed research methodologies. Nunamaker et al. [3] dedicated a distinct element of their methodology to theory building/development that interacts with other elements of the methodology: systems development, experimentation, and observation. Conversely, Peffers et al. [24] recognized that a theory foundation should drive the design science research effort, particularly artifact design and development. Finally, Sein et al. [25] proposed a methodology, or action design, which further highlights this theory-driven approach to DSR for a single DSR study.

However, none of the above prominent DSR-specific methodologies seek to illustrate how theory is gathered through an accumulation process across different studies, as originally argued by Walls et al. [4]. The argument of this paper is that there is a need to understand this accumulation of ISDT and how it iteratively transpires across DSR studies. Next, we review literature that offers potential organizing devices for this.

3   Potential Organizing Devices for ISDT Accumulation Across DSR Studies

This paper focuses on how a theory accumulates in but also potentially across DSR studies. We argue that we need an organizing device to structure and support such theory accumulation processes. The organizing device should enable convergent thinking through theoretical consensus by enabling, and not inhibiting, the type of thinking needed for path-breaking contributions [16]. Furthermore, researchers involved should be well versed in ways to recognize gaps and opportunities for creating something truly new. For this purpose, the concept of multiple search spaces for setting new directions was developed in Klahr and Simon's study [9] of discovery in science. According to them, discovery in science involves search spaces with distinct but interdependent interests and actors.

How to do this remains a challenge, especially when the search involves many actors and takes place over an extended period of time [14]. A particular difficulty of developing a logic or heuristic for discovery is that the problem situation needs to be represented when the problem is not yet or only partly known. Organizing devices in the form of paradigms is needed to describe what is already there so that it can be challenged and changed in the creation of something new [12].

In this paper, we build on ISDT [2] and search for an appropriate organizing device to structure and support its incremental accumulation. We seek an organizing device for ISDT that supports the use and improvement of ISDT from implementation to implementation, across studies, between actors, and over time. We start out by considering existing organizing devices for ISDT development and application. The organizing devices that we consider are means-ends propositions [9, 26–28], design patterns [29, 30], PICO [31], and CIMO [32, 33]. By combining distinctive elements of existing devices, we proceed to develop an organizing device specifically for ISDT accumulation across studies, which is elaborated on in the next section.

3.1 Means-Ends Proposition

The early design science of Herbert Simon relies on the simple organizing device of the means-ends proposition [9]. Means-ends propositions are similar to the technological rules of Popper [28] and Bunge [26] or the technical norms proposed by Niiniluoto [27]. This structure builds on "purpose-oriented logic," i.e., proposals indicating that it is logical (in a practical rather than deductive sense) to do X if you want A and you believe that you are in a situation B [6]. This type of practical inference provides a methodological basis for reasoning about designs [35]. Using this logic, it is possible to articulate the problem to be solved and a proposed solution, linking different types of knowledge ([36], p. 41). Means-ends propositions can be used to describe how ISDT relates to the "know-what," "know-when," and "know-how" needed to apply the knowledge as illustrated in Table 1. We elaborate on this below.

Van Aken's notion of a design exemplar is linked to "know-what" search space and the "if you want A" part of the means-ends proposition [6]. He defines a design exemplar as a general prescription that has to be translated to the specific problem at hand. In solving that problem, one has to design a specific variant of that design exemplar. Gregor and Jones [2] have in turn defined the ISDT Purpose and Scope as "What the system is for," or the set of meta-requirements or goals that specify the type of artifact to which the theory applies and also defines the scope, or boundaries, of the theory. Gregor and Jones [2] provide an example of such from Iversen et al.

Table 1 Using a means-ends proposition as an organizing device for ISDT

Means-ends [6]	Design pattern [30]	ISDT component [2] with example(s) from [34]
If you want A, ("Know-what")	Problem	**Purpose and scope**: The aim is to develop an approach for understanding and managing risk in software process improvement (SPI).
		Principles of form and function: A risk framework is given to aid in the identification and categorization of risks. A process with four steps is then given to show heuristics that can be used to relate identified risk areas to resolution strategies.
and you believe you are in situation B, ("Know-when")	Solution	**Constructs**: Examples are: risk item, risky incident, resolution actions.
		Artifact mutability: Suggestions for improving the approach are given for further work: one example is that parts of the approach could be packaged as a self-guiding computer-based system.
then do X ("Know-how")	Consequences	**Principles of implementation**: It is stated that the approach requires facilitation by someone experienced in risk management, SPI and running collaborative workshops.
		Justificatory knowledge: The approach proposed is derived from other risk management approaches (other design theories).

[34], which focuses on software process improvement and risk management. According to Gregor and Jones [2], the ISDT Purpose and Scope for this study can be characterized as, "The aim is to develop an approach for understanding and managing risk in software process improvement."

Consequently, we see that Gregor and Jones [2] describe the general prescription of a design exemplar [6] with their definition of the ISDT Purpose and Scope. Van Aken [6] himself gives an example from civil engineering and bridge building. In his terms, the general prescription is the concept of bridge, and an exemplar of it is a suspension bridge. Wikipedia gives a definition of a bridge in Gregor and Jones's terms, i.e., what it is for or its purpose and scope: ". . . a structure built to span physical obstacles such as a body of water, valley, or road, for the purpose of providing passage over the obstacle." However, in order to define what a suspension bridge is, we need further conceptual tools.

Here, Gregor and Jones's ISDT Principles of Form and Function becomes a valuable way to define the "know-what" search space further, which they define as "the abstract 'blueprint' or architecture that describes an IS artifact." For example, this blueprint or architecture is needed to understand how to build a suspension bridge. A general prescription does not allow this. Gregor and Jones illustrate this with an example from Iversen et al. [34]: "A risk framework is given to aid in the identification and categorization of risks and a process with four steps is given to show heuristics that can be used to relate identified risk areas to resolution strategies." The example from Iversen et al. [34] gives a more detailed blueprint of what the framework proposed in the paper is supposed to accomplish. Similarly, if we use van Aken's bridge example, Wikipedia gives an architectural, though abstract, plan of a suspension bridge: "A suspension bridge is a type of bridge in which the deck (the load-bearing portion) is hung below suspension cables on vertical suspenders." However, for a civil engineer, this description does provide an understanding how build such a bridge. Similarly, an IS researcher who has knowledge of contingency-theory-based risk management models (see, e.g., [37, 38]) can understand how Iversen et al. [34] propose to identify and resolve risks in their area of study.

Next, we look at van Aken's [6] "and you believe you are in situation B" part of the means-ends proposition and the search space "know-when." Van Aken links the application of a design exemplar in a specific time and/or place. For example, you need a certain design to build a suspension bridge over the Grand Canyon where the length of the opening, soil structure, weather, etc. impact the design. These features of the place where the bridge is built are representations of the entities of interest, or ISDT Constructs [2]. Gregor and Jones describe these to be the risk items, risky incidents, and resolution actions that impact the use of the risk management approach in the Iversen et al. [34] study. However, we also need to know how the changes in the state of the artifact impact the design or what degree of artifact change is encompassed by the theory that the design is based on. Gregor and Jones define this as the ISDT Artifact Mutability. This is similarly exemplified by Gregor and Jones in the Iversen et al. [34] study. In this study, they see that in ISDT Artifact Mutability, "suggestions for improving the approach are given for further work: one example is that parts of the approach could be packaged as a self-guiding computer-based system." For bridge building, this could be, e.g., for example how bridge carrying capacity alters after a certain length of time or how the bridge reacts to change of the temperature, or an earthquake.

Finally, we examine van Aken's "then do X" part of the means-ends proposition and the "know-how" search space [6]. These describe the processes for implementing the theory (either product or method) in specific contexts, i.e., ISDT Principles of implementation [2]. In bridge building, these would be the work processes, e.g., fixing the suspension of cables of the bridges. In Iversen et al. [34], Gregor and Jones depicted this as "it is stated that the approach requires facilitation by a facilitator experienced in risk management, SPI and running collaborative workshops." Similarly, we need to know how, e.g., the length of the suspension bridge impacts the design. For this, we need to have the underlying knowledge or theory from natural or social or design sciences that gives a basis and explanation for the design, or ISDT Justificatory knowledge [2]. Gregor and Jones give an example of this from the Iversen et al. [34] paper as follows: "the approach proposed is derived from other risk management approaches." Similarly, civil engineering provides an amplitude of theoretical knowledge about how the length of the suspension bridge should impact its design; for an example, see [39].

The shortcoming in using means-ends propositions for organizing ISDT is that although the purpose, solution, and context are articulated for the design, the structure does not help to identify unintended or surprising outcomes. Thus, it does not identify why a solution does or does not work, i.e., the "know-why" of

ISDT is not articulated because the proposition leaves ISDT Testable Propositions and ISDT Expository Instantiation outside the structure.

3.2   Design Patterns Proposition

The purpose of design patterns is to identify and develop the common elements of successful designs [29, 30, 40, 41]. Alexander, a student of city planning and design [29], originally defined design patterns this way: "The elements of this language are entities called patterns. Each pattern describes a problem that occurs over and over again in our environment, and then describes the core of the solution to that problem, in such a way that you can use this solution a million times over, without ever doing it the same way twice." Alexander's book described in detail more than 250 such design patterns that impact the design of cities. Later, the design proposition was especially applied in software engineering and object oriented programming [30, 40] where it has greatly impacted the way current programming languages address the reusability of software components.

We argue that there is a clear congruence between means-ends and design pattern propositions and consequently the ISDT components. This argument is threefold, in following we present a logical argument to tie means-ends proposition's three search spaces—"know-what," "know-when," and "know-how"—to three design pattern search spaces proposed by Gamma et al. [30]: (1) problem, (2) solution, and (3) consequences (cf. Table 1).

Gamma et al. [30] have defined the problem search space as what explains the problem and its context. Furthermore, according to Gamma et al. [30], this can be a specific design problem, such as how to represent algorithms or their structures as objects. Sometimes the problem will include a list of conditions for the pattern. This corresponds with van Aken's definition for search space "know-what," which we described in the earlier section. More specifically, van Aken addresses the need to understand a general prescription of a problem, which can be further translated to a specific problem at hand. Gregor and Jones's [2] definitions of ISDT Purpose and Scope and ISDT Principles of Form and Function support this argument. The first of these depicts the need to understand the problem at hand, whereas the second highlights the importance of understanding the structures, i.e., form and function, of the problems.

Second, Gamma et al. [30] argue for the need to have a solution search space, which describes the elements that make up the design as well as their relationships, responsibilities, and collaborations. According to them, the solution does not need to describe "a particular concrete design or implementation, because a pattern is like a template that can be applied in many different situations." This corresponds to the means-ends proposition definition of "know-when" search spaces, which highlights the need for understanding when to apply a design exemplar in a specific time and/or place. Gregor and Jones' ISDT Constructs and ISDT Justificatory Knowledge provide conceptual tools for how to operationalize this. More specifically, ISDT

Constructs represent the entities, whereas ISDT Justificatory Knowledge forms the basis for and explanation of the design [2].

Finally, Gamma et al. [30] present the consequences search space, which essentially deals with how to apply the patterns as well as the trade-offs of applying them. Gamma et al. [30] highlight that some of the consequences are "often unvoiced when we describe design decisions; they are critical for evaluating design alternatives and for understanding the costs and benefits of applying the pattern." We see that these are linked to van Aken's "know-how" search space, which we argue describes the processes for implementing the theory in specific contexts, i.e., ISDT Principles of implementation, and how the changes of the artifact impact the design, i.e., ISDT Artifact Mutability [2].

However, there are also some significant differences. Means-ends propositions do not emphasize outcomes, as design patterns do, for their consequences, i.e., articulate the trade-offs and outcomes of using a design pattern. However, Gamma et al. [30] argue that design patterns should be observed from sample code or implemented artifacts. Therefore, the consequence element of design patterns indicates a possible form, i.e., the ISDT Expository instantiation for an organizing device that also captures the question of why a solution does or does not work, i.e., "know-why." However, it does not depict how this would come about, especially when considering ISDT development and ISDT Testable Propositions. Consequently, we argue that design pattern propositions only offer limited support for the "know-why" search space, and further understanding is needed.

3.3 PICO/CIMO Propositions

PICO and CIMO are two very similar propositions put forward to organize research findings in their selected fields. The PICO proposition was developed as an organizing device for medicine and nursing to solve patient-specific clinical questions [31]. More specifically, PICO is used to articulate clinical questions in terms of four logical elements: problem/population (P), intervention (I), comparison (C), and outcome (O). Consequently, the focus of PICO is to select between available treatment alternatives for a specific patient. To aid in the selection, the problem (or population) for alternative interventions needs to be identified as well as available evidence of outcomes. Conversely, the CIMO proposition was developed as an organizing device to evaluate social policy interventions [33]. Later, CIMO was also applied to management research and organizational design [32], but also more recently to IS research [42]. The CIMO proposition distinguishes the problem context (C) clearly from the outcomes (O), making it explicit that a design may or may not work as intended. Furthermore, to aid in the improvement of designs, the intervention (I) is also distinguished from generative mechanisms (M). Separating the intervention from the mechanism that it triggers in different contexts provides the basis for dealing with intended and unintended outcomes of research. This separation also allows for interventions that work in different way through activating

Table 2 Organizing device for ISDT accumulation based on means-ends, design patterns, and PICO and CIMO propositions

ISDT search space	ISDT component	Supported by
"Know-What"	Purpose and scope	Means-ends, design pattern, and PICO/CIMO propositions
	Principles of form and function	
"Know-When"	Constructs	Means-ends, design pattern, and PICO/CIMO propositions
	Artifact mutability	
"Know-How"	Principles of implementation	Means-ends, design pattern, and CIMO proposition
	Justificatory knowledge	
"Know-Why"	Expository instantiation	Design pattern and CIMO proposition
	Testable propositions	

different mechanisms in different problem contexts. More specifically, Denyer et al. [32] defined the CIMO as follows:

- Context (C): The problem and its surrounding (external and internal) factors.
- Intervention (I): The interventions through which actors aim to influence outcomes.
- Mechanisms (M): The mechanism triggered in a certain context by an intervention.
- Outcome (O): The outcomes of an intervention, both intended and unintended.

Therefore, the CIMO and PICO propositions provide a possible way to organize ISDT, the question of knowing why, and the possibility of not knowing, which are not covered by the means-ends proposition (cf. Table 1) or the design patterns proposition (cf. Table 2). Falsification, or "not-knowing," is vital for knowledge accumulation as it is not only a mechanism for understanding gaps in theories but also identifying potential new research agendas [16, 28]. However, the weakness of using CIMO as an organizing device is that it is not unambiguous how ISDT components are to be mapped. In the next section, we develop a logical argument for how the ISDT components can be mapped to specific search spaces. Furthermore, we depict four different situations in which these search spaces can potentially interact with each other. In other words, in this section, we will propose an organizing device for incremental ISDT accumulation.

4 Proposed Organizing Device for Incremental ISDT Accumulation

Here, we build on the means-ends [6, 9] and design patterns [29, 30] propositions to provide a logical argument that links ISDT components to specific ISDT search spaces. We have labeled these search spaces as "know-when," "know-what,"

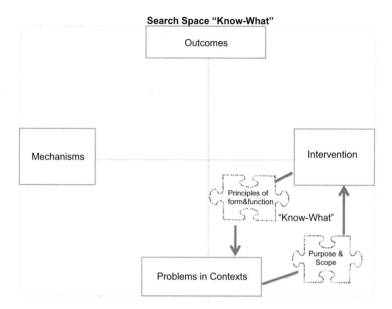

Fig. 1 ISDT search space "know-what"

"know-how," and "know-why." These are summarized in Table 2. We furthermore develop an argument of how PICO/CIMO propositions support the three above-mentioned search spaces but also the "know-why" search space that is not supported by the means-ends proposition and only partly supported by the design patterns proposition. More specifically, we propose a logical argument to link these search spaces together with the ISDT components identified by Gregor and Jones [2] to describe how ISDT accumulates not only within a DSR study but also potentially across different DSR studies. This organizing device is summarized in Table 2 and Figs. 1, 2, 3 and 4 and elaborated in the sections below.

4.1 Search Space: "Know-What"

This search space builds on the means-ends proposition "If you want A" and the design patterns proposition's definition of "Problem." We earlier argued that ISDT Purpose & Scope links to this specific search space based on the means-ends proposition illustrated in Table 1. Similarly, we stated that the design patterns proposition supports a similar connection when considering how "Problem" can be defined, and we depicted this in Table 1.

From the PICO/CIMO perspective, the connection to ISDT Purpose & Scope is clear. PICO and CIMO focused on understanding either problem (PICO) or context (CIMO). We use the term "Problems in Context" to summarize these two definitions. This directly links to how Gregor and Jones [2] have defined the ISDT Purpose &

Scope, i.e., what the artifact is for, its goals, scope, and/or boundaries and how these impact the ISDT and the problem definition for the study in a specific context.

Furthermore, we have argued that this ISDT component is linked to the search space "know-what" for ISDT Principles of Form & Function. This argumentation is based on the means-ends and design patterns propositions and the examples given in Table 1. ISDT principles of form and function depict how there is a need for an abstract "blueprint" or architecture that depicts the artifact, either product or method [2]. We see that this ISDT component is connected to PICO/CIMO's "intervention" element, and that when ISDT Purpose & Scope are fed in the search process through an intervention by the actors, this creates a new understanding of ISDT Principles of Form & Function that further explicates the problem(s) impacting the theory in a specific context. This interaction is illustrated in Fig. 1.

4.2   Search Space: "Know-When"

This search space builds on the means-ends proposition "and you believe you are in situation B" and design patterns proposition's definition of "solution." Based on the means-ends proposition, we argued earlier that ISDT constructs link to this specific search space. We depicted this link with the examples given in Table 1. Similarly, we showed that the design patterns proposition supports a similar connection when considering how "solution" can be defined, and we illustrated this relationship in Table 1.

Similarly, we see that there is a connection between PICO/CIMO and the definitions by the means-ends and design patterns propositions. The PICO proposition looks at how to select between available treatment alternatives for a specific patient, whereas CIMO looks at a problem and its surrounding environment as well as the external and internal factors that impact the problem. Therefore, both PICO and CIMO focus on understanding the representations of the entities of interest in a theory [2] or a solution in a certain context [30] or providing understanding when you are in a specific situation [9]. Consequently, we argue that ISDT construct is linked to problems in contexts and especially to the contextual internal and/or external factors depicted by the CIMO proposition.

Furthermore, the PICO and CIMO proposition, but CIMO in particular, can explain what happens when ISDT construct(s) is/are applied and the effect, which could potentially change the state of the artifact anticipated in the theory to a degree encompassed by the theory. This is how Gregor and Jones [2] define ISDT artifact mutability. This, in turn, feeds the creation of new knowledge and understanding of how mechanisms work as well as how ISDT constructs should be revised, renewed or changed. Potentially, the result may also indicate that the ISDT constructs do not apply, and they may be expunged from the ISDT. This interaction is illustrated in Fig. 2.

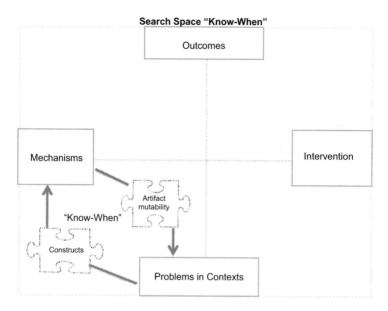

Fig. 2 ISDT search space "know-when"

4.3   Search Space: "Know-How"

The search space "know-how" builds on the means-ends proposition "then do X" and the design patterns proposition's definition of "consequences." Based on the means-ends proposition, we argued earlier that ISDT Principles of Implementation link to this specific search space. This argumentation is summarized in Table 1. We also argued that based on the design patterns proposition, there is a similar connection to the "consequences" of a study. This connection is shown in Table 1. Consequently, we see that this search space also links to CIMO's mechanisms, like the earlier search space discussed in the previous section. However, mechanisms can often also be hidden, just as the inner workings of a clock cannot be seen but drive the patterned movements of the hands [33]. Here Gregor and Jones's [2] definition of ISDT Principles of implementation is particularly helpful; it includes a description of processes for implementing a theory in specific contexts. We argue that this definition in part defines what a mechanism is in the context of ISDT.

Interestingly, this makes the connection to another element of the CIMO proposition and ISDT. Denyer et al. [32] have argued that mechanisms are triggered in a certain context. We have also argued that ISDT Justificatory Knowledge is linked to the search space "know-how" (cf. Table 1) based on the means-ends and design patterns propositions. We therefore argue that this interaction between the problem-in-context knowledge and the mechanisms that are triggered in certain contexts

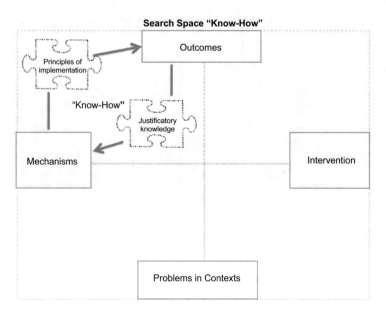

Fig. 3 ISDT search space "know-how"

resolves into understanding the underlying theory that gives a basis and explanation for a design [2]). In other words, the ISDT Principles of Implementation that are fed in the search process "know-how" trigger "outcomes" that in turn create new ISDT Justificatory Knowledge, which further explains the problems in contexts, and more specifically from the point of contextual internal and/or external factors impacting the theory. This interaction is depicted in Fig. 3.

4.4 Search Space: "Know-Why"

Our final search space, "know-why," is based on the CIMO and design patterns propositions. CIMO explicitly argues that a design may or may not work as intended [32, 33]. Similarly, the CIMO proposition makes a separation of interventions and mechanisms, which the PICO, means-end, and design patterns propositions do not. Linking these two CIMO elements together is argued to provide a platform for understanding the basis for dealing with intended and unintended outcomes of research. This is also supported by the design patterns proposition as described in below. Here, we also develop a logical argument as to why ISDT Expository Instantiation and ISDT Testable Propositions are linked to this search space.

First of all, the results of applying Iversen et al. [34] risk management approach in different contexts may have both intended and unintended results for the ISDT Expository Instantiation. In their case, the four variants of the approach are for each of the iterations of an action research cycle. Here, the design patterns proposition and the argument that design patterns should be studied from artifact implementations in order to understand the underlying patterns [30] are particularly helpful. Four variations provide a way to study the design patterns in the ISDT Expository Instantiation and the means to study both intended and unintended results. Furthermore, the test results of McKenna et al. [43] demonstrate how the artifact can assist in representing the theory not only for exposition but also for the purposes of testing the theory [2]. McKenna et al.'s [43] results also demonstrated how this can be operationalized in terms of both connecting the kernel theories to the design of the artifact and how the outcomes can impact the artifact itself, e.g., how the design should be altered for the next intervention so it can provide a better explanation of the theory.

Gregor and Jones [2] have defined ISDT Testable Propositions as the truth statements about design theory. These propositions can be considered to be heuristics or rules for a framework or model, e.g., what Iversen et al. [34] described in their work that develops a contingency model (see, e.g., [37, 38]). Gregor and Jones [2] claim that the ISDT Testable Proposition in this paper is the described risk management approach, which is adaptable to different organizational contexts, although it is seen as a generalizable approach. However, other kinds of testable propositions should also be considered. McKenna et al. [43] have described one such approach by investigating how different information service components affect consumers' potential adoption of such services. The paper first develops a conceptual model that uses the theory of organizational information services (TOIS) [37] and the unified theory of acceptance and use of technology (UTAUT) [44] as a basis. Furthermore, the ISDT Testable Propositions are developed based on an IS artifact that was developed based on the kernel theories. McKenna et al. [43] then proceed with a controlled experiment to test the propositions and the connection between the TOIS and the UTAUT. Finally, based on the results, McKenna et al. [43] then provided an argument that individual constructs can be linked to specific service components.

Consequently, we argue that both ISDT Expository Instantiation and ISDT Testable Propositions are linked to the CIMO proposition's "intervention" and "outcomes" elements, which in turn portray the "know-why" search space also partly supported by the design patterns proposition. Furthermore, we argue that the linkage between the ISDT components, and the CIMO proposition enables us to deal with intended and unintended outcomes of research [32] and further the understanding of why certain things happen when the artifact is tested or used. This interaction is illustrated in Fig. 4.

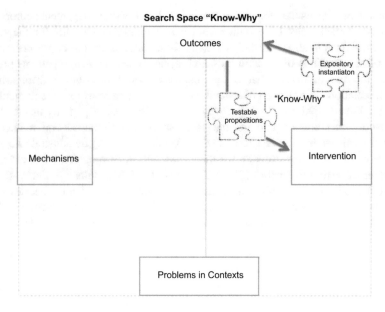

Fig. 4 ISDT search space "know-why"

5 Guiding Principles of Combination and Transfer Between Search Spaces

In the DSR literature, the received view is that theory development is done within a particular DSR study (see, e.g., [3, 24, 25]). What's more, none of the prominent DSR-specific methodologies seek to illustrate how theory is accumulated across studies, as originally argued by Walls et al. [4]. For this purpose, we have provided a logical argument of how to link ISDT components by Gregor and Jones [2] and the four depicted ISDT search spaces in the previous section (cf. Tables 1 and 2 and Figs. 1–4).

However, we see that this is not sufficient to fully understand how accumulation of ISDT components transpires iteratively and incrementally across ISDT search spaces within a DSR study, but also between DSR studies. To accomplish this, we propose that there are two guiding principles that support this: transfer and combination. In the following, we go through these two guiding principles, and these are illustrated in Fig. 5.

First, we argue that there are challenges related to the transfer of theoretical knowledge between ISDT search spaces. When different actors build and use a common theoretical knowledge base, i.e., ISDT, there is a need to link different types of ISDT search spaces. Furthermore, in the absence of an organizing device to facilitate communication between different actors, it is more difficult to find and use results from previous studies and contribute to the efforts of others. We see that the

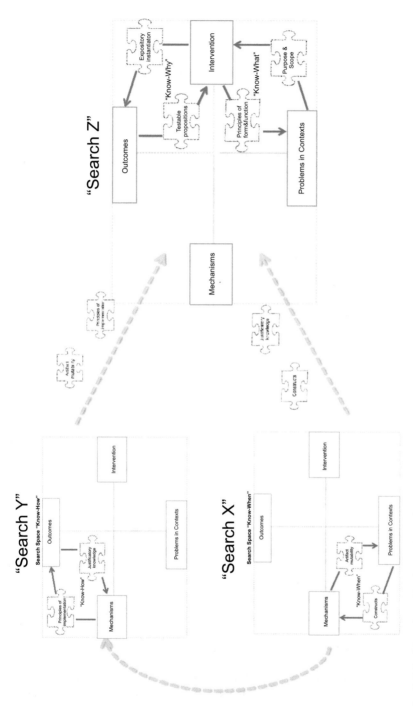

Fig. 5 Principles of combination and transfer between search spaces

value of an organizing device is especially important when there are interdependent DSR studies with dedicated ISDT search spaces [25]. Otherwise, the transfer of ISDT components is more reduced to the transfer of artifacts [13]. This guiding principle of transfer is illustrated in Fig. 5 as a transfer of theoretical knowledge from Search X to Search Y. The transfer is also conceptualized to happen between CIMO elements, e.g., from mechanisms to mechanisms (as illustrated in Fig. 5) following the pre-described interactions of the search spaces and ISDT components in Figs. 1–4.

However, access to an artifact is not sufficient for determining its use and potential purposes. To achieve satisfactory and progressive outcomes, we argue that a combination of the new and pre-existing is required for an ISDT search space, such as Search X or Y in Fig. 5 [13]. In addition, we see that the organizing device should also support the combination of ISDT components by different actors [11]. The findings of a DSR study are potentially a platform for further ISDT development by another actor [45]. This, in turn, enables increasing returns through a division of labor in ISDT accumulation [14]. Thus, the important factors of ISDT accumulation are in addition to the combination within a dedicated ISDT search space and the possibility to transfer and enable the combination of ISDT components across ISDT search spaces by different actors. This is illustrated in Fig. 5 as the combination and transfer of ISDT components from Searches X and Y to Search Z.

6   Discussion

Our paper proposes an organizing device to assist in structuring accumulation of ISDTs between different search processes [5], different actors, and studies (ref. Table 2). The framework facilitates the transfer and combination of ISDT components over a length of time across different studies (see Fig. 5). Our proposition rests on the notion that by representing an organizing device for incremental ISDT accumulation, it is easier to understand how different ISDT components are related to each other and how ISDT accumulation is realized in practice.

With this paper, we make the argument that in order to allow generalization across different projects, we should take a more refined view of the contribution the DSR studies make in terms of eight ISDT components proposed by Gregor and Jones [2], or alternatively, another definition of an ISDT if such is presented by the literature. Therefore, our organizing device proposes that in order for the findings of a DSR study, i.e., ISDT component or components, to be generalized, we need to consider if and how they could be re-applicable in other DSR projects or possibly in other research domains as well. The further the ISDT components are applicable from the point of their origin, i.e., the context of the specific DSR study, the stronger the type of generalization is. However, the reader should note that the different ISDT components are not equally easy to apply to other projects. That said, we also see that all types of ISDT components should be re-applicable in other DSR projects if an argument for generalization is made. In the exemplary study [46], the purpose and scope from previous research were transferred to define a new context, and a simulation was reused in developing a proof-of-concept for the novel aspects of ISDT. Thus, we should neither discount the value of ISDTs that remain context specific and never transferred or combined. These can be highly valuable to resolve particular problems faced by the practitioners or researchers. Thus, in our view, there can be ISDTs that have a varying degree of generalization, and we should embrace these both. More likely, there is a continuum of generalizability of ISDTs and we should embrace this in our DSR.

ISDT, being a theory, needs instantiations. However, we argue that ISDT does not require a fully implemented instantiation to contribute to research. In contrast to the literature requiring an artifact (of some kind) to be considered a DSR study [4, 19, 24, 47], our proposed organizing device allows for contributions to ISDT well before implemented instantiations. The question of the nature of the artifact is perhaps a more interesting issue than having a fully implemented instantiation. Similar to Lee et al. [48], we propose that instead of information technology artifact, we should instead treat IS artifact as the focus of DSR. According to Lee et al. [48], IS artifact is comprised of information artifact, technology artifact, and social artifact. To us, this is a compelling argument, and we see that this would make ISDT more relevant for the wider IS research community. Finally, other artifacts may be of interest. For example, services and operational processes are man-made artifacts that often include or are enabled by information technology.

Thus, whether DSR requires an instantiation our position is that due to the incremental nature of how ISDTs accumulate, it is not necessary that all DSR studies present an instantiation. This is directly related to the maturity of the ISDT. In our view, we can expect an instantiation for well-developed ISDTs, but not for initial and explorative designs. Consequently, we do not see that every DSR project should always go through all four presented search spaces. However, we also see that a project or research program can go through all search spaces several times until a well-developed ISDT is achieved.

In seeking to accumulate ISDT, we need to tackle both the generalization and specialization issues related to ISDT development. As long as problem models, solution models, explanation models and their relations do not refer to common and cross-project reference hierarchies, there will be incompatible and conflicting perceptions of what are general concepts and what are instances so that generalizations can only be made within the context of a single DSR project. Therefore, there are likely to be challenges in terms of the intended aim of our organizing device in supporting ISDT accumulation across different projects. This is a serious concern inhibiting ISDT accumulation, but it is linked not only to our proposed organizing device but to ISDTs in general.

7 Conclusions and Future Research

We see that further research is needed to fully develop the proposed use of the organizing device. At the moment, our framework is based on iterations within a search space. We see that more research is needed to determine whether this is a sound and feasible tactic, or simply reflects a preference for a logical division of ISDT development. Previous research by Goldenberg [49] found evidence that the best outcomes from new combinations in product innovations were achieved with focused searches of either different contexts or designs. Thus, further studies are needed to understand the possible combinations between different studies. It would also be fascinating to understand how this varies between different domains of research and possibly also with artifact types. We should also venture to other fields of design. Given the recent interest in service design and engineering [50], it would be highly interesting to see whether the wider service research community would consider the approach to be feasible for conducting research in its field. Similarly, we feel that the current evidence-based management research community would consider our approach interesting. Our framework can similarly be applied to studies that aim to develop new management approaches and methods [51]. Correspondingly, engineering communities could also potentially find our research valuable for structuring their own research and providing the means to manifest the underlying theories as designs.

References

1. Gregor, S.: The nature of theory in information systems. MIS Q. **30**(3), 611–642 (2006)
2. Gregor, S., Jones, D.: The anatomy of a design theory. J. Assoc. Inf. Syst. **8**(5), 312–335 (2007)
3. Nunamaker, J.F., Chen, M., Purdin, T.D.M.: Systems development in information systems research. J. Manag. Inf. Syst. **7**(3), 89–106 (1991)
4. Walls, J.G., Widmeyer, G.R., El Sawy, O.A.: Building an information system design theory for vigilant EIS. Inf. Syst. Res. **3**(1), 36–59 (1992)
5. Vom Brocke, J., Winter, R., Hevner, A., Maedche, A.: Special Issue Editorial–Accumulation and evolution of design knowledge in design science research: a journey through time and space. J. Assoc. Inf. Syst. **21**(3), 520–544 (2020)
6. Aken, J.E.V.: Management research based on the paradigm of the design sciences: the quest for field-tested and grounded technological rules. J. Manag. Stud. **41**(2), 219–246 (2004)
7. Briner, R.B., Denyer, D., Rousseau, D.M.: Evidence-based management: concept cleanup time? Acad. Manag. Perspect. **23**(4), 19–32 (2009)
8. Feldman, D.H., Csikszentmihalyi, M., Gardner, H.: Changing the World: A Framework for the Study of Creativity. Praeger Publishers/Greenwood Publishing Group (1994)
9. Simon, H.A.: The Sciences of the Artificial. (1969)
10. Klahr, D., Simon, H.A.: Studies of scientific discovery: complementary approaches and convergent findings. Psychol. Bull. **125**(5), 524 (1999)
11. Allen, D.K., Colligan, D., Finnie, A., Kern, T.: Trust, power and interorganizational information systems: the case of the electronic trading community TransLease. Inf. Syst. J. **10**(1), 21–40 (2000)
12. Kuhn, T.S.: The Structure of Scientific Revolutions. University of Chicago press (2012)
13. Arthur, W.B.: The Nature of Technology: What It Is and How It Evolves. Simon and Schuster (2009)
14. De Langhe, R.: The division of labour in science: the tradeoff between specialisation and diversity. J. Econ. Methodol. **17**(1), 37–51 (2010)

15. Gregor, S.: Building theory in the sciences of the artificial. Paper presented at the Proceedings of the 4th International Conference on Design Science Research in Information Systems and Technology (2009)
16. Colquitt, J.A., Zapata-Phelan, C.P.: Trends in theory building and theory testing: a five-decade study of the Academy of Management Journal. Acad. Manag. J. **50**(6), 1281 (2007)
17. Gregor, S., Hevner, A.R.: Positioning and presenting design science research for maximum impact. MIS Q. **37**(2) (2013)
18. Baskerville, R., Vaishnavi, V.: Pre-theory design frameworks and design theorizing. Paper presented at the 49th Hawaii International Conference on System Sciences, Kauai (2016)
19. Hevner, A.R., March, S.T., Park, J.: Design research in information systems research. MIS Q. **28**(1), 75–105 (2004)
20. Kuechler, W., Vaishnavi, V.: On theory development in design science research: anatomy of a research project. Eur. J. Inf. Syst. **17**(5), 489–504 (2008)
21. Pries-Heje, J., Baskerville, R.: The design theory nexus. MIS Q. **32**(4), 731–755 (2008)
22. Kuechler, W., Vaishnavi, V.: A framework for theory development in design science research: multiple perspectives. J. Assoc. Inf. Syst. **13**(6) (2012)
23. Merton, R.K.: Social Theory and Social Structure. Simon and Schuster (1968)
24. Peffers, K., Tuunanen, T., Rothenberger, M., Chatterjee, S.: A design science research methodology for information systems research. J. Manag. Inf. Syst. **24**(3), 45–78 (2007)
25. Sein, M.K., Henfridsson, O., Purao, S., Rossi, M., Lindgren, R.: Action design research. MIS Q. **35**(1) (2011)
26. Bunge, M.: Scientific Research, I-II. Springer, Berlin (1967)
27. Niiniluoto, I.: The aim and structure of applied research. Erkenntnis. **38**(1), 1–21 (1993)
28. Popper, K.R.: The logic of scientific discovery. (1959)
29. Alexander, C., Ishikawa, S., Silverstein, M.: A Pattern Language: Towns, Buildings, Construction, vol. 2. Oxford University Press. (1977)
30. Gamma, E., Helm, R., Johnson, R., Vlissides, J.: Design Patterns: Elements of Reusable Object-Oriented Software. Pearson Education (1994)
31. Sackett, D.L., Rosenberg, W.M., Gray, J., Haynes, R.B., Richardson, W.S.: Evidence based medicine: what it is and what it isn't. BMJ Br. Med. J. **312**(7023), 71 (1996) http://www.ncbi.nlm.nih.gov/pmc/articles/PMC2349778/pdf/bmj00524-0009.pdf
32. Denyer, D., Tranfield, D., Van Aken, J.E.: Developing design propositions through research synthesis. Organ. Stud. **29**(3), 393–413 (2008)
33. Pawson, R., Tilley, N.: Realistic Evaluation. Sage (1997)
34. Iversen, J.H., Mathiassen, L., Nielsen, P.A.: Managing risk in software process improvement: an action research approach. MIS Q. **28**(3), 395–433 (2004)
35. Holmström, J., Ketokivi, M., Hameri, A.P.: Bridging practice and theory: a design science approach. Decis. Sci. **40**(1), 65–87 (2009)
36. Mahoney, J.T., Sanchez, R.: Building new management theory by integrating processes and products of thought. J. Manag. Inq. **13**(1), 34–47 (2004)
37. Mathiassen, L., Saarinen, T., Tuunanen, T., Rossi, M.: A contingency model for requirements development. J. Assoc. Inf. Syst. **8**(11), 569–597 (2007)
38. Weill, P., Olson, M.H.: An assessment of the contingency theory of management information systems. J. Manag. Inf. Syst., 59–85 (1989)
39. Timoshenko, S.P.: Theory of suspension bridges. J. Franklin Inst. **235**(3), 213–238 (1943) http://www.sciencedirect.com/science/article/pii/S0016003243906271
40. Lea, D.: Christopher Alexander: an introduction for object-oriented designers. ACM SIGSOFT Softw. Eng. Notes. **19**(1), 39–46 (1994)
41. Leitner, H.: Pattern Theory: Introduction and Perspectives on the Tracks of Christopher Alexander. CyberSpace, Graz (2015)
42. Henfridsson, O., Bygstad, B.: The generative mechanisms of digital infrastructure evolution. MIS Q. **37**(3), 896–931 (2013)

43. McKenna, B., Tuunanen, T., Gardner, L.: Consumers' adoption of information services. Inf. Manag. **50**(5), 248–257 (2013) http://www.sciencedirect.com/science/article/pii/ S0378720613000323
44. Venkatesh, V., Morris, M.G., Davis, G., Davis, F.: User acceptance of information technology: toward a unified view. MIS Q. **27**(3), 425–278 (2003)
45. Eisenmann, T., Parker, G., Van Alstyne, M.W.: Strategies for two-sided markets. Harv. Bus. Rev. **October**, 92–101 (2006)
46. Arnäs, P.O., Holmström, J., Kalantari, J.: In-transit services and hybrid shipment control: the use of smart goods in transportation networks. Transport. Res. C Emerg. Technol. **36**, 231–244 (2013)
47. March, S.T., Smith, G.F.: Design and natural science research on information technology. Decis. Support. Syst. **15**(4), 251–266 (1995)
48. Lee, A.S., Thomas, M., Baskerville, R.L.: Going back to basics in design science: from the information technology artifact to the information systems artifact. Inf. Syst. J. **25**(1), 5–21 (2015)
49. Goldenberg, J., Lehmann, D.R., Mazursky, D.: The idea itself and the circumstances of its emergence as predictors of new product success. Manag. Sci. **47**(1), 69–84 (2001)
50. Ostrom, A.L., Bitner, M.J., Brown, S.W., Burkhard, K.A., Goul, M., Smith-Daniels, V., et al.: Moving forward and making a difference: research priorities for the science of service. J. Serv. Res. **13**(1), 4–36 (2010)
51. Kaplan, R.S.: Innovation action research: creating new management theory and practice. J. Manag. Account. Res. **10**, 89–118 (1998)

Assessing the Temporal Validity of Design Knowledge

Jannis Beese

Abstract Design science research (DSR) aims to generate generalizable knowledge on how to design effective solutions to real-world problems. In some instances, however, previously evaluated design knowledge may no longer be suitable to build effective solutions for current-day problems. This paper therefore proposes a framework to assess the temporal validity of extant design knowledge. By analysing inferences made in the creation of design knowledge, I identify four preconditions that must be met to apply previously evaluated designs in a similar way to more recent problem instances. Furthermore, specific checks are proposed to guide practitioners and researchers in their verification of previously evaluated design knowledge. The proposed framework and checks support the reuse of previous design knowledge to solve new problem instances and complement ongoing efforts in the scientific community to facilitate the cumulative collection of design knowledge over time.

Keywords Design science research · Cumulative knowledge · Temporal validity

1 Introduction

Scientific objectivity refers to a fundamental "*characteristic of scientific claims, methods and results, [. . .expressing] the idea that the claims, methods and results of science are not, or should not be influenced by particular perspectives, value commitments, community bias or personal interests*" [1]. This goal of achieving a scientifically objective truth also permeates discussions of research paradigms for behavioral science in the Information Systems (IS) discipline [2]. An accepted outcome of a behavioral IS research paper constitutes, for example, the proposition and validation of a generic cause-effect relation. Genericity thereby refers to the

J. Beese (✉)
Institute of Information Management, University of St. Gallen, St. Gallen, Switzerland
e-mail: jannis.beese@unisg.ch

© The Author(s), under exclusive license to Springer Nature Switzerland AG 2021
S. Aier et al. (eds.), *Engineering the Transformation of the Enterprise*,
https://doi.org/10.1007/978-3-030-84655-8_11

invariance of the proposed cause-effect relation to the specific research context, i.e. it should be reasonably argued that the same cause-effect relation will also apply to other, not yet observed situations that are within the given research limitations.

In contrast to this focus on the truth of a general cause-effect relation in natural and social sciences, the Design Science Research (DSR) paradigm in IS emphasizes utility, i.e. the construction, evaluation, and (situated) instrumentalization of generic means-ends relations in the design of real-world artefacts [3, 4]. Simply stated, the overall goal of DSR is to gain knowledge on how to design effective solutions to real-world problems [4, 5]. In this context, again, genericity refers to the invariance of a purposefully constructed means-ends relation, i.e. the researcher needs to provide arguments that the same means will lead to the same ends in other, not yet observed situations. A generic evaluation with regard to utility, however, would then also depend on an objective understanding of what constitutes desirable ends to achieve. Therefore, contrary to the time-invariant scientific objectivity in the natural sciences, design science has a fundamentally subjective teleology, targeting pre-scriptive—and thereby ultimately moral—"ends", which may be influenced by temporally instable individual perspectives, value commitments, personal interests, and community bias [6].

Consequently, efforts within the DSR community to support the cumulative collection of design knowledge over time (e.g. [7]) need to consider (and continuously re-evaluate) the temporal validity of the individual contributions. To facilitate such an accumulation of design knowledge, this essay discusses several pre-conditions that need to be met in order to successfully apply previously evaluated designs in a similar way to more recent problem instances. Stated concisely, I aim to understand *under which circumstances existing design knowledge can be applied to build effective artefacts that solve current problems.*

In particular, I discuss four preconditions that must be fulfilled so that a purposefully designed artefact, which has worked well in the past, will similarly work well for current problem instances:

1. *Scientific reproducibility*: The originally identified cause-effect relation must still hold true.
2. *Suitable manipulation*: The employed means must still be suitable to manipulate the targeted causal constructs (i.e. the independent variables of the scientific cause-effect relation).
3. *Invariant normativity*: The general perception on what constitutes desirable ends must be unchanged, so that the purpose of the original artefact is still valid.
4. *Suitable instantiation*: Reconstructing the original artefact must still be feasible, e.g. similar resources or infrastructure must be available and not be replaced by new, fundamentally different entities.

The application of these pre-conditions have a clear practical contribution: If a problem that has been solved previously re-occurs in a similar way at a different point in time, can one expect the old design knowledge that has been gained from the previous solution to still apply for building a new solution? Can one simply re-build the old solution, or are further investigations and adaptations required? The identified preconditions provide a simple framework to check the central inferences that were made in the creation and application of design knowledge.

From a scientific perspective, this framework complements efforts to support DSR researchers in better managing the already accumulated design knowledge in IS. We should not only strive to continuously add to the overall body of design knowledge, but also to carefully curate and clean up existing knowledge. While outdated and no longer feasible design knowledge and related designs can still provide interesting insights, this knowledge should be clearly identifiable as outdated. In particular, both researchers and practitioners who are looking for solutions, but are not very familiar with the existing body of knowledge, should be able to distinguish currently working solution designs and related design knowledge from outdated information.

In the following, I first review existing models on inferences in DSR and on the accumulation of design knowledge over time. Then, I discuss the temporal validity of inferences in DSR, leading to the identification of the four identified preconditions. And finally, I discuss the usage and implications of these preconditions in more detail.

2   Related Literature and Positioning

Recently, vom Brocke et al. [7] published a special issue on the *Accumulation and Evolution of Knowledge in Design Science Research* in the Journal of the AIS. Their editorial [7] provides an excellent overview on the current state of the art in this area.

The first central distinction made by vom Brocke et al. [7] splits design knowledge into three separate aspects. Knowledge in the *problem space* covers information about the problem to be solved, including contextual aspects (such as descriptions of key stakeholders) and goodness criteria (i.e. how we know that the problem has been adequately solved) [8]. Notably, the authors highlight that problem spaces are neither spatially nor temporally invariant, since, for example, currently highly relevant problems might not be nearly as relevant in the next year [7, 9].

Knowledge in the *solution space* encompasses both the key results of DSR as well as related activities. Key results come in various forms, for example as designed artefacts in the form of constructs, algorithms, methods, and other actual instantiations [10–12], or as supporting design principles and overarching design theories [13]. Related activities cover a description of the process that was used to identify and construct the result, e.g. explaining why a specific artefact is considered to be an appropriate candidate in the solution space.

Finally, *evaluation* refers to knowledge and related data that connects problems and solutions. Giving sufficient evidence on the extent to which a proposed solution actually solves a targeted problem is essential for DSR and therefore has thoroughly been investigated in extant research [10, 14–16].

2.1   Linking Design Knowledge and Explanatory Knowledge

In the creation of design knowledge, researchers usually rely on explanatory knowledge that allows them to describe, analyze, understand, and predict cause-effect relations in the targeted research context [17]. I use the term "explanatory knowledge"—in contrast to Ω-knowledge, which is employed by vom Brocke et al. [7]—to highlight the focus on cases where there is an investigated cause-effect relation. This does not include, for example, purely descriptive research without any observed relations.

There is a clear relation between the scientific investigation of cause-effect relations and DSR investigations of means-ends relations, in that the means are expected to purposefully manipulate causal variables that contribute to specific effects, which in turn show a normative correspondence to the desired ends. Starting with such explanatory knowledge about a cause-effect relation, investigators within a design research project rely on this explanatory knowledge to identify and construct prescriptive means-end relations that support the design of the targeted artefacts (see Fig. 1).

Essentially, the translation between explanatory knowledge and design knowledge reduces the development of an effective artefact to a search for a suitable means-ends relation, which (i) allows the development of specific means that are effective in manipulating the causal constructs of the cause-effect relation, and which (ii) has sufficient evidence that the evoked effects correspond to the targeted ends (e.g. fulfill identified goodness criteria). In consequence, however, the validity of design knowledge hinges, to some extent, on the validity of the underlying cause-effect relations.

2.2   Generalizability and Reliability of Design Knowledge

Vom Brocke et al. [7] use the term λ-knowledge to refer to design knowledge, i.e. knowledge about the construction of specific design entities (e.g. solution artefacts or design processes) or overarching design theories. They suggest that accumulated design knowledge (in the course of a single DSR project or spanning multiple projects) should be described along the three dimensions: *Projectability* (i.e. the extent to which design knowledge remains invariant to changes in the

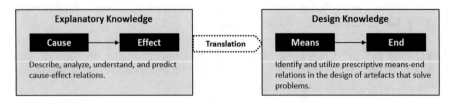

Fig. 1 Link between explanatory knowledge and design knowledge

problem space), *fitness* (i.e. the extent to which design knowledge remains invariant to changes in the solution space), and the confidence in the *evaluation* (i.e. the mapping between problem and solution space). So essentially, the terms *projectability* and *fitness* correspond to the generalizability of design knowledge in the problem and solution space respectively (what is the set of problem and solution instances that this knowledge applies to?), and *confidence* refers to the reliability of the design knowledge (if we have problems and solutions within the described scope, how confident are we that an application of the solution will fulfill the identified goodness criteria?) [7, 10].

3   Analysis of the Temporal Validity of Inferences in DSR

The scope of the analysis in the subsequent section now focuses on how this confidence may change over time. In this scenario we assume that we have a relevant current problem and we have already identified previous design knowledge, which claims to cover this problem in its problem space. We also assume that this design knowledge was generated and evaluated rigorously, so that at the time the research was conducted, solutions in the solution space really solved the problems in the problem space with reasonable confidence [10]. The question of whether this design knowledge will help us to solve our current problem then can be answered by checking if the original inferences made in the development of the design knowledge still hold true today.

To facilitate this analysis, Fig. 2 connects the previously discussed cause-effect relations and means-ends relations with the design of instantiated artefacts in DSR [18].

Starting with explanatory knowledge about a cause-effect relation, we have some evidence that certain constructs (causes/independent variables) have at least a partially significant causal contribution to observable effects (dependent variables). This cause-effect relation has been proven through previous studies. Consequently, we believe in its scientific reproducibility, i.e. if we manage to manipulate the causal constructs in our current problem context a suitable way, we can induce specific changes in the effect constructs (see 1, *Scientific reproducibility* in Fig. 2).

Design knowledge in IS is often grounded in cause-effect relations that were observed in social settings (including, for example, explanatory knowledge about user's perceptions and intentions) [19]. Consequently, the validity of such cause-effect relations is tied to the social context, which may change over time. How technology is perceived and used might change over time, and fundamental break-throughs (for example the increased modern-day interconnectivity, the prevalence of mobile devices, or future developments in the area of AI/machine learning) might fundamentally change previously observed cause-effect relations in this context [6]. Therefore, one step in the evaluation of previous design knowledge should be to consider the scientific reproducibility of the underlying cause-effect relations in current times. Any doubts that question whether purposeful changes in the causal

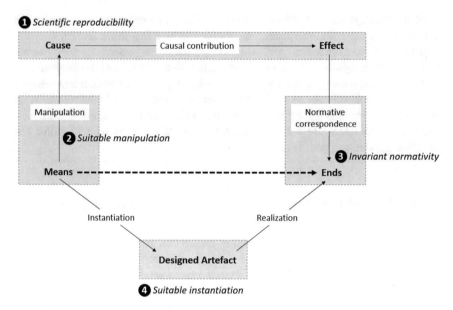

Fig. 2 Link between explanatory knowledge and design knowledge

constructs still evoke the expected changes in the effect constructs could translate into concerns that the means will not effectively achieve the desired ends.

Additionally, we have some design knowledge about potential ways to effectively manipulate the causal constructs [13, 19]. In other words, we know that previously specific means were identified to be suitable manipulations that affect the potentially abstract causal constructs in a targeted way. If we want to re-apply the previous design knowledge to our new problem instance, we therefore assume that this manipulation is still suitable in the sense that it will still evoke similar changes in the causal constructs of the cause-effect relation (see 2, *Suitable manipulation* in Fig. 2).

This concern becomes particularly important abstract social constructs are targeted, such as employing humor to achieve higher customer engagement in online interactions. Whether such means (e.g. humor) are suitable to effectively manipulate the targeted construct (e.g. customer engagement) can change over time and might even lead to adverse effects. Similarly, we might observe changes in the causal constructs over time even without any interactions (such as fears and resilience against new technologies), so that some parts of an originally highly effective manipulation may not be necessary anymore.

Regarding the other side of the cause-effect relation, we have previously established that the changes in the effect constructs have a normative correspondence to some desirable ends. Such a correspondence may, for example, be established by clearly linking the effect constructs to the goodness criteria that were identified in the analysis of the problem space. For a successful re-application of a previous design, we need to confirm that this normative correspondence has remained invariant (see 3, *Invariant normativity* in Fig. 2). This entails both, invariance of the ends in themselves (i.e. what used to be desirable in the past still is considered to be desirable today), as well as their correspondence to the effect constructs (i.e. the effect constructs still provide a valid description of the ends).

Finally, we need to consider the actual instantiation of an artefact. Such instantiations are naturally tied to a specific context, including a specific point in time [18]. If we want to directly re-employ such designs (i.e. re-build old solutions), we need to ensure that these are still suitable instantiations at present (see 4, *Suitable instantiation* in Fig. 2). In particular this requires ensuring that we still have access to the necessary resources to re-instantiate old designs and that these artefacts are still interpreted and used in a similar way by affected stakeholders. For example, specific infrastructure that was employed in the design of old artefacts might no longer be readily available or might have been replaced with new and fundamentally different components.

3.1 Checks and Practical Recommendations

Following the preceding analysis of the temporal validity of inferences made in DSR projects, we now aim to reframe this analysis as a list of pre-conditions and checks that facilitate the application of design knowledge to new problem instances. Table 1 provides an overview of the identified preconditions and exemplary checks.

First, one should identify the sources used to argue for any cause-effect relations that were employed in the design of the artefact. In particular psychology and the

Table 1 Preconditions and recommended checks for the application of old design knowledge

Precondition	Description	Exemplary checks
Scientific reproducibility	The original explanatory cause-effect relation still needs to be reliable.	• How old is the original research on the employed cause-effect relations? • Are there any updates, contrasting findings, or other advances?
Suitable manipulation	The original means must still be suitable to manipulate the causal constructs.	• Are the original means intuitive or do they feel out-of-place? • Do the original means target seemingly unimportant aspects of the problem?
Normative correspondence	The ends remained largely unchanged and still correspond to the effect constructs.	• Are the originally formulated goals still valid? • Would you still measure success in the same way?
Suitable instantiation	It is still feasible to re-construct previous instantiations.	• Is any specific technology or infrastructure outdated? • Can you think of any fundamentally different newer technologies that might provide a superior approach?

social sciences have recently faced what some term a "reproducibility crisis" [20], indicating that many published cause-effect relations could not be reproduced with comparable effect sizes [21]. Consequently, it would be wise to note the age of the original publications and to check if there have been any more recent confirmations, contradictions, or other related advances.

Second, one should confirm that the original means are still suitable to manipulate the targeted causal constructs [4]. This essentially corresponds to checking whether the original argument for choosing exactly these means still holds true today. Potentially, even a simple intuitive check of the means may help to see if these feel currently outdated. Furthermore, one should check that all targets of the manipulation are valid by confirming that all aspects of the originally identified problem are still present.

Third, one should confirm that there was no major shift in what constitutes desirable ends and that these ends still correspond to the identified effect constructs. Regarding the former, this includes checking that the originally identified goals and success criteria are still relevant and applicable. More concisely: If you were to evaluate the success of your artefact, would you still apply the same measures?

Fourth, one needs to evaluate whether it is still feasible to re-construct a previous instantiation. In particular, this includes checking if any specific technology or infrastructure, which was essential for the previous instantiation, is still relevant and available today. Furthermore, one should investigate if any of the employed technologies (e.g. statistical models, algorithms, or specific software) are still the state of the art, or if they have been replaced by any fundamentally different newer technologies that might provide a superior approach.

Finally, we note that the non-fulfillment of any pre-condition does not imply that the artefact must not work in current-day problem instances. For example, even though the employed cause-effect relation might not be statistically reliable, you might still be in a particular setting where your manipulation just by chance corresponds with an increase in the effect construct. Consequently, these are pre-conditions that allow you to reliably reuse extant design knowledge without a new evaluation to protect against random chance. Furthermore, even if one of the pre-conditions is not fulfilled, this framework allows for a more targeted re-design and re-evaluation, which only focusses on the identified defects and uncertainties.

4 Discussion and Limitations

The analysis of the temporal validity of inferences in the creation of design knowledge (see Fig. 2) in combination with the identified pre-conditions and checks for employing previous design knowledge to solve new problem instances (see Table 1) provides a practical tool that is meant to facilitate the application of design knowledge. Most fundamentally, this framework helps to answer the question of whether an old solution can simply be re-used to solve a known problem, which has occurred before and which is now occurring again. The preceding analysis shows that the answer to this question is by no means trivial, since a typical DSR project makes various inferences in the creation of design knowledge and the instantiation of effective solution artefacts [19]. Since the temporal invariance of these inferences is not guaranteed, simply reusing old solutions for recurring problems is by no means guaranteed to work. The checks in Table 1 are meant to provide a simple list of things that could go wrong, or conversely, a list of preconditions that, if met, enable the naïve reuse of an old solution.

Regarding the application of the proposed framework in DSR itself, a simple application can be found in supporting what vom Brocke et al. [7] refer to as *Mode 5* and *Mode 6* design knowledge contributions, i.e. contributions that build on and complement extant designs. Mode 5 contributions thereby describe the application of previously effective designs to inform novel designs for new problem instances. Mode 6 contributions comprise complementing designs that build on and further support existing solutions. In both situations, it is essential to understand the extent to which the extant design knowledge still reliably supports the development of solution artefacts for current problem instances.

Even more generally, it might also be valuable to continuously and systematically re-evaluate and comment on extant design knowledge. Most DSR studies carefully review related literature on related designs. The scholars who conduct such reviews should not be afraid to doubt the current-day validity of old design knowledge. In quickly and continuously changing contexts (such as information systems research) the expectation should be that knowledge may change over time and become outdated (which can happen for multiple reasons, as our discussion has indicated). Considering the growth and the vast amount of design knowledge that is already accessible today, not only efforts that add to this body of knowledge should be valued, but also efforts that check, curate, and revise already existing knowledge.

Regarding limitations, the application of the proposed framework and the checks depends on not only rigorously conducted, but also thoroughly reported DSR. I therefore would like to highlight the importance of the design knowledge principles proposed by vom Brocke et al. [7] in this context. Design researchers must clearly describe the problem- and solution spaces of their design knowledge (*Positioning*). Otherwise, we are, for example, not able to check whether a new problem instance really falls into the analyzed problem space, so that we can try to reuse an old solution. Furthermore, researchers must be transparent with regard to their use of prior (explanatory and design) knowledge (*Grounding*), so that we can re-check the underlying assumptions about cause-effect relations. Finally, DSR studies should clearly describe the evolution of the design process (*Aligning*) and how they aim to advance prior design knowledge (*Advancing*), both of which facilitate our understanding of why specific decisions were made and whether the underlying logic still holds true today.

Furthermore, we also note that the proposed framework and the checks do not readily apply to all kinds of design knowledge. Detailed descriptions of problem situations, for example, also provide valuable design knowledge, since they may facilitate subsequent DSR projects. However, the proposed framework does not apply, since no explanatory cause-effect relation is employed. Similarly, some parts of the framework might not apply in specific cases. Some design research with a technical focus (for example descriptions of specific algorithms) has no social components and thus remains invariant over time, so that some of the proposed checks are not readily applicable.

References

1. Reiss, J., Sprenger, J.: Scientific objectivity. In: The Stanford Encyclopedia of Philosophy, Winter 2020 edn. Stanford University (2020)
2. Hassan, N.R., Mingers, J.: Reinterpreting the Kuhnian paradigm in information systems. J. Assoc. Inf. Syst. **19**(7) (2018)
3. Goldkuhl, G.: Pragmatism vs interpretivism in qualitative information systems research. Eur. J. Inf. Syst. **21**(2), 135–146 (2012)
4. Winter, R.: Design science research in Europe. Eur. J. Inf. Syst. **17**(5), 470–475 (2008)
5. Holmström, J., Ketokivi, M., Hameri, A.-P.: Bridging practice and theory: a design science approach. Decis. Sci. **40**(1), 65–87 (2009)
6. Lawrence, T.B., Winn, M.I., Jennings, P.D.: The temporal dynamics of institutionalization. Acad. Manag. Rev. **26**(4), 624–644 (2001)
7. vom Brocke, J., Winter, R., Hevner, A.R., Maedche, A.: Accumulation and evolution of design knowledge in design science research – a journey through time and space. J. Assoc. Inf. Syst. (2020) forthcoming
8. Venable, J.R., Pries-Heje, J., Baskerville, R.L.: A comprehensive framework for evaluation in design science research. In: Peffers, K., Rothenberger, M., Kuechler, B. (eds.) 7th International Conference on Design Science Research in Information Systems and Technology (DESRIST 2012), Las Vegas, NV, vol. 7286, pp. 423–438 (2012)
9. Baskerville, R.L., Kaul, M., Storey, V.C.: Genres of inquiry in design-science research: justification and evaluation of knowledge production. MIS Q. **39**(3), 541–564 (2015)
10. Hevner, A.R., March, S.T., Park, J., Ram, S.: Design science in information systems research. MIS Q. **28**(1), 75–105 (2004)
11. March, S.T., Smith, G.F.: Design and natural science research on information technology. Decis. Support Syst. **15**(4), 251–266 (1995)
12. Offermann, P., Blom, S., Schönherr, M., Bub, U.: Artifact types in information systems design science – a literature review. In: Winter, R., Zhao, J.L., Aier, S. (eds.) 5th International Conference on Design Science Research in Information Systems and Technology (DESRIST 2010). St. Gallen (2010)
13. Gregor, S., Hevner, A.R.: Positioning and presenting design science research for maximum impact. MIS Q. **37**(2), 337–355 (2013)
14. Abraham, R., Aier, S., Winter, R.: Fail Early, Fail Often: Towards Coherent Feedback Loops in Design Science Research Evaluation. 35th International Conference on Information Systems (ICIS 2014), Auckland, New Zealand. Association for Information Sytems (2014)
15. Prat, N., Comyn-Wattiau, I., Akoka, J.: A taxonomy of evaluation methods for information systems artifacts. J. Manag. Inf. Syst. **32**(3), 229–267 (2015)
16. Venable, J.R., Pries-Heje, J., Baskerville, R.: FEDS: a framework for evaluation in design science research. Eur. J. Inf. Syst. **25**(1), 77–89 (2016)
17. Winter, R., Albani, A.: Restructuring the design science research knowledge base – a one-cycle view of design science research and its consequences for understanding organizational design problems. In: Baskerville, R., de Marco, M., Spagnoletti, P. (eds.) Designing organizational systems: an interdisciplinary discourse, 1st edn, pp. 63–81. Springer (2013)

18. Lukyanenko, R., Evermann, J., Parsons, J.: Instantiation Validity in IS Design Research, pp. 321–328. Cham (2014)
19. Drechsler, A., Hevner, A.R.: Utilizing, producing, and contributing design knowledge in DSR projects. In: Chatterjee, S. (ed.) DESRIST 2018, Chennai LNCS, vol. 10844, pp. 82–97 (2018)
20. Baker, M.: 1,500 scientists lift the lid on reproducibility. Nature. **533**, 452–454 (2016)
21. Collaboration, O.S.: Estimating the reproducibility of psychological science. Science. **349** (6251), aac4716 (2015)

Pedagogy for Doctoral Seminars in Design Science Research

Alan R. Hevner

Abstract Doctoral instruction in design science research (DSR) must surpass the learning of fundamental concepts and processes. Doctoral students should be prepared to perform cutting edge research that extends prescriptive knowledge bases of design artifacts and design theories. This chapter proposes a two-dimensional pedagogy of research challenges and fields of information systems (IS) research with a robust focus on doctoral education. Experiences with a pilot course using this novel instructional approach are discussed.

Keywords Design science research · Doctoral education · Research challenges · Research fields · Design artifacts · Design theories · Evaluation · Problem space · Solution space

1 Introduction

The Design Science Research (DSR) paradigm has its roots in the sciences and engineering of the artificial [1]. DSR seeks to enhance human knowledge with the creation of innovative artifacts and the understanding of how and why the artifacts improve the human condition. These artifacts embody the ideas, practices, technical capabilities, and products through which information systems and computing technologies can be efficiently developed and effectively used. Artifacts are not exempt from natural laws or behavioral theories. To the contrary, their creation relies on existing laws and theories that are applied, tested, modified, and extended through the experience, creativity, intuition, and problem solving capabilities of the researcher. Thus, the results of DSR include both the newly designed artifact and a fuller understanding of the theories of why the artifact is an improvement to the relevant application context [2].

A. R. Hevner (✉)
School of Information Systems and Management, Muma College of Business, University of South Florida, Tampa, FL, USA
e-mail: ahevner@usf.edu

© The Author(s), under exclusive license to Springer Nature Switzerland AG 2021
S. Aier et al. (eds.), *Engineering the Transformation of the Enterprise*,
https://doi.org/10.1007/978-3-030-84655-8_12

Design activities are central to most applied disciplines. Research in design has a long history in many fields including architecture, engineering, education, psychology, anthropology, and the fine arts. The Information Systems (IS) field since its advent in the late 1940s has identified with a research focus on the design and use of socio-technical systems [3]. Socio-technical systems are composed of inherently mutable and adaptable hardware, software, and human interfaces that provide many unique and challenging design problems that call for new and creative research methods.

Graduate courses in IS research methods typically include a module on the basic concepts of DSR. Professional seminars on DSR methods are also available.[1] The curriculum content of a standard DSR module or course is described by the following statement of purpose from the DSR syllabus in the AIS Education Reference Syllabi [4]:[2]

> This course provides a comprehensive introduction to the basic concepts and principles of design science research applied to the IS field. The course develops skills for implementing and evaluating the techniques and methods that are used in the various stages of a DSR project. Research methods and techniques are discussed in the context of exemplar case studies. Common methods that are used in the important activities of design research, namely, building and evaluation, will be covered. The key to appreciating the core ideas and goals of DSR is a clear understanding of how DSR relates to human knowledge. The appropriate and effective consumption and production of knowledge are related issues that researchers should consider throughout the research process—from initial problem selection, to the use of sound research methods, to reflection, and to communication of research results in journal, magazine, and conference articles. Each of the course units includes a list of learning objectives that give the student the understanding and the skills to perform rigorous and relevant DSR in a range of selected application areas.

The goal of this chapter is to present a proposal for a full semester Doctoral Seminar that goes beyond DSR fundamentals and prepares doctoral students for rigorous and relevant research dissertations and publications using DSR methods. A two-dimensional pedagogy is outlined. Section 2 presents a set of research challenges for performing DSR and Sect. 3 overviews prominent fields of IS research in which DSR methods can be applied. Then, using these dimensions to structure the content, Sect. 4 outlines a semester curriculum for a DSR Doctoral Seminar. The chapter concludes with a discussion of experiences in piloting this course during the Fall 2020 semester.

---

[1] See the Design Science seminar by Jan vom Brocke and Robert Winter—https://vhbonline.org/en/veranstaltungen/prodok/kurse-2020/2005ms04

[2] https://eduglopedia.org/design-science-research-in-information-systems-syllabus

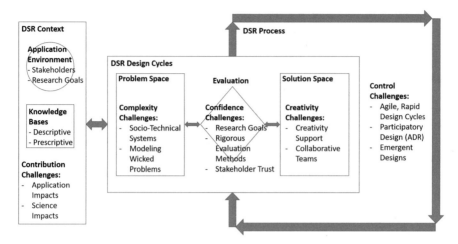

Fig. 1 Design science research challenges

2 Design Science Research Challenges

Researchers using DSR methods face a number of key challenges in the design and execution of their research projects. An understanding of these challenges and the means to address them in specific application environments are essential learning activities in a doctoral seminar. I presented an initial taxonomy of DSR challenges in a keynote address given at the 2016 DESRIST Workshop in St. Johns, Newfoundland. Over the past 5 years, I have expanded and refined the DSR challenge taxonomy as it has been applied to research projects in different application fields. Figure 1 illustrates five DSR challenges considered essential to include in a doctoral seminar curriculum. This section provides brief descriptions of each DSR challenge with required student readings.[3]

2.1 Complexity Challenges

Research in information systems has long studied complexity by recognizing the need to understand complex socio-technical systems, which are diverse, interdependent, connected, and adaptive. Simon [1] identifies the importance of studying complexity because of the need to be able to understand the large-scale systems in the world, including the diverse application environments in which the systems operate. In DSR, complexity is addressed by bounding, capturing, and representing the relevant *Problem Space* and the specific wicked problems to be

---

[3] Suggested course readings in this chapter can be altered based on the instructor's preferences.

addressed by the research project. Capturing and representing the problem space involves domain knowledge to provide the context as well as an understanding of the research objectives. The context is influenced by the domain, stakeholders, time, and space. The goodness of the solution is assessed by goals and evaluation measures to assess achievement of the goals.

Students gain an understanding of the challenges of problem space complexity via an appreciation of the socio-technical system focus of the IS field [3]. Nielsen and Persson [5] discuss issues of formulating IS research problems. The importance of capturing both fitness and sustainability goals in the DSR research project is addressed in Gill and Hevner [6]. Pragmatic advice for identifying, defining, and applying research goals and respective evaluation criteria is provided in Hevner, Prat, Comyn-Wattiau, and Akoka [7].

2.2   Creativity Challenges

Once the research problem has been understood and represented, the DSR project moves to the *Solution Space* in which satisfactory solutions are designed. This is the stage of creating novel ideas and of reasoning in the choice of the best idea to move forward to implementation. According to Burkus [8], "creativity is the starting point for all innovation" where creativity is defined as the process of developing ideas that are both novel and useful. Amabile [9] posits that four components are necessary for a creative response:

- Domain-relevant skills include intelligence, expertise, knowledge, technical skills, and talent in the particular domain in which the innovator is working.
- Creativity-relevant processes include personality and cognitive characteristics that lend themselves to taking new perspectives on problems, such as independence, risk taking, self-discipline in generating ideas, and a tolerance for ambiguity.
- Intrinsic task motivation is seen as a central tenet. "People are most creative when they feel motivated primarily by the interest, enjoyment, satisfaction and challenge of the work itself—and not by extrinsic motivators." [9]
- The social environment, the only external component, addresses the working conditions that support creative activity. Positive organizational settings stimulate creativity with clear and compelling management visions, work teams with diverse skills working collaboratively, freedom to investigate ideas, and mechanisms for developing new ideas and norms of sharing ideas.

Effective solution design requires more than just the generation of many creative ideas. Successful innovation also requires the intellectual control to refine creative thinking into practical IT solutions. Such control is dependent on the cognitive skills of reason and judgment. Human reason reflects thinking in which plans are made, hypotheses are formed, and conclusions are drawn on the basis of evidence in the form of data, past experience, or knowledge. While creativity often calls for divergent thinking to break out of mindsets; reason calls for convergent thinking to refine ideas into practical artifacts and actions. Moving design ideas from 'blue sky' to artifact instantiations requires goal setting. The goal setting activity in the problem space now comes into play as the criteria for ranking the creative ideas produced to address the problem into one design candidate to move forward into implementation and evaluation. The iterative DSR build and refinement activities of the creative design cycles are studied in Baskerville, Kaul, Pries-Heje and Storey [10].

2.3 Confidence Challenges

Rigorous evaluation methods link solutions (in the solution space) to problems (in the problem space) and provide evidence of the extent to which a solution solves a problem using the chosen evaluation methods. Conceptually, both formative and summative evaluations can be distinguished in the DSR process [11]. DSR evaluation can be described as a continuously organized process [12] throughout all stages of a DSR project. Evidence produced by DSR evaluations promote stakeholder confidence in the research results. The level of research confidence assesses such qualities as the types of evaluation performed, the rigor of the evaluation methods, and the convincing nature of the evaluation results.

Not all DSR projects have the opportunity to test new design artifacts in realistic environments. In such cases, opportunities for evaluations in artificial environments should be considered (e.g., simulation) [13]. Given the great variety of different methods and application scenarios for evaluations, transparency of both the process and the results of the evaluation are important confidence criteria for DSR contributions.

2.4 Control Challenges

The performance of a DSR project requires attention to process control of research activities and intellectual control of the emerging problem and solution artifacts. DSR projects emphasize adaptive learning based on applying incremental, controlled search methods [14]. This approach can be used with problem environments that are fast-changing and have great amounts of uncertainty. The DSR team begins immediately the iterative cycles of building and refining the artifact in a controlled manner. Later, upon reflection of the design results, identification and extension of relevant design theories may occur [15].

Several proposed process models for scheduling and coordinating design activities exist. Peffers, Tuunanen, Rothenberger, and Chatterjee [16] propose and develop a design science research methodology (DSRM) for the production and presentation of DSR activities. This process model includes six steps: problem identification and motivation, definition of the objectives for a solution, design and development, demonstration, evaluation, and communication; and four possible entry points: problem-centered initiation, objective-centered solution, design and development-centered initiation, and client/context initiation.

By combining the research methods of action research with DSR, Sein, Henfridsson, Purao, Rossi, and Lindgren [17] propose the Action Design Research (ADR) process model. Their model begins with a problem formulation stage followed by multiple iterations of the build, intervention, and evaluation stage along with reflection and learning in each iteration. The ADR project completes with a stage of formulation of learning for system evolution. Action research principles of guided emergence, iterative intervention, and co-creation between research and practitioner are highlighted. An elaborated ADR (eADR) process model has been proposed by Mullarkey and Hevner [18]. This model identifies separate ADR stages of diagnosis, design, implementation, and evolution in order to provide distinct entry points into the project and novel artifacts produced by iterative eADR stages.

2.5   Contribution Challenges

Two dominant types of design knowledge contributions are defined as research outcomes from a DSR project—design artifacts and design theories [15, 19]. Students must understand how to position DSR contributions toward providing both real-world solutions and rigorous contributions to design knowledge. A DSR project needs to meet the theoretical requirements of IS journal publication in the form of new or extended design theories [20], and at the same time, to solve a practical problem or to address an interesting class of problems.

Basic knowledge can be represented by two major types: (1) research activities that primarily grow Ω-knowledge (comprising descriptive, explanatory and predictive knowledge), and (2) research activities that primarily grow λ-knowledge (prescriptive, and design knowledge). Contributions to Ω-knowledge enhance our understanding of the world and the phenomena that technologies harness (or cause). Contributions to λ-knowledge typically deal with technological (in the sense of means-end) innovations that directly impact individuals, organizations, or society and also enable the development of future technological innovations. Research projects may combine both genres of inquiry and contribute to both knowledge bases [21].

The relationships of specific design knowledge created in DSR projects and the general knowledge bases (Ω and λ) are analyzed in Drechsler and Hevner [22]. Paired modes of consuming and producing knowledge between the DSR project and the descriptive and prescriptive knowledge bases are described. Knowledge can be projected from the application research project into nascent theories around solution actions, entity realizations, and design processes based on the new and interesting design knowledge produced in a DSR project. Avdiji and Winter [23] identify a number of knowledge gaps that must be bridged in DSR projects as researchers move between the problem space and solution space in the consumption and production of design knowledge.

Many DSR projects are longitudinal efforts involving multiple research teams. Vom Brocke, Winter, Hevner, and Maedche [24] propose models for the accumulation and evolution of design knowledge in an organized DSR body of knowledge. Guidance is presented on how to position design knowledge contributions in wider problem and solution spaces via (1) a model conceptualizing design knowledge as a resilient relationship between problem and solution spaces, (2) a model that demonstrates how individual DSR projects consume and produce design knowledge, (3) a map to position a design knowledge contribution in problem and solution spaces, and (4) principles on how to use this map in a DSR project.

3   Fields of IS Research

The second important dimension of the seminar covers the wide range of research fields in IS. Doctoral students will gain an appreciation of how the DSR challenges are applied in a selected set of IS research fields that can change with each semester offering of the course. I survey the students to ensure that areas of particular interest to each student are covered in the seminar. The following sections briefly describe the research fields with the papers assigned during the Fall 2020 semester.

3.1   Digital Innovation

Design Science Research in the IS field is, at its essence, about Digital Innovation (DI). Innovative sociotechnical design artifacts involve digital information technologies (IT) being used in ways that result in profound disruptions to traditional ways of doing business and to widespread societal changes. The phenomena of DI encompasses new digital technologies, information digitization, digitally-enabled generativity, entrepreneurship, and innovation management with a greater range and reach of innovation across organizational boundaries [25, 26].

Kohli and Melville [27] provide a comprehensive review and synthesis of the DI literature. Winter and Aier [28] study the use of DSR in business innovation. The alignment of DSR and DI is explored by Hevner and Gregor [29]. They propose a novel process model of DI that supports a richer understanding of different types of entrepreneurship for the investment of DI in organizations.

3.2 Neuroscience and Information Systems (NeuroIS)

Research in the fields of neuroscience and IS can connect to identify and frame fundamental questions about the relationships between human cognitive abilities for creativity and design innovations. The goals of such NeuroIS studies should include the development of new neuroscience models of creativity, new paradigms for designing IT artifacts, novel approaches for education to optimize creative design thinking, and the development of creativity-enhancing IT tools for specific application domains.

Many critical cognitive and affective functions are involved in performing DSR projects. Vom Brocke, Riedl and Léger [30] present ideas on how to apply NeuroIS in DSR projects. They identify three strategies, (1) to apply NeuroIS theories to inform the design of IS artifacts, (2) to apply NeuroIS methods and tools to support the evaluation of IS artifacts as well as to (3) apply NeurosIS methods and tools in order to build neuro-adaptive IS artifacts. Hevner, Davis, Collins, and Gill [31] offer a concise conceptual model of NeuroIS for use in DSR projects. Riedl, Davis, and Hevner [32] provide an extensive survey of research methods, instruments, tools, and measurements for performing NeuroIS projects. A recent proposal for a NeuroIS research agenda is presented in vom Brocke, Hevner, Leger, Walla, and Riedl [33]. They discuss four key areas for future NeuroIS research: (1) IS design, (2) IS use, (3) emotion research, and (4) neuro-adaptive systems.

3.3 Data Analytics

IS research in data sciences can benefit from greater attention to the use of DSR methods to support the effective interplay of data analytics, data artifacts, and theory development. The creative design of novel data artifacts and causal models can inform methods of inductive, deductive, and abductive reasoning [34, 35]. The roles of data artifacts and causal models are largely unexplored in IS research due to a lack of common terminologies and research approaches [36]. An important goal is to explore an initial understanding of how to build a framework for integrating the scientific method with novel design contributions into data science research projects [37].

3.4 Cybersecurity

The use of DSR methods in cybersecurity research is rare but has great potential. Most IS research in cybersecurity has focused on human behaviors regarding security and privacy [38, 39]. One DSR exemplar is by Benjamin, Valacich, and

Chen [40]. They design a cybersecurity framework which provides guidelines for conducting research on Dark-net forums.

A primary mission of Security Analysts (SAs) in security operations centers (SOCs) is to investigate suspicious cyber events as an integral part of the process of assuring systems and data security in client organizations. We are applying DSR methods to work closely with a leading cybersecurity firm to systematize and improve the efficiency and effectiveness of these investigations [41]. The engaged scholarship, multi-method approach leads to the design of an intelligent system for improving the cognitive tasks and the resultant decisions made by SAs in SOCs while executing cybersecurity event investigations.

3.5 Artificial Intelligence

Advances in artificial intelligence (AI) technologies and systems, underpinned with the availability of new sources of big data, are impacting and changing our lives in many disruptive ways. The design and use of socio-technical information systems increasingly requires new approaches for finding the right balance of synergies between human behaviors and AI-based machine behaviors. As AI research and development generate new and unprecedented capabilities for enhancing speed, scale, flexibility, decision-making, and personalization in systems [42, 43], our abilities to design systems to take advantage of these advances are greatly challenged. IS research must appropriately integrate human and AI capabilities into systems that realize effective synergies among the component human and machine behaviors [44]. A human-centered research is a promising direction for designing AI systems that support human self-efficacy, promote creativity, clarify responsibility, and facilitate social participation [45]. These human aspirations also encourage consideration of privacy, security, environmental protection, social justice, and human rights.

3.6 Collaboration in Teams

DSR projects are performed by teams with diverse skill sets and an equally diverse range of stakeholders [46]. Producing a satisfactory design artifact for release into an application context brings the cognitive challenges of collaboration among members of the research team and effective communication to and from stakeholder audiences into sharp relief [47]. In design tasks the goal is collaborative emergence of a design based on contributions from the full design team.

The central research challenge regarding collaborative design is to understand how to assemble and support design teams that interact effectively to produce great designs [48]. To meet this challenge we must study how individuals work alone and together on all design processes, as they solve complex problems in creative ways with appropriate controls [49]. Such research requires methods that reveal individual cognitions (e.g., neuroscience); the knowledge, skills and abilities that each individual brings to the team (e.g., survey measures); team interactions and representations (e.g., video and audio recordings of interactions, collection of models and other external representations); as well as design outcomes (e.g., design artifacts). This approach can leverage multi-method knowledge to open up the black box on individual cognition along with the more traditional ways of investigating collaboration to draw a more complete picture of collaborative design.

4   DSR Doctoral Seminar Curriculum

A standard 15-week semester curriculum for the DSR Doctoral Seminar can be designed around the two dimensions of DSR challenges and IS research fields. I piloted the following semester structure during Fall 2020 in the IS program at the University of South Florida.

4.1   DSR Basics (2 Weeks)

The first two weeks are devoted to a review of the fundamental ideas and concepts of the DSR paradigm. Readings included Hevner, March, Park, and Ram [50], Hevner [51], Gregor and Hevner [15], and Baskerville, Baiyere, Gregor, Hevner, and Rossi [19]. References to exemplar DSR case studies are provided for further study (e.g. [52]). The range of IS research fields are described and each student selects one of the research fields as a semester focus for study.

4.2   DSR Challenges (6 Weeks)

One week is devoted to an in-depth study of each of the five DSR Challenges discussed in Sect. 2. As the challenges are analyzed, each student prepares and interacts with the class as to how the challenges apply to their chosen research field. During the sixth week, each student makes a formal presentation and delivers a white paper on the five DSR challenges in their research field.

4.3   IS Research Fields (6 Weeks)

Each of the selected IS research fields for that semester is presented and discussed in one class session. If one of the students has chosen that week's field, then the student and the instructor jointly present that session. The broad coverage of multiple IS research fields exposes the students to multiple research opportunities with a focus on the DSR challenges across the fields of study.

4.4 Final Research Presentation (1 Week)

Over the final 6 weeks of the semester, the students are required to refine their mid-term white papers into research papers that can be targeted to appropriate conferences in the chosen IS research field. The research contributions of the papers should address one or more DSR challenges in the chosen field.

5 Conclusion

Doctoral instruction in design science research (DSR) must address the significant challenges of using DSR to perform impactful IS research leading to a successful dissertation and publications in top IS journals and conferences. Doctoral students should be prepared to perform cutting edge research that extends prescriptive knowledge of design artifacts and design theories. This chapter proposes a two-dimensional pedagogy of research challenges and fields of research application with a robust focus on rigorous and relevant educational outcomes.

I piloted the proposed doctoral curriculum during the Fall 2020 semester with three students. The students chose individually to focus on the research fields of Data Analytics, Cybersecurity, and Artificial Intelligence. During the class periods on DSR challenges, each student discussed how that challenge impacts their chosen research field and what research opportunities exist to extend DSR thinking to provide better research outcomes.

I received very positive assessments from the students on how the class was presented and educational results. In particular, they commented that the well-defined pedagogy of challenges and research fields provides a learning structure to the course that is rational and highly motivating. The final course papers are in the process of refinement for submission to IS conferences.

Acknowledgements I gratefully acknowledge the enthusiastic participation of Thomas Gill, Arindam Ray, and Zheyi Xu as students in the Fall 2020 Design Science Research Seminar.

References

1. Simon, H.: The Sciences of the Artificial, 3rd edn. MIT Press (1996)
2. Hevner, A., Chatterjee, S.: Design Research in Information Systems: Theory and Practice. Springer (2010)
3. Sarker, S., Chatterjee, S., Xiao, X., Elbanna, A.: The sociotechnical axis of cohesion for the IS discipline: its historical legacy and its continued relevance. MIS Q. **43**(3), 695–719 (2019)
4. Hevner, A., Chatterjee, S.: Design Science Research in Information Systems. Syllabus shared on EDUglopedia.org by the Association for Information Systems (2016)
5. Nielsen, P., Persson, J.: Engaged problem formulation in IS research. Commun. Assoc. Inf. Syst. **38**, 720–737 (2016) Paper 35
6. Gill, T.G., Hevner, A.: A fitness-utility model for design science research. ACM Trans. Manag. Inf. Syst. **4**(2), Article 5, 24 pages (2013)
7. Hevner, A., Prat, N., Comyn-Wattiau, I., Akoka, J.: A pragmatic approach for identifying and managing design science research goals and evaluation criteria. Proceedings of the SigPrag Workshop, San Francisco, 2018 (2018)
8. Burkus, D.: The Myths of Creativity. Jossey-Bass (2014)
9. Amabile, T.: Componential Theory of Creativity. Working Paper, Harvard Business School, April (2012)
10. Baskerville, R., Kaul, M., Pries-Heje, J., Storey, V.: Inducing creativity in design science research. Proceedings of DESRIST Workshop. Springer, Worcester, MA (2019)
11. Venable, J., Pries-Heje, J., Baskerville, R.: FEDS: a framework for evaluation in design science research. Eur. J. Inf. Syst. **25**(1), 77–89 (2016)
12. Sonnenberg, C., vom Brocke, J.: Evaluations in the science of the artificial – reconsidering the build-evaluate pattern in design science research. In: Peffers, K., Rothenberger, M., Kuechler, B. (eds.) Advances in Theory and Practice, pp. 381–397. Springer (2012)
13. Prat, N., Comyn-Wattiau, I., Akoka, J.: A taxonomy of evaluation methods for information systems artifacts. J. Manag. Inf. Syst. **32**(3), 229–267 (2015)
14. Hevner, A.: Intellectual control of complexity in design science research, in A. Rai, Editor's Comments: Diversity of Design Science Research. MIS Q. **41**(1), iii–xviii (2017)
15. Gregor, S., Hevner, A.: Positioning and presenting design science research for maximum impact. MIS Q. **37**(2), 337–355 (2013)
16. Peffers, K., Tuunanen, T., Rothenberger, M., Chatterjee, S.: A design science research methodology for information systems. J. MIS. **24**(3), 45–77 (2007)
17. Sein, M., Henfridsson, O., Purao, S., Rossi, M., Lindgren, R.: Action design research. MIS Q. **35**(1), 37–56 (2011)
18. Mullarkey, M., Hevner, A.: An elaborated action design research process model. Eur. J. Inf. Syst. **28**(1), 6–20 (2019)
19. Baskerville, R., Baiyere, A., Gregor, S., Hevner, A., Rossi, M.: Design science research contributions: finding a balance between artifact and theory. J. Assoc. Inf. Syst. **19**(5), Article 3 (2018)
20. Gregor, S., Jones, D.: The anatomy of a design theory. J. Assoc. Inf. Syst. **8**(5), 312–335 (2007)
21. Baskerville, R., Kaul, M., Storey, V.: Genres of inquiry in design-science research: justification and evaluation of knowledge production. MIS Q. **39**(3), 541–564 (2015)
22. Drechsler, A., Hevner, A.: Utilizing, producing, and contributing design knowledge in DSR projects. Proceedings of the Design Science Research in Information Systems and Technology (DESRIST 2018), Chennai, India, pp. 82–97 (2018)
23. Avdiji, H., Winter, R.: Knowledge gaps in design science research. Proceedings of the 40th International Conference on Information Systems, Munich, Germany (2019)
24. vom Brocke, J., Winter, R., Hevner, A., Maedche, A.: Accumulation and evolution of design knowledge in design science research: a journey through time and space. J. Assoc. Inf. Syst. **21**(3), Article 9 (2020c)

25. Nambisan, S., Lyytinen, K., Majchrzak, A., Song, M.: Digital innovation management: reinventing innovation management research in a digital world. MIS Q. **41**(1), 223–238 (2017)
26. Yoo, Y., Henfridsson, O., Lyytinen, K.: Research commentary – The new organizing logic of digital innovation: an agenda for information systems research. Inf. Syst. Res. **21**(4), 724–735 (2010)
27. Kohli, R., Melville, N.: Digital innovation: a review and synthesis. Inf. Syst. J. **29**, 200–223 (2019)
28. Winter, R., Aier, S.: Design science research in business innovation. In: Hoffmann, C., Lennerts, S., Schmitz, C., Stölzle, W., Uebernickel, F. (eds.) Business Innovation: Das St. Galler Modell, pp. 475–498. Wiesbaden (2016)
29. Hevner, A., Gregor, S.: Envisioning entrepreneurship and digital innovation through a design science research lens: a matrix approach. Inf. Manag. In Press (2020)
30. vom Brocke, J., Riedl, R., Léger, P.: Application strategies for neuroscience in information systems design science research. J. Comput. Inf. Syst. **53**(3), 1–13 (2013)
31. Hevner, A., Davis, C., Collins, R., Gill, T.G.: A NeuroDesign model for IS research. Informing Sci. Int. J. Emerging Transdiscipl. **17**, 103–132 (2014)
32. Riedl, R., Davis, F., Hevner, A.: Towards a NeuroIS research methodology: intensifying the discussion on methods, tools, and measurement. J. Manag. Inf. Syst. **15**, i–xxxv (2014)
33. vom Brocke, J., Hevner, A., Léger, P.M., Walla, P., Riedl, R.: Advancing a NeuroIS research agenda with four areas of societal contributions. Eur. J. Inf. Syst. **29**(1), 9–24 (2020a)
34. Gregor, S., Hevner, A.: The essential role of design science research for the effective interplay of analytics and theory. SIGPHIL Workshop on the Death of Theory in IS and Analytics, Munich, Germany (2019)
35. Pearl, J.: The seven tools of causal inference with reflections on machine learning. Commun. ACM. **62**(3), 54–60 (2019)
36. Abbasi, A., Sarkar, S., Chiang, R.: Editorial – Big data research in information systems: toward an inclusive research agenda. J. AIS. **17**(2), i–xxxii (2016)
37. Stodden, V.: The data science life cycle: a disciplined approach to advancing data science as a science. Commun. ACM. **63**(7), 58–66 (2020)
38. Bélanger, F., Crossler, R.: Privacy in the digital age: a review of information privacy in IS literature. MIS Q. **35**(4), 1017–1041 (2011)
39. Lu, Y.: Cybersecurity research: a review of current research topics. J. Indus. Integr. Manag. **3**, 4, 25 pages (2018)
40. Benjamin, V., Valacich, J., Chen, H.: DICE-E: a framework for conducting darknet identification, collection, evaluation with ethics. MIS Q. *43*, 1 (2019)
41. Daniel, C., Mullarkey, M., Hevner, A.: Cyber Analysis Methodology (CAM) assistant, demonstration and presentation. Workshop on Information Technology and Systems (WITS), Munich, Germany (2019)
42. Malone, T.: How human-computer 'superminds' are redefining the future of work. MIT Sloan Manag. Rev. **59**(4), Summer 2018 (2018)
43. Wilson, H.J., Daugherty, P.: Collaborative intelligence: humans and AI are joining forces. Harv. Bus. Rev. **July–August** (2018)
44. Hevner, A., Storey, V.: Research challenges of human-artificial intelligence systems design., Under Journal Review (2021)
45. Shneiderman, B.: Human-centered artificial intelligence: three fresh ideas. AIS Trans. Human-Comput. Interaction. **12**(3), 109–124 (2020)
46. Otto, B., Osterle, H.: Principles for knowledge creation in collaborative design science research. Proceedings of the International Conference on Information Systems, Orlando, FL (2012)
47. Weedman, J.: Client as designer in collaborative design science research projects: what does social science design theory tell us? Eur. J. Inf. Syst. **17**(5), 476–488 (2008)
48. Arias, E., Eden, H., Fischer, G., Gorman, A., Scharff, E.: Transcending the individual human mind – creating shared understanding through collaborative design. ACM Trans. Comput. Human Interaction. **7**(1), 84–113 (2000)

49. Kolfschoten, G., de Vreede, G.J.: A design approach for collaboration processes: a multimethod design science study in collaboration engineering. J. Manag. Inf. Syst. **26**(1), 225–256 (2009)
50. Hevner, A., March, S., Park, J., Ram, S.: Design science research in information systems. MIS Q. **28**(1), 75–105 (2004)
51. Hevner, A.: A three cycle view of design science research. Scand. J. Inf. Syst. **19**(2), 87–92 (2007)
52. vom Brocke, J., Hevner, A., Maedche, A.: Design Science Research. Cases. Springer Nature (2020b)

Part III
Applied Fields

Management of Enterprise-Wide Information Systems

Stephan Aier, Barbara Dinter, and Joachim Schelp

Abstract This article offers a short retrospective on the research streams about enterprise-wide IS management at the chair of Robert Winter. Both research project streams on analytical integration (data warehousing, information integration etc.) and transactional integration (application integration, enterprise architecture, transformation management) reside in the same understanding of the extended application landscape developed by Robert Winter.

Keywords Analytical information systems · Data warehousing · Information integration · Application integration · Enterprise architecture · Transformation management · Enterprise-wide information systems

1 Introduction

Many contributions in information systems (IS) research focus on the design, development, adoption, and use of individual IS, or they address certain properties of those IS such as security, privacy, or trust. In contrast the paper at hand takes a perspective beyond the individual IS and emphasizes the management of the entire IS landscape of an organization, i.e., it centers on the *enterprise-wide IS*. The management of the enterprise-wide IS can be considered as one of the core research

S. Aier (✉)
Institute of Information Management, University of St. Gallen, St. Gallen, Switzerland
e-mail: stephan.aier@unisg.ch

B. Dinter
Chemnitz University of Technology, Chemnitz, Germany
e-mail: barbara.dinter@wirtschaft.tu-chemnitz.de

J. Schelp
Helsana Versicherungen, Zürich, Switzerland

University of St. Gallen, St. Gallen, Switzerland
e-mail: joachim.schelp@unisg.ch

© The Author(s), under exclusive license to Springer Nature Switzerland AG 2021
S. Aier et al. (eds.), *Engineering the Transformation of the Enterprise*,
https://doi.org/10.1007/978-3-030-84655-8_13

perspectives at the chair of Robert Winter. In this article we offer a retrospective on the research about this topic in the years between about 2000 and 2020 as well as a discussion of future research opportunities.

Although the complexity of IS landscapes has been both a research and a practical problem in the past, many approaches have focused on their redesign by replacing them with a set of newly built systems—either self-developed or completely off the shelf. The recurring integration activities in the management of IS landscapes have led to Robert Winter's view of an extended application landscape as he described it, e.g., in [1] (Fig. 1).

In contrast to previous approaches, he has put transactional and analytical applications into a common context. Integration management was then further described for both transactional and analytical perspectives (see e.g. [3]) and provides references to general IS management.

The remainder of this article is structured as follows: After this short introduction the second section reflects the basic tensions forming the management challenges in complex, enterprise-wide IS landscapes. These tensions will give a hand when describing the research topics of the subsequent research streams in Sect. 3. The initial research stream has been developed in the data warehouse context and dates back to Robert Winter's early years at the Institute of Information Management in St. Gallen (Sect. 3.1). Shortly after the turn of the millennium the second industry-agnostic research stream focusing on transactional integration started (Sect. 3.2). Later, this research stream transformed into research on enterprise architecture management (Sect. 3.3) and enterprise transformation support (Sect. 3.4). Many of the early and more recent publications have shaped the idea of an *architectural coordination* within and between organizations, which will be finally reflected in the implications of previous and for future research, concluding this contribution.

2 Challenges for Managing Enterprise-Wide Information Systems

Information systems research and practice is often concerned with the design or management of a particular IS serving a certain purpose for a specific stakeholder group in an organization. However, if we extend our perspective beyond the individual IS to cover the entirety of IS within an organization or even a group of organizations in an ecosystem, we take an enterprise-wide perspective on IS. Taking such a perspective reveals the tensions that exist in IS landscapes. Those tensions can be found in competing user requirements, diverse and sometimes incompatible technologies of different generations, and potentially conflicting stakeholder concerns such as quality requirements, budgets, and varying priorities for business, IT, or compliance driven initiatives.

On a more generic level, these tensions often have common underlying patters. First, there is a *local-global tension*. From a local perspective of, e.g., a business unit,

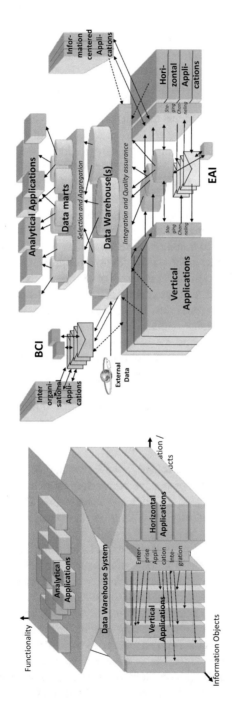

Fig. 1 From the application landscape [1] to the extended application landscape [2]

a project, a process, or a systems owner perspective, simple and locally effective solutions such as direct point-to-point interfaces, copies of datasets for local purposes, or a specific technology platform often seem reasonable. Apparently, they benefit from limited complexity, short implementation cycles, and little coordination efforts with other stakeholders in the organization. From an enterprise-wide perspective, however, such local solutions lead to redundancies, inconsistencies, and in total result in high IS complexity that is difficult and expensive to maintain.

Closely related to the local-global tension there is a *short-term-long-term tension*. Short-term solutions that typically respond to symptoms of problems or quickly deliver newly requested features often do neither address the need to adapt the underlying fundamental structures to solve the problems' root causes nor do they build sustainable and capable foundations for new feature sets. From an isolated, often local, perspective short-term solutions are very effective and efficient, however, from an enterprise-wide perspective a collection of short-term solutions does not solve any problem fundamentally.

In addition to the short-term-long-term tension most solutions are considered to solve a problem for a specific *point of time*, whereas the problems often develop over time. Furthermore, there are different rhythms of change on the various abstraction levels of an organization, as they result from diverse lifespans of the solutions [4].

Beyond the varying scopes an enterprise-wide perspective is inevitably confronted with the *diversity of stakeholder concerns,* which are potentially conflicting. Prioritizing the concerns of some stakeholders over those of others' leads to tensions that are reflected in discourses on organizational norms and values, and thus questions of legitimacy of stakeholder concerns.

While enterprise-wide perspectives often strive for finding standardized and thus synergetic solutions, standards can also hinder innovation. In some contexts, generativity, diversity, and individual solutions may be preferrable. However, differentiating *opportunities for synergies from opportunities for innovation* remain challenging.

These and other challenges are rooted in the increasing levels of *complexity* that come with an enterprise-wide perspective comprising more elements and relations than local perspectives as well as higher dynamics [5]. The consequences of increasing levels of IS complexity are among others decreasing comprehensibility and predictability [6].

Finally, a common problem of enterprise-wide IS or enterprise-wide perspectives on IS is related to the challenges of presenting convincing *business cases*. These challenges are rooted in the infrastructure-like character of such systems and perspectives. Upfront investments into infrastructures are rather large while their payoffs are distributed over diverse stakeholders, use cases, and over time. Consequently, the one-off invest is visible for many stakeholders in an organization, while the total returns are only visible from an enterprise-wide perspective.

As a result of these challenges, the management of enterprise-wide IS requires continuous efforts that need to be constantly adapted to the environmental trends and requirements prevailing at a specific point in time. In the following we will describe some of the efforts and contributions of Robert Winter's chair over time and for different enterprise-wide IS topics.

3 Contributions in Competence Centers and Beyond

A range of research activities at Robert Winter's chair has addressed integration from different perspectives as laid out in the introduction. It all started in the late 90s with research projects focusing on data warehousing: The research group "Competence Center Data Warehouse Strategy" (see Sect. 3.1) constituted the starting point for a series of research projects on data warehousing, business intelligence and corporate decision processes.

Feedback from practitioners in the field of analytical information systems (AIS) led to the conclusion that research on integration among operational systems would strike on a rich vein of research problems and exhibit a great supplement. Therefore, an additional line of research on integration was started in 2001. This stream of research projects is described in Sect. 3.2 and following.

In the beginning most research projects have been driven by research consortia, so-called Competence Centers [7]. Research has been funded by industry partners, which in addition delegated staff into these consortia to extend the research capacity. Industries involved have been among others banking, insurance, financial service providers, IT service providers, public services, transportation, and utilities—mostly medium and large sized companies. Furthermore, the activities have been complemented by a cross-industry practitioner forum, the *St. Gallen Anwenderforum*, which has frequently been hosted as a 1-day event at the University of St. Gallen. Up to 250 representatives from small to large sized companies in various industries shared their experiences in the context of research challenges at that time. These by now 50 instantiations of the forum provided valuable opportunities to access a broad audience for collecting empirical data. Over time the percentage of competitive public funding of foundational research has grown, with successfully acquired research grants, e.g., from the Swiss National Science Foundation.

Both research streams, illustrated in Fig. 2 have been industry agnostic, although financial services with their complex, evolutionarily grown application landscapes often offered practical research grounds for data and transactional integration, as well as architectural and transformational challenges. Beyond these two research streams there have been other streams at Robert Winter's chair, not being covered in this paper, focusing on industry specific research problems.

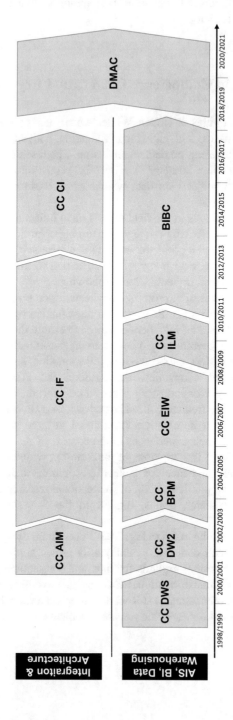

Fig. 2 Research projects on integration, architecture, and transformation over two decades

3.1   Results Area 1: Analytical Information Systems

The concept of data warehousing (DWH) and business intelligence (BI) can be considered as one of the earliest exemplars for enterprise-wide IS. Already in 1958, when Hans Peter Luhn introduced the term and the basic idea of BI, he claimed that a "comprehensive system may be assembled to accommodate all information problems of an organization. We call this a Business Intelligence System" [8]. Since then, DWH & BI have increasingly gained relevance and remain indispensable components in most enterprise IS landscapes while changing their shape over time to address new requirements and to integrate new technologies. Nowadays, they are often part of an analytical ecosystem, and therefore not being replaced by, but rather serving as a meaningful supplement to modern big data & business analytics (BA) architectures. In the following we will use the term *analytical information systems* (AIS) as an umbrella term for IS that are supposed to analyze data and by that to support any kind of organizational decisions.

Having a closer look at the nature of AIS it can be observed that (most of) the aforementioned tensions of enterprise-wide IS also apply here. Several tensions have been captured by the concept of *information logistics* (IL), which has extended the common understanding of DWH & BI to overcome some of their limitations in practice. According to [9] IL refers to "the planning, implementation, and control of the entirety of cross-unit data flows as well as the storage and provisioning of such data". In order to differentiate IL and operational data integration, only those data flows are attributed to IL that support decision making. The local-global tension of enterprise wide IS is addressed in IL in particular by its "holistic approach", which originates from the total system concept and two of its major assumptions: the impact of subsystems on other subsystems and on the overall system, and the idea of synergies (the whole is greater than the sum of its parts) [9]. The idea of cross-unit data flows in IL also supports the local-global tension as well as the diversity of stakeholders and their needs.

A broad range of AIS-related topics has been subject to research at Robert Winter's chair since 1998, i.e., for more than two decades now, mainly in the context of the following Competence Centers (CC):

- Competence Center Data Warehousing Strategy (CC DWS) 1998–2000
- Competence Center Data Warehousing 2 (CC DW2) 2001–2002
- Competence Center Business Performance Management (CC BPM) 2003–2005
- Competence Center Enterprise Information Warehousing (CC EIW) 2005–2009
- Competence Center Information Logistics Management (CC ILM) 2009–2011
- Business Intelligence in Banking Community (BIBC) 2012–2019
- Data Management and Analytics Community (DMAC): since 2019

This approach of consortial research with industry partners has, among others, resulted in about 60 workshops (most of them as 2-day events) over the years in which academic research on the one side and practitioners' needs, experiences, and feedback on the other side have led to fruitful discussions and benefits for both sides.

The CC history reflects the increasing perception of AIS as enterprise-wide IS, too. Not only one CC has been named as "Enterprise Data Warehousing" (CC EIW), also many topics that have been addressed in workshops and projects with industry partners referred to challenges and characteristics of enterprise-wide IS.

In the following, while discussing how the enterprise-wide perspective has changed the perception and realization of AIS over time, we also take the opportunity to compare the CC history (which, as mentioned, has been driven to a large extent by the needs of industry partners) with the scientific progress. For this purpose, we draw on a publication by Marjanovic et al. [10] who investigated by means of semantic text mining the history of BI & BA. Although this analysis was based on the publications of the longest-running minitrack on BI & BA at the Hawaii International Conference on Systems Sciences (HICSS), it can be considered as representative for the research activities in the BI & BA community that Robert Winter has been an active member of. Robert Winter has not only served as one of the minitrack co-chairs (2010–2013), he has also been identified as the most active author with eight papers in the analyzed period (1990–2017), and within the minitrack his chair has represented the most active group with 12 publications. In addition, two papers, co-authored by Robert Winter, have been among the three most-cited publications.

Marjanovic et al. have distinguished four historical phases [10]. The first one, called *Executive Information Systems* (1990–1996) is not in our focus. However, the subsequent phases can well be aligned with the aforementioned CCs. Table 1 provides an overview of both historical perspectives—the BI & BA phases according to [10] and the CC history—and the main topics in those, respectively. We have identified the CC topics by an analysis of workshops and industry projects in each CC. To illustrate the scientific impact of the CCs we have added references to selected publications that resulted from this research.

The BI & BA phase *Data Warehousing* matches with CC DWS and CC DW2. During that time dedicated DWH solutions have been stepwise introduced in organizations. Therefore, the CC industry partners have mainly been interested in "how to" guidance and best practices to set up such IS. Consequently, in particular technical and methodological solutions were needed. The enterprise-wide perspective has not yet been the primary focus.

The subsequent BI & BA phase *DW extended with BI* emphasized—besides advanced architecture topics—the business side (especially business value) and organizational issues. The corresponding CCs BPM, EIW, and ILM also shifted their focus from implementation aspects to operations (BI service management, BI billing, etc.) and the strategic management of AIS (BI strategy, BI governance, BI maturity model, etc.). In particular in this stage the enterprise-wide perspective on AIS gained attention by the dedicated focus on *Enterprise Data Warehousing* and *Information Logistics Management* as the primary vision of those CCs. The CC EIW operated with mixed teams from the industry partners. While in before CC participants were mainly IT representatives, in the CC EIW now also business representatives have contributed and by that have emphasized the growing relevance of the

Table 1 AIS research in Competence Centers in comparison with BI & BA scientific publications

BI & BA phases [10]	BI & BA key themes according to [10]	CC	CC topics
(1) Executive Information Systems (1990–1996)	Not in our focus	–	–
(2) Data Warehousing (1997–2003)	– Strong emphasis on data – Focus on DWH technical aspects and infrastructure – Metadata – Technical/query performance	CC DWS (1998–2000)	– DWH methodology/ processes—[11–14] – DWH architecture—[11] – Organizational structure for DWH—[11] – Metadata mgt. (MDM) – Data quality mgt. (DQM)
		CC DW2 (2001–2002)	– Integration of operational applications—[15] – Data privacy/security – MDM/DQM—[16–18]
(3) DWH extended with BI (2004–2011)	– Focus on BI rather than DWH – Various organizational issues – Turning data into information – Deriving business value from BI – Operational BI – Data quality – Data integration	CC BPM (2003–2005)	– Realtime DWH, operational BI – BI service mgt.—[19] – BI cost estimation/ billing—[20] – BI strategy – BI benchmarking/ maturity model – Business performance mgt.—[21] – DWH architecture mgt.
		CC EIW (2005–2009)	– Concept of IL—[9, 22] – BI governance—[23] – Process centric BI—[24, 25] – BI marketing – BI strategy—[26, 27] – BI service mgt. – MDM/DQM
		CC ILM (2009–2011)	– IL benchmarking/ maturity model—[28, 29] – IL project mgt.
(4) BI extended with BA and big data (2012–2017)	– Big data – Agile BI – Realtime DW/BI	BIBC (2012–2019)	– Big data – BI value and continuous use—[30] – Disruptive BI/DWH technologies

(continued)

Table 1 (continued)

BI & BA phases [10]	BI & BA key themes according to [10]	CC	CC topics
			– Data lake
			– Cloud computing in BI
			– BI self service
			– Agile BI
			– Regulatory requirements
			– BI operations (release mgt., testing, etc.)
			– BI cost allocation—[31, 32]
			– MDM/DQM
–	–	DMAC (since 2019)	– Data driven organization
			– Digital platforms
			– AI/ML
			– Cloud, data lake, agile BI
			– Data mgt. (MDM, DQM, etc.)—[33]

business perspective for AIS topics. It has also addressed the challenges of the *diversity of stakeholders* tension in enterprise-wide IS.

The final BI & BA period *BI extended with BA and big data* corresponds mainly to BIBC. In both streams the increasing awareness and application of big data and advanced analytics have resulted in new use cases, technologies and analytics techniques. At HICSS at that time several new minitracks have been established, explaining why not all those topics became a new focus of the analyzed minitrack. However, the topic portfolio of BIBC illustrates that despite the hype about big data and BA (including artificial intelligence and machine learning) rather "traditional" BI has still been a major concern of the industry partners—not surprisingly, since data management and governance have still required significant efforts just to provide a foundation for new big data and BA use cases.

Since the analysis of [10] ended in 2017, the latest CC (DMAC) cannot be aligned with a BI & BA phase in their historical perspective. Nevertheless, DMAC continues the history of AIS-related research and considers the current megatrend of digital transformation by shifting its focus on the role of AIS and data management in digital and analytics ecosystems. Its new perspective on data as an indispensable resource in organizations and its potential for digital innovation could also be observed in recent publications in the HICSS minitrack.

Comparing both streams results in two major observations. On the one hand, "new" topics in the CCs correspond well with the research themes addressed in HICSS publications. This supports the assumption of consortial research that industry-driven research may lead to valuable scientific outcomes. On the other hand, while research not surprisingly focuses on such new topics, the CCs over time rather have added then substituted topics. Consequently, the topic range in the CCs has increased and some topics are still in focus, even after two decades—in particular data management issues such as data quality management and meta data management. Having a closer look at the "long runner" topics reveals that they are often related to the aforementioned tensions of enterprise-wide IS as they constitute organizational challenges that cannot be overcome in solutions that are limited in terms of their scope and/or their temporal impact. Interestingly, they also exhibit that the original idea of DWH, to transform newly generated data into valuable information, remains a major concern in modern AIS.

We conclude the discussion about AIS research at Robert Winter's chair by assigning the focal points of the CCs to the *components of an AIS framework*. Figure 3 illustrates well how the scope of the AIS-related CCs has grown over time and by now covers all relevant design questions. Each circle indicates in which BI & BA phase according to [10] and in which CC the framework component has been addressed.

Not only the research foci have evolved over time, also the portfolio of research methods applied in the AIS-related CCs has continuously been extended. The *design science research (DSR) paradigm* has always been a core competence at Robert Winter's chair. At the same time, researchers, in particular Ph.D. students, could benefit from great resources and opportunities in the CCs for their publications and dissertations due to the extensive collaboration with industry partners. In the early years, often case studies and action design research, have constituted a profound basis for the design and evaluation of artifacts, such as methods and reference models. With the increasing application of behavioral research in IS, events such as the "St. Gallen Anwenderforum", offered the opportunity to conduct surveys and to collect high quality data for empirical research. Consequently, the mutual use of DSR and behavioral research had a great fit with the IS research cycle [34].

3.2   Results Area 2: Integration Methods and Models

Early DWH research offered a broad range of approaches to deal with data integration and data transformation. In addition to having dedicated data integration storages being accessible for transactional write access, i.e., *operational data stores* (ODS) as described by [35], transferring concepts from DWH to the transactional/ operational integration discussion was the starting point of the second general research stream. At the end of the 1990s the overall application landscapes in certain industries—especially the financial services industry—had grown that complex that operational integration became a major issue. This called for systematic and enterprise-wide integration approaches in analogy to data warehousing.

When facing these challenges, organizations had different options at hand. First, they could drop their self-developed systems and migrate to standardized application packages. This was—and still is—an option that was well established for solving the

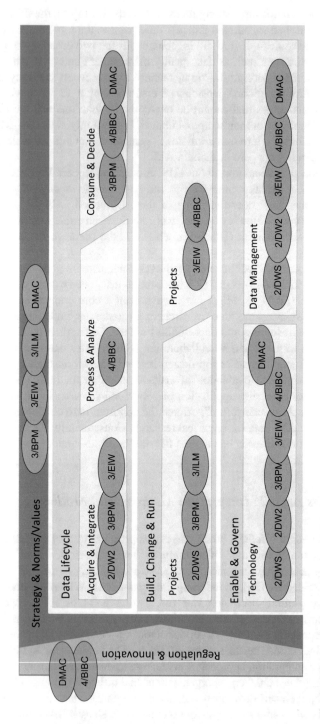

Fig. 3 AIS framework (based on the *DMAC Big Picture*)

complexity issues of self-developed software from the 1990s onwards. SAP is a well-known vendor offering such an approach. Organizations, whose core competency is not the software development, often opted for this type of systems when realigning their IT and business strategy [36]. Second, in cases where no standardized application package is available—or is considered insufficient—the redesign of the existing core system and its redevelopment is the other option at hand.

However, in contrast to the less complex situation in the 1980s the problem could not be solved anymore by replacing the old systems by a new one: In the now large and complex IS landscapes, the challenge of integrating a multitude of systems with each other persists. As the business-driven integration requirements are growing, as are the overall IS complexity and thus the challenges to integration.

Research in the CCs Application Integration Management (CC AIM) and Integration Factory (CC IF) addressed this broad range of problems with various approaches. On the IS development level, integration patterns for data and application integration have been identified (i.e., [37]), leading to a methodology for designing integration architectures [38].

Several projects with industry partners showed that an increased focus had to be given to the architectural perspective in general, which was still in its infancy at that time, so that Robert Winter came up with the request for a dedicated management of architecture [39]. Consequently, subsequent research contributed to the management of IS architectures. Based on the Business Engineering methodology developed in St. Gallen, results often added enhancements to this methodology, as, e.g., in [40].

Furthermore, a range of contributions focused on modelling techniques by enhancing the Business Engineering framework accordingly. E.g., [2] introduced a visualization technique for application landscapes, which has been successfully adopted in several cases in practice. Further contributions added metrics, i.e., [41, 42], and systematized the overall modelling framework [43], which was then implemented as *ADOben* with a modelling tool vendor [44]. The research stream has been further complemented by an abstraction of integration archetypes that allow for conceptualizing different integration settings and their requirements and implications [45].

Most of the research in this period was deeply rooted in the St. Gallen Business Engineering framework and focused on extending or adapting it to the research problems at hand. While the Business Engineering framework has mostly been driven through case studies, the set of research methods being employed at the chair of Robert Winter at that time has been broadened. More and broader empirical work was added, e.g., in [46]. The knowledge acquired on integration and architectural perspectives and the extension of research methods being applied, laid the foundation for the next cycle of research activities continued in the CC IF [47].

3.3   Results Area 3: Enterprise Architecture Management
Methods and Models

The integration complexity has driven the demand for methodological support and for architecture management in particular. It was again propelled by new technological advances. *Service Oriented Architectures* (SOA) were introduced to harness this complexity and to increase the corporate IT agility, which soon proved to create additional challenges calling for management attention. Finding the appropriate level of service granularity and heuristics for service definition were among the initial challenges influencing the re-use of services. Over time the number of services and their variants added to an increasing structural and dynamic complexity of a service mesh with faltering re-use and exploding maintenance costs [48, 49].

Early contributions focused on analyzing the root causes of growing service complexity [50]. Understanding the relationship to agility [51], and the aspects of service design [52] were important to shape further research. Design approaches for services [53, 54] and management recommendations [55] have led to contributions in enhancing the Business Engineering framework. Regarding business/IT alignment the introduction of an additional layer, the integration (later: *alignment* [54]) *layer*, to the Business Engineering framework was an important step [56]. It explained the mechanisms and value contributions of the artifact types populating it. This resulted in fruitful (and reoccurring) discussions on the differentiation of software systems vs. applications: While applications represent a logical cluster of business capabilities, a particular software system is just one of many possible implementations of that application. Most notably, however, this discussion led to the introduction of the idea of capabilities as a central alignment artifact that while remaining abstract in the beginning, is widely adopted in practice today [54].

Additional contributions focused on the management of these complexities with enterprise architecture (EA) management. Either by introducing an explicit EA governance perspective [57–60], EA principles [61, 62], and EA planning [63, 64], or by extending EA modelling [61, 65, 66] and EA management (EAM) in general [3, 63, 67, 68].

Later the focus shifted from foundational EAM method support to making available methods effective in different situations [69–72] and to make EAM part of an organization, i.e., to institutionalize EAM [73–75]. Here Robert Winter, among others [76], shaped the term *architectural thinking* [77], which had significant impact in practice [78] and research [79, 80]. It was also a starting point for designing new types of interventions, e.g., nudges, to operationalize architectural thinking in organizations [81].

Even though, later research was not directly contributing to EA anymore, it was still significantly infused by the architectural perspective and by the idea of the necessity for *architectural coordination* in large and complex sociotechnical systems. Exemplarily we may mention the still ongoing work on digital platforms [82, 83]. The shift to architectural thinking and architectural coordination helped to focus again on the underlying tensions of managing enterprise-wide IS [84].

The research methodology to be applied was discussed intensely. In addition to previous case study research, action research, and empirical research, simulation modelling [85, 86] and behavioral experiments [87] were added to the portfolio. The reflection of design research became a topic of its own, spanning from discussing method construction [88] to design research itself [89, 90], often in the context of EA research [81, 91]. These discussions facilitated the exchange with other research groups on Enterprise Architecture both from an analytical viewpoint [92] and from practical cooperation (e.g. as in [63, 93]).

As mentioned before, a significant part of the research on EA was concerned with creating value by using EA. One major field of EA use were large scale transformations, which the following section will report about.

3.4 Results Area 4: Enterprise Transformation Methods and Models

Taking an enterprise-wide perspective on IS does not only include the components and their relations, but also their evolution and fundamental transformation. Enterprise-wide perspectives such as EAM should be able to provide efficient and effective (architectural) coordination support for enterprise transformation initiatives [94–96].

The *Competence Center Corporate Intelligence* (CC CI) as well as the SNSF-funded research project *Architectural Coordination of Enterprise Transformation* (ACET) developed the conceptual and methodological foundations for such a support function [97]. Corporate intelligence is based on the idea to collect local transformation-related information, to consolidate and integrate them, and to provide project specific and regular analysis from an architectural perspective.

In particular the CC developed the Transformation Intelligence Capability Catalogue (TICC, Fig. 4) [98]. It constitutes a response to the finding that enterprise transformation initiatives require an information support that may be delivered by EAM [99]. Still, EAM often is not involved in such initiatives. Thus, TICC strives for leveraging EAM for supporting enterprise transformations through architectural coordination [100].

The underlying assumption of TICC is that large transformations involve several organizational units of an enterprise and that these organizational units operate based on their local goals, information, resources, etc. Architectural coordination aims at integrating these local perspectives to an enterprise-wide perspective [101–103]. Enterprise architects and EAM may therefore provide major parts of the architectural coordination to an enterprise transformation [104].

The catalogue shows which parts of an enterprise transformation may benefit from architectural coordination, and it shows where architectural coordination, and therefore EAM, may be involved. For architects, it reveals where EA services can contribute. For transformation managers, it describes for which parts of a

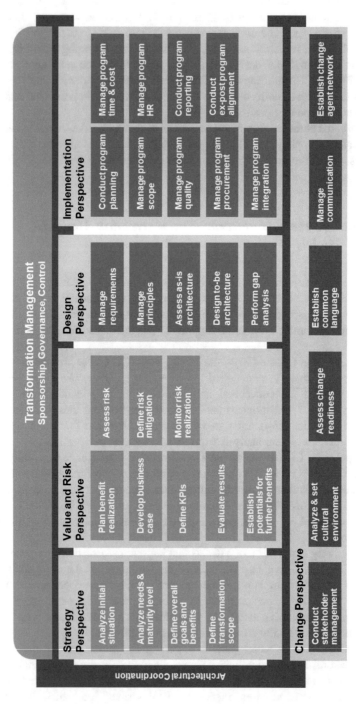

Fig. 4 Transformation Intelligence Capability Catalogue [98]—© 2017 Springer International Publishing; reprinted with permission

transformation they may seek advice from the enterprise architects [105, 106]. It is important to emphasize that neither can EAM support every aspect of an enterprise transformation nor does an enterprise transformation require every EA artifact. Instead, TICC provides guidance for using EA artifacts to support respective aspects of an enterprise transformation.

TICC offers an integrated view of different yet complimentary perspectives on an enterprise transformation. The catalogue shows how disciplines as different as change management, program management, value management, or EAM all contribute to the toolbox of enterprise transformation. It aims to support enterprise transformation by orchestrating different perspectives from an architectural vantage point.

The catalogue comprises the perspectives of strategy, value and risk, design, implementation, and change. These perspectives support transformation management, which is concerned with the management tasks at the overall transformation level, and the architectural coordination function, which forms an umbrella function of integrating the individual perspectives into a consistent whole. These perspectives do not represent a phase or process model. Instead, the general assumption is that all of the perspectives are relevant throughout an enterprise transformation. For example, the value and risk perspective is not only relevant when planning a transformation. It will also be important during the actual implementation of the transformation for making sure that planned benefits are actually realized.

Each of these perspectives comprises a set of capabilities. TICC does not prescribe how to implement each of these capabilities since for most of these capabilities, academic literature as well as corporate practice provides a plethora of method fragments and techniques.

Eventually, TICC's implicit idea, which is reflected by TICC's multiple perspectives, is to ease some of the tensions of enterprise-wide IS at least for the course of a transformation initiative by the means of EAM and by overcoming some of the inevitable knowledge boundaries that result from the diversity of stakeholders [101].

The CC CI with its industry partners and the concurrent fundamental research project ACET provide a nice example for how fundamental research can be inspired and driven by corporate practice on the one hand, and how fundamental research can return structure to and insights being adopted and employed by corporate practice.

4 Implications for Research and Practice, Today and in the Future

Looking back at those 20 years of research on enterprise-wide IS provides the opportunity to identify the aspects that have changed and those that have remained. From those observations we may derive implications for the future of research on and the practice of enterprise-wide IS.

We reviewed research on enterprise-wide IS for the instances of decision support & data analytics, integration, enterprise architecture, and enterprise transformation. All of those instances have exhibited significant progress in the last 20 years with regards to the methodological support being available, the tool and technology support, the adoption in practice, and their overall maturity. They created visible impact in academia and practice. In academia, we see tracks at academic conferences, journals focusing on the respective instance, and many special issues in the general IS journals over the years. In academic education, respective bachelor and master courses or even entire study programs are well established at many universities. In practice this development is reflected in specific roles and job profiles, dedicated organizational units as well as service providers such as consulting firms. Thus, it may be appropriate to refer to these instances of enterprise-wide IS as *disciplines*—the disciplines of analytical information systems, application integration, enterprise architecture, and enterprise transformation.

Obviously, the disciplines that deal with enterprise-wide IS topics can never be developed in isolation as closed systems. In fact, they have needed to adopt and integrate novel, more agile paradigms for new ways to plan, coordinate, and deliver change. They also have benefited from new environmental constraints such as the increase of regulatory requirements after the financial crisis in 2008 that brought enterprise-wide perspectives forward, e.g., for an integrated financial and risk reporting. And of course, they face new challenges and receive new momentum through organizations' adoption of new and partially game changing technologies such as the distributed processing of large data sets and the data lakes challenging classical DWH technologies, or cloud computing, which changes timelines, business cases, requirements, etc. of large and small IS initiatives.

In summary, we observed continuous opportunities and needs to evolve the disciplines of enterprise-wide IS in order to remain relevant and respond to changing requirements. In many cases organizations could benefit from responses delivering such useful, adequate method and/or technology support.

However, coming back to the challenges of managing enterprise-wide IS that we discussed in Sect. 2, we have to state that most challenges and their underlying tensions will remain. It seems they cannot be solved completely. Indeed, Robert Winter's chair provided support to explain and understand those tensions, to negotiate them, and, partially, to find common ground within an organization on how to deal with a tension locally as well as on an enterprise-wide basis. Yet, such understanding and common ground is ephemeral. It needs to be constantly assured, renewed, and reestablished. It requires continuous efforts that need to be adapted to changing environmental settings, requirements, and prevalent IS management fashions. Those tensions are the reflection of the continuous aspiration for legitimacy of goals and perspectives of stakeholder groups within and beyond the organization.

This has implications for future research: The methodological support is to be adapted to better address the continuously moving goals and rules of the transformation game. Furthermore, the set of tools and techniques has to be extended and refined to any new knowledge in the underlying fields. Due to the rapidly evolving technologies further adaption is needed to address them in the enterprise-wide IS disciplines. And most of all, striving for new lenses and explanations means to deal with the classical tensions inherent in an enterprise-wide perspective on IS in evolving environments. The latest developments of *cloud transformation, corporate agility*, and *digital platform ecosystems* provide fundamentally new and inspiring perspectives on classical and outlasting challenges for managing enterprise-wide IS.

References

1. Winter, R.: Modelle, Techniken und Werkzeuge im Business Engineering. In: Österle, H., Winter, R. (eds.) Business Engineering – Auf dem Weg zum Unternehmen des Informationszeitalters, pp. 87–118. Springer, Berlin (2003)
2. Winter, R.: Ein Modell zur Visualisierung der Anwendungslandschaft als Grundlage der Informationssystem-Architekturplanung. In: Schelp, J., Winter, R. (eds.) Integrationsmanagement, pp. 1–29. Springer, Berlin (2006)
3. Winter, R. (ed.): Management von Integrationsprojekten, mit Grundlagenbeiträgen von Stephan Aier, Christian Fischer, Bettina Gleichauf, Christian Riege, Jan Saat, Joachim Schelp und Robert Winter. Business Engineering. Springer, Berlin (2009)
4. Gericke, A., Winter, R.: Geschäftslösungen – Gegenstand der Analyse und Gestaltung mit BEN. In: Winter, R. (ed.) Business Engineering Navigator: Gestaltung und Analyse von Geschäftslösungen "Business-to-IT", pp. 15–54. Springer, Berlin (2011)
5. Schilling, R.D., et al.: Revisiting the impact of information systems architecture complexity: a complex adaptive systems perspective. In: 38th International Conference on Information Systems (ICIS 2017), Seoul, South Korea (2017)
6. Beese, J., et al.: Drivers and effects of information systems architecture complexity: a mixed-methods study. In: 24th European Conference on Information Systems (ECIS), Istanbul, Turkey (2016)
7. Österle, H., Otto, B.: Consortium research. a method for researcher-practitioner collaboration in design-oriented IS research. Bus. Inf. Syst. Eng. 2(2), 273–285 (2010)
8. Luhn, H.P.: A business intelligence system. IBM J. Res. Dev. 2(4), 314–319 (1958)
9. Dinter, B., Lahrmann, G., Winter, R.: Information logistics as a conceptual foundation for enterprise-wide decision support. J. Decis. Syst. 19(2), 175–200 (2010)
10. Marjanovic, O., Dinter, B.: Learning from the history of business intelligence and analytics research at HICSS: a semantic text-mining approach. Commun. Assoc. Inf. Syst. 43 (2018)
11. Jung, R., Winter, R. (eds.): Data Warehousing Strategie - Erfahrungen, Methoden, Visionen. Springer, Berlin (2000)
12. Meyer, M., Winter, R.: Organisation des unternehmensweiten Data Warehousing. In: Jung, R., Winter, R. (eds.) Data Warehousing 2000 – Methoden, Anwendungen, Strategien, pp. 309–331. Physica, Heidelberg (2000)
13. Winter, R., Meyer, M.: Organization of data warehousing in large service companies – a matrix approach based on data ownership and competence centers. J. Data Warehousing. 6(4), 23–29 (2001)
14. Strauch, B.: Entwicklung einer Methode für die Informationsbedarfsanalyse im Data Warehousing. Universität St, Gallen, Bamberg (2002)
15. Winter, R.: The Current and Future Role of Data Warehousing in Corporate Application Architecture. IEEE Computer Society (2001)
16. Helfert, M.: Planung und Messung der Datenqualität in Data-Warehouse-Systemen. Difo-Druck GmbH, Bamberg (2002)
17. von Maur, E., Winter, R. (eds.): Data Warehouse Management. Business Engineering. Springer, Berlin (2003)

18. Melchert, F., et al.: Using Reference Models for Data Warehouse Metadata Management. In: AMCIS2005, Omaha, NE (2005)
19. Winter, R., Klesse, M.: Organizing data warehouse service providers. Bus. Intell. J. **14**(3), 31–39 (2009)
20. Klesse, M.: Leistungsverrechnung im Data Warehousing – Entwicklung einer Methode. Universität St. Gallen, St. Gallen (2007)
21. Melchert, F., Winter, R., Klesse, M.: Aligning process automation and business intelligence to support corporate performance management. In: AMCIS 2004. Association for Information Systems, New York (2004)
22. Dinter, B., Winter, R. (eds.): Integrierte Informationslogistik. Business Engineering. Springer, Berlin (2008)
23. Dinter, B., et al.: Governance in der Informationslogistik am Beispiel eines Energieversorgers. In: DW2008: Synergien durch Integration und Informationslogistik. St.Gallen, Köllen (2008)
24. Bucher, T., Dinter, B.: Situational method engineering to support process-oriented information logistics: identification of development situations. J. Database Manag. **23**(1), 31–48 (2012)
25. Bucher, T., Dinter, B.: Process orientation of information logistics – an empirical analysis to assess benefits, design factors, and realization approaches. In: The Forty-First Annual Hawaii International Conference on System Sciences (HICSS-41). IEEE Computer Society, Waikoloa, Big Island, Hawaii (2008)
26. Dinter, B., Winter, R.: Information logistics strategy – analysis of current practices and proposal of a framework. In: 42nd Hawaii International Conference on System Sciences (HICSS-42). IEEE Computer Society, Big Island, Hawaii (2009)
27. Dinter, B.: Success factors for information logistics strategy — an empirical investigation. Decis. Support. Syst. **54**(3), 1207–1218 (2013)
28. Raber, D., Wortmann, F., Winter, R.: Towards the measurement of business intelligence maturity. In: European Conference on Information Systems 2013, Utrecht (2013)
29. Lahrmann, G., et al.: Business intelligence maturity: development and evaluation of a theoretical model. In: Forty-Fourth Annual Hawaii International Conference on System Sciences (HICSS-44). IEEE Computer Society, Koloa, Kaua'i, Hawaii (2011)
30. Bischoff, S., et al.: Understanding continuous use of business intelligence systems: a mixed methods investigation. J. Inf. Technol. Theory Application. **16**(2), 5–38, Article 2 (2015)
31. Epple, J., Bischoff, S., Aier, S.: Management objectives and design principles for the cost allocation of business intelligence. In: Pacific Asia Conference on Information Systems (PACIS 2015). Association for Information Systems, Singapore (2015)
32. Epple, J., et al.: Business intelligence is no 'free lunch': what we already know about cost allocation – and what we should find out. Int. J. Bus. Intell. Res. **9**(1), 1–15, Article 1 (2018)
33. Schilling, R.D., et al.: Design dimensions for enterprise-wide data management: a Chief Data Officer's journey. In: Proc. 53rd Hawaii International Conference on System Sciences (HICSS 53), Grand Weilea, Maui, Hawaii (2020)
34. Schelp, J., Winter, R.: Language communities in enterprise architecture research. In: Diversity in Design Science – 4th Conference on Design Science Research in Information Systems and Technologies (DESRIST2009). ACM, Philadelphia, PA (2009)
35. Inmon, W.H.: Building the Operational Data Store, 2nd edn. Wiley, New York (1999)
36. Luftman, J.N., Lewis, P.R., Oldach, S.H.: Transforming the enterprise: the alignment of business and information technology strategies. IBM Syst. J. **32**(1), 198–221 (1993)
37. Schwinn, A., Schelp, J.: Data integration patterns. In: 6th International Conference on Business Information Systems BIS 2003. Department of Management Information Systems at The Poznan University of Economics, Colorado Springs (2003)
38. Schwinn, A.: Entwicklung einer Methode zur Gestaltung von Integrationsarchitekturen für Informationssysteme. Difo-Druck, Bamberg (2006)
39. Winter, R.: Architektur braucht Management. Wirtschaftsinformatik. **46**(4), 317–319 (2004)

40. Hafner,   M.:   Entwicklung   einer   Methode   für   das   Management   der Informationssystemarchitektur im Unternehmen. Universität St. Gallen Institut für Wirtschaftsinformatik Difo-Druck, Bamberg (2005)
41. Hagen, C., Schwinn, A.: Measured Integration - Metriken für die Integrationsarchitektur. In: Schelp, J., Winter, R. (eds.) Integrationsmanagement. Planung, Bewertung und Steuerung von Applikationslandschaften, pp. 268–292. Springer, Berlin (2005)
42. Schwinn, A., Winter, R.: Success factors and performance indicators for enterprise application integration. In: AMCIS2005. Association for Information Systems, Omaha, NE (2005)
43. Braun, C.: Modellierung der Unternehmensarchitektur: Weiterentwicklung einer bestehenden Methode und deren Abbildung in einem Meta-Modellierungswerkzeug. Universität St. Gallen, St. Gallen (2007)
44. Aier, S., et al.: Business engineering navigator – a "Business to IT" approach to enterprise architecture management. In: Bernard, S., et al. (eds.) Coherency Management – Architecting the Enterprise for Alignment, Agility, and Assurance, pp. 77–98. Author House, Bloomington (2009)
45. Aier,   S.,   et   al.:   Empirische   Validierung   von   Integrationstypen   am   Beispiel unternehmensübergreifender Integration. In: 9. Internationale Tagung Wirtschaftsinformatik. Wien, Österreichische Computer Gesellschaft (2009)
46. Klesse,   M.,   Wortmann,   F.,   Schelp,   J.:   Erfolgsfaktoren   der   Applikationsintegration. Wirtschaftsinformatik. **47**(4), 259–267 (2005)
47. Schelp, J., Winter, R. (eds.): Auf dem Weg zur Integration Factory. Physica, Heidelberg (2004)
48. Aier, S., Saat, J.: Wertbeitrag serviceorientierter Architekturen – Ein Framework für Business Cases als Ergebnis einer empirischen Studie. HMD – Praxis Der Wirtschaftsinformatik. **45** (273), 107–115 (2010)
49. Aier, S., et al.: Economic Justification of Service-Oriented Architecture (SOA) – Research Study: Experiences and Guidelines on Building SOA Business Cases (2008)
50. Schelp, J., Stutz, M., Winter, R.: SOA-Risiken und SOA-Governance. In: Starke, G., Tilkov, S. (eds.) SOA-Expertenwissen - Methoden, Konzepte und Praxis serviceorientierter Architekturen, pp. 661–668. dpunkt, Heidelberg (2007)
51. Schelp, J., Winter, R.: Agilität und SOA. In: Starke, G., Tilkov, S. (eds.) SOA-Expertenwissen - Methoden, Konzepte und Praxis serviceorientierter Architekturen, pp. 41–47. dpunkt, Heidelberg (2007).
52. Schelp, J., Winter, R.: Business application design and enterprise service design: a comparison. Int. J. Service Sci. **1**(3/4), 206–224 (2008)
53. Aier, S., Gleichauf, B.: Towards a sophisticated understanding of service design for enterprise architecture. In: 3rd Workshop on Trends in Enterprise Architecture Research (TEAR 2008) at the 6th International Conference on Service Oriented Computing (ICSOC 2008). Springer, Sydney (2009)
54. Aier, S., Winter, R.: Virtual decoupling for IT/business alignment – conceptual foundations, architecture design and implementation example. Bus. Inf. Syst. Eng. **1**(2), 150–163 (2009)
55. Schelp, J., Winter, R.: Integration management for heterogeneous information systems. In: Desouza, K.C. (ed.) Agile Information Systems – Conceptualizations, Construction, and Management, pp. 134–149. Butterworth-Heinemann, Oxford (2007)
56. Winter, R., Fischer, R.: Essential layers, artifacts, and dependencies of enterprise architecture. In: EDOC Workshop on Trends in Enterprise Architecture Research (TEAR 2006) within The Tenth IEEE International EDOC Conference (EDOC 2006). IEEE Computer Society, Hong Kong (2006)
57. Schelp, J., Stutz, M.: SOA Governance. HMD - Praxis der Wirtschaftsinformatik. **42**(253), 66–73 (2007)
58. Winter, R., Schelp, J.: Dienst-Orientierung im Business Engineering. Hmd - Praxis Der Wirtschaftsinformatik. **42**(241), 45–54 (2005)

59. Winter, R., Schelp, J.: Dienstorientierte Architekturgestaltung auf unterschiedlichen Abstraktionsebenen. In: Reussner, R., Hasselbring, W. (eds.) Handbuch der Software-Architektur, pp. 229–242. dpunkt, Heidelberg (2006)
60. Winter, R., Schelp, J.: Enterprise architecture governance: the need for a business-to-IT approach. In: The 23rd Annual ACM Symposium on Applied Computing (SAC2008), Fortaleza, Ceará, Brazil, Mar 16–20, 2008. ACM Press, Fortaleza, Ceará, Brazil (2008)
61. Aier, S., Fischer, C., Winter, R.: Construction and evaluation of a meta-model for enterprise architecture design principles. In: The 10th International Conference on Wirtschaftsinformatik WI 2011, Zurich, Switzerland (2011)
62. Winter, R., Aier, S.: How are enterprise architecture design principles used? In: The Fifteenth IEEE International EDOC Conference Workshops, Trends in Enterprise Architecture Research (TEAR). IEEE, Helsinki (2011)
63. Aier, S., et al.: Towards a more integrated EA planning: linking transformation planning with evolutionary change. In: The 4th International Workshop on Enterprise Modelling and Information Systems Architectures (EMISA 2011). Gesellschaft für Informatik Köllen, Hamburg (2011)
64. Gericke, A., Winter, R.: BEN-Gestaltungsmethodik für Geschäftslösungen. In: Winter, R. (ed.) Business Engineering Navigator: Gestaltung und Analyse von Geschäftslösungen "Business-to-IT", pp. 55–84. Springer, Berlin (2011)
65. Aier, S., Gleichauf, B.: Towards a sophisticated understanding of service design for enterprise architecture. In: 3rd Workshop on Trends in Enterprise Architecture Research (TEAR 2008), Sydney (2008)
66. Schelp, J., Winter, R.: (Re-) Design for Agility – Components of an Incremental Method for Integration Architecture Evolution in Large Companies (2009)
67. Schelp, J., Winter, R.: Management der Unternehmensarchitektur. In: Reussner, R., Hasselbring, W. (eds.) Handbuch der Software-Architektur, pp. 249–266. dpunkt, Heidelberg (2008)
68. Stutz, M., Aier, S.: SOA-Migration und Integration auf Basis von Services-Repositories. Hmd - Praxis Der Wirtschaftsinformatik. **42**(257), 20–27 (2007)
69. Aier, S., Gleichauf, B., Winter, R.: Understanding enterprise architecture management design – an empirical analysis. In: The 10th International Conference on Wirtschaftsinformatik (WI 2011), Zurich, Switzerland (2011)
70. Aier, S., Riege, C., Winter, R.: Classification of enterprise architecture scenarios – an exploratory analysis. Enterprise Modell. Inf. Syst. Architect. **3**(1), 14–23 (2008)
71. Riege, C., Aier, S.: A contingency approach to enterprise architecture method engineering (extended version). J. Enterprise Architect. **5**(1), 36–48 (2009)
72. Aier, S.: The role of organizational culture for grounding, management, guidance and effectiveness of enterprise architecture principles. Inf. Syst. E-Bus. Manag. **12**(1), 43–70 (2014)
73. Weiss, S., Aier, S., Winter, R.: Institutionalization and the effectiveness of enterprise architecture management. In: 34th International Conference on Information Systems (ICIS 2013), Milano, Italy (2013)
74. Haki, K., et al.: The evolution of information systems architecture: an agent-based simulation model. MIS Q. **44**(1), 155–184 (2020)
75. Brosius, M., et al.: Enterprise architecture assimilation: an institutional perspective. In: Proceedings of the 39th International Conference on Information Systems (ICIS 2018), San Francisco, USA (2018)
76. Ross, J.W., Quaadgras, A.: Enterprise Architecture Is Not Just for Architects. Center for Information Systems Research Sloan School of Management Massachusetts Institute of Technology, Cambridge, MA (2012)
77. Winter, R.: Architectural thinking. Bus. Inf. Syst. Eng. **6**(6), 361–364 (2014)
78. Aier, S., Labusch, N., Pähler, P.: Implementing architectural thinking: a case study at Commerzbank AG. In: Proceedings of the CAiSE 2015 Workshops, Stockholm, Sweden (2015)

79. Burmester, F., Drews, P., Schirmer, I.: Leveraging architectural thinking for large-scale E-government projects. In: Fortieth International Conference on Information Systems (ICIS 2019), Munich (2019)

80. Horlach, B., et al.: Everyone's going to be an architect: design principles for architectural thinking in agile organizations. In: Proceedings of the 53rd Hawaii International Conference on System Sciences, Wailea (2020)

81. Schilling, R.D., Aier, S., Winter, R.: Designing an artifact for informal control in enterprise architecture management. In: Proceedings of the 40th International Conference on Information Systems (ICIS 2019), Munich, Germany (2019)

82. Blaschke, M., et al.: Capabilities for digital platform survival: insights from a business-to-business digital platform. In: 39th International Conference on Information Systems (ICIS2018). Association for Information Systems, San Francisco, CA (2018)

83. Schmid, M., et al.: Developing design principles for digital platforms: an agent-based modeling approach. In: 15th International Conference on Design Science Research in Information Systems and Technology (DESRIST 2020). Springer Nature Switzerland AG, Kristiansand, Norway (2020)

84. Haki, M.K., Aier, S., Winter, R.: A stakeholder perspective to study enterprisewide IS initiatives. In: 24th European Conference on Information Systems (ECIS), Istanbul, Turkey (2016)

85. Beese, J., et al.: Simulation-based research in information systems: epistemic implications and a review of the status quo. Bus. Inf. Syst. Eng. **61**(4), 503–521 (2019)

86. Spagnoletti, P., et al.: Exploring foundations for using simulations in IS research. Commun. Assoc. Inf. Syst. **42**(1), 268–300 (2018)

87. Beese, J., et al.: Enterprise architecture as a public goods dilemma: an experimental approach. In: Aveiro, D., Guizzardi, G., Borbinha, J. (eds.) Advances in Enterprise Engineering XIII, pp. 102–114. Springer, Cham (2020)

88. Winter, R., Schelp, J.: Reference modeling and method construction – a design science perspective. In: 21st Annual ACM Symposium on Applied Computing (SAC2006), Dijon, France, April 23–27, 2006. ACM Press, Dijon, France (2006)

89. Aier, S., Fischer, C.: Scientific progress of design research artefacts. In: Proceedings of the 17th European Conference on Information Systems (ECIS 2009), Verona (2009)

90. Gericke, A., Winter, R.: Notwendigkeit und Priosisierung einer betriebswirtschaftlichen Konstruktionslehre. In: Winter, R. (ed.) Business Engineering Navigator: Gestaltung und Analyse von Geschäftslösungen "Business-to-IT", pp. 1–13. Springer, Berlin (2011)

91. Schilling, R.D., et al.: Extending CCM4DSR for collaborative diagnosis of socio-technical problems. In: 12th International Conference on Design Science Research in Information Systems and Technology (DESRIST 2017). Springer, Karlsruhe, Germany (2017)

92. Schelp, J., Winter, R.: On the interplay of design research and behavioral research—a language community perspective. In: Third International Conference on Design Science Research in Information Systems and Technology (DESRIST2008), Georgia State University (2008)

93. Aier, S., Johnson, P., Schelp, J.: TEAR 2008. Pre-Proceedings of the 3rd Workshop on Trends in Enterprise Architecture Research. In: The 3rd Workshop on Trends in Enterprise Architecture Research (TEAR 2008) (2008)

94. Abraham, R., et al.: Understanding coordination support of enterprise architecture management – empirical analysis and implications for practice. In: Americas Conference on Information Systems (AMCIS), Chicago, IL (2013)

95. Labusch, N., et al.: Architectural support of enterprise transformations: insights from corporate practice. In: Multikonferenz Wirtschaftsinformatik 2014. Universität Paderborn, Paderborn (2014)

96. Labusch, N., et al.: The architects' perspective on enterprise transformation: an explorative study. In: 6th Working Conference, PRET 2013. Springer, Utrecht (2013)

97. Proper, H.A., et al. (eds.): Architectural Coordination of Enterprise Transformation. The Enterprise Engineering Series. Springer, Cham (2017)
98. Abraham, R., et al.: Transformation intelligence capability catalogue. In: Proper, H.A., et al. (eds.) Architectural Coordination of Enterprise Transformation, pp. 175–181. Springer, Cham (2017)
99. Lahrmann, G., et al.: Management of large-scale transformation programs: state of the practice and future potential. In: 7th Workshop, TEAR 2012, and 5th Working Conference, PRET 2012 at The Open Group Conference 2012. Springer, Barcelona (2012)
100. Labusch, N., Winter, R.: Method support of large-scale transformation in the insurance sector: exploring foundations. In: 7th Workshop, TEAR 2012, and 5th Working Conference, PRET 2012 at The Open Group Conference 2012. Springer, Barcelona (2012)
101. Abraham, R., Aier, S., Winter, R.: Crossing the line: overcoming knowledge boundaries in enterprise transformation. Bus. Inf. Syst. Eng. **57**(1), 3–13 (2015)
102. Abraham, R., et al.: Can boundary objects mitigate communication defects in enterprise transformation? Findings from expert interviews. In: 5th International Workshop on Enterprise Modelling and Information Systems Architectures (EMISA 2013). Gesellschaft für Informatik (GI), St. Gallen (2013)
103. Abraham, R., Tribolet, J., Winter, R.: Transformation of multi-level systems – theoretical grounding and consequences for enterprise architecture management. In: Advances in Enterprise Engineering VII, pp. 73–87 (2013)
104. Labusch, N., Aier, S., Winter, R.: Beyond enterprise architecture modeling – what are the essentials to support enterprise transformations? In: 5th International Workshop on Enterprise Modelling and Information Systems Architectures (EMISA 2013). Gesellschaft für Informatik (GI), St. Gallen (2013)
105. Labusch, N.: The ACET information requirements reference model. In: Proper, H.A., et al. (eds.) Architectural Coordination of Enterprise Transformation, pp. 211–220. Springer, Cham (2017)
106. Labusch, N.: Information requirements for enterprise transformation. In: Proper, H.A., et al. (eds.) Architectural Coordination of Enterprise Transformation, pp. 111–121. Springer, Cham (2017)

The Competence Center Health Network Engineering: A Retrospective

Lars Baacke, René Fitterer, Anke Helmes, Tobias Mettler, and Peter Rohner

Abstract Founded in 2005 at the Institute of Information Systems at the University of St. Gallen (IWI-HSG), the Competence Center Health Network Engineering (CC HNE) represented an association of researchers and practitioners whose goal was to support the transformation of the Swiss healthcare system with models and methods from the St. Gallen business engineering approach. This paper provides a retrospective of the work of the CC HNE. Starting with a motivation for the research focus as well as a classification in the research of the IWI-HSG, the main research results of the Competence Center are presented. This includes in particular work on networkability, performance management and maturity models as well as a Networkability Maturity Model. Subsequently, it will be discussed how the research results have found their way into practice (keyword: relevance). Here, the focus is on established communities of practice, whereby the application of the results in the context of the IT community of practice is examined in more detail. Finally, the results are subjected to a critical appraisal and an outlook on the need for further research is given.

L. Baacke
BEG Analytics AG, Schaffhausen, Switzerland
e-mail: lars.baacke@beganalytics.com

R. Fitterer
SAP (Switzerland) AG, Regensdorf, Switzerland
e-mail: rene.fitterer@sap.com

A. Helmes
BOC Information Technologies Consulting GmbH, Berlin, Germany
e-mail: anke.helmes@boc-group.com

T. Mettler
University of Lausanne, Lausanne, Switzerland
e-mail: tobias.mettler@unil.ch

P. Rohner (✉)
Institute of Information Management, University of St. Gallen, St. Gallen, Switzerland
e-mail: peter.rohner@unisg.ch

© The Author(s), under exclusive license to Springer Nature Switzerland AG 2021 225
S. Aier et al. (eds.), *Engineering the Transformation of the Enterprise*,
https://doi.org/10.1007/978-3-030-84655-8_14

Keywords Applied research · E-health · Healthcare · Center of excellence research · Community of practice · Benchmarking · Maturity models

1 Introduction

In 2005, the Swiss healthcare system appeared to be facing major financial challenges due to changing demographic, health, social, political and economic conditions as well as new pharmaceutical and technical possibilities. A transformation of the hospital landscape and thus of the entire service provision was under discussion. This was the trigger for the launch of the Competence Center "Health Network Engineering" (CC HNE) in spring 2005. Robert Winter had set himself the goal of transferring the methods and models for the transformation of companies and business networks, which had been developed at the Institute of Information Systems at the University of St.Gallen (IWI-HSG) since the mid-1990s, to the healthcare sector. Against this background, he put together a group of young researchers who were to deal with the systematic optimization of services, cooperations, processes, structural organizations, etc. jointly by "business" and "IT". The purpose was to strengthen the strategic freedom of action and operational excellence of Swiss hospitals or their networks.

Between 2005 and 2012, 12 large-scale workshops were held with a total of 260 participants from hospitals (management, clinical staff, employees from medical services, employees from support functions and administration). Surveys (e.g. on the status of cooperation management, on process orientation or on the practice of information management) as well as around 300 individually conducted qualitative and quantitative interviews were used to gain insights. On this basis, it was possible, together with hospital partners, to design and test new methods and models for solving the problems that were supposed to arise soon. The results were directed on the one hand to the practice with the aim of offering good instruments to those responsible for hospitals (management, cadres from the medical profession and nursing as well as in the support services) and on the other hand to the scientific community dealing with the field. The dissertations of the authors of this report, Anke Helmes, Lars Baacke, René Fitterer and Tobias Mettler, as well as the habilitation of Peter Rohner emerged from this.

After a few cycles of research and development, it became clear that the CC HNE methods and models, which were well received at scientific conferences and in journals, were (still) "solutions looking for a not yet identified problem" from the hospitals' perspective. The CC HNE was ahead of the curve in terms of the pressures on effectiveness, quality, and efficiency in hospitals. In addition, the medical and nursing staff, whose personal commitment to patients is arguably the real "treasure" of the health care system, naturally had reservations about the business-driven projects. It was to take several more years before the instruments found the hoped-for acceptance in practice. This makes it all the more gratifying to look back on the intensive work in the CC HNE from the present time, in which the topics launched by the CC HNE are moving to the center of the development of Swiss hospitals.

2 The Research Focus Health Network Engineering

2.1 Motivation

The Competence Center "Health Network Engineering" (CC HNE) was founded in 2005 at the Institute of Information Systems (IWI) of the University of St. Gallen (HSG). A Competence Center (CC) is understood to be an association of researchers and practitioners who jointly solve practice-related problems in a domain. The CC HNE focuses on various problems in the Swiss health care system [1].

In the early 2000s, the Swiss health care system was faced with major challenges due to the increasingly rapid changes in social, political and economic conditions in conjunction with ever new technical possibilities (see also Sect. 1) [1–3]. In particular, the question of how to shape the transformation process of the Swiss healthcare system to the information age (keyword: e-health) had to be solved. In this context, the focus is on various aspects—from strategy to organizational structure and process organization to information technology: starting with the definition of services, solutions must be found for service provision and quality assurance as well as service recording and billing in the healthcare sector.

The ability of the individual players in the healthcare system to network is seen as a success factor for implementation. These actors include, for example, hospitals and doctors' practices, care facilities, laboratories and pharmacies, medical technology and pharmaceutical suppliers as well as insurers, logistics companies and other service providers [2, 3]. Networking capability is "[...] the ability to connect as quickly as possible and at low cost with other actors in the health care system for joint service provision [...]" [4].

Against the background described above, the Competence Center Health Network Engineering has set itself the task of supporting the transformation of the Swiss healthcare system as a neutral partner. For the implementation of a successful transformation, various focal points have been set in the CC HNE—also through the orientation of the various partners [5]. In addition to the networking capability already mentioned, these include process management in hospitals, performance management in the healthcare system, and maturity models for the further development of the networking of the individual players in the healthcare system.

2.2   Classification in the Research of the IWI-HSG

The research of the Competence Center Health Network Engineering builds on the research results of the IWI-HSG or integrates with various parallel research initiatives.

First of all, CC HNE applies the methods and models of the St. Gallen Business Engineering approach [6–8], which has been developed and refined at IWI-HSG for decades. The St. Gallen Business Engineering approach is a framework that provides methods and (reference) models to systematically design networked, efficient structures at all levels of organizations, i.e., from the strategy to the organizational to the (IT) system level [2–4].

In addition to the St. Gallen Business Engineering approach, the research of the CC HNE also builds on or integrates various fundamental works of the IWI-HSG. This includes, among others, work dealing with fundamental questions on the topics of result types model vs. method [9], situational method engineering [10, 11] or situational maturity models [12, 13].

Finally, in parallel to the CC HNE, there are other Competence Centers at IWI-HSG that deal with application-oriented research in various domains (such as the CC Integration Factory with the topic of Enterprise Architecture Management (EAM)) and cross-fertilize the research of the CC HNE.

3   Research Results of the Competence Center Health Network Engineering

3.1   Networking Capability and Component-Based Modeling

In the wake of rising costs and increasingly restrained budgets for healthcare [14, 15], networking capability (see Sect. 2.1) is a key requirement at the strategic, organizational, and technical levels. It is thus a key design object for benefiting from specialization and collaboration with business partners without incurring greater costs for each partnership initiated.

A representation of the artifacts of a design object, such as the networking capability of the healthcare system, in the form of models pursues the goal of explicating the fundamental structuring of the organization, which serves for analysis purposes and as a basis for making decisions about its design. The basis for modeling a complex phenomenon is a suitable framework. Frameworks are conceptual and heuristic aids to represent an object system. "Conceptual means that they help to conceptualize and structure an object. Heuristic means that they can support the finding of a solution" [16].

Existing frameworks integrate methods and models for the design and development of the respective design object and define corresponding meta-models or vocabularies to ensure an intersubjectively comprehensible description of the models [17, 18]. However, a corresponding adaptation to the respective concerns of the stakeholders of an organization is usually not methodically supported. As described in Sect. 2.2, numerous frameworks have been defined in EAM in various contributions by researchers and practitioners [19–22]. However, the frameworks described usually only define generic modeling approaches, for example, for coverage analysis [23].

As part of the work on the EU-funded PICTURE project [24], the usefulness of semantically annotated and standardized building blocks for modeling processes was explored. Based on such models, process characteristics can be measured and corresponding potential weaknesses can be identified. The measurement is not limited to the scope of individual processes, but the analysis can be carried out across the entire process landscape, enabling prioritization of ICT investments based on indicators such as process complexity, number of organizational interfaces or media discontinuities. Such rankings also make it possible to prioritize specific modernization projects.

Building on these findings, a comprehensive metamodel of the specific entities from the perspective of a hospital was described in [25]. By means of focus group discussions, a total of 21 influencing factors were identified which lead to an increase in networking capability. These were assigned to one of the five dimensions of consideration (environment, strategy, organization, system, values and culture) of the business engineering approach adapted to healthcare (cf. Sect. 2.2). By means of an explorative survey, the identified influencing factors were given to a broad audience for evaluation. These influencing factors form the basis for deriving rules and norm strategies for the systematic development of networking capability in healthcare organizations.

3.2 Performance Management and Maturity Models

Public sector organizations are different compared to their commercial counterparts in the private sector. There is no focus on profit maximization, little potential for revenue generation, and, generally speaking, no end result against which performance can ultimately be measured [26]. Performance measurement is therefore seen as a somewhat daunting endeavor. However, from a management perspective, performance is defined as a valuable contribution to the achievement of an organization's goals [27].

Mettler and Rohner [28] stated that at the strategic level, key performance indicators (KPIs) must be defined for shaping the economy, efficiency and effectiveness of service delivery (Strategize) and the redesign and operationalization of processes must be initiated (Plan). In addition, the operational level must focus on measuring and reporting performance (Monitor and Analyze) and optimizing and adjusting processes (Take Corrective Action). By linking the strategic and operational levels, performance management (PM) provides feedback based on specifics rather than generalizations [29]. This gives both clinical and administrative decision makers the ability to know at any point in time whether the strategy they are formulating is actually working, and if not, why.

Building on the findings of this work (see [28] and [29]), the focus was on prioritizing areas for action in terms of a roadmap to optimize PM quality, efficiency, and effectiveness of healthcare organizations, particularly in the area of networking capability and supply chain management.

A particular focus is on the development of maturity models. Maturity assessment approaches originate mainly from the field of quality management. Maturity, "the state of being complete, perfect, or ready" [30], as an assessment criterion for quality management was first introduced in Crosby's Quality Management Maturity Grid (CQMM) [31]. Crosby defines five evolutionary stages of how an organization adopts quality practices based on similar concepts to those of Gibson and Nolan [32], who stated that an organization goes through different stages when adopting technologies.

3.3   Networkability Maturity Model

Initial work by CC HNE already pointed to the need to create "development and maturity stages" [33] to enable an assessment of an organization's current networking capability and to provide recommendations for action for its further development. Based on these initial findings, a total of 24 maturity models were examined for their applicability in creating a maturity model for networking capability [34]. This serves to define a method for identifying and structuring functional and technical design objects that determine the maturity level of networking among healthcare providers. The maturity model of networking capability consists of six components and corresponding factors (cf Fig. 1) and, as described in the following chapter, forms a methodological basis for the benchmarking of the performance of Swiss hospitals used in Switzerland to date.

4   Relevance of Research and Current Trends

Despite the high level of complexity and the rather low pressure to change, digitization has now also picked up speed in the Swiss healthcare system—not only in the core areas of medical and nursing service provision, but also in cross-organizational collaboration and in the area of management and support processes. The models and methods of CC HNE contributed to this.

For every research work, the question arises as to its practical applicability and its contribution to problem solving. The work produced at CC HNE is still used today in various communities of practice, including IT (www.it-benchmark.ch) and procurement & logistics (www.beschaffungsbenchmark.ch). Every year, well over 100 support areas from hospitals, psychiatric clinics, rehabilitation and special clinics as well

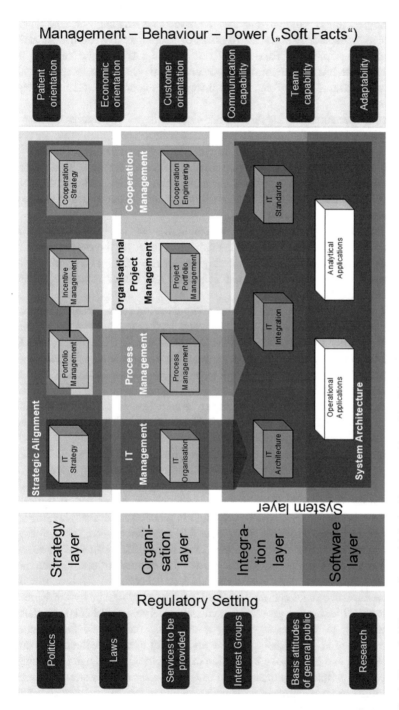

Fig. 1 Networkability maturity model for healthcare providers [34]. © 2010 BEG Analytics AG, reprinted with permission

as retirement and nursing homes in Switzerland and Germany participate in the systematic benchmark comparisons and the associated exchange of experience: In the first step, transparency is created (through own, comparative and historical data). In the second step, knowledge is derived on the basis of the methods used (e.g. maturity models). In the third step, impact is achieved by the companies taking appropriate measures. The effect can be measured in concrete terms in subsequent benchmarks.

The measurement and analysis methods—consisting of key figures on costs and performance (efficiency), information on effectiveness, and qualitative surveys—provide a comprehensive view of the company's own organization. The classification into reference groups and the presentation of trends ensure a high degree of comparability and relevance of the statements, even for companies with different structures. A few examples will be used to illustrate this system and at the same time present some current trends.

The Community of Practice in IT was created in 2008 and has been continuously developed since then. The associated benchmark is based on the assumption that an IT service provider should ensure both high efficiency of the IT organization and high business application benefit. Both efficiency and benefit score are systematically quantified and compared.

For IT as a percentage of total healthcare organization costs, recent values ranged from 2.3% to 6.9%, with half of the participants having values between 3.62% and 4.95%. The median in 2019 was 4.29%, with a mean of 4.42% (see Fig. 2, left). Over time, it has become clear in recent years that IT costs are steadily increasing—not only in absolute terms, but also relative to the healthcare organization's total costs and total revenue (cf. Fig. 2 right). In a benchmark comparison with other companies in the same reference group, these values can be an indication of the need to catch up or an investment backlog (cf. trend lines in Fig. 2 on the right) as well as providing indications of future strategic orientation.

It can therefore be observed that more and more is being invested in IT. The reason for this can also be seen in the benchmark: IT is providing more and more services—from telephony and mobile device management, through logistics and home automation, to medical technology, sensor technology and data analytics. The increase in services is disproportionately high in most organizations, i.e., the scope of services has been growing faster than IT costs have been rising for years (cf. typical scissor shape of the two trend lines in Fig. 3). It can thus be seen that the efficiency of IT—understood as the measurable quotient of performance points (output) and IT costs (input)—is also steadily increasing.

The performance trend can be explained, among other things, by the increasing penetration of IT resources, growing virtualization (servers and clients) and mobility (smart devices), as well as a growing number of small applications (apps) in particular. The rapid growth requires new approaches to manage the complexity of IT architectures and to improve innovation capability (e.g., with agile methods).

While the IT of many healthcare organizations was historically strongly rooted in the infrastructure area, application management and, above all, innovation management are now playing an increasingly important strategic role (see Fig. 4, left).

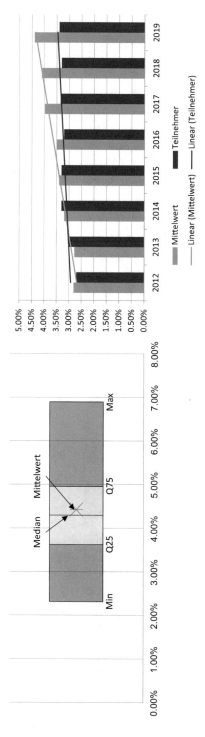

Fig. 2 Share of IT costs in total organizational costs (IT benchmark 2019, BEG Analytics AG, www.it-benchmark.ch). © 2019 BEG Analytics AG, reprinted with permission

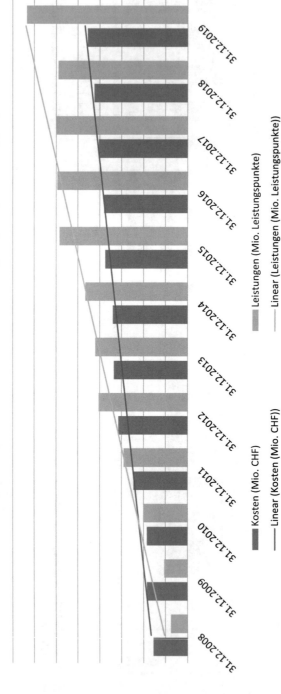

Fig. 3 Development of costs and scope of services (IT benchmark 2019, BEG Analytics AG, www.it-benchmark.ch). © *2019 BEG Analytics AG, reprinted with permission*

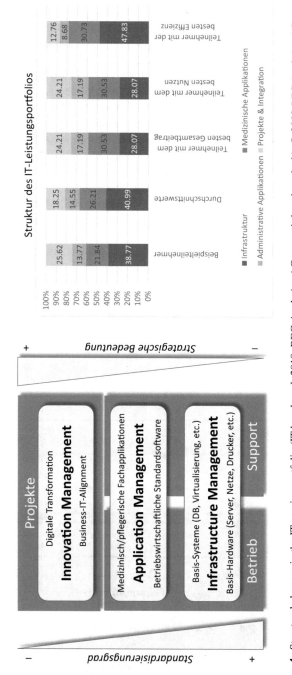

Fig. 4 Structural changes in the IT service portfolio (IT benchmark 2019, BEG Analytics AG, www.it-benchmark.ch). © 2019 BEG Analytics AG, *reprinted with permission*

Accordingly, the service portfolio, the role and strategy, the sourcing concepts, and the qualifications, methods and tools of the IT department are also changing. Figure 4 (right-hand side) shows, for example, that benchmark participants with high efficiency often provide a disproportionately high share of infrastructure services. On the other hand, participants with a high proportion of services in application management and innovation (projects, integration, etc.) are able to provide greater benefits and a higher overall contribution to the organization as a whole. These comparisons can also be used in benchmarking with other participants to derive insights for one's own organization and measures for future alignment.

In addition to efficiency, the benchmark also measures and compares the benefit of specialist applications (calculation of benefit scores between 0 and 100% depending on the respective functional maturity and the range of use of the application functions). The measurement methodology was developed in CC HNE [35]. It is used to assess the entire application landscape in an industry comparison. On this basis, potential for improvement and backlog demand in the support of the various business processes can be identified and concrete measures for digitization can be derived.

In addition to a large number of other specific indicators and comparative variables (e.g., personnel structure, support, IT security, business-IT alignment), the strategic orientation of an IT organization in terms of efficiency and benefit can also be derived from the data (see Fig. 5). The following diagram shows the distribution of the benchmark participants (differentiated by reference group) in the area of

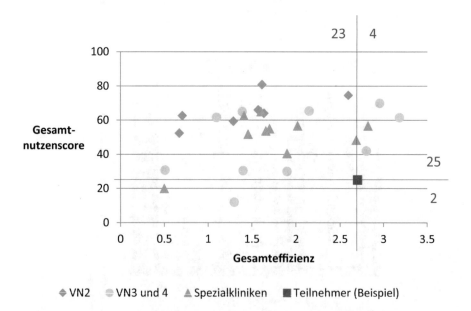

Fig. 5 Strategic positioning in the area of tension between efficiency and application benefit (IT benchmark 2019, BEG Analytics AG, www.it-benchmark.ch). © *2019 BEG Analytics AG, reprinted with permission*

conflict between efficiency and benefit. For each individual participant, it can be concluded whether the focus should be on increasing efficiency or benefits in the future, e.g., through higher standardization and consolidation or by increasing investment in digitization and integration projects.

For the participant marked in red in Fig. 5, it can be seen that only two participants have an even lower application benefit, while at the same time only four participants have an even higher efficiency. In this case, the strategic thrust should be aimed at consistent further development of the application benefit.

The community approach also encourages the exchange of experience beyond pure data analysis. Joint annual events and workshops, individual follow-up discussions, presentations and management summaries, as well as annually changing additional surveys on current focus topics (e.g., business-IT alignment, megatrends, or IT security) and further innovation and research projects round out the collaboration of the community members and their business and scientific partners. The findings flow directly into the strategic, organizational and systems development of the support organization.

The community approach has proven to be a sustainable link between science and practice. The key performance indicator and maturity models developed as part of CC HNE's research still form a powerful basis for continuous business engineering and networking in the healthcare sector and are continuously developed along current digitization trends.

5 Discussion and Outlook

5.1 Critical Appraisal

The work of the CC HNE shows that research within the framework of the St. Gallen Business Engineering approach can both be used beneficially in practice and produce new theoretical insights for research [36]. Numerous methods and models, which were developed during the existence of the CC HNE, have passed the so-called "applicability check" [37] and are still being used in practice after the activities of the CC HNE have ceased. In this context, the developed maturity models, benchmarking tools and other artifacts have taken on the function of "boundary objects" [38], which are used to create a common understanding of complex or paradoxical problems in healthcare (e.g. intra- and interorganizational collaboration and coordination of certain activities such as material procurement, digitalization, etc.). The pragmatic research-orientation of the CC HNE has not only produced concrete and tangible results, but has also fostered the establishment of communities of practice [39] and thus created a continuous transfer of knowledge (even after the end of a research project or program). This seems to be a major challenge for many research groups [40].

From a scientific point of view, the research work within the framework of the CC HNE has attracted attention in particular because of its transdisciplinary character

Informationsfluss vom Ärztehaus in das Spital

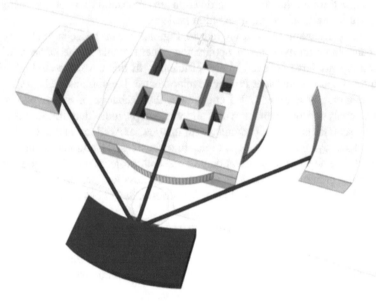

Fig. 6 Merging business process management and architectural design as the basis for hospital construction

[41]. Thus, not only has an intensive exchange between practitioners and researchers been cultivated, but disciplinary divides have often been overcome. Examples include the application of business process management to hospital construction (see Fig. 6) or the networking of hospital pharmacy and logistics. Accordingly, the research results of CC HNE have been widely published in the relevant scientific journals and conferences of different domains (e.g., business informatics, health economics, public administration, medical informatics).

5.2 Outlook on the Need for Further Research

The current Covid 19 pandemic is not the only reason why the healthcare sector will face major challenges in the future. Hospitals are confronted with numerous technological innovations, such as the increased use of process automation and decision-making based on applications in artificial intelligence, Internet of Things or service robots [42]. This requires rethinking and adapting existing structures, processes, and organizational culture, which in turn suggests that designing networking capability will remain a key management task to ensure successful adoption and smooth operations.

The pandemic, however, has shown that not only crisis management but also organizational preparedness is an important issue. The work of the CC HNE at the chair of Robert Winter, in particular the basic research in the field of maturity modeling [3, 12, 34], has made a valuable contribution in this respect and forms the basis of numerous new artifacts for the measurement of maturity or preparedness of hospitals and other health care providers [43–45]. In this respect, the methods and models of CC HNE are not only "boundary objects" for practitioners, but can also be further refined, adapted and extended in the context of research projects.

References

1. Rohner, P.: Den Weg in ein Vernetztes Gesundheitswesen fundiert erarbeiten. SIR Medical - Die Fachzeitschrift für ICT und neue Trends in Medizin & Gesundheitswesen. **2005**, 2–3 (2005)
2. Helmes (née Gericke), A., Rohner, P., Winter, R.: Netzwerkfähigkeit im Gesundheitswesen. Swiss Med. Inform. **59** (2006)
3. Helmes (née Gericke), A., Rohner, P., Winter, R.: Vernetzungsfähigkeit im Gesundheitswesen – Notwendigkeit, Bewertung und systematische Entwicklung als Voraussetzung zur Erhöhung der Wirtschaftlichkeit administrativer Prozesse. HMD – Praxis der Wirtschaftsinformatik **251** (2006)
4. Mettler, T., Rohner, P.: Faktoren zur Steigerung der Vernetzungsfähigkeit im Gesundheitswesen: Herleitung und Empirische Validierung. Gesundheitsökonomie & Qualitätsmanagement. **14**, 311–316 (2009)
5. Back, A., von Krogh, G., Enkel, E.: The CC model as organizational design striving to combine relevance and rigor. Syst. Pract. Action Res. **20**, 91–103 (2007)
6. Österle, H., Winter, R. (eds.): Business Engineering: Auf dem Weg zum Unternehmen des Informationszeitalters. Springer, Berlin (2003)
7. Österle, H., Back, A., Winter, R., Brenner, W. (eds.): Business Engineering—Die ersten 15 Jahre. Springer, Berlin (2004)
8. Winter, R.: Business Engineering Navigator: Gestaltung und Analyse von Geschäftslösungen "Business-to-IT". Springer, Berlin (2011)
9. Winter, R., Gericke, A., Bucher, T.: Method versus model–two sides of the same coin? In: Albani, A., Barjis, J., Dietz, J.L.G. (eds.) Advances in Enterprise Engineering Iii, pp. 1–15. Springer, Berlin (2009)
10. Helmes (née Gericke), A.: Konstruktion Situativer Artefakte: Beiträge zur Konstruktionsforschung Und Zur Artefaktkonstruktion. Institut für Wirtschaftsinformatik, Dissertation. Universität St. Gallen (2009)
11. Helmes (née Gericke), A., Winter, R.: Situational Change Engineering in Healthcare. In: Proceedings of the European Conference on eHealth 2006, pp. 227–238. Fribourg, Schweiz (2006)
12. Mettler, T., Rohner, P.: Situational maturity models as instrumental artifacts for organizational design. In: Proceedings of the 4th International Conference on Design Science Research in Information Systems and Technology, pp. 1–9. Philadelphia (2009)
13. Mettler, T.: Supply Management im Krankenhaus: Konstruktion und Evaluation eines konfigurierbaren Reifegradmodells zur zielgerichteten Gestaltung. Institut für Wirtschaftsinformatik, Dissertation. Universität St.Gallen (2010)
14. Slembeck, T.: Kostentreiber im Schweizer Gesundheitswesen: Eine Auslegeordnung. Santésuisse. (2006)
15. Weisbrod, B.A.: The health care quadrilemma: an essay on technological change, insurance, quality of care, and cost containment. J. Econ. Lit. **29**, 523–552 (1991)

16. Schwaninger, M.: Was ist ein Modell? In: Dubs, R., Euler, D., Rüegg-Stürm, J., Wyss, C. (eds.) Einführung in die Managementlehre, pp. 53–63. Haupt Verlag, Bern (2004)
17. The Open Group (ed.): Togaf Version 9 – the Open Group Architecture Framework. The Open Group, San Francisco (2009)
18. Winter, R., Fischer, R.: Essential layers, artifacts, and dependencies of enterprise architecture. In: Proceedings of the 10th IEEE International Enterprise Distributed Object Computing Conference Workshops, pp. 30. Hong Kong (2006)
19. Zachman, J.A.: A framework for information systems architecture. IBM Syst. J. **26**, 276–292 (1987)
20. IFIP-IFAC Task Force on Architectures for Enterprise Integration: Geram: The Generalised Enterprise Reference Architecture and Methodology: Version 1.6.3 (Final). In: Bernus, P., Nemes, L., Schmidt, G. (eds.) Handbook on Enterprise Architecture, pp. 21–63. Springer, Berlin (2003)
21. Goethals, F.G., Snoeck, M., Lemahieu, W., Vandenbulcke, J.: Management and enterprise architecture click: the Fad (E) E framework. Inf. Syst. Front. **8**, 67–79 (2006)
22. CIO Council: Federal Enterprise Architecture Framework (FEAF). United States Office of Management and Budget. (1999)
23. Aier, S., Riege, C., Winter, R.: Unternehmensarchitektur–Literaturüberblick und Stand der Praxis. Wirtschaftsinformatik. **50**, 292–304 (2008)
24. Baacke, L., Becker, J., Bergener, P., Fitterer, R., Greiner, U.: ICT-enabled optimization of government processes. In: Weerakkody, V., Janssen, M., Dwivedi, Y.K. (eds.) Handbook of Research on ICT-Enabled Transformational Government: A Global Perspective, pp. 117–139. IGI Global, Hershey (2009)
25. Mettler, T., Rohner, P., Baacke, L.: Improving data quality of health information systems: a holistic design-oriented approach. In: Proceedings of the 16th European Conference on Information Systems, pp. 1883–1893. Galway, Ireland (2008)
26. Boland, T., Fowler, A.: A systems perspective of performance management in public sector organisations. Int. J. Public Sect. Manag. **13**, 417–446 (2000)
27. Hoffmann, O.: Performance Management – Systeme und Implementierungsansätze. Haupt, Bern (2002)
28. Mettler, T., Rohner, P.: Performance management in health care: the past, the present, and the future. In: Tagungsband der 9. Internationale Tagung Wirtschaftsinformatik, pp. 699–708. Wien (2009)
29. Amaratunga, D., Baldry, D.: Moving from performance measurement to performance management. Facilities. **20**, 217–223 (2002)
30. Simpson, J.A., Weiner, E.S.C.: The Oxford English Dictionary. Oxford University Press, Oxford (1989)
31. Crosby, P.B.: Quality Is Free—the Art of Making Quality Certain. McGraw-Hill, New York (1979)
32. Gibson, C.F., Nolan, R.L.: Managing the four stages of EDP growth. Harv. Bus. Rev. **52**, 76–88 (1974)
33. Helmes (née Gericke), A., Rohner, P., Winter, R.: Networkability in the health care sector-necessity, measurement and systematic development as the prerequisites for increasing the operational efficiency of administrative processes. In: Proceedings of the 17th Australasian Conference on Information Systems, pp. 1–9. Adelaide, Australia (2006)
34. Fitterer, R., Rohner, P.: Towards assessing the networkability of health care providers: a maturity model approach. IseB. **8**, 309–333 (2010)
35. Fitterer, R.: Anforderungsbasierte Bewertung der Informationssystemarchitektur von mittelgrossen gemeinnützigen Krankenhäusern. Institut für Wirtschaftsinformatik. Dissertation. Universität St. Gallen (2010)
36. Nunamaker, J.F., Briggs, R.O., Derrick, D.C., Schwabe, G.: The last research mile: achieving both rigor and relevance in information systems research. J. Manag. Inf. Syst. **32**, 10–47 (2015)

37. Rosemann, M., Vessey, I.: Toward improving the relevance of information systems research to practice: the role of applicability checks. MIS Q. **32**, 1–22 (2008)
38. Abraham, R., Aier, S., Winter, R.: Crossing the line: overcoming knowledge boundaries in enterprise transformation. Bus. Inf. Syst. Eng. **57**, 3–13 (2015)
39. Mettler, T.: Contextualizing a professional social network for health care: experiences from an action design research study. Inf. Syst. J. **28**, 684–707 (2018)
40. Rai, A.: Engaged scholarship: research with practice for impact. MIS Q. **43**, iii–viii (2019)
41. Mettler, T., Rohner, P., Winter, R.: Transdisciplinary and transformative research at the intersection between management, healthcare, and innovation. Gaia. **23**, 272–274 (2014)
42. Mettler, T., Sprenger, M., Winter, R.: Service robots in hospitals: new perspectives on niche evolution and technology affordances. Eur. J. Inf. Syst. **26**, 451–468 (2017)
43. Carvalho, J.V., Rocha, Á., van de Wetering, R., Abreu, A.: A maturity model for hospital information systems. J. Bus. Res. **94**, 388–399 (2019)
44. Gastaldi, L., Pietrosi, A., Lessanibahri, S., Paparella, M., Scaccianoce, A., Provenzale, G., Corso, M., Gridelli, B.: Measuring the maturity of business intelligence in healthcare: supporting the development of a roadmap toward precision medicine within Ismett Hospital. Technol. Forecast. Soc. Chang. **128**, 84–103 (2018)
45. Van Dyk, L.: The development of a telemedicine service maturity model. Stellenbosch University. (2013)

A Research Agenda for Studying Platform Ecosystems

Kazem Haki

Abstract Platform ecosystems are complex ecologies of firms with individual and collective, intertwined interests, whose expansion and growth follows through the co-evolution of the digital platform core and the ecosystem participants' interests and stakes. Adhering to a sociotechnical perspective, this chapter proposes a research agenda to study the co-evolution of platform ecosystems' technical and social aspects comprising the digital platform and its ecosystem of heterogeneous stakeholders. The proposed research agenda seeks to provide a basis to generate both descriptive and design theories when studying platform ecosystems.

Keywords Digital platforms · Platform ecosystems · Descriptive theories · Design theories

1 Motivation to the Research Agenda

Digitalization and digital transformation have become an essential part of contemporary organizations' life and fabric. The use of novel digital means has not only facilitated business operations, but also created new ways of economic exchange and novel types of institutional arrangements. One of the prevalent means to leverage digital transformation is *digital platform*—a technological foundation upon which other firms can develop complementary products, technologies, or services [1].

With the rise of the platform economy [2, 3], digital platforms have become omnipresent in various industries and change the fabric of organizations. In catching up with the platform economy, in recent years a plethora of platform native companies were founded (e.g., Uber, Airbnb) and many technology incumbents strongly invested in entering the platform business (e.g., Apple's iOS, Google's Android). Further, many companies also considered *platformization* of their established

K. Haki (✉)
Institute of Information Management, University of St. Gallen, St. Gallen, Switzerland
e-mail: kazem.haki@unisg.ch

© The Author(s), under exclusive license to Springer Nature Switzerland AG 2021
S. Aier et al. (eds.), *Engineering the Transformation of the Enterprise*,
https://doi.org/10.1007/978-3-030-84655-8_15

business, i.e., shifting from a product-based competition strategy to a platform-based competition strategy such as the key players in the enterprise software market (e.g., SAP, Salesforce).

Such phenomenal rise of the platform economy has resulted in the emergence of the world's most valuable companies such as Apple, Google, Microsoft, and Amazon, [4], each of them marked by a digital platform [5–7]. In such an unleased rise of the platform economy, while few digital platforms thrive and grow, like those of Apple (*iOS*), Google (*Android*), or *Amazon.com*, many others fail to sustain in the long run. An example of digital platform failure is Microsoft's operating system *Windows Phone*. In 2017, Microsoft discontinued its support for *Windows Phone* [8] with only 0.2% of all smart-phones running the *Windows Phone* operating system [9]. Therefore, *digital platform success and its sustained evolution* is an interesting and timely topic of investigation in digitalization era.

The concept of platform is not a new one (e.g., [10]). Platform and its peripherals shape an *ecosystem* of heterogeneous stakeholders that take advantage of the platform to develop innovative value propositions for their customers [11–13]. Nevertheless, the inherent capabilities of digital technologies have extended the use cases of platforms and accelerated the platformization of established businesses (e.g., telecommunication firms) and systems (e.g., enterprise systems). Therefore, "digital" platforms have become the central hub of platform ecosystems, which are, thanks to digital technologies, able to attract a plethora of business actors contributing to the success and growth of the platform and its ecosystem. Therefore, we ground our research on the premise that *digital platform success and its sustained evolution* is contingent on the contribution of a critical mass of actors within each of the relevant actor roles of the respective *ecosystem* such as owner, complementors, and end users [6, 7, 14]. Each of these actor roles offer complementary resources to the respective ecosystem to serve a wide range of end users and to satisfy various requirements [15].

Due to a multitude of actors' engagement in the ecosystem, digital platform success and sustained evolution becomes considerably depend on the digital platform's ability to *simultaneously* allow for structural stability (exploitation)—to reliably serve networked business activities—and for change and innovation (exploration)—to make the ecosystem attractive and open for new actors [16]. Thus, to thrive in the long run, digital platforms require a delicate balance of control by an owner (*control*) and autonomy among the other independent actors (*generativity*) [5, 17–22]. Extant literature approaches generativity and control as a *duality* [21, 23]. That is, the paradoxical combination of control and generativity presents the requirement of digital platforms *simultaneously* being governed by the owner's centralized top-down control and distributed actors' autonomy [5]. This *generativity-control* paradox is thus central in understanding digital platform success and sustained evolution [16].

Beyond the technical aspect, digital platforms are sociotechnical phenomena and viewed as a central point of gravity within their business ecosystems. For instance, Android and iOS have become the cornerstone and the *raison d'être* of their respective mobile telecommunications ecosystems. Through exploiting digital technologies, digital platforms facilitate the integration of resources among multiple, varied, and interdependent actors in different roles. Since these actors *and* their relations evolve over time in varied patterns [12], digital platform success and sustained evolution is considerably dependent on how the relation between different actors with various roles (e.g., owner, complementors, end user) are dynamically configured to *jointly* create value for the particular needs of specific end users [24]. Therefore, the nature of value creation in ecosystems is networked, emergent, and contingent on the digital platform's capabilities in bringing together a critical mass of diminutive resource sets [14, 20]. In case of malfunction, these specificities can substantially impede digital platform success [5]. Digital platform success and sustained evolution is thereby highly dependent on its abilities to ensure efficient and effective *value co-creation* processes among actors in the ecosystem [14, 25–27]. Thus, digital platforms derive much of their value from the business ecosystems they serve. That is, digital platforms become more valuable and can sustainably grow when more actors join the ecosystem to co-create value through their complementary business and technological resources [5, 6].

The main goal of this chapter is to provide a research agenda on how digital platforms and their pertinent business ecosystems co-evolve with regard to ongoing changes in requirements and technologies, and consequently in configurations of both digital platforms and business ecosystems, and how this co-evolutionary process relates to a platform's success and sustained evolution. In other words, we aim to understand how digital platforms transform economic exchanges and enable the emergence of business ecosystems as well as how novel economic exchanges and dynamic configurations of business ecosystems stimulate the emergence of digital platforms.

2 An Overview of the Current State of Research

The concept of *platform* dates back to the late 1990s [10, 28], where research started to focus technology as a mediating factor on innovation activities of two cooperating actors [29]. In the mid-2000s, due to the ever-growing rise of business ecosystems [30], research started to focus platforms as a mediator for networked, multi-lateral innovation activities. Recently platform is defined as "a business based on enabling value-creating interactions between external producers and consumers. The platform provides an open, participative infrastructure for these interactions and sets governance conditions for them. The platform's overarching purpose is to consummate matches among users and facilitate the exchange of goods, services, or social currency, thereby enabling value [co-]creation for all participants" [2]. Platforms invert companies, blur business boundaries, and transform companies' traditional inward focus into an outward focus toward business ecosystems [2].

Platform is a simple-sounding yet transformative concept that is radically changing business, the economy, and society at large [2]. This is the reason why digital platforms have become a major research topic in IS and organization science research [16, 21, 31, 32]. As sociotechnical systems, digital platforms coordinate business actors that innovate and/or compete, and consist of a modular technological architecture with a core and extensions by complementors [31, 33]. A digital platform can function as a central hub and a technological foundation of a business ecosystem, where peripheral firms or individuals facilitate complements and are connected via boundary resources [13].

Digital platforms co-create value employing resources they do not own or control, but that are possessed and controlled by their constituent actors in their business ecosystem [2, 22]. Therefore, digital platforms and their pertinent business ecosystems (co-)evolve much faster than traditional businesses. Consequently, such co-evolutionary processes challenge the structure of ownership, roles, and institutional arrangements among participating actors, often bringing about the emergence of new configurations in both the digital platform and its corresponding business ecosystem. This has two major implications in studying digital platforms:

1. *Top-down control* is necessary, but not sufficient, to ensure structural stability of digital platforms and their business ecosystems. When digital platforms and their embedded business ecosystems are not stable, they bear the risk of becoming too fragmented and less useful for networked business activities [11, 21].
2. Digital platforms and their embedded business ecosystems should account for generativity to allow for *bottom-up emergence* of new roles, ownerships, and institutional arrangements among their involved actors [7, 12, 21].

The latter is necessary to make the business ecosystem attractive for more actors, to obtain more complementary resources, and to eventually satisfy a wider range of customers, which makes the (co-)evolution of the business ecosystem and its digital platform inherently emergent. Thus, in studying platform ecosystems we argue for a co-existence of top-down control and bottom-up emergence, both of which need to be simultaneously considered and legitimated [34–36]. This co-existence of top-down control and bottom-up emergence concerns *balancing* of what may be allowed to emerge and what can be purposefully controlled [37–40] so as to *guide* and constrain digital platforms' emergent behavior. Despite considerable research attention to digital platforms [5, 6, 41–43] and notwithstanding several calls to simultaneously considering generativity and control in digital platforms development [21], we still lack insights on how to leverage both (top-down) *control* and *generativity* (bottom-up emergence) in digital platforms.

3   Conceptual Bases of the Research Agenda

To account for the previously elaborated research gap in digital platform research, we opt for a complexity theory perspective and employ its notion of complex adaptive systems (CAS) [44–46]. Complexity theory in general and CAS in particular conceptualize (co-)evolution as resulting from the interactions of a system's constituent actors [44, 45], which in the context of our study relates to the interactions between constituent actors of the business ecosystem, enabled by the respective digital platform. Therefore, we conceptualize digital platforms and their embedded business ecosystems as CAS.

CAS are representative of systems that have non-linear properties (on the global level) resulting from the interactions among the system's actors (on the local level) [44, 45]. Such systems adapt and evolve through their dynamic interactions with an environment [39] and their adaptive behaviors are characterized by *self-organization* and *emergence* [39, 40]:

3. *Self-organization* [34, 46] is the ability to generate new internal structures and forms of behavior [39] owing to system actors' spontaneous restructuring of relationships with neighboring actors. Self-organization brings about the emergent behavior of a system as a whole [39].
4. *Emergence* postulates that the overall state of a system results from the individual actors' local actions [39, 40], their complex interactions within and across levels of analysis, as well as the constant changes in the modes of interaction over time. Emergence makes the outcomes of local actors' interactions unpredictable [38, 44, 45].

The CAS perspective, and its approach to self-organization and emergence, provides a distinct lens to examine the co-evolution of digital platforms and their corresponding business ecosystems. To comprehend self-organization and emergence in CAS, we focus on the CAS components that underlie such behaviors [35, 47]:

5. *Agents*: CAS comprise a large number of interacting agents. Agents are persons (i.e., individuals, groups, or coalitions of groups), organizations, objects, or concepts that share certain attributes and behavioral rules.
6. *Interactions*: Interactions reflect mutually adaptive behaviors by agents, which are realized through connections as well as resources flows among agents.
7. *Environment*: Interactions among agents are mediated by their surrounding environmental properties. That is, the environment provides the conditions of interactions among agents.

In translating CAS components and behaviors to the study of co-evolving digital platforms and business ecosystems, we adopt Orlikowski and colleagues' [48–50] structurational model of technology. They distinguish between two dynamically interacting agents: actors (e.g., platform owners, complementors, and customers) and technology components (i.e., digital platform's components that mediate the co-creation of value). Actors build, use, and change the technology components to fulfill their business tasks, while technology components enable, facilitate, and constrain business tasks. These interactions among actors and technology components occur over time and evolve to the technology structure status quo in the ecosystem (i.e., current configuration and architecture of the digital platform). Further, these interactions are affected by (and can also affect) institutional properties of the ecosystem in which such interactions occur. Thus, digital platforms and their corresponding business ecosystems co-evolve over time in an emergent way through the dynamic interactions between actors and technology components to fulfill continuously changing business tasks.

We acknowledge that conceptualizing digital platforms and their corresponding business ecosystems as merely emergent phenomena is an oversimplification [51]. On the one hand, their co-evolution is emergent, since self-organized and loosely coupled groups of actors interact with one another to fulfill constantly changing business tasks (bottom-up emergence). On the other hand, platform owners strongly invest in establishing roles, standards, and principles to align actors' behavior with platform's and the corresponding business ecosystem's global objectives (top-down control) [52]. The result is a co-existence of top-down control and bottom-up emergence, both of which need to be simultaneously considered and legitimated [34]. We account for both in terms of balancing what may be allowed to emerge and what can be purpose-fully controlled [37, 38, 40, 53] so as to guide and constrain the emergent behavior of digital platforms.

To account for the abovementioned co-existence of top-down control and bottom-up emergence, we posit that CAS's behavior may be constrained and guided via their institutional properties [44, 45, 54, 55] since these properties define interaction conditions among actors. To conceptualize the institutional properties prevalent in the behavior of CAS, we opt for institutional theory as a theoretical lens.

The key assumption of institutional theory is that organizations (here: the actors in the platform ecosystem) are social constructions that constantly seek to gain legitimacy in their social context (here: the platform ecosystem as a whole). That is, in order to survive, organizations must adhere to the rules and beliefs that prevail in their ecosystem [56, 57].

A main discourse in institutional theory is based on institutional pressures, outlined by DiMaggio and Powell [56] and later adapted by Scott [58]. Institutional pressures, as mechanisms of institutional isomorphism, comprise *coercive*, *normative*, and *mimetic* pressures.

8. *Coercive pressures* are a set of forces that constrain and regularize behavior.
9. *Normative pressures* are forced by organizational counterparts that introduce an obligatory dimension into social life via values and norms. While values are the desired conceptions to which existing behaviors can be compared, norms are legitimate means to pursue valued ends.
10. *Mimetic pressures* create the frames through which shared conceptions are made. Mimetic pressures are evident when actors encounter uncertain causes and solutions. In this case, they unconsciously model themselves on other, successful actors.

Institutional pressures help us understand local actors' actions and their interactions: In building, using, interacting with, or changing a digital platform, actors seek to gain legitimacy in their ecosystem by interpreting and applying the surrounding institutional pressures. This understanding of local actors' actions and interactions helps us elaborate *how the co-evolution of digital platforms and business ecosystems can be purposefully guided through institutional pressures* toward platform success and its sustained evolution.

4   The Research Agenda

This research agenda seeks to provide a basis to generate theories of two types, i.e., *descriptive* and *design* theories [59, 60] on the co-evolution of digital platforms and business ecosystems. In the following, we explain the objectives of these two theorization paths (and their relation) and recommend research methods to obtain these objectives.

Toward descriptive theories: this research agenda aims at theorizing the co-evolution of digital platforms and their business ecosystems as emergent phenomena that arise through a series of multi-level and episodic, punctuated sociotechnical changes [61]. The objective is thus to extend the extant body of knowledge through the following distinct approaches:

11. Through following a *longitudinal and process-based approach* [62–65], this research agenda encourages the prospective studies to go beyond existing often conceptual and/or variance-based views on digital platforms. Variance-based views have a limited utility as they examine digital platforms in a specific point of time, which fails to reveal the *de facto* complexity of such platforms—as a co-evolving phenomenon that continuously responds to dynamically changing business and technological environments [10, 40, 66]. Instead, we need to incorporate the *time* dimension into theorizing the complexity of digital platforms, to allow for investigating the move from an initial to emergent states [61].

12. Through following a *guided evolution* approach [35, 36], this research agenda encourages the prospective studies to go beyond existing either-or approaches to govern platform ecosystems. While theorizing platform ecosystems as complex, emergent phenomena, we posit that their emergent evolution can be purposefully guided through a set of institutional arrangements. Therefore, this research agenda promotes the incorporation of the (top-down) *control* and *generativity* (bottom-up emergence) perspectives in studying platform ecosystems.

The dynamics of *simultaneously* obtaining control and generativity over time are under-researched. While digital platform research provides fruitful foundations for understanding the dynamics of digital platforms, it has only slowly started moving away from an *either-or* approach toward delicately *balancing* control and generativity. This is problematic as pure control makes adaptation difficult and pure generativity comes at the cost of experimentation without gaining associated benefits. As a result, digital platform research predominantly sees control and generativity as incompatible and mutually exclusive goals [67], *without* integrating these foundations into a coherent model that sheds light on the dynamics of balancing these goals. This lack compromises theoretical accounts of how conflicting goals can be *balanced* to obtain both control and generativity at the same time. Consequently, little is known about the (co-)evolutionary processes of *simultaneously* obtaining control and generativity, and *dynamically and continuously* maintaining the co-existence of the two. Therefore, we are lacking empirical evidence from the real-world digital platforms to capture and understand such (co-)

evolutionary processes. Further, owing to ever-evolving and emergent characteristics of digital platforms, using simple causal models or explanations, to be explored or tested through research methods such as snapshot case studies or surveys, would not do justice to the complexity of the phenomenon of interest. Therefore, we suggest longitudinal, process-based case studies to collect data on the evolution of platform ecosystems as a longitudinal chain of events over time that explain how platform ecosystems emerge to their status quo.

While the longitudinal case studies provide detail empirical accounts from the real-world platform ecosystems, the derived theories would be bounded to the limited number of studied cases and to the cases' particular conditions. This is particularly relevant since such research approaches do hardly allow to isolate and vary the potentially large number of parameters of the respective CAS in a controlled environment and produce appropriate amounts of data to capture non-linearity and emergence of the phenomenon. Therefore, next to longitudinal case studies, we encourage scholars to also opt for simulation-based experimentations that allow for not only observing the non-linearity and emergence of platform ecosystems, but also for conducting what-if analyses to investigate how platform ecosystems behave under various circumstances [35].

Scholars have acknowledged the potential of simulation-based research in advancing organizational [68–71] and IS research [72–75], particularly for investigating complex systems since they exhibit non-linear behavior and their emergent properties unfold over time [69, 71]. Simulation experiments enable researchers to study emergent behavior based on the mechanisms that lead from specific decisions to high-level consequences [76]. Among the various approaches to simulation, agent-based simulation specifically allows scholars to describe interactions between individual actors according to prescribed rules, and eventually to observe the emerging behavior from these interactions in an environment [51, 70, 77, 78]. Agent-based simulations re-quire a precise conceptualization of the objects themselves and of their relations to immediately affected entities [79]. Depending on these descriptions on a local level, the overall system behavior can then be observed without requiring a precise understanding of the intermediate relations that lead to this emergent behavior. Such characteristics of agent-based simulation would allow researchers to explore and explain the overall behavior of platform ecosystems under various experimental conditions while only the constituent agents' behavioral rules and interactions are modeled [35, 80].

Toward design theories: Even though descriptive theories are required to provide "what" knowledge about the phenomenon of interest, design theories complement scientific inquiries on the respective phenomenon by providing "how" knowledge [59]. Therefore, design theories build on and go beyond descriptive theories [59] by offering projectable guidelines [81]. In the proposed research agenda, while the descriptive aspect focuses digital platforms' underlying mechanisms of sustainable evolution, it is also important to delineate and rigorously develop prescriptive design knowledge on the design and evolution of digital platforms [26]. Therefore, this research agenda also encourages the development of design theories on how control and generativity can be balanced for digital platforms to thrive sustainably. Following the design science research (DSR) approach [59, 60], such prescriptive knowledge can be developed through deriving a set of interrelated design principles and their corresponding design requirements and features [82]. Design requirements represent the problem space of design in that they capture generic requirements of sustainable digital platforms [83, 84]. Design principles embody prescriptive knowledge that bridges the problem space (design requirements) and solution space (design features) of design [59, 85]. Design principles thus serve as a means to con-vey design knowledge that contributes beyond context-bound instantiations of digital platforms [85]. Design principles also constitute general solution components that can be instantiated into several exemplars of digital platforms [86]. Design features represent the solution space of design in that they denote specific ways to implement a design principle in an actual digital platform [82]. While design principles abstract from technical specifics, design features explain why a technical specificity leads to a specific goal.

As a part of design science endeavors, we also encourage prospective research to derive and delineate design archetypes [87–89] for digital platforms whose configurations particularly well balance control and generativity. The digital platforms' requirements, principles, and features can be used as differentiating aspects of digital platforms to identify emerging dominant patterns that consistently reoccur across different digital platform instances. Further, owing to the dichotomy between descriptive and design theorizing and their reciprocal relationship [59, 90], the descriptive and design aspects of the research agenda are interrelated. The descriptive aspect relates to understanding and analyzing the co-evolution of digital platforms and business ecosystems. Informed by the insights from descriptive studies, design science studies aim at deriving design principles to guide the design and evolution of digital platforms.

5 Concluding Remarks

Notwithstanding digitalization's *sociotechnical* nature, a plethora of academic and practical endeavors focus its *technical* aspect such as the need for novel technologies (e.g., Blockchain) or new applications of existing technologies (e.g., Internet of Things). Therefore, what humanities and social sciences may contribute does not only concern the *social* aspect of digitalization, but, even more importantly, the consideration of *both social and technical* aspects and their *co-evolution*. With this inclusive perspective, the proposed research agenda in this chapter concerns how digital platforms, as a sociotechnical phenomenon, transform economic exchanges and how novel theories in and practices of economic exchanges stimulate the emergence of digital technologies.

On the socioeconomic end, the focus lies on *business ecosystems* as actor-to-actor networks of heterogeneous economic players that engage in service-for-service economic exchanges beyond their organizational boundaries. On the technical end, the focus lies on *digital platforms* as the point of gravity within their business ecosystem in enabling service-for-service economic exchanges. Relying on this sociotechnical perspective, the research agenda concerns the *co*-evolution of business ecosystems and digital platforms. We focus on how digital platforms transform economic exchange and enable the emergence of business ecosystems, and on how novel forms of economic exchange and dynamic configurations of business ecosystems stimulate the emergence of digital platforms. Owing to the co-evolutionary changes in both social and technical aspects, we argue for the *emergent and complex* nature of both digital platforms and business ecosystems. Since digital platforms are the *raison d'être* of their pertinent business ecosystems, we yet acknowledge the need for *controlling* the evolution of digital platforms (through e.g., institutional arrangements) to manage this co-evolution. This results in accounting for both a platform's *generativity* (bottom-up emergence) and (top-down) *control*, and their *balance* in purposefully *guiding* the co-evolution of digital platforms and their business ecosystems.

Owing to particularities of digital platforms and platform ecosystems as a research topic, we expect that resulted theories of the proposed research agenda go beyond merely employing CAS and institutional theory and contribute in their dominant discourses. Going beyond the bottom-up emergence notion of complexity science, the resulted studies from the proposed research agenda can contribute in discussing the necessity of balancing both top-down control and bottom-up emergence mechanisms in institutional contexts. This will contribute to complexity theory by demonstrating that the emergent behavior of complex adaptive systems can be purposefully guided to reach a balance between top-down control and bottom-up emergence. While a theorization of evolution must comprise a mixture of both deterministic and emergent elements [91], the discussion of the balance between top-down control and bottom-up emergence has not yet been a research focus [37, 40]. This is a multifaceted approach in examining organizational and IS phenomena beyond their sole theorization as either emergent phenomena or phenomena that are subject to top-down control. Concerning institutional theory, this grand theory has been criticized for its static view to organizations [56] and of largely being used to explain the persistence (inertia, stability) of organizational arrangements [92]. To demonstrate the full power of institutional theory and contribute to recent discourses in this theory [93], the resulted studies from the proposed research agenda can focus on change and dynamics in institutional arrangements and discover the dynamic combination of institutional pressures over time to cope with changing situations.

References

1. Gawer, A.: Platforms, Markets and Innovation. Edward Elgar, Cheltenham (2011)
2. Parker, G.G., Van Alstyne, M., Choudary, S.P.: Platform Revolution: How Networked Markets Are Transforming the Economy and How to Make Them Work for You. WW Norton (2016)
3. Kenney, M., Zysman, J.: The rise of the platform economy. Iss. Sci. Technol. **32**, 61 (2016)

4. Statista: Most Valuable Companies in the World 2017. https://www.statista.com/statistics/263264/top-companies-in-the-world-by-market-value/ (2017)
5. De Reuver, M., Sorensen, C., Casole, R.C.: The digital platform: a research agenda. J. Inf. Technol. **33**, 124–135 (2017)
6. Parker, G., Van Alstyne, M., Jiang, X.Y.: Platform ecosystems: how developers invert the firm. MIS Q. **41**, 255–266 (2017)
7. Tiwana, A.: Evolutionary competition in platform ecosystems. Inf. Syst. Res. **26**, 266–281 (2015)
8. Briegleb, V.: End of Life: Windows Phone ist offiziell tot. https://www.heise.de/ho/meldung/End-of-Life-Windows-Phone-ist-offiziell-tot-3769434.html (2017)
9. Gartner: Gartner Says Worldwide Sales of Smartphones Grew 9 Percent in First Quarter of 2017. https://www.gartner.com/newsroom/id/3725117 (2017)
10. Ciborra, C.U.: The platform organization: recombining strategies, structures, and surprises. Organ. Sci. **7**, 103–118 (1996)
11. Yoo, Y., Boland, R.J., Lyytinen, K., Majchrzak, A.: Organizing for innovation in the digitized world. Organ. Sci. **23**, 1398–1408 (2012)
12. Tiwana, A., Konsynski, B., Bush, A.A.: Platform evolution: coevolution of platform architecture, governance, and environmental dynamics. Inf. Syst. Res. **21**, 675–687 (2010)
13. Jacobides, M.G., Cennamo, C., Gawer, A.: Towards a theory of ecosystems. Strateg. Manag. J. **39**, 2255–2276 (2018)
14. Grover, V., Kohli, R.: Cocreating it value: new capabilities and metrics for multifirm environments. MIS Q. **36**, 225–232 (2012)
15. Wareham, J., Fox, P.B., Giner, J.L.C.: Technology ecosystem governance. Organ. Sci. **25**, 1195–1215 (2014)
16. Ghazawneh, A., Henfridsson, O.: Balancing platform control and external contribution in third-party development: the boundary resources model. Inf. Syst. J. **23**, 173–192 (2013)
17. Ciborra, C.U., Braa, K., Cordella, A., Dahlom, B., Failla, A., Hanseth, O., Hepso, V., Ljungberg, J., Monteiro, E., Simon, K.: From Control to Drift: The Dynamics of Corporate Information Infrastructures. Oxford University Press, Oxford (2000)
18. Henfridsson, O., Bygstad, B.: The generative mechanisms of digital infrastructure evolution. MIS Q. **37**, 907–931 (2013)
19. Lusch, R.F., Nambisan, S.: Service innovation: a service-dominant logic perspective. MIS Q. **39**, 155–175 (2015)
20. Tan, B., Pan, S.L., Lu, X.H., Huang, L.H.: The role of IS capabilities in the development of multi-sided platforms: the digital ecosystem strategy of Alibaba.com. J. Assoc. Inf. Syst. **16**, 248–280 (2015)
21. Tilson, D., Lyytinen, K., Sørensen, C.: Research Commentary – Digital infrastructures: the missing IS research agenda. Inf. Syst. Res. **21**, 748–759 (2010)
22. Blaschke, M., Haki, K., Aier, S., Winter, R.: Capabilities for digital platform survival: insights from a business-to-business digital platform. In: 39th International Conference on Information Systems (ICIS2018). Association for Information Systems, San Francisco, CA, pp. 1–17 (2018)
23. Farjoun, M.: Beyond dualism: stability and change as in duality. Acad. Manag. Rev. **35**, 202–225 (2010)
24. Sarker, S., Sarker, S., Sahaym, A., Bjorn-Andersen, N.: Exploring value cocreation in relationships between an ERP vendor and its partners: a revelatory case study. MIS Q. **36**, 317–338 (2012)
25. Friend, S.B., Malshe, A.: Key skills for crafting customer solutions within an ecosystem: a theories-in-use perspective. J. Serv. Res. **19**, 174–191 (2016)
26. Blaschke, M., Riss, U., Haki, K., Aier, S.: Design principles for digital value co-creation networks: a service-dominant logic perspective. Electron. Mark. **29**, 443–472 (2019)
27. Haki, K., Blaschke, M., Aier, S., Winter, R.: A value co-creation perspective on information systems analysis and design. Bus. Inf. Syst. Eng. **61**, 487–502 (2019)

28. Kim, D.J., Kogut, B.: Technological platforms and diversification. Organ. Sci. **7**, 283–301 (1996)
29. Rochet, J.C., Tirole, J.: Platform competition in two-sided markets. J. Eur. Econ. Assoc. **1**, 990–1029 (2003)
30. Gupta, A.K., Tesluk, P.E., Taylor, M.S.: Innovation at and across multiple levels of analysis. Organ. Sci. **18**, 885–897 (2007)
31. de Reuver, M., Sørensen, C., Basole, R.C.: The digital platform: a research agenda. J. Inf. Technol. **33**, 124–135 (2018)
32. Cennamo, C., Santaló, J.: Generativity tension and value creation in platform ecosystems. Organ. Sci. **30**, 617–641 (2019)
33. Gawer, A., Cusumano, M.A.: Industry platforms and ecosystem innovation. J. Prod. Innov. Manag. **31**, 417–433 (2014)
34. Benbya, H., McKelvey, B.: Toward a complexity theory of information systems development. Inf. Technol. People. **19**, 12–34 (2006)
35. Haki, K., Beese, J., Aier, S., Winter, R.: The evolution of information systems architecture: an agent-based simulation model. MIS Q. **44**, 155–184 (2020)
36. Haki, K., Legner, C.: The mechanics of enterprise architecture principles J. Assoc. Inf. Syst. (Forthcoming)
37. Choi, T.Y., Dooley, K.J., Rungtusanatham, M.: Supply networks and complex adaptive systems: control versus emergence. J. Oper. Manag. **19**, 351–366 (2001)
38. Dooley, K.J.: A complex adaptive systems model of organization change. Nonlin. Dyn. Psychol. Life Sci. **1**, 69–97 (1997)
39. Merali, Y.: Complexity and information systems: the emergent domain. J. Inf. Technol. **21**, 216–228 (2006)
40. Vessey, I., Ward, K.: The dynamics of sustainable IS alignment: the case for IS adaptivity. J. Assoc. Inf. Syst. **14**, 283–311 (2013)
41. Barrett, M., Oborn, E., Orlikowski, W.: Creating value in online communities: the sociomaterial configuring of strategy, platform, and stakeholder engagement. Inf. Syst. Res. **27**, 704–723 (2016)
42. Ceccagnoli, M., Forman, C., Huang, P., Wu, D.J.: Cocreation of value in a platform ecosystem: the case of enterprise software. MIS Q. **36**, 263–290 (2012)
43. Huang, P., Tafti, A., Mithas, S.: Platform sponsor investments and user contributions in knowledge communities: the role of knowledge seeding. MIS Q. **42**, 213–240 (2018)
44. Anderson, P.: Complexity theory and organization science. Organ. Sci. **10**, 216–232 (1999)
45. Holland, J.H.: Hidden Order: How Adaptation Builds Complexity. Addison Wesley Longman, Cambridge, MA (1995)
46. Axelrod, R., Cohen, M.D.: Harnessing Complexity: Organizational Implications of a Scientific Frontier. Free Press, New York (1999)
47. Nan, N.: Capturing bottom-up information technology use processes: a complex adaptive systems model. MIS Q. **35**, 505–532 (2011)
48. Orlikowski, W.J., Yates, J., Okamura, K., Fujimoto, M.: Shaping electronic communication: the metastructuring of technology in the context of use. Organ. Sci. **6**, 423–444 (1995)
49. Orlikowski, W.J., Robey, D.: Information technology and the structuring of organizations. Inf. Syst. Res. **2**, 143–169 (1991)
50. Orlikowski, W.J.: The duality of technology: rethinking the concept of technology in organizations. Organ. Sci. **3**, 398–427 (1992)
51. Curşeu, P.L.: Emergent states in virtual teams: a complex adaptive systems perspective. J. Inf. Technol. **21**, 249–261 (2006)
52. Cram, W.A., Brohman, M.K., Gallupe, R.B.: Information systems control: a review and framework for emerging information systems processes. J. Assoc. Inf. Syst. **17**, 216–266 (2016)
53. Merali, Y., McKelvey, B.: Using complexity science to effect a paradigm shift in information systems for the 21st century. J. Inf. Technol. **21**, 211–215 (2006)

54. Lyytinen, K., Newman, M.: Explaining information systems change: a punctuated socio-technical change model. Eur. J. Inf. Syst. **17**, 589–613 (2008)
55. McLeod, L., Doolin, B.: Information sevelopment as situated socio-technical change: a process approach. Eur. J. Inf. Syst. **21**, 176–191 (2012)
56. DiMaggio, P.J., Powell, W.W.: The iron cage revisited: institutional isomorphism and collective rationality in organizational fields. Am. Sociol. Rev. **48**, 147–160 (1983)
57. Meyer, J.W., Rowan, B.: Institutionalized organizations: formal structure as myth and ceremony. Am. J. Sociol. **83**, 340–363 (1977)
58. Scott, W.R.: Institutions and Organizations: Ideas, Interests, and Identities. SAGE, Thousand Oaks, CA (2014)
59. Gregor, S., Hevner, A.R.: Positioning and presenting design science research for maximum impact. MIS Q. **37**, 337–355 (2013)
60. Gregor, S.: The nature of theory in information systems. MIS Q. **30**, 611–642 (2006)
61. Haki, M.K., Aier, S., Winter, R.: A stakeholder perspective to study enterprisewide IS initiatives. In: 24th European Conference on Information Systems (ECIS), Istanbul, Turkey (2016)
62. Markus, M.L., Robey, D.: Information technology and organizational change – causal structure in theory and research. Manag. Sci. **34**, 583–598 (1988)
63. Mohr, L.B. (ed.): Explaining Organizational Behavior. Jossey-Bass, San Francisco, CA (1982)
64. Pettigrew, A.M.: What is a processual analysis? Scand. J. Manag. **13**, 337–348 (1997)
65. Van de Ven, A.H., Huber, G.P.: Longitudinal field research methods for studying processes of organizational change. Organ. Sci. **1**, 213–219 (1990)
66. Tanriverdi, H., Rai, A., Venkatraman, N.: Research commentary-Reframing the dominant quests of information systems strategy research for complex adaptive business systems. Inf. Syst. Res. **21**, 822–834 (2010)
67. He, Z.-L., Wong, P.-K.: Exploration vs. exploitation: an empirical test of the ambidexterity hypothesis. Organ. Sci. **15**, 481–494 (2004)
68. Burton, R.M., Obel, B.: Computational modeling for what-is, what-might-be, and what-should-be studies—and triangulation. Organ. Sci. **22**, 1195–1202 (2011)
69. Davis, J.P., Eisenhardt, K.M., Bingham, C.B.: Developing theory through simulation methods. Acad. Manag. Rev. **32**, 480–499 (2007)
70. Fioretti, G.: Agent-based simulation models in organization science. Organ. Res. Methods. **16**, 227–242 (2013)
71. Harrison, J.R., Zhiang, L., Carroll, G.R., Carley, K.M.: Simulation modeling in organizational and management research. Acad. Manag. Rev. **32**, 1229–1245 (2007)
72. Zhang, M., Gable, G.G.: Rethinking the value of simulation methods in the information systems research field: a call for reconstructing contribution for a broader audience. International Conference on Information Systems, Auckland, New Zealand (2014)
73. Beese, J., Haki, M.K., Aier, S., Winter, R.: Simulation-based research in information systems: epistemic implications and a review of the status quo. Bus. Inf. Syst. Eng. **61**, 503–521 (2019)
74. Spagnoletti, P., Za, S., Winter, R., Mettler, T.: Exploring foundations for using simulations in IS research. Commun. Assoc. Inf. Syst. **42**, 268–300 (2018)
75. Beese, J., Haki, K., Aier, S.: On the conceptualization of information systems as socio-technical phenomena in simulation-based research. In: 2015 International Conference on Information Systems (ICIS 2015). Association for Information Systems, Fort Worth, TX (2015)
76. Helbing, D., Balietti, S.: How to do agent-based simulations in the future: from modeling social mechanisms to emergent phenomena and interactive systems design. In: Helbing, D. (ed.) Social Self-Organization, pp. 25–70. Springer, Berlin (2012)
77. Bonabeau, E.: Agent-based modeling: methods and techniques for simulating human systems. Proc. Natl. Acad. Sci. **99**, 7280–7287 (2002)
78. Hedström, P., Manzo, G.: Recent trends in agent-based computational research. A brief introduction. Sociol. Methods Res. **44**, 179–185 (2015)
79. Borgatti, S.P., Halgin, D.S.: On network theory. Organ. Sci. **22**, 1168–1181 (2011)

80. Schmid, M., Haki, K., Aier, S., Winter, R.: Developing design principles for digital platforms: an agent-based modeling approach. In: International Conference on Design Science Research in Information Systems and Technology (DESRIST). Springer, Kristiansand, Norway (2020)
81. Baskerville, R., Pries-Heje, J.: Projectability in design science research. J. Inf. Technol. Theory Appl. **20** (2019)
82. Meth, H., Müller, B., Mädche, A.: Designing a requirement mining system. J. Assoc. Inf. Syst. **16**, 799–837 (2015)
83. Baskerville, R.L., Pries-Heje, J.: Explanatory design theory. Bus. Inf. Syst. Eng. **2**, 271–282 (2010)
84. Walls, J.G., Widmeyer, G.R., El Sawy, O.A.: Building an information system design theory for vigilant EIS. Inf. Syst. Res. **3**, 36–59 (1992)
85. Chandra, L., Seidel, S., Gregor, S.: Prescriptive knowledge in IS research: conceptualizing design principles in terms of materiality, action, and boundary conditions. In: 2015 48th Hawaii International Conference on System Sciences, pp. 4039–4048. IEEE (2015)
86. Iivari, J.: Distinguishing and contrasting two strategies for design science research. Eur. J. Inf. Syst. **24**, 107–115 (2015)
87. Schilling, R.D., Haki, M.K., Aier, S.: Introducing archetype theory to information systems research: a literature review and call for future research. In: 13th International Conference on Wirtschaftsinformatik (WI 2017), St. Gallen, Switzerland (2017)
88. Blaschke, M., Haki, K., Aier, S., Winter, R.: Taxonomy of digital platforms: a platform architecture perspective. In: 14th International Conference on Wirtschaftsinformatik (WI2019). Association for Information Systems, Siegen, Deutschland (2019)
89. Staub, N., Haki, K., Aier, S., Winter, R.: Taxonomy of digital platforms: a business model perspective. In: Hawaii International Conference on System Sciences (HICSS) (2021)
90. March, S.T., Smith, G.F.: Design and natural science research on information technology. Decis. Support. Syst. **15**, 251–266 (1995)
91. Radzicki, M.J.: Institutional dynamics, deterministic chaos, and self-organizing systems. J. Econ. Iss. **24**, 57–102 (1990)
92. Greenwood, R., Hinings, C.R.: Understanding radical organizational change: bringing together the old and the new institutionalism. Acad. Manag. Rev. **21**, 1022–1054 (1996)
93. Pache, A.-C., Santos, F.: When worlds collide: the internal dynamics of organizational responses to conflicting institutional demands. Acad. Manag. Rev. **35**, 455–476 (2010)

A Concept for an IT-Supported Integrated Earnings and Risk Management to Strengthen the Resilience of Companies in Times of Crisis

Hans-Ulrich Buhl, Björn Häckel, and Christian Ritter

Abstract In this article, a multi-purpose performance measurement system is developed enabling companies from all industries to manage their business activities with uniform enterprise-wide earnings and risk measures as a value-oriented corporate management geared towards sustainability and resilience. In particular, the developed KPI system consistently supports continuous performance measurement and risk monitoring as well as ex ante decision support as core tasks of an IT-supported integrated earnings and risk management. Its application, especially in good times, strengthens the resilience of companies in times of crisis.

Keywords Value-based management · Sustainability · Resilience · Integrated earnings · Risk management

1 Introduction

The December 2019 outbreak of the novel virus SARS-CoV-2 and the resulting disease COVID-19 developed into a global pandemic, which, in addition to the health threat, leads to significant impacts on the world population in social, environmental, and economic dimensions [1]. Public health policies aimed at pandemic containment generated difficult trade-offs. Measures such as self-isolation, physical distancing, school and business closures, and travel restrictions were intended to protect the health of the population and avoid overloading the health care system. On

H.-U. Buhl (✉) · C. Ritter
Research Center Finance and Information Management, University of Augsburg, Project Group Business and Information Systems Engineering of Fraunhofer FIT, Augsburg, Germany
e-mail: hans-ulrich.buhl@fim-rc.de; christian.ritter@fim-rc.de

B. Häckel
Research Center Finance and Information Management, Augsburg University of Applied Sciences, Project Group Business and Information Systems Engineering of Fraunhofer FIT, Augsburg, Germany
e-mail: bjoern.haeckel@fim-rc.de

© The Author(s), under exclusive license to Springer Nature Switzerland AG 2021 257
S. Aier et al. (eds.), *Engineering the Transformation of the Enterprise*,
https://doi.org/10.1007/978-3-030-84655-8_16

the other hand, these measures can have a negative impact on the social cohesion of societies, increase inequality, and thus cause a significant decrease in economic output and the loss of many jobs, not only in the short term [2]. The economic consequences of the COVID-19 pandemic also included supply shortages and production losses due to the disruption of production systems, a decrease in demand due to consumers' delayed purchases, and the postponement of investments by companies [3]. In particular, industries such as aviation, tourism, hospitality, and the event industry were and are severely affected, as operations had to be completely halted at times and then curtailed. Thus, in addition to the serious health and social consequences, a worldwide economic crisis and recession loomed. In Germany, a historic economic slump as a result of the COVID-19 pandemic was demonstrated by the 9.7% decline in economic output in the second quarter[1] of 2020. This decline set in much more abruptly than in the financial crisis of 2009, when even in the worst 3 months (Q1/2009) gross domestic product shrank by only 4.7%[1] [4]. From today's perspective, it is almost impossible to predict globally how further infection events and the health policy measures that depend on them will develop and to what extent the numerous government rescue and support measures will have their hoped-for effect. Many companies were caught unprepared by this crisis because—as in the financial crisis—they severely underestimated the extent of such an external shock. It became apparent from insufficient strategic and operational actions in good times to be able to react appropriately to such a crisis situation and thus ensure the company's ability to survive without government intervention that there is often only a limited understanding of the company's own risks [5]. To survive this cross-industry and global crisis, but also to be prepared for further times of crisis in the future, integrated earnings and risk management makes an important contribution to the resilience of each individual company and thus also to the stability of the overall economic system. In this context, we understand the resilience of a company as the "ability of an organization to absorb and adapt in a changing environment to enable it to deliver its objectives and to survive and prosper" [6]. To ensure the survivability of a company in the sense of resilience, the task of integrated earnings and risk management includes long-term risk provisioning, especially in economically good times, to be able to bridge short-term volatility in times of crisis, as well as to ensure the long-term continuity of a company through appropriate strategic and operational control measures. Increasing possibilities in the field of information technology such as increasing availability of data, transmission and processing in real time as well as analyses with the help of main memory databases and artificial intelligence (AI) support earnings and risk management to fulfill this task. Thus, the question arises what contribution Business & Information Systems Engineering can make as an interdiscipline and design-oriented transdiscipline to increase the resilience of companies. Digital technologies penetrate and accelerate almost all areas of life and work and lead to an ongoing cross-industry transformation of business models and value creation systems. Coordination and communication systems support a

---

[1]Price-adjusted, calendar- and seasonally adjusted rate of change over previous period.

worldwide division of labor and specialization, resulting in globally distributed and fragmented value creation systems. Increasing networks of companies and individuals through physical objects and information systems is generating a steadily growing volume of control-relevant internal and external data. The analysis of this data—especially through the use of AI—offers companies the potential to improve their control concepts, to react quickly to changing circumstances and thus to implement a dynamically acting integrated earnings and risk management in an increasingly complex environment. However, against the backdrop of such a crisis, IT is proving to be both a blessing and a curse. The fragmentation of corporate value creation systems made possible by IT networking creates global dependencies that were previously limited to local areas. In recent years, this has resulted in increasing complexity and, in some cases, intransparency for all parties involved. The resulting rapid spread from local to global crises has been enabled by IT as an enabler of an increasingly global, interconnected and fast-paced world [7]. In particular, the current crisis caused by the COVID-19 pandemic showed that the tight coupling in global value systems massively amplified the negative economic implications of the crisis and acted as a fire accelerator. Thus, production stoppages and supply gaps were favored by measures driven by international competition and enabled by IT, such as the fragmentation of value creation, low inventory levels, and just-in-time or just-in-sequence control concepts. Thus, as a design- and solution-oriented transdiscipline, Business & Information Systems Engineering today faces even more than before the challenge of making digital technologies usable in such a way that the opportunities outweigh the disadvantages in good times as well as in times of crisis. To be able to derive the right control measures both for risk prevention and in a crisis in the sense of corporate management geared to sustainability and resilience, it is essential to be able to evaluate and use the constantly increasing flood of data available to a company from internal and external sources in a targeted manner. For this reason, companies need a consistent enterprise-wide data basis of earnings and risk variables to support integrated earnings and risk management. Such a data basis should be used in particular for the core tasks of integrated earnings and risk management, performance measurement within the existing corporate portfolio, continuous monitoring of risk-bearing capacity, and ex ante decision support [8]. Fulfilling these three core tasks strengthens a company's resilience by identifying changing conditions and threats at an early stage and by anticipating their impact on the risk positions of the entire corporate portfolio. This enables appropriate, proactive decisions to be made and management measures to be derived. At the same time, particularly in good economic times, appropriate risk provisioning can be realized by building up financial reserves and investing in sustainable products, services and business models that increase crisis resilience. To date, however, there is still a lack of suitable financial methods and key performance indicator systems for building up a consistent, multi-purpose data basis for integrated earnings and risk management throughout the company. In particular, the commonly used modeling of uniform risk measures, with which consistent aggregation across several aggregation levels is possible, as well as the transfer of the earnings and risk measures used for multiple purposes, continue to cause considerable difficulties for companies. The consequence of this deficit is that, in many cases, value-oriented corporate management geared to sustainability and resilience does not take place because the effects of an impending crisis event on the risk positions of the entire corporate portfolio cannot be anticipated and, consequently, no appropriate management measures can be derived.

Even in the extensive literature on integrated earnings and risk management, most of the time only one of the three core tasks mentioned above is considered in isolation. For the purpose of performance measurement, numerous works discuss in particular risk-adjusted profitability measures [9], such as the class of Risk Adjusted Performance Measures (RAPM), as well as residual profit concepts [10], such as Economic Value Added (EVA). Furthermore, there is a large body of work dealing with methods for measuring the overall risk of a company in the context of continuous monitoring of risk-bearing capacity [11, 12]. The purpose of decision support under return and risk aspects is the subject of the diverse literature in financing and investment theory under uncertainty [13] as well as decision theory [14]. Thus, it should be noted that although a variety of methods and concepts exist for the individual core tasks of integrated earnings and risk management, the literature generally does not take an integrated view of these core tasks. This paper therefore develops a solution approach for creating an enterprise-wide consistent, multi-purpose data basis for integrated earnings and risk management. To this end, uniform enterprise-wide return and risk variables are first defined, taking into account in particular the requirement of consistent aggregability across all aggregation levels of the company portfolio. Based on this, the consistent use of these variables for performance measurement within the existing portfolio, risk monitoring and ex ante decision support is presented. It is shown how purpose-specific key performance indicators for the above-mentioned core tasks of integrated earnings and risk management can be formed from the uniform enterprise-wide earnings and risk variables enabling a company to consistently evaluate and manage its business activities on this basis.

In summary, the following research questions are explored:

- How must uniform enterprise-wide earnings and risk measures be designed, in particular to enable value-additive aggregation across all aggregation levels? What financial consistency requirements must be met for this?
- How can uniform enterprise-wide return and risk measures be used in a multi-purpose manner to simultaneously support performance measurement in the existing portfolio, risk monitoring, and ex ante decision support in a consistent manner?

These research questions are explored in the following sections. Already in [15] the information systems aspects of these questions, in particular the requirements for consistent return and risk databases, were examined. This paper in contrast focuses on the conceptual financial aspects and operationalizes and extends the solution approach developed in [15]. First, the state of research is briefly presented.

2   Financial Methods for Integrated Earnings and Risk Management

Integrated earnings and risk management should support the objective of value-oriented corporate management and thus contribute to increasing the value of the company [16, 17]. Integrated earnings and risk management must therefore be based on a system of business targets that has a target function for maximizing the long-term value of the company under sustainability requirements [18]. In addition, such a target system must take into account constraints such as, in particular, limits on risk-bearing capacity to ensure the resilience of the company. In addition to the basic theories of classical decision theory [19] or portfolio and capital market theory [20, 21], a large number of financial methods, concepts and performance measurement systems have been developed over time for integrated earnings and risk management. Especially for performance measurement, risk-adjusted profitability ratios such as the class of RAPM and residual profit concepts such as EVA have become established in practice across industries due to their ease of application. However, the following problems arise in the application of RAPM and EVA: Risk assessments at low aggregation levels are usually performed as stand-alone valuations of individual businesses or sub-portfolios. Existing diversification effects are only taken into account after aggregation to a portfolio at a higher aggregation level. Therefore, the sum of the stand-alone risk valuations of the individual businesses (or sub-portfolios) is usually not equal to the overall risk valuation of the portfolio. A simple additive aggregation of the individual risk scores to an overall risk score is therefore not possible. Since these ratios also mostly assess new investments only with their stand-alone risk, numerous contributions note that management based on them can lead to systematically wrong decisions [22]. The periodic and generally non-cash flow-oriented design of these ratios further limits their suitability for forward-looking management. Furthermore, if the earnings and risk variables used are already linked to a key figure at lower levels of aggregation, there is a loss of information at higher levels of aggregation.

Even if the input variables are kept separate at each aggregation level, RAPM has an additional problem due to the formation of quotients: By linking return and risk variables to relative variables, (meaningful) aggregation is not readily possible, which calls into question their suitability in the context of a KPI system for integrated return and risk management. In principle, cases can arise where, despite an improvement in the RAPM of all individual businesses (or sub-portfolios) in a portfolio, a deterioration occurs at the overall portfolio level and vice versa.

The financial ratio concepts that have are widespread in practice to date are therefore only suitable to a limited extent for building up a consistent, multi-purpose data basis across the company [15]. To the best of our knowledge, it has not yet been investigated how a performance measurement, risk monitoring and ex ante decision support can be enabled on the basis of a multi-purpose data basis consisting of earnings figures, risk figures and value contributions. The aim of this paper is to provide an approach to close this research gap.

3   Financial Requirements and Solutions for a Consistent, Multi-purpose Data Basis Throughout the Company

Based on the fundamental tasks and requirements of integrated earnings and risk management, this section presents a financial solution approach for establishing a consistent, multi-purpose data basis across the company.

3.1   Tasks of a Multipurpose Data Basis

To be able to fulfill the tasks of value-oriented corporate management, a multi-purpose data basis of earnings and risk parameters must enable consistent earnings and risk management and monitoring across all hierarchy levels, taking diversification effects into account. In relation to the existing portfolio, this data basis should be able to be used both for performance analysis of the subdivisions on the basis of their earnings and risk contributions and for monitoring the risk-bearing capacity of the existing corporate portfolio. In addition, it is intended to support decisions on changes to the existing portfolio. In the following, a multi-purpose data basis is defined and applied to support these different purposes.

3.2   Earnings and Risk Measures for the Valuation of Uncertain Payment Flows

The following approach focuses on payment flows or present values of payment flows and their fluctuations. In the following, it is assumed that the distribution of uncertain payment flows is known for each individual business or can be estimated on the basis of historical data.

For the purpose of evaluating uncertain payment flows, income and risk measures are to be conceptualized as follows. The term income measure corresponds to the expected net present value from cash surpluses, while the corresponding risk measure is intended to assess the fluctuations in the uncertain net present value under consideration. Based on uncertain payment flows, the following assumptions are made for the return and risk measures of the multi-purpose data basis:

A1) Uncertain payment flows and net present values of individual businesses i
One company owned at the time $t = 0$ in total $I \geq 2$ current individual businesses, which are combined in the portfolio U. For each individual business $i \in I$ and time period $t \in T$ there is an uncertain payment surplus $z_{i,\,t}$. These can then be combined into $Z^i = (z_{i,0}, \ldots, z_{i,T})$. The uncertain net present value $BW(Z^i)$ is calculated by discounting the payment surpluses $z_{i,\,t}$ to the point in time $t = 0$ with the risk-free interest rate $r_{i,\,p}$ (for each period $p = 1, \ldots, T^i$):

$$BW\left(Z^i\right) = z_{i,0} + \sum_{t=1}^{T^i} \frac{z_{i,t}}{\prod_{p=1}^{t}\left(1+r_{i,p}\right)}$$

The density functions $f(z_{i,\,t})$ and $f(BW(Z^i))$ respectively of the considered random variables $z_{i,\,t}$ and $BW(Z^i)$ and the risk-free interest rates $r_{i,\,p}$ are known or can be estimated on the basis of historical data.

A2) Earnings

As a measure of earnings E^i we use the expectancy value $E^i = \mathbb{E}[X] = \int_{-\infty}^{\infty} f(X) \cdot X dX$ for $X = BW(Z^i)$.

A3) Risk

The uncertain payment flows Z^i of the individual businesses i become an uncertain total payment flow Z^U of the portfolio U of the company aggregated as $Z^U = \sum_i Z^i$.

A risk measure R^i evaluates the absolute risk contribution of the uncertain net present value $BW(Z^i)$ of an individual business i to the absolute total risk R^U of the uncertain net present value $BW(Z^U)$ of the company. For the valuation, the covariance between the net present value $BW(Z^i)$ of the individual business i and the net present value $BW(Z^U)$ of the portfolio U of the company at the time $t = 0$ is used [23]. This definition of the risk corresponds to a covariance-based risk allocation using the global risk variance [24]. It holds:

$$R^i = \mathbb{C}ov\left(BW\left(Z^i\right), BW\left(Z^U\right)\right) = \rho_{i,U} \cdot \sigma_i \cdot \sigma_U,$$

with ρ as correlation coefficient, σ as standard deviation and $\mathbb{C}ov$ as covariance, each at time $t = 0$. The (net present value) risk measure $R^i \in \mathbb{R}$ is scalar and is expressed in monetary units and, by taking correlations into account, can assume any value between $(-\infty, \infty)$. In the following sections, the consistent use of the return and risk measures defined above for enterprise-wide performance analysis, risk monitoring and for ex ante decision support is presented. In particular, it will be shown that a consistent aggregation of these variables across multiple aggregation levels is possible.

3.3 Enterprise-Wide Performance Analysis of Earnings and Risk Contributions

To be able to perform an enterprise-wide performance analysis of the subdivisions of a company on the basis of their earnings or risk contributions, it must be possible to consistently summarize the earnings or risk variables of the individual businesses defined in A2 and A3 over any number of aggregation levels. For this purpose, a hierarchical tree structure is defined in A4 to represent a hierarchical organizational structure.

A4) Hierarchical Tree Structure

The individual businesses i of a company can be successively combined via sub-portfolios on n aggregation levels in a hierarchical tree structure to form more general groups up to the portfolio U of the company. The overall portfolio is at the highest level of aggregation A_1 while the individual businesses i are located on the lowest aggregation level A_n. The aggregation level A_1 consists of only one node x (A_1) (root node) and represents the entire portfolio U. The lower aggregation levels A_k for $k > 1$ consist of several disjoint nodes $x(A_k)$, ..., $y(A_k)$. The nodes on the lowest aggregation level correspond to the individual businesses (leaves). In order to enable a clear aggregation of single businesses via sub-portfolios on different aggregation levels up to the portfolio U of the company, each node $x(A_{k+1})$ of the aggregation level A_{k+1} is assigned through the edges in the hierarchical tree structure to exactly one node $y(A_k)$ of the next higher aggregation level A_k ($\forall k \in \{1, ..., n-1\}$): Thus, each individual business $i \in U$ is part of exactly one sub-portfolio $y(A_{n-1})$ of the company at the next higher level of aggregation A_{n-1} and the nodes $x(A_k)$ on the aggregation levels A_k with $k \in \{2, .., n\}$ are disjoint. The result is a hierarchical tree structure for aggregating the individual businesses of a company over all aggregation levels. For each sub-portfolio or portfolio $x(A_k)$ an earnings figure and a risk figure are to be determined by aggregating the corresponding figures of the individual businesses. Such a multi-level aggregation of the single businesses, via sub-portfolios up to the portfolio of the company, is substantially facilitated, if for the considered earnings and risk variables applies that $V(X + Y) = V(X) + V(Y)$, with $V(X)$ being representative for $E(X)$ or $R(X)$. In the following, this property is referred to as value-additive.

Value additivity of earnings

We consider two payment flows Z^i and Z^j with $i, j \in \{1, ..., I\}$, $i \neq j$. Value additivity applies to their earnings valuation E^i and E^j if the following consistency requirement K1 is met.

Consistency requirement K1:

The consistency requirement K1 consists of the uniform use of a risk-free interest rate $r_p = r_{p,i}$, $p \in T$, $i \in I$ used for discounting the respective payment surpluses $z_{i,t}$ (see Appendix A1).[2]

Result 1:

If the assumptions A1, A2 and A4 as well as the consistency requirement K1 are fulfilled, then the earnings variables can be linked value-additively to any aggregation level of a hierarchical tree structure and thus enable an enterprise-wide performance analysis of the earnings contributions of the subareas: The total earnings E^{i+j} from the individual businesses i and j corresponds to the sum of the earnings E^i and

---

[2]The appendix of this article is available at the following link: https://www.fim-rc.de/increasing-resilience-with-risk-management

E^j of the individual businesses i and j: $E^{i+j} = E^i + E^j$, with $i, j \in \{1, \ldots, I\}$, $i \neq j$. If one considers the portfolio $y(A_k)$ on a higher aggregation level A_k, $\forall\, k$ with $1 \leq k \leq n$ with its disjoint sub-portfolios $x(A_{k+1})$ of a lower aggregation level A_{k+1}, value additivity applies to the earnings variables $E^{x(A_{k+1})}$:

$$E^{y(A_k)} = \sum_{x(A_{k+1}) \subseteq y(A_k)} E^{x(A_{k+1})}.$$

For the portfolio U of the company, the earnings E^U result from a value-additive linkage of the earnings variables $E^{x(A_k)}$ of the sub-portfolios $x(A_k)$ of a certain aggregation level A_k, $\forall\, k$ with $1 < k \leq n$:

$$E^U = \sum_{x(A_k)} E^{x(A_k)} = \sum_i E^i.$$

The total earnings of the portfolio U of the company is thus always the same, independent of the aggregation level A_k on which the earnings variables $E^{x(A_k)}$ of the sub-portfolios $x(A_k)$ are linked in a value-additive manner.

In the following, we show that value-added aggregation is possible for appropriate covariances when they are used as risk measures.

Value additivity of risks

For the risk assessments R^i and R^j of any two payment flows Z^i and Z^j with $i, j \in \{1, \ldots, I\}$, $i \neq j$ using the covariances between the individual businesses i and j and the portfolio U of the company, value additivity applies [21] (see Appendix A2). This relation can be applied to any two levels of aggregation (such as business units and enterprise or individual businesses and business units) and holds regardless of the underlying distribution of the random variables under consideration (see Appendix A3). In practice, the correlations between neighboring aggregation levels of a hierarchical tree structure are likely to be easier to estimate on the basis of historical data, or tend to be available sooner than is the case for the correlations $\rho_{i,U}$ between the individual businesses i and the portfolio U of the company. The compliance with the following consistency requirement K2a enables the consistent estimation of the correlations $\rho_{i,U}$ between the individual businesses i and the portfolio U of the company based on the product of the correlations between the sub-portfolios at the intermediate aggregation levels of a hierarchical tree structure. Furthermore, in addition to K2a, the following consistency requirements K2b and K2c are also required to enable value-added aggregation of risks (see Appendix A3):

Consistency requirement K2:

K2a): The correlation $\rho_{i,\,U}$ between a single business i and the portfolio of the company U corresponds to the product of the $n-1$ correlations between the sub-portfolios at the intermediate levels of aggregation:[3]

---

[3] $n-1$ factors for correlations between sub-portfolios at respective adjacent aggregation levels.

$$\rho_{i,U} = \rho_{i,x(A_{n-1})} \cdot \cdots \cdot \rho_{y(A_2),U}$$

K2b): For the correlations between the sub-portfolios of different aggregation levels $1 \leq m < k < n$ it must be true that the correlation $\rho_{x(A_{k+1}),y(A_m)}$ between a sub-portfolio $x(A_{k+1})$ and a portfolio $y(A_m)$ of the higher aggregation level A_m is equal to the product of the correlations between the sub-portfolios at the intermediate aggregation levels:

$$\rho_{x(A_{k+1}),y(A_m)} = \rho_{x(A_{k+1}),j(A_k)} \cdot \cdots \cdot \rho_{l(A_{m+1}),y(A_m)}$$

$$\text{with } x(A_{k+1}) \subseteq j(A_k) \subseteq \ldots \subseteq l(A_{m+1}) \subseteq y(A_m)$$

K2c): The standard deviation $\sigma_{y(A_k)}$ of a portfolio $y(A_k)$ at any aggregation level A_k with $1 \leq k < n$ it must be equal to the sum of the products of the standard deviations $\sigma_{x(A_{k+1})}$ of the sub-portfolios $y(A_k)$ contained in the portfolio $x(A_{k+1})$ and the respective correlations $\rho_{x(A_{k+1}),\ y(A_k)}$:

$$\sigma_{y(A_k)} = \sum_{x(A_{k+1}) \subseteq y(A_k)} \left(\rho_{x(A_{k+1}),y(A_k)} \cdot \sigma_{x(A_{k+1})} \right)$$

When using empirical estimation procedures to determine correlations and standard deviations, it must be ensured that the formulated consistency requirement K2 is met.

Result 2:
If assumptions A1, A3 and A4 as well as consistency requirements K1 and K2 are met, then risk measures can be linked in a value-added manner at any aggregation level, thus enabling an enterprise-wide performance analysis of the risk contributions of the subsectors: The total risk R^{i+j} from the individual businesses i and j is equal to the sum of the risks R^i and R^j of the individual businesses i and j: $R^{i+j} = R^i + R^j$ with $i, j \in \{1, \ldots, I\}$, $i \neq j$. If we consider the sub-portfolios $x(A_{k+1})$ of a lower aggregation level A_{k+1} assigned to a portfolio $y(A_k)$ value additivity applies to the risks $R^{x(A_{k+1})}$:

$$R^{y(A_k)} = \sum_{x(A_{k+1}) \subseteq y(A_k)} R^{x(A_{k+1})}.$$

The risk R^U for the portfolio U of the company results from a value-additive linkage of the risks $R^{x(A_k)}$ of the sub-portfolios $x(A_k)$ of a certain, arbitrary aggregation level A_k ($\forall k$ mit $1 < k \leq n$):

$$R^U = \sum_{x(A_k)} R^{x(A_k)}.$$

The overall risk of the portfolio U of the company is thus always the same regardless of the considered aggregation level A_k, on which the risks $R^{x(A_k)}$ of the sub-portfolios $x(A_k)$ are value-additively linked. If value-additive risk variables are used as a basis, they can be linked in a very simple manner over any number of aggregation levels without the need for complex simulation procedures. In the following, we will show how earnings and risks can be linked to value contributions in the sense of safety equivalents over any number of aggregation levels for the purpose of enterprise-wide performance analysis. The present contribution follows the explanations in [19] where, for an alternative definition of value contribution metrics, reference is made to e.g. [25].

Additive linking of earnings and risks to value contributions

In terms of value-based management, a (net present value) value contribution is a risk-adjusted measure of absolute value added, which is calculated by linking earnings and risk measures. While the previously defined earnings and risk variables are defined for all distributions, we assume a normal distribution in the following assumption A5. This enables us to determine value contributions in terms of safety equivalents based on decision theory.

A5) (Net present value) value contribution

It is assumed that the uncertain net present values $BW(Z^i)$ of the individual businesses i of the company can be regarded as normally distributed random variables (with the notation $BW^*(Z^i)$). With the help of an integration function $V_{Int,BW^*}\left(E^i_{BW^*}, R^i_{BW^*}\right)$ based on a classical preference function of the form $\phi(\mu, \sigma) = \mu - \frac{\alpha}{2}\sigma^2$ from decision theory [26] a (net present value) earnings variable $E^i_{BW^*}$ and a (net present value) risk variable $R^i_{BW^*}$ can be additively linked to a (net present value) value contribution $W^i_{BW^*}$:

$$W^i_{\ BW^*} = V_{Int,BW^*}\left(E^i_{BW^*}, R^i_{BW^*}\right) = a^i \cdot E^i_{BW^*} - b^i \cdot R^i_{BW^*}$$

$$= a^i \cdot \mathbb{E}\left(BW(Z^i)\right) - b^i \cdot Cov_{i,U,BW^*},$$

with $a^i \in \mathbb{R}^+$, $b^i \in \mathbb{R}$ as constants. The (net present value) value contribution $W^i_{BW^*}$ is scalar and is expressed in monetary units. $W^i_{BW^*}$ is referred to in the following as value contribution. The value contributions for the individual businesses i or the sub-portfolios $x(A_k)$ are formed in analogy to the preference function, since instead of the variance σ^2 the covariances Cov_{i,U,BW^*} are used [23].

Result 3a:
For the individual businesses i and a given portfolio, the absolute risk-adjusted contribution to the total value of the company can be determined based on the value contribution $W^i_{BW^*}$. The constant a^i in the integration function above expresses the individual return attitude, whereas b^i reflects the individual risk attitude: $b^i = 0$: risk neutrality; $b^i > 0$: risk aversion; $b^i < 0$: risk appetite.

Value additivity of value contributions

Value contributions—for linking the earnings and risk variables—are value-additive, provided that enterprise-wide, constant parameters a and b are applied in the integration function $V_{Int,BW^*}\left(E^i_{BW^*}, R^i_{BW^*}\right)$ (see Appendix A4). For value contributions to be value-additive, it is therefore assumed that the following consistency requirement K3 is met:

Consistency requirement K3:
Enterprise-wide, constant parameters a and b with $a = a^i = a^U$ and $b = b^i = b^U \; \forall \; i \in \{1,\ldots,I\}$ are to be used in the integration function $V_{Int,BW^*}\left(E^i_{BW^*}, R^i_{BW^*}\right)$ for all sub-portfolios $x(A_k)$.

Result 3b:
If value-additive earnings and risk measures are used, and at the same time earnings and risk measures are linked additively, and in addition assumption A5 and consistency requirement K3 are met, then value contributions are value-additive. Value-additive contributions can be linked for all individual businesses via sub-portfolios up to the portfolio of the company U. The consistent use of a and b ensures a uniform earnings/risk attitude throughout the company and thus uniform 'prices' per unit of earnings (valued with the factor a) or per unit of risk (evaluated with the factor b) when determining the value contributions.

In the following section, the analysis is extended from the risk measure R into the shortfall risk measure value-at-risk, which can be used in particular to monitor the risk-bearing capacity of a company.

3.4 Continuous Risk Monitoring Based on Consistent Value-at-Risk Figures

The value-at-risk concept is one possible concept for determining the level of shortfall risk of the company: Value-at-risk (VaR) is according to [27] defined as "the negative change in value of a risky asset position, measured in monetary units, that will not be exceeded with a specified probability within a specified period of time". While the concept of value-at-risk has a number of weaknesses in general distributions [11], it also has great importance due to its regulatory recognition. The following simple relationship between (net present value) risk measures and corresponding value-at-risk measures can be established for normally distributed net present values.

If assumption A5 is fulfilled, the uncertain net present values $BW(Z^i)$ of the individual businesses i of the company are normally distributed. Therefore, the uncertain net present value $BW(Z^U)$ of the portfolio U of the company is normally distributed. The value-at-risk $VaR^U_{1-\gamma,BW^*}$ (adjusted by the expectancy value $\mathbb{E}[BW(Z^U)]$) of the uncertain net present value $BW(Z^U)$ of the portfolio U of the company can be calculated for a given confidence level $(1 - \gamma)$ by multiplying the standard deviation $\sigma^U_{BW^*}$ by the quantile q_γ or $q_{1-\gamma}$ of the standard normal distribution (e.g. $q_{\gamma = 1\%} = 2.33$; $q_{\gamma = 5\%} = 1.65$):

$$VaR^U_{1-\gamma,BW^*} = q_{1-\gamma} \cdot \sigma^U_{BW^*} = -q_\gamma \cdot \sigma^U_{BW^*}$$

By adjusting for the expectancy value of the underlying stochastic net present value, the value-at-risk is obtained as a position-independent risk measure. In order to determine the value-at-risk contribution $VaR^{x(A_k)}_{1-\gamma,BW^*}$ of a sub-portfolio $x(A_k)$ at any level of aggregation A_k mit $1 \le k \le n$ the following formula can be used:

$$VaR^{x(A_k)}_{1-\gamma,BW^*} = -q_\gamma \cdot \rho_{x(A_k),U,BW^*} \cdot \sigma^{A_k}_{BW^*} = -q_\gamma \cdot \frac{R^{x(A_k)}_{BW^*}}{\sigma^U_{BW^*}}$$

with $\rho_{x(A_k),U(A_1),BW^*}$ as the correlation between the net present value of the sub-portfolio $x(A_k)$ and the net present value of the portfolio U of the company. Analogous to the proofs in the appendix for the risk variables $R^{x(A_k)}_{BW^*}$ it is possible to prove value additivity for the value-at-risk contributions $VaR^{x(A_k)}_{1-\gamma,BW^*}$ at any level of aggregation if the following additional consistency requirement K4 is met:

Consistency requirement K4:
The quantile q_γ of the standard normal distribution is uniform, i.e., at a uniform confidence level $1 - \gamma$, for the value-at-risk assessment for all sub-portfolios $x(A_k)$ (with $1 \le k \le n$) in the hierarchical tree structure.

Result 4:
Value-at-risk can be used to monitor the company's risk-bearing capacity and can be used for risk limitation and internal equity management. On the basis of integrated earnings and risk databases, value-at-risk figures—for individual businesses, sub-portfolios or for the portfolio of the company—can be generated in a simple manner as the product of the respective risk figures and the corresponding enterprise-wide quantile if assumption A5 and consistency requirement K4 are met.

3.5 Incremental Decision Support on the Expansion or Reduction of the Existing Portfolio

While the previous sections on enterprise-wide performance analysis and monitoring of risk-bearing capacity were based on an existing portfolio, the following section examines whether incremental changes to the existing portfolio by adding an additional individual business (or an additional sub-portfolio) or a corresponding reduction in the portfolio is advantageous from the company's perspective. For this purpose, the individual businesses or sub-areas of the company are considered as sub-portfolios $x(A_k)$ at a certain aggregation level A_k with $1 \leq k < n$ according to the hierarchical tree structure defined in A4. It denotes N the number of sub-portfolios considered $x(A_k)$ of the company portfolio. The aim is to investigate whether, in the case of N existing sub-portfolios $x(A_k)$ the expansion or reduction of the company portfolio by one sub-portfolio $y(A_k)$ is advantageous and thus increases the overall value of the company. First, the expansion of the existing portfolio of the company by a $(N + 1)th$ sub-portfolio will be examined. The net present value earnings E^U of the company changes by the addition of the sub-portfolio $y(A_k)$ by the incremental net present value earnings variable $IE^{y(A_k)}$:

$$IE^{y(A_k)} = E^{U(N+1)} - E^{U(N)} = \mathbb{E}\left[BW\left(Z^{y(A_k)}\right)\right] = E^{y(A_k)}$$

$$= \int_{-\infty}^{\infty} f\left(BW\left(Z^{y(A_k)}\right)\right) \cdot BW\left(Z^{y(A_k)}\right) dBW\left(Z^{y(A_k)}\right),$$

with $y(A_k)$ as the additional sub-portfolio at the aggregation level A_k on which the addition is to be decided and $U(N)$ and $U(N + 1)$ the existing or new portfolio of the companies after the addition of the sub-portfolio $y(A_k)$ respectively. In this context, the incremental, net present value earnings figure corresponds to $IE^{y(A_k)}$ the net present value earnings figure $E^{y(A_k)}$ of the sub-portfolio $y(A_k)$. The change in the net present value risk variable R^U of the company as a result of the addition of the sub-portfolio $y(A_k)$ is expressed by the incremental, net present value risk variable $IR^{y(A_k)}$:

$$IR^{y(A_k)} = R^{U(N+1)} - R^{U(N)} = \sigma^2_{U(N+1)} - \sigma^2_{U(N)} = \sigma^2_{y(A_k)} + 2 \cdot Cov_{y(A_k),U(N)}$$

For the additional sub-portfolio $y(A_k)$ the following incremental, (net present value) value contribution can therefore be given $IW_{BW^*}^{y(A_k)}$:

$$IW_{BW^*}^{y(A_k)} = V_{Int,BW^*}^{y(A_k)}\left(IE_{BW^*}^{y(A_k)}, IR_{BW^*}^{y(A_k)}\right) = a \cdot IE_{BW^*}^{y(A_k)} - b \cdot IR_{BW^*}^{y(A_k)}$$

$$= a \cdot E_{BW^*}^{y(A_k)} - b \cdot \left(\sigma^2_{y(A_k),BW^*} + 2 \cdot Cov_{y(A_k),U(N),BW^*}\right)$$

Provided that beyond the given sub-portfolio $y(A_k)$ there are no further opportunities to add sub-portfolios or individual businesses and no other constraints (such as risk-bearing capacity) have a restrictive effect, a decision-maker acts rationally in accordance with Bernoulli's principle if he or she

- in the case $IW_{BW^*}^{y(A_k)} > 0$ expands the existing portfolio of the company by the $(N + 1)th$ sub-portfolio $y(A_k)$
- or in case of $IW_{BW^*}^{y(A_k)} \leq 0^4$ rejects the addition of the $(N + 1)th$ sub-portfolio $y(A_k)$.

Analogously, for the reduction of the existing portfolio $U(N)$ by one sub-portfolio $v(A_k)$ the following incremental, net present value earnings and risks can be specified:

Incremental net present value earnings $IE_{BW^*}^{v(A_k)}$:

$$IE_{BW^*}^{v(A_k)} = E_{BW^*}^{U(N-1)} - E_{BW^*}^{U(N)} = -E_{BW^*}^{v(A_k)}$$

Incremental net present value risks $IR_{BW^*}^{v(A_k)}$:

$$IR_{BW^*}^{v(A_k)} = R_{BW^*}^{U(N-1)} - R_{BW^*}^{U(N)} = -\sigma_{v(A_k),BW^*}^2 - 2 \cdot Cov_{v(A_k),U(N-1),BW^*}$$

Therefore, the following incremental (net present value) value contribution $IW_{BW^*}^{y(A_k)}$ of selling the sub-portfolio $v(A_k)$ can be specified:

$$IW_{BW^*}^{v(A_k)} = V_{Int,BW^*}^{v(A_k)}\left(IE_{BW^*}^{v(A_k)}, IR_{BW^*}^{v(A_k)}\right) = a \cdot IE_{BW^*}^{v(A_k)} - b \cdot IR_{BW^*}^{v(A_k)}$$

$$= a \cdot E_{BW^*}^{v(A_k)} - b \cdot \left(-\sigma_{v(A_k),BW^*}^2 - 2 \cdot Cov_{v(A_k),U(N-1),BW^*}\right)$$

A decision-maker acts rationally according to Bernoulli's principle if he or she

- in case $IW_{BW^*}^{v(A_k)} > 0$ sells the $(N)th$ sub-portfolio $v(A_k)$
- or in case $IW_{BW^*}^{v(A_k)} \leq 0^4$ does not sell the $(N)th$ sub-portfolio $v(A_k)$.

The outlined incremental value contributions can thus be used to support enterprise-wide investment and divestment decisions, both for individual businesses and for entire sub-portfolios at a certain level of aggregation A_k. In this way, decisions ranging from an arbitrarily small customer transaction to larger transactions, such as the purchase or sale of entire sub-portfolios of the company, can be consistently achieved. By considering incremental risk measures, the following consistency requirement for the pairwise covariances $Cov_{i,j}$ is also met between the

---

[4] Strictly speaking, the decision-maker in the case $IW_{BW^*}^{y(A_k)} = 0$ $[IW_{BW^*}^{v(A_k)} = 0]$ would be indifferent. In this case, it is assumed that due to the lack of a positive incremental value contribution from the additional [considered] sub-portfolio $y(A_k)[v(A_k)]$, the decision-maker will not add [sell] it.

individual businesses in a sub-portfolio or between the sub-portfolios in an overall portfolio:

Consistency requirement K5:
For each individual business (sub-portfolio) i it must hold that the sum of the pairwise covariances $Cov_{i,j}$ between all individual businesses (or sub-portfolios) of a company must correspond to the covariance $Cov_{i,U}$ between the single business (sub-portfolio) i and the company U: $Cov_{i,U} = \sum_j Cov_{i,j} \ \forall i$. Based on this for the correlations $\rho_{i,U}$ the following relationship must be met: $\forall i : \rho_{i,U} = \dfrac{\sum_j \rho_{i,j} \cdot \sigma_j}{\sigma_U}$. After the existing company portfolio has been expanded or reduced by a sub-portfolio, the consistency requirements K2 and K5 must be checked again.

Consistency requirement K6:
In the event of an expansion of the company portfolio by a sub-portfolio $y(A_k)$ with $\rho_{y(A_k),U(N)} \neq 1$ that is not fully correlated with the original portfolio U (N), the remaining sub-portfolios' $x(A_k)$ correlations to the company U change: I.e., from $\rho_{y(A_k),U(N)} \neq 1$ follows $\rho_{x(A_k),U(N+1)} \neq \rho_{x(A_k),U(N)}$. Therefore, the correlations $\rho_{x(A_k),U(N+1)}$ have to be recalculated. Similarly, if the company portfolio is reduced by a sub-portfolio $v(A_k)$ with $\rho_{v(A_k),U(N)} \neq 1$ that is not fully correlated with the old portfolio $U(N)$, the correlations of the remaining sub-portfolios $x(A_k)$ with the company U change: I.e., from $\rho_{v(A_k),U(N)} \neq 1$ follows $\rho_{x(A_k),U(N-1)} \neq \rho_{x(A_k),U(N)}$. Therefore, the correlations $\rho_{x(A_k),U(N-1)}$ must be recalculated. In practical implementation, it must be analyzed whether, in the case of minor changes in the company portfolio, a costly recalculation of the correlations and the subsequent verification of the consistency requirements K2 and K3 can be waived and how threshold values for such recalculations can be defined. Finally, the risk measures and value contributions for ex ante decision support are compared with the risk measures and value contributions for performance measurement in the following. A comparison between the risk measures $R^{y(A_k)}$ and value contributions $W_{BW^*}^{y(A_k)}$ used for continuous performance measurement, and the incremental risk measures $IR^{y(A_k)}$ and value contributions $IW_{BW^*}^{y(A_k)}$ used in ex ante decision support shows that these generally differ. For the standard case of a positive covariance $Cov_{y(A_k),U(N)}$ between the new sub-portfolio y (A_k) to be added and the existing corporate portfolio $U(N)$ the result is, e.g., a larger incremental risk value $IR^{y(A_k)}$ of the continuous performance measurement compared to the risk value $R^{y(A_k)}$. This is due to the fact that in the case of incremental risk measurement, all correlation effects of the sub-portfolio $y(A_k)$ with the corporate portfolio $U(N)$ are attributed exclusively to the new sub-portfolio $y(A_k)$. Since, for a given company portfolio, the addition of a new sub-portfolio causes the change in the risk position of the company, this represents an adequate risk attribution. Conversely, ex ante decision support based on the risk measure of continuous performance measurement is not meaningful, since the change in the risk position induced by a newly added sub-portfolio $y(A_k)$ is not adequately attributed to the new

sub-portfolio. Rather, in this case, part of the newly induced risk is attributed to other businesses or sub-portfolios. In the standard case of a positive covariance $Cov_{y(A_k),U(N)}$ this procedure leads to an underestimation of the risk and thus to an overestimation of the value contribution of the newly added sub-portfolio $y(A_k)$. This illustrates that integrated earnings and risk indicators must always be used with regard to the respective application purpose. If, for example, the company's internal incentive systems in decentralized decision-making structures are based on the value contributions of performance measurement, this can lead to misaligned incentives. If decision-makers make decisions for self-benefit optimization on the basis of the value contributions to performance measurement instead of on the incremental value contributions, systematically wrong decisions may be the result.

4 Conclusion and Outlook

In this paper, a financial approach was developed to create a consistent, multi-purpose data basis across the company for integrated earnings and risk management geared to sustainability and resilience. The first step was to define uniform enterprise-wide earnings and risk measures that allow aggregation across any number of aggregation levels (e.g., individual businesses, business units, company). Under the additional assumption of normally distributed net present values, the earnings and risk variables were linked to (risk-adjusted) value-additive contributions that support consistent performance measurement across all hierarchical levels of the company portfolio. Furthermore, if normally distributed net present values are available, the risk variables under consideration can be converted into value-at-risk figures using simple quantile factors, which can be used to continuously monitor risk-bearing capacity. In addition, the incremental risk quantities and value contributions of an additional sub-portfolio or individual business, or the sale of a sub-portfolio or individual business can be calculated for ex ante decision support. The successful implementation of these three core tasks of earnings and risk management strengthens the resilience of a company by supporting both forward-looking, proactive risk management in economically good times and, at the same time, better reactive management in times of crisis. With the help of the concept developed, dependencies can be identified across all hierarchical levels and the effects of possible crisis scenarios on the company portfolio can be anticipated at an early stage. This enables decision-makers to build up financial reserves in the sense of sustainability and resilience-oriented corporate management and to invest in good times in the sustainable orientation of a company, which increases its crisis resilience. The enterprise-wide aggregation of earnings and risk positions also provides the information basis in times of crisis to detect the realized crisis effects on the overall portfolio at an early stage and to decide in good times on measures to increase crisis resilience. The approach developed can be used throughout a company, provided that the incoming variables and parameters are known or can be estimated for the sub-areas of the companies under consideration. However, the concept presented still has the following limitations. The underlying variables and parameters only represent the first and second moments of the distribution of random variables (here: uncertain net present values). Although a consideration of higher moments could provide decision-makers with further information about the underlying distributions, a value-additive aggregation in integrated earnings and risk databases is usually not possible for them. Furthermore, the mapped correlations only describe linear relationships between the random variables under consideration and are assumed to be constant over the period under consideration, which is often not the case, especially in crises, and therefore requires cautious estimation. Therefore, in addition to changes in correlations over time that can be observed in the real world, non-linear correlations between random variables in particular are not considered. It should also be noted that a previously multilevel aggregation of earnings and risk variables is possible for all underlying distributions of uncertain net present values of individual businesses, but value contributions in the sense of certainty equivalents presuppose normally distributed net present values of individual businesses. Since this paper focuses on the internal earnings and risk management of the company, there is a need for further research, especially regarding the extension of the earnings and risk variables and the key figures derived from them with regard to regulatory requirements as well as reporting requirements. From the perspective of the Business & Information Systems Engineering discipline, the developed financial methodology represents an important conceptual basis for IT-supported management systems. In this context, IT-supported earnings and risk management is to be understood as an important component of initiatives for the digital transformation of the financial area of a company. Based on the project work of the Research Center Finance & Information Management, the Fraunhofer Project Group Business & Information Systems Engineering and the accompanying support of companies in the digitalization of the finance area, the following findings and recommendations for action can be derived: The use of digital technologies such as Robotic Process Automation and AI can increase the degree of automation, especially of repetitive tasks and processes in the finance area, and thus increase the freedom for discretionary tasks. The integration of various data sources as well as the use of modeling, simulation and analysis software have the potential to automate standard reporting and consolidation processes. In addition, AI-based data analysis as well as methods from the field of predictive analytics enable complex processes such as scenario analyses and forecasting to be carried out in real time without a high level of manual effort. This can improve and accelerate decision-making processes in a volatile market environment in particular [28, 29]. By reducing manual activities, resources in finance can be increasingly allocated to analytical and interpretative tasks to favor a shift in task focus to the derivation of recommended actions as well as decision support. As innovative technologies increasingly take on repetitive and decision-making tasks, the function of finance is changing from data provider to business partner or business advisor. However, this also has implications for the requirements profile of employees in finance. In the future, interdisciplinary knowledge at the interface of digital technologies and business contexts will become even more important to use IT support effectively and to be able to interpret the results of data and AI-supported analysis tools in a business context and derive recommendations for action. At the same time, interdisciplinarily trained employees are required to derive a dedicated digitalization strategy and implement it in a targeted and coordinated manner as part of initiatives and projects. Therefore, Business & Information Systems Engineering as an interdiscipline can make an important contribution to the digital transformation of the finance function of companies.

References

1. Thomas, O., Hagen, S., Frank, U., et al.: Global crises and the role of BISE. Bus. Inf. Syst. Eng. **62**, 385–396 (2020)
2. Nicola, M., Alsafi, Z., Sohrabi, C., et al.: The socio-economic implications of the coronavirus pandemic (COVID-19): a review. Int. J. Surg. **78**, 185–193 (2020)
3. Baldwin, R., Tomiura, E.: Thinking ahead about the trade impact of COVID-19. Economics in the Time of COVID-19 **59** (2020)
4. Bundesministerium für Wirtschaft und Energie. Die wirtschaftliche Lage in Deutschland im September 2020. https://www.bmwi.de/Redaktion/DE/Pressemitteilungen/Wirtschaftliche-Lage/2020/20200914-die-wirtschaftliche-lage-in-deutschland-im-september-2020.html (2020). Accessed 28 Sep 2020
5. Belelieu, A., Barton, M.E., Blake, M., et al.: Building a more resilient and sustainable world. https://www.bain.com/globalassets/noindex/2020/wef_building_a_more_resilient_and_sustainable_world_2020.pdf (2020). Accessed 26 Sep 2020
6. DIN e.V., Beuth Verlag: AS ISO 22301:2017 Societal security – Business continuity management systems – Requirements (2017)
7. Buhl, H.U.: IT as curse and blessing. Bus. Inf. Syst. Eng. **55**, 377–381 (2013)
8. Steiner, M., Kinder, C., Willinsky, C.: Kapitalallokation und Verrechnung von Risikokapitalkosten in Kreditinstituten. ZfB. **71**, 281–300 (2001)
9. Gebhardt, G., Mansch, H.: Wertorientierte Unternehmenssteuerung in Theorie und Praxis. ZfbF (2005)
10. Dutta, S., Reichelstein, S.: Accrual accounting for performance evaluation. Rev. Account. Stud. **10**, 527–552 (2005)
11. Szegö, G.: Measures of risk. J. Bank. Financ. **26**, 1253–1272 (2002)
12. Kürsten, W., Brandtner, M.: Kohärente Risikomessung versus individuelle Akzeptanzmengen - Anmerkungen zum impliziten Risikoverständnis des "Conditional Value-at-Risk". ZfbF. **61**, 358–381 (2009)
13. Kruschwitz, L.: Investitionsrechnung. Oldenbourg (2014)
14. Laux, H., Gillenkirch, R.M., Schenk-Mathes, H.Y.: Entscheidungstheorie, vol. 4. Springer (1998)
15. Faisst, U., Buhl, H.U.: Integrated enterprise balancing mit integrierten Ertrags- und Risikodatenbanken. Wirtschaftsinf. **47**, 403–412 (2005)
16. Coenenberg, A.G., Salfeld, R., Schultze, W.: Wertorientierte Unternehmensführung: Vom Strategieentwurf zur Implementierung. Schäffer-Poeschel (2015)
17. Rappaport, A.: Creating shareholder value: a guide for managers and investors. Simon and Schuster (1999)
18. Weber, J., Bramsemann, U., Heineke, C., et al.: Wertorientierte Unternehmenssteuerung. Springer (2004)
19. Bamberg, G., Dorfleitner, G., Krapp, M.: Unternehmensbewertung unter Unsicherheit: Zur entscheidungstheoretischen Fundierung der Risikoanalyse. J. Bus. Econ. **76**, 287–307 (2006)

20. Markowitz, H.M.: Portfolio Selection: Efficient Diversification of Investments. Yale University Press (1959)
21. Copeland, T.E., Weston, J.F., Shastri, K.: Finanzierungstheorie und Unternehmenspolitik: Konzepte der kapitalmarktorientierten Unternehmensfinanzierung. Pearson (2008)
22. Froot, K.A., Stein, J.C.: Risk management, capital budgeting, and capital structure policy for financial institutions. J. Financ. Econ. **47**, 55–82 (1998)
23. Huther, A.: Integriertes Chancen- und Risikomanagement: Zur ertrags- und risikoorientierten Steuerung von Real- und Finanzinvestitionen in der Industrieunternehmung, Gabler Edition Wissenschaft. Deutscher Universitätsverlag, Wiesbaden (2003)
24. Albrecht, P., Koryciorz, S.: Methoden der risikobasierten Kapitalallokation im Versicherungs- und Finanzwesen. ZVersWiss. **93**, 123–159 (2004)
25. Franck, E. (ed.): Marktwertorientierte Unternehmensführung: Anreiz- und Kommunikationsaspekte ZfbF Sonderheft, vol. 50. Verl.-Gruppe Handelsblatt, Düsseldorf (2003)
26. Schneeweiß, H.: Entscheidungskriterien bei Risiko. Springer, Berlin (1967)
27. Uhlir, H., Aussenegg, W.: Value-at-Risk (VaR)-Einführung und Methodenüberblick. Bankarchiv. **44**, 831–836 (1996)
28. Röglinger, M., Bolsinger, M., Häckel, B., et al.: How to structure business transformation projects: the case of Infineon's Finance IT Roadmap. J. Inf. Technol. Theory Appl. **17**, 2 (2016)
29. Federmann, F., Häckel, B., Isbruch, F., et al.: Treiberbasierte Simulation im Controlling bei Infineon. ZfC. **32**, 28–35 (2020)

Data Vault as a Modeling Concept for the Data Warehouse

Peter Gluchowski

Abstract The choice of appropriate data models has been intensively discussed since the early days of the debate on the design of data warehouse architectures. Initially, the two camps of the multidimensional and the normalized relational modeling paradigm opposed each other.

However, since both modeling techniques prove to be suboptimal due to the specifics of the data warehouse concept, data vault models are increasingly used today. Data Vault not only supports the requirement for agility, but also enables complete traceability and auditability of any changes. Data Vault has therefore established itself as the standard in large core data warehouses.

Keywords Core data warehouse · Data modeling · Data vault

1 Data Modeling in the Data Warehouse

Ever since the early days of the discussion about the design of a data warehouse landscape and the associated multidimensional view of business data, intensive thought has been given to suitable forms and techniques of data modeling. The chosen way of storing relevant data determines not least on the one hand the flexibility in reacting to changed or extended user requirements and on the other hand the access possibilities for the end user, especially with regard to navigation functionality and response time.

Unfortunately, the established practices and methods of data modeling from the operational system environment can only be used to a limited extent, since the corresponding systems are designed more towards the fast and consistent recording of numerous individual transactions and less towards the comprehensive evaluation of large data volumes.

P. Gluchowski (✉)
Chemnitz University of Technology, Chemnitz, Germany
e-mail: Peter.Gluchowski@wirtschaft.tu-chemnitz.de

© The Author(s), under exclusive license to Springer Nature Switzerland AG 2021
S. Aier et al. (eds.), *Engineering the Transformation of the Enterprise*,
https://doi.org/10.1007/978-3-030-84655-8_17

Against this background, data modeling in the data warehouse, especially in the core data warehouse or in the integration layer of a layered architecture, still proves to be a red-hot topic even after more than 20 years of intensive discussion. In the past, it was particularly the disputes that arose between the advocates of dimensional modeling (star and snowflake schema) on the one hand and normalized data models (data models in third normal form) on the other, which sometimes resulted in true religious wars.

Especially for larger data warehouse implementations, modeling according to the third normal form was often preferred, which can be traced back to one of the "forefathers" of the data warehouse concept, William Inmon [1]. The goal here is to build a comprehensive, enterprise-wide data model for the core data warehouse that holds the relevant data in the highest possible level of detail and quality assurance. New data marts can then be quickly created from this data pool. In addition, it is easy to ensure that the key figures used are defined uniformly. The considerable complexity that arises from the large number of tables to be created, including the associated links, proves to be problematic. In addition to the initial set-up, the further development of the data model in particular is associated with great effort and long project times. At the same time, users want agile solutions that are capable of implementing new requirements in a timely manner.

In contrast to Inmon, Ralph Kimball propagated the development of a dimensional data model for the core data warehouse more than 20 years ago, which organizes relevant data in dimension and fact tables using star or snowflake schema modeling [2]. In this way, it is possible to realize both the initial structure and the iterative further development comparatively quickly, which is very close to the ideas and business understanding of the users. The central design feature are "conformed dimensions", i.e. dimensions and the associated dimension tables that can be used flexibly in different contexts, e.g. in interaction with various fact tables. A major criticism of dimensional modeling for the core data warehouse is its lack of robustness in the face of changes to the source systems or to the business logic, which usually entail extensive and costly modifications to the data model along with the associated development and testing tasks. Today, dimensional modeling is used primarily at the level of data marts.

However, both modeling approaches often lead to difficulties that are more or less pronounced [3]. Over time, for example, very complex ETL structures with numerous dependencies almost inevitably build up to an extensive warehouse architecture. On the way from the source systems to usage by the end user, the data objects pass through a wide variety of preparation and refinement steps, making traceability of the entire data flow a laborious undertaking. However, this is unavoidable if, for example, the user questions individual value specifications or if data types or structures change in the systems supplying the data. The need for serial processing in individual areas can also lead to time bottlenecks when loading the target system. In addition, individual ETL jobs prove difficult to track and modify due to deep nesting. Decoupling and standardization of the modules would be desirable.

From the user's point of view, a decision-supporting systems must be able to react quickly to changing requirements. After all, the business logic to be mapped changes with increasing volatility. Existing decision data must therefore be adaptable and expandable within a short period of time, and new data sources must be integrated quickly. The associated demand for agility also requires short release cycles, which poses major challenges for the operation and further development of big data architectures.

In this context, however, classic data warehouses often prove to be cumbersome and sluggish, especially since all modifications are linked to extensive testing and quality assurance processes. It is therefore not surprising that some business users are already increasingly questioning the concept of the single point of truth, which has been sustainable for many years, due to a lack of flexibility.

2 Data Vault Modeling

This is where a concept that aims to overcome the disadvantages of classic approaches and focuses on a special type of data modeling promises to be a remedy: Data Vault [4]. The Data Vault approach extends beyond pure data modeling and today also addresses aspects such as architecture or suitable process models (Data Vault 2.0) [5]. With this comprehensive approach, the Data Vault concept promises to be able to support the agility demanded by the business side in an excellent manner and to offer both stable and flexible BI solutions that can be quickly adapted to expanded or changed requirements. This should result in future-proof architectures that take into account the character of a core data warehouse as a long-term investment. The method favors a "single version of the facts" over a "single version of the truth" by initially continuing to process even data containing errors (bad data, e.g., transaction data for undefined master data).

At its core, the Data Vault concept is a modeling methodology that ensures scalability and, above all, auditing capability through consistent model separation of keys (hub tables), descriptive attributes (satellite tables), and relationship information (link tables) through conceptual clarity, in addition to flexibility and adaptability.

Figure 1 visualizes the distribution of the object types key, context information and relations on tables in the relational schema with third normal form, in the Star schema and in the Data Vault.

The left part initially contains an operational customer table with typical fields for the primary key (Customer_ID), for foreign key links to other tables (customer group and sales employee) and further, descriptive attributes. These different object types are all found in a table in third normal form. In the Star schema, on the other hand, the dimension tables contain key information and context information, and the fact tables also contain relationship information. Data Vault modeling, on the other hand, manages business keys exclusively in hubs, all relationship information in links, and all other attributes in the associated satellites. The three model components each contain mandatory information about the data source (record source) and the load time (load date or Date_Time_Stamp).

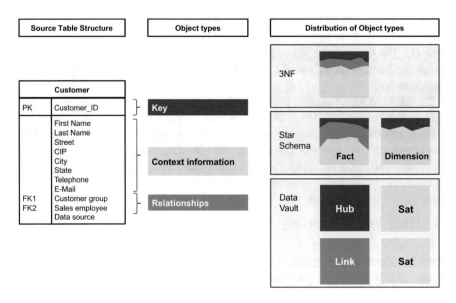

Fig. 1 Distribution of object types on tables (based on [6])

Hub Customer

Hub Customer	
PK	H_Customer_SID
	Customer_ID
	Date_Time_Stamp
	Data_Source

H_Customer_SID	Customer_ID	Date_Time_Stamp	Data_Source
1	1003456	10.04.2020	ECC Europe
2	1003457	10.04.2020	ECC Europe
3	1003458	11.04.2020	ECC Europe
4	1003459	11.04.2020	ECC Europe

Fig. 2 Hub customer

2.1 Core Objects of the Data Vault Modeling

Hubs represent core objects of the respective business logic. In addition to an artificial surrogate key (SK, sometimes also referred to as sequence key) for linking the other structures, which is usually formed as a continuous integer number or as a hash value, there is also always a business key that is unique throughout the company, e.g., a customer number. A hub does not contain any relationship information or descriptive attributes. Hubs are created once and are not changed thereafter. This allows ETL processes to be limited to insert statements for those objects for which no business key exists in the target system. The load date or the timestamp (here a current date, in case of multiple updates per day also more detailed) represents the first loading of this business key (the customer_ID) into the core data warehouse. On the other hand, the source (data source) describes from which system this business key originates (see Fig. 2).

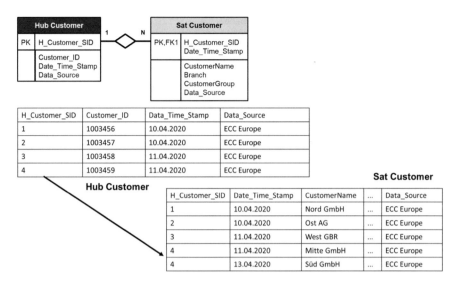

H_Customer_SID	Customer_ID	Data_Time_Stamp	Data_Source
1	1003456	10.04.2020	ECC Europe
2	1003457	10.04.2020	ECC Europe
3	1003458	11.04.2020	ECC Europe
4	1003459	11.04.2020	ECC Europe

Hub Customer

Sat Customer

H_Customer_SID	Date_Time_Stamp	CustomerName	...	Data_Source
1	10.04.2020	Nord GmbH	...	ECC Europe
2	10.04.2020	Ost AG	...	ECC Europe
3	11.04.2020	West GBR	...	ECC Europe
4	11.04.2020	Mitte GmbH	...	ECC Europe
4	13.04.2020	Süd GmbH	...	ECC Europe

Fig. 3 Satellite customer

L_CustOrder_SID	H_Customer_SID	H_Order_SID	Date_Time_Stamp	Data_Source
KA4711	1	A12345	16.04.2020	ECC Europe
KA4712	2	A23456	17.04.2020	ECC Europe
KA4713	2	A34567	19.04.2020	ECC Europe
KA4714	3	A45678	23.04.2020	ECC Europe

Sat CustomerOrder

L_CustOrder_SID	Date_Time_Stamp	OrderDate	ContactName	Data_Source
KA4711	16.04.2020	15.04.2020	Meier	ECC Europe
KA4711	24.04.2020	15.04.2020	Müller	ECC Europe

Fig. 4 CustomerOrder link

Satellites store all descriptive attributes of hubs and links, which can also have multiple satellites. The primary key is composed of the surrogate ID of the hub (or link) and a load timestamp. In addition to a reference to the associated source system, the other associated attributes can be found here. If several satellites exist for a hub or link, then these are usually divided according to the type of data, the frequency of changes or the source, for example. Furthermore, the satellites also map the historization, as in the example of Fig. 3 for the customer with ID 4. Filling the satellites also proves to be a pure insertion process, since changes to attribute characteristics are reflected in a new table row.

Links map all relationships in Data Vault models by representing links between two (or more) hubs, using the surrogate keys of the hubs as references in the form of foreign keys (see Fig. 4). Although links do not have their own business keys, they

Table 1 Modeling rules for data vault data models

• Hub
— There are no direct relationships between different hubs.
— Hubs are connected exclusively by links.
— Surrogate keys and business keys of hubs are immutable.
• Link
— Links link two or more hubs together (linking link and hub via a link is also allowed).
— Links also have an immutable artificial key (surrogate key).
— The alternate key of a link then contains the composite key from the surrogate keys of the linked hubs.
• Satellite
— Satellites always point clearly to a hub or link.
— Satellites usually use the hub or link key in conjunction with a timestamp as the primary key.

also have unique surrogate keys. The load timestamp records the first occurrence of the relationship. Just like hubs, links can also have satellites.

To ensure the construction of correct Data Vault models, there are several modeling rules that must be followed in the design process (see Table 1).

Extensive and complex data vault data models can be built on the basis of these rules. Figure 5 below shows an example of a core data warehouse for order processing.

In detail, different modeling philosophies arise in the Data Vault context. For example, it can be argued whether an end-date attribute is required in the satellite tables. In practical use, however, this results in advantages for validity queries. Also, a separate hub can be defined for the order item in Fig. 5 if it proves necessary for the application.

Overall, it should be noted that a data vault model produces more data artifacts (tables or fields) than a dimensional or normalized data model. When filling the model with data from the upstream systems, this proves to be a manageable deficit, especially since the representatives of the individual object types hub, link and satellite have great structural similarities, which opens up automation potentials in the context of creating ETL processes.

2.2 Auxiliary Constructs of Data Vault Modeling

However, compiling data from the Data Vault to fill further data layers, such as the Data Mart layer, requires very complex SQL statements with considerable scope. For this reason, auxiliary constructs are often used for the further preparation steps, which do not represent mandatory components of the Data Vault modeling, but lead to a significant simplification of subsequent transformation processes. Bridge tables and point-in-time tables are two different approaches that can be implemented as physical tables or views [7]. These tools for technical performance tuning for further

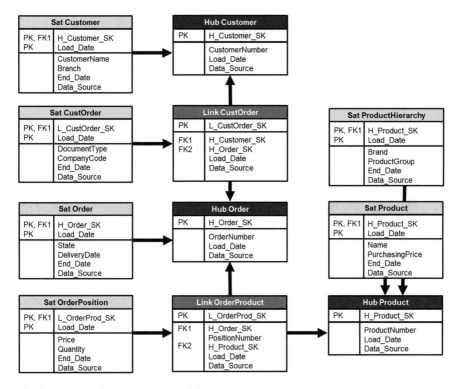

Fig. 5 Exemplary Data Vault data model

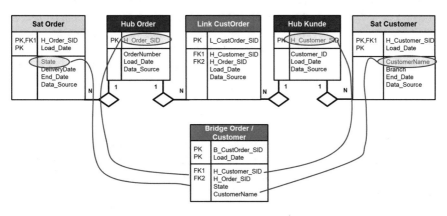

Fig. 6 Exemplary bridge table

processing can be deleted at any time without affecting the information content in the enterprise data warehouse.

Bridge tables bring together individual elements from hub, link and satellite tables in an integrated object (see Fig. 6). The data contained there is either

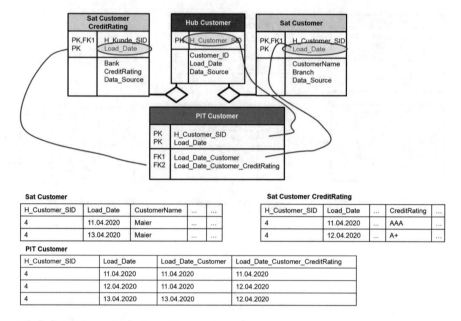

Fig. 7 Exemplary point-in-time table

physically stored in separate tables or materialized views, or exists as logical views of the data vault data structures. Corresponding mergers can extend over several links and then include objects from completely different data areas.

In contrast, point-in-time tables bring together the elements of different satellites of a hub in such a way that the validity of the value characteristics of a data object at an arbitrary point in time can be easily derived from them. This simplifies the process of reading out the status of validity at any point in time across different satellites, especially since calculating the respective validity can prove to be a challenging undertaking.

Figure 7 uses an example to illustrate the basic procedure for point-in-time tables.

The Customer hub has two different satellites. While "Sat Customer" contains general information about the customer, "Sat Customer CreditRating" contains, among other things, information about the customer's ability to pay. In both satellites, the attribute values change over time. The PIT table refers to the respective valid "Load_Date" in the satellite tables on a given date. This makes it easy to determine the respective validities at any given time almost immediately. To ensure data consistency, the point-in-time tables do not have any further descriptive information from satellites apart from the link to the business object (here the H_Customer_SID).

2.3   Advantages of Data Vault Modeling

Loading data into a Data Vault model follows simple and consistent patterns. The associated ETL processes consist of key lookups, delta determinations and insert commands (if not additionally working with end dates) on hubs, links and satellites. Furthermore, a parallelized execution of ETL processes proves to be feasible, especially since the different tables of a type can be loaded independently of each other. The loading process follows a predefined pattern. First, all hubs are loaded, if necessary in parallel. Parallel loading can then also be performed for the links and hub satellites before the link satellites are finally filled.

Automation concepts are used above all in the creation of ETL processes. Based on the metadata of the data models, loading routes can be generated very well automatically, since the structure of hubs, links and satellites proves to be comparatively uniform in each case. In this respect, template-based and automated generation of ETL processes leads to extensive effort reductions. In addition, the automatic generation of SQL-based test cases and their automatic execution up to logging of the test results is proving to be common. This ensures integrated quality assurance of ETL development as well as data modeling.

Furthermore, the Data Vault data model proves to be comparatively easy to extend, especially since existing structures are not changed by new data objects and testing efforts are therefore kept to a minimum.

Since the required transformations of the data before filling the data vault are limited to a few standard operations, some of which can be automated, the compilation of data in a core data warehouse can be designed in a very agile manner. Further functional transformations are shifted to higher data warehouse layers. For this purpose, the data is often divided into a raw data vault (with only slightly processed raw data) and a business data vault (with more extensive processing, such as data cleansing, type conversion, calculation of key figures or aggregation).

3   Summary

In summary, it can be said that the Data Vault modeling methodology offers a powerful set of tools for building consistent and coordinated data models for the core data warehouse that are based on predefined rules. Although this tends to increase the effort required for the pure creation of the data model, there is potential for savings in other areas. The relatively low-effort changeability favors use in agile environments, which are becoming increasingly widespread.

References

1. Inmon, W.H.: Building the Data Warehouse, 3rd edn. Wiley, New York (2002)
2. Kimball, R.: The Data Warehouse Toolkit – Practical Techniques for Building Dimensional Data Warehouses. Wiley, New York (1996)
3. Hüsemann, B.: Data Vault - Zentralisierung von Businesslogik und Data-Mart-Anbindung. TDWI-Tagung, München (2015)
4. Linstedt, D.: Super Charge your Data Warehouse, o. O. (2011)
5. Linstedt, D., Olschimke, M.: Building a Scalable Data Warehouse with Data Vault 2.0. Morgan Kaufmann, Waltham, MA (2015)
6. Hultgren, H.: Modeling the Agile Data Warehouse with Data Vault. New Hamilton, Stockholm (2012)
7. Hahne, M.: Modellierung von Business-Intelligence-Systemen. dpunkt, Heidelberg (2014)

Evaluating a Forward-Looking Maturity Model for Enterprise Performance Management

Jörg H. Mayer, Christian Hebeler, Markus Esswein, Moritz Göbel, and Reiner Quick

Abstract Enterprise performance management (EPM) helps in executing a company's strategy. As current benchmarking approaches against the so-called "first quartile" are backward-looking and, thus, fail to capture the disruptive nature of digital technologies, a new zero-quartile benchmarking compares companies against the expected (collectively deemed best possible) state. However, its relevance was not yet demonstrated. Therefore, the objective of this article is to evaluate this new zero-quartile benchmarking approach with the help of a case study at a global supplier of natural ingredients and nutrition solutions which currently improves their EPM by leveraging digital technologies. We subsume our findings towards digital EPM as follows: (1) From playground to pitch: It is not easy to implement a digital enterprise platform. However, it should be a company's future single source of truth. (2) Powering up a company's crystal ball: Leveraging predictive analytics, companies should rethink their budgeting and forecasting. (3) Setting the scene: Companies should continue harmonizing their ERP while automating their standard reporting and analysis using finance bots.

Keywords Digital transformation · Enterprise performance management (EPM) · Maturity model (MM) · Benchmarking · Digital technologies: automation, analytics, digital enterprise platform · Survey · Rasch Algorithm · Design science research (DSR) in information systems (IS)

J. H. Mayer (✉) · M. Esswein · M. Göbel · R. Quick
Darmstadt University of Technology, Darmstadt, Germany
e-mail: jmayer@bwl.tu-darmstadt.de; esswein@bwl.tu-darmstadt.de;
moritz.goebel@tu-darmstadt.de; quick@bwl.tu-darmstadt.de

C. Hebeler
Döhler GmbH, Darmstadt, Germany
e-mail: christian.hebeler@doehler.com

© The Author(s), under exclusive license to Springer Nature Switzerland AG 2021
S. Aier et al. (eds.), *Engineering the Transformation of the Enterprise*,
https://doi.org/10.1007/978-3-030-84655-8_18

287

1   Introduction

The onset of the COVID-19 global pandemic is highlighting the importance of digital technologies. The basic understanding is that organizations with a higher level of digital maturity are more flexible and can better cope with challenging situations like the present one [1].

Improving their digital maturity, companies can resort to *benchmarking* as a continuous process of identifying highest standards of excellence for products, services, and processes [2]. However, current benchmarking approaches against the so-called "first quartile"—defined as the top 25% target state of top performing companies [3]—are backward-looking and fail to capture the disruptive nature of digital technologies such as automation, analytics, and digital enterprise platforms [4].

Addressing this shortcoming, a new *zero-quartile benchmarking* compares companies against the *expected* (collectively deemed best possible) state of benchmarking objects [5]. Accordingly, the zero quartile marks a target state which is a step ahead of (existing) best practices of top performing companies today.

Comparing digitalization efforts between companies' departments shows that the *finance function*—once a frontrunner for digitalization—is falling behind. This could be attributed to a lack of guidance from academia. Taking enterprise performance management (EPM) as a case example, Esswein et al. [5] constructed a zero-quartile-benchmarking towards a future EPM leveraging digital technologies. Their *maturity model (MM)*—defined as a conceptual model incorporating a sequence of discrete maturity levels and representing an anticipated, desired, or typical path of evolution [6]—serves not only as a self-assessment for companies to evaluate their as-is situation, but also to derive design guidelines for reaching the next to-be level.

Emphasizing a staged research process with iterative "build" and "evaluate" activities Peffers et al. [7], *evaluating* artefacts is a key element of design science research, (DSR) in information systems (IS, [8]). Some researchers such as Straub and Ang [9] appraise an object of interest along the two basic dimensions, that is rigor and relevance. Other authors apply a series of more detailed criteria such as completeness, efficiency, consistency, and robustness [10].

As the EPM MM by Mayer et al. [11] is based on a comprehensive literature review and a survey among 203 participants, it should be rigorous. However, its *relevance* was not yet demonstrated. Therefore, the objective of this article is to *evaluate this (new) zero-quartile benchmarking MM towards digital EPM at a global supplier of natural ingredients and nutrition solutions*. We raise two research questions:

- Does the proposed model fulfill what it is meant to do (validity)?
- Is it useful beyond the environment in which it was initially developed (utility)?

To create things that serve human purposes [12], ultimately to build a better world [13], we follow DSR in IS [14, 15], for which the publication schema by Gregor and Hevner [16] gave us directions. We motivate this article on the basis of current challenges associated with a new benchmarking towards digital EPM (*introduction*). Based on the state of the art, we highlight research gaps (*literature review*). Addressing these gaps, we substantiate an evaluation framework and apply it in a case study (*method*). Then, we present our *results*. Comparing them with prior work and examining how they relate back to the article's objective and research questions, we end with a summary, the limitations of our work, and avenues for future research (*discussion and conclusion*).

2 Literature Review

Following Webster and Watson [17], we commenced our literature review with a (1) *journal search* focusing on leading IS research and accounting journals, complemented by proceedings from major IS conferences.[1,2,3] In line with Mayer et al. [11], we also considered papers from MIS Quarterly Executive and the Harvard Business Review. For our (2) *database search*, we used ScienceDirect, EBSCO host, Springer Link, AIS eLibrary, and Google Scholar. Assessing the publications through their titles, abstracts, and keywords, we performed an iterative (3) *keyword search*.

As a result, we complemented the 69 publications examined by Mayer et al. [11] with another six publications. They focus on evaluation activities contributing to our staged research process (Sect. 1). Finally, we conducted a (4) *backward and forward search*. Including references from all relevant publications, we identified another three publications such as Alturki et al. [21] and ended up with *78 publications* in total (Fig. 1).

The **gap analysis** was structured in three clusters (Fig. 1): (1) The *benchmarking object* encompasses the two key EPM process activities "planning, budgeting, and forecasting" as well as "reporting and analysis". "Others" subsume articles that do not focus on a specific EPM process activity. (2) The cluster *"peer-group partner"* refers to what the benchmarking object is compared to [22]. (3) Last, but not least, we differentiated between research methods, addressing the way in which researchers collect and understand data [23]. Quantitative research includes

---

[1] Based on the AIS senior scholars' basket of leading IS Journals [18]: European Journal of Information Systems; Information Systems Research; Information Systems Journal; Journal of the Association for Information Systems; Journal of Information Technology; Journal of Management Information Systems; Journal of Strategic Information Systems; MIS Quarterly.

[2] In order to focus on leading accounting journals, we used the Scimago Journal Ranking [19]. We selected the subject area "Business, Management, and Accounting" and, herein, the subject category "accounting." The resulting top 50 journal ranking includes outlets such as Accounting Review, Journal of Accounting Research, and the Journal of Finance.

[3] We followed the AIS' list of leading IS conferences [20]: Americas Conference on Information Systems; European Conference on Information Systems; International Conference on Information Systems; Pacific and Asia Conference on Information Systems.

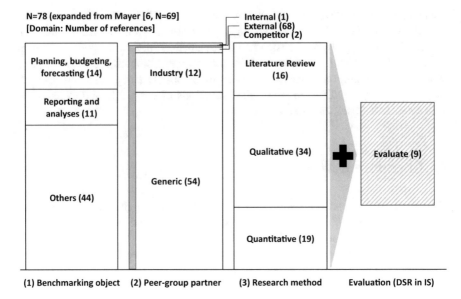

Fig. 1 Overview of relevant publications including the results from Mayer et al. [11]

empirical studies such as surveys, (laboratory) experiments, and archival studies. In turn, qualitative research covers case studies, focus group observations, interviews, document and text analyses, as well as researchers' impressions and reactions. Literature reviews are a third category, because they summarize both quantitative and qualitative research outcomes. Finally, we complemented the work of Mayer et al. [11] with nine articles focusing on (4) *evaluation activities*.

(1) Benchmarking object: We differ three digital technologies, namely automation, analytics, and digital enterprise platform. The latter serves as a single source of truth of a company's data. Efficiencies can be realized by automation, when transferring data between IS [24]. Companies will become more effective when applying (predictive) analytics on big data as a "modern" crystal ball [25]. However, summarizing our observations, neither of these articles offered design guidelines on how to improve EPM processes by leveraging digital technologies. Furthermore, as most of the articles incorporate only past data, we follow Mayer et al. [11] in suggesting a more *forward-looking EPM MM based on the zero-quartile definition* (Sect. 1).

(2) Peer-group partner: Internal benchmarking compares different sites or employees' skills within a company [26]. 68 articles referred to external benchmarking. 54 out of these 78 articles incorporate *generic benchmarking* across industries [2]. Ensuring sufficient data for their novel benchmarking, Mayer et al. [11] and Esswein et al. [5] applied a *generic benchmarking across industries.*

(3) Research method: A majority of 34 researchers such as Hess et al. [27], Pinto [28], and Sjödin et al. [29] opted for case studies. Kane et al. [30] and Plaschke et al. [31] chose a survey as their research method. Articles from practitioners most often describe the impact of digital technologies on the Finance function [32, 33]. However, they often lack a rigorous foundation [34], lack validation [35], or fail to provide guidelines on how to reach a next level of maturity. In this context, the *Rasch algorithm* is a well-established method. Leem et al. [36] surveyed managers from 312 companies and came up with a MM based on the analytical hierarchy process. Mayer et al. [11] applied the Rasch algorithm for design guidelines in order to align reporting, planning, and consolidation from functional, organizational, and IT perspectives.

Determining how well they perform against a predefined set of metrics there are different approaches how to **evaluate** artefacts [37]: (a) A basic differentiation is rigor and relevance [10]. While *rigor* covers the scientific adequacy of a research project, *relevance* addresses its applicability in practice. (b) Gregor and Hevner [16] propose more evaluation criteria, in particular validity, utility, quality, and efficacy. Whereas the latter refers to the value the artifact brings to the field, a *valid* artifact works and does what it is meant to do. *Utility* criteria assess whether the achievement of goals has value outside the development environment. (c) Prat et al. [11] recommend a larger series of criteria such as goal (efficacy, validity, and generality), environment, structure, activity, and evolution. They clarify efficacy to be the degree to which the artifact produces its desired effect, subordinating quality under utility as the quality of the artifact in practical use. (d) Other authors developed *evaluation frameworks*. Examples are Sonnenberg and vom Brocke [38] who proposed to differentiate between when, what, and how to evaluate. The "when" question covers the two alternatives of an *ex-ante evaluation*, which is the evaluation of an uninstantiated artifact, while an *ex-post evaluation* is after instantiation. This distinction is similar to the differentiation of a formative evaluation, which takes place during artifact creation and forms the artifact, while a summative evaluation summarizes the artefact and evaluates for given criteria after the fact. The "what" question distinguishes product artefacts like *tools, diagrams, and software* from process artifacts like *methods and procedures*. Finally, the "how" question refers to methods used for evaluation. Venable et al. [39] proposed a *framework for evaluation in Design Science (FEDS)* that takes the two differentiators of "when" and "what" along with other factors and requirements to provide evaluation methods such as case studies or surveys for a naturalistic ex-post evaluation or a mathematical or logical proof for an artificial ex-post evaluation.

Combining the findings from these four approaches, we propose a naturalistic, summative ex-post evaluation by triangulating three sources of data [21, 40]: Receiving basic information about the reference company, we propose to start with *desk research*. To evaluate the reference company regarding their digitalization status (as the outcome of the proposed MM) and especially if the MM does what it is meant to do (RQ 1), we propose *expert interviews*. Finally, we propose to discuss the results from the manager perspective and do that with another interview to check if the proposed MM is useful beyond the environment in which it was initially developed (RQ 2).

3   Method

Applying our findings from Sect. 2, we evaluated the MM from Mayer et al. [11] at a global *supplier of natural ingredients and nutrition solutions* (1.7 bn EUR sales; 7000 employees, [41]). Guided by our research questions, we focused on *validity* and *utility*.

We started with *desk research* in the accounting department of the reference company and focused on the EPM processes and their status of applying digital technologies. After six weeks we had gained a comprehensive overview of EPM process activities and got to know the most important processes and IS experts to, finally, select the following five experts: the team lead of Sales Controlling; the Head of Financial Services; the team lead of IT Business Solutions; the Head of Supply Chain Controlling; the Head of Group Controlling.

Based on the questionnaire from the survey by Mayer et al. [11], we continued with five *expert interviews* of about 60 min per interview. In doing so, we explained the six EPM processes with their activities, the three digital technologies automation, analytics, and digital enterprise platform (Sect. 2), and filled out the questionnaire according to their answers. Then, we averaged the individual results and, with reference to RQ 1, we positioned the reference company within the maturity model for each of the EPM processes (in detail, Sect. 4).

In order to evaluate not only the company, but even the MM itself (RQ 2), we discussed the results with the Head of Group Controlling, Supply Chain Controlling, and Financial Services. These interviews lasted about 60 min. We laid out the maturity of the reference company and then discussed design guidelines from Mayer et al. [11] towards the next steps within the MM. We concluded the interviews with their feedback regarding the ease of use of the MM as well as asking about other areas of implementation within the reference company and across their industry.

4   Results

4.1   Evaluating the Company (Validity)

Our reference company can be considered as a *"digital beginner"* (category I) in terms of **strategic business planning**. While they have a digital enterprise platform set up, they do not use it for strategic business planning. Since regional strategy plans are created manually in MS Excel by the regional heads and then evaluated by the group management, this can be classified as a manual process. Analytics is used to judge market potential, but data is often manually derived from external data sources. Automation is not realized at any scale. However, the reference company is currently updating their data sources to implement a peer-customer basis in their digital enterprise platform, that is a cloud for customer data (C4C) by SAP. However, these developments have not been fully integrated, yet. Therefore, there is room for a single source of truth target and enabling analytics on big data. This is in line with Mayer et al. [11] as they propose to implement a digital enterprise platform allowing managers to back their experience with data from market analytics and social media listening. The Head of Group Controlling agreed with this design guideline, seeing a digital enterprise platform implementation as an important step. He added that such a platform should be used to quantify qualitative goals like "exploit full market potential," great people, great workplace" (employee wellbeing), and help to form "guard rails" for processes like increase in market potential or employee retention rate. These guard rails should incorporate performance indicator thresholds that can then be used to control these processes.

With respect to **budgeting**, our reference company is a *digital student* (II). The budget is obtained in a bottom-up approach derived from both last year's performance and the forecasts until the end of the current year. It is uploaded as MS Excel data to the digital enterprise platform and checked against group management's top-down strategy. Multiple systems are used simultaneously. Analytics are sometimes used—for example to forecast the market potential and adjust the regions' budgets accordingly. No automation is in place. In order to advance their maturity level, the reference company should benefit from the use of their digital enterprise platform and incorporate predictive analytics for a more accurate budgeting. The Head of Group Controlling laid out a shift in the budgeting process towards a rolling forecast model. Both the budgeting and forecasting process have to be built on the same basis. The budget will serve as the performance goal whereas the forecast indicates deviations. Predictive analytics is therefore an essential component of the 2025 budgeting process. He argued that the budget will be a mix of the predicted outcome and the guide rails provided by strategic business planning.

Forecasting is on the same level as budgeting, judging from a technical standpoint, as the consolidation units' forecasts are still based on managers' experience and then aggregated by the company headquarter. There are both a digital enterprise platform and analytics for all sales order data, but no automation in the forecast creation, yet. However, the reference company is already working on an automated forecast solution. Based on that, the reference company is ranked on maturity level II *"digital student"* progressing towards level III. As they will be rolling out a forecasting solution for automatic forecast creation, tapping into their rich analytics, they are on track to level IV and V. The design guidelines of Mayer et al. [11] propose to ground forecasts on predictive analytics and advise managers to shift their attention to irregularities and sudden changes to adjust developments which cannot be foreseen by the model such as the current corona virus, which is aligned with the reference company's efforts.

Regarding the fourth process activity, **standard reporting and analysis**, we evaluate the reference company as a *digital driver* (level IV). Reports are most often generated on a daily basis and provided via dashboards with drill-down capabilities incorporating several filters. Mayer et al. [11] proposed that more standard reports should be automated and that reports should be available for "self-service" reporting. It was evident that the reference company already accomplished this design guideline and can focus their work on implementing this technology in other sectors and activities. The Head of Group Controlling saw further development potential in standard reporting in the combination of data with causation. He mentioned tying the automated reports together with notifications to, finally, inform stakeholders of what needs attention and with necessary transactions to solve the issue.

Ad-hoc analyses can be found in a similar state, although often less automated than standard reporting and analysis. Ad-hoc analyses are often accomplished by managers utilizing dashboards in a "self-service fashion." However, since they do not utilize predictive analytics yet and ad-hoc analyses are sometimes stitched together using multiple dashboards, the reference company is situated as a digital practitioner (maturity level III). Here, the design guideline by Mayer et al. [11] proposes that managers should start working with data themselves, "...analyzing in a self-service fashion." This is already accomplished by the reference company, but there is potential in connecting multiple dashboards to intelligently create views on specific situations much like a person would create a top management presentation combining different data sources.

Since ad-hoc analyses at the reference company are mainly defined by ordering an analysis from employees when dashboards are not sufficient, the question arises, where to draw the line between deep-diving into an automated reporting dashboard or an ad-hoc analysis. Especially when daily reports start automatically reporting underlying issues and offering transactions for solving the problem in the future, like indicated by the Head of Group Controlling, this differentiation will be increasingly difficult to make.

Finally, **business decision support,** was evaluated to be on the level of a digital practitioner (maturity level III) as the reference company already has a modern infrastructure including analytics which is just not weaved into other processes yet. The digital enterprise platform is used for accessing automatically imported customer market data as well as for dashboards. Looking forward, similar actions as for ad-hoc analyses can be recommend. With increasing levels of digitalization, the reference company wants to merge ad-hoc analyses, business decision support and the daily reporting dashboards into one system supplying employees with relevant information. The sixth design guideline by Mayer et al. [11] establishing a digital enterprise platform for business decision support to enable views in different granularities from a top-down to the line-item level was already accomplished by the reference company.

According to the Head of Group Controlling, ad-hoc analyses and business decision support are only necessary when the standard reporting is not sufficiently automated. He said that the design guidelines recommending the development of the digital enterprise platform supported by analytics to enable managers to work with data themselves as the next development step provide good advice, but at the same time he perceives these processes as a sign of insufficient control through technology itself. Today, these processes still exist and, in the future, they will be a part of the combined process. But as technology will improve, he predicted daily reporting, ad-hoc analyses, and business decision support to merge into one when the decision and correction process become part of an automated reporting.

4.2 Evaluating the Model (Utility)

After applying the maturity model at our reference company, we evaluated the *utility* of both the MM and design guidelines from Mayer et al. [11], (RQ 2). For the latter, we focused on the proposed critical paths from one to the next higher level.

During the questionnaire-based interviews, we observed that managers of different departments sometimes evaluated the company's maturity quite differently. The most striking difference was the use of a digital enterprise platform for forecasting. This can be attributed to different degrees of technology implementation and its use in different areas like Supply Chain Controlling and Financial Services. The Head of Group Controlling added that, firstly, age and technology understanding might play a role. The young team lead of Sales Controlling was regularly disappointed by the lower level of automation. She and her supply chain colleague were often manually enhancing reports and forecasts, while the more positive results came from IT and accounting, which already have many automated dashboards live.

Regarding utility, we focused on the structure of the model regarding (I) the choice of technologies and (II) the six processes. The Head of Group Controlling laid out that a model should not only measure the level of technology implementation, but also the level of control. For that, a careful selection of technology is important. He found our selection quite fitting, covering the important areas of data aggregation (digital enterprise platform), interpretation (analytics), and process automation (automation). As for the six EPM process activities, he agreed with the differentiation, but foresaw a shift towards merging processes in future. More specifically, automated reports are supposed to merge with ad-hoc analyses and business decision support. In addition to their usual function, they will enable solutions such as business decision support. This can be accomplished by not only reporting on anomalies, but also offering the necessary transactions to accomplish the strategy.

The Head of Group Controlling evaluated the MM as a useful tool for benchmarking. He proposed the model to be used as a metric when a new company is to be bought and its digital fitness needs to be evaluated. When asked, if he preferred the traditional "first quartile" benchmarking, he answered that he is in favor of the forward-looking zero-quartile approach. He was convinced that the model could also be applied to other processes like order-to-cash and purchase-to-pay. Nevertheless, frequent updates would be necessary as the pace of digitization is high and new technologies will emerge.

To start future discussions beyond our reference company, we subsume our findings in three categories. **(1) From playground to pitch:** The feedback regarding the MM was good throughout all evaluation steps. The critical path and the design guidelines from Mayer et al. [11] provide a useful EPM development. For example, when it came to the first process activity "strategic business planning," the managers from the reference company laid out that they currently do not have a digital enterprise platform integrating data within one single source of truth. Furthermore, they agreed with the associated first design guideline that a digital enterprise platform should be the new *single source of truth* allowing managers to back their experience with internal and external data. However, two interviewees expected more guidance on how to proceed in detail, for instance, how to select the "right" data and the appropriate mix of internal and external data. Another issue that was mentioned by the Head of Financial Services is that there was no differentiation between rule-based and cognitive-based automation.

(2) Powering up a company's crystal ball: In future, *machine-based forecasts* will complement the management judgement within the company and, thus, will help to better navigate in a volatile world. This is in line with the second and third design guideline driving predictive analytics by Mayer et al. [11]. Looking forward, so the Head of Financial Services, the so-called W-budgeting with its first estimations from the business units will be replaced by a "V-budgeting." He argued that this new kind of budgeting and forecasting should start with machine-based estimates for the next year, derived from their group strategy and leveraging latest internal and external data. Then, these guidelines should be discussed with the business units, aligned, and, finally, fixed. This will be relevant for all functions and business units alike, our interviewees agreed. However, only digital masters have such a machine-based budgeting already in place.

(3) Setting the scene: With a focus on the reporting and analysis processes, the Head of Financial Services and the Head of Group Controlling stated that experiencing digital technologies in a "trial and error" mode was accepted in the years of global economic prosperity. Today, even digital technologies had to pay off. Nonetheless, this should not be understood too literally. As an example, they highlighted that *software robots* relieve Finance personnel from repetitive tasks when transferring data between different IS. Furthermore, they improve data accuracy and speed, but rarely result in full-time equivalent (FTE) savings. Accordingly, they proposed to consider *effectiveness* equal to efficiency when measuring digital technology success. Only when assessing digital technologies and their benefits and drawbacks comprehensively will a company be able to advance to higher levels of digital maturity.

5   Discussion and Conclusion

Evaluating a MM which should lead *towards future EPM* leveraging digital technologies, we answered two RQs about the model's validity and utility. The MM is based on a new zero-quartile benchmarking and focuses on three digital focus technologies, that is automation, analytics, and the digital enterprise platform.

We answered RQ 1 about validity with the help of five expert interviews and gave answers to RQ 2 about utility by three complementing manager interviews. The *validity* of the model by Mayer et al. [11] should be higher than Imgrund et al. [42] as we applied a triangulation approach to evaluate it (Sect. 3). Furthermore, multiple participants within the reference company increased the validity of our results. In other words: Personal biases as discussed in Sect. 4.2 were mitigated by the number of interviews. In comparison to Berger et al. [43] and Eremina et al. [44], the model by Mayer et al. [11] provides better *utility* incorporating three waves towards digitalization beyond the EPM processes.

For practice, our findings should help companies to better understand the forward-looking MM by Mayer et al. [11], finally, evolve better towards digital EPM. The input by our interviewees provides insights into how managers engage with the omnipresent topic of digitalization and where they see challenges and opportunities.

For *research purposes*, our method mix constitutes a rigorous starting point for future evaluation activities. Our approach is more comprehensive than Alturki et al. [21] and Venable et al. [45] as we focus on the application of evaluation in greater detail applying a naturalistic approach not only on the evaluated artifact (MM) but at the same time on the topic of evaluation itself.

Our article reveals *avenues for future research*: As we have seen different perspectives of maturity within the same reference company, the validity can be increased by a *larger sample sizes of interviews*. Thus, the impact of our evaluation results should be tracked in *other companies*. They should evaluate if our findings are relevant and could be converted into concrete actions.

Besides digital technologies, even EPM processes will change over time. Thus, we recommend to *continuously update* our results. This is also true for the *questionnaire of the survey* from Mayer et al. [11] as more and more building blocks like processes, digital technologies, the method per se, and the outcomes of the MM may change. Furthermore, there could be more unpredictable developments in the future such as the current COVID-19 pandemic which may shift the key topics of corporate management towards treasury. In other words, the zero-quartile benchmarking from Mayer et al. [11] and even our findings should be tested in *other domains of a company*.

Last, but not least, companies should suggest a *continuous benchmarking* of their "as is" status in order to track digital progress over time. Our findings on hand may help in doing so.

References

1. Fletcher, G., Griffiths, M.: Digital transformation during a lockdown. Int. J. Inf. Manag. **55**, 102–185 (2020)
2. Bhutta, K.S., Huq, F.: Benchmarking – best practices: an integrated approach. Benchmarking. **6** (3), 254–268 (1999)
3. Joo, S.-J., Nixon, D., Stoeberl, P.A.: Benchmarking with data envelopment analysis: a return on asset perspective. Benchmarking. **18**(4), 529–542 (2011)
4. Chanias, S., Hess, T.: How digital are we? Maturity models for the assessment of a company's status in the digital transformation. Management Report/Institut für Wirtschaftsinformatik und Neue Medien. **2016**(2), 1–14 (2016)
5. Esswein, M., Mayer, J.H., Stoffel, S., Quick, R.: Predictive analytics – a modern crystal ball? Answers from a case study. In: Johannesson, P., Ågerfalk, P., Helms, R. (eds.) Information Systems for a Sharing Society. Proceedings of the Twenty-Sixth European Conference on Information Systems (ECIS, 2019), Stockholm and Uppsala, Sweden, pp. 1–18

6. de Bruin, T., Freeze, R., Kulkarni, U., Rosemann, M.: Understanding the main phases of developing a maturity assessment model. In: Proceedings of the 16th Australasian Conference on Information Systems (ACIS, 2005), Sydney, Australia, pp. 8–19
7. Peffers, K., Tuunanen, T., Gengler, C.E., Rossi, M., Hui, W., Virtanen, V., Bragge, J.: The design science research process: a model for producing and presenting information systems research. In: First International Conference on Design Science Research in Information Systems and Technology (DESRIST, 2006), Claremont, CA, pp. 83–106
8. Hevner, A., Chatterjee, S. (eds.): Design Research in Information Systems: Theory and Practice. Integrated Series in Information Systems, vol. 22. Springer Science+Business Media LLC, Boston, MA (2010)
9. Straub, D., Ang, S.: Editor's Comments: Rigor and relevance in IS research: redefining the debate for future research. MIS Q. **35**(1), iii (2011)
10. Prat, N., Comyn-Wattiau, I., Akoka, J.: Artifact evaluation in information systems design-science research – a holistic view. In: Proceedings of the 19th Pacific Asia Conference on Information Systems (PACIS, 2014), Chengdu, China, pp. 1–16
11. Mayer, J.H., Göbel, M., Esswein, M., Quick, R.: Getting Digital Technologies Right – A Forward-Looking Maturity Model For Enterprise Performance Management. In: Cuel, R., Winter, R. (eds.) Digital Resilience and Sustainability: People, Organizations, and Society. Proceedings of the Eighteenth Conference of the Italian chapter of (ItAIS), pp. 1–14. Trento, Italy (2021)
12. Simon, H.A.: The Science of the Artificial, 3rd edn. MIT Press, Cambridge, MA (1996)
13. Walls, J.G., Widmeyer, G.R., El Sawy, O.A.: Building an information system design theory for vigilant EIS. Inf. Syst. Res. **3**(1), 36–59 (1992)
14. Hevner, A.R., March, S.T., Park, J., Ram, S.: Design science in information systems research. MIS Q. **28**(1), 75–105 (2004)
15. vom Brocke, J., Winter, R., Hevner, A., Maedche, A.: Accumulation and evolution of design knowledge in design science research – a journey through time and space. J. Assoc. Inf. Syst. **21**(3), 520–544 (2019)
16. Gregor, S., Hevner, A.R.: Positioning and presenting design science research for maximum impact. MIS Q. **37**(2), 337–355 (2013)
17. Webster, J., Watson, R.T.: Analyzing the past to prepare for the future: writing a literature review. MIS Q. **26**(2), xiii–xxiii (2002)
18. AIS: Senior Scholar's Basket of Journals. https://aisnet.org/page/SeniorScholarBasket (2020). Accessed 14 July 2020
19. SJR: Scimago Journal & Country Rank. https://www.scimagojr.com/journalrank.php ? area=1400&category=1402 (2020). Accessed 6 June 2021
20. AIS: Conferences. https://aisnet.org/page/Conferences (2020). Accessed 14 July 2020
21. Alturki, A., Gable, G.G., Bandara, W.: The design science research roadmap: in progress evaluation. In: Proceedings of the 18th Pacific Asia Conference on Information Systems (PACIS, 2013), Jeju Island, Korea, pp. 1–15
22. Schmaus, P.A.: Peer group benchmarking for the relative performance evaluation of companies. University of St Gallen, Business Dissertations, p. 128. Epubli GmbH, Berlin (2018)
23. Myers, M.D.: Qualitative research in information systems. MIS Q. **21**(2) (1997)
24. Ahmad, M., Botzkowski, T., Klötzer, C., Papert, M.: Behind the blackbox of digital business models. In: Proceedings of the 53rd Hawaii International Conference on System Sciences (HICSS, 2020), Wailea, HI, pp. 4547–4557
25. LaValle, S., Lesser, E., Shockley, R., Hopkins, M.S., Kruschwitz, N.: Big data, analytics and the path from insights to value. Reprint Number 52205. MIT Sloan Manag. Rev. **52**(2), 21–31 (2011)
26. Spendolini, M.J.: The benchmarking process. Compensation Benefits Rev. **24**(5), 21–29 (1992)
27. Hess, T., Benlian, A., Matt, C., Wiesböck, F.: Options for formulating a digital transformation strategy. MISQE. **15**(2), 123–139 (2016)

28. Pinto, J.L.: Assessing the relationship between bpm maturity and the success of organizations, NOVA Information Management School (NIMS, 2020)
29. Sjödin, D.R., Parida, V., Leksell, M., Petrovic, A.: Smart factory implementation and process innovation. Res. Technol. Manag. **61**(5), 22–31 (2018)
30. Kane, G.C., Palmer, D., Phillips, A.N., Kiron, D., Buckley, N.: Achieving digital maturity: adapting your company to a changing world. Reprint Number 59180. MIT Sloan Manag. Rev. **59**(1), 21–31 (2017)
31. Plaschke, F., Seth, I., Rob, W.: Bots, algorithms, and the future of the finance function. McKinsey Financ. **65**, 18–23 (2018)
32. Accenture: From bottom line to front line. https://www.accenture.com/_acnmedia/pdf-85/accenture-cfo-research-global.pdf (2020). Accessed 9 June 2021
33. Lucas, S.: The Benefits of the SAP Digital Enterprise Platform. https://blogs.saphana.com/2016/02/03/the-benefits-of-the-sap-digital-enterprise-platform/ (2016). Accessed 9 June 2021
34. Lasrado, L.A., Vatrapu, R., Andersen, K.N.: Maturity models development in IS research: a literature review. In: Selected Papers of the Information Systems Research Seminar in Scandinavia (IRIS, 2015), Oulu, Finland, pp. 1–12
35. Williams, C., Boardman, L., Lang, K., Schallmo, D.: Digital maturity models for small and medium-sized enterprises: a systematic literature review. In: Proceedings of the 30th International Society for Professional Innovation Management (ISPIM, 2019), Florence, Italy, pp. 1–15
36. Leem, C.S., Wan Kim, B., Jung Yu, E., Ho Paek, M.: Information technology maturity stages and enterprise benchmarking: an empirical study. Indus. Manag. Data Syst. **108**(9), 1200–1218 (2008)
37. March, S.T., Smith, G.F.: Design and natural science research on information technology. Decis. Support Syst. **15**(4), 251–266 (1995)
38. Sonnenberg, C., vom Brocke, J.: Evaluation Patterns for Design Science Research Artefacts. European Design Science Symposium, vol. 286, pp. 71–83. Springer (2012)
39. Venable, J., Pries-Heje, B.J., Baskerville, J., Baskerville, R.: A comprehensive framework for evaluation in design science research. In: Proceedings of the 7th International Conference on Design Science Research in Information Systems and Technology (DESRIST, 2012), Las Vegas, NV, pp. 423–438
40. Teddlie, C., Tashakkori, A.: Foundations of Mixed Methods Research: Integrating Quantitative and Qualitative Approaches in the Social and Behavioral Sciences. SAGE, Los Angeles (2010)
41. North Data: Döhler Group SE, Darmstadt. https://www.northdata.de/D%C3%B6hler+Group+SE,+Darmstadt/HRB+95005 (2020). Accessed 9 June 2021
42. Imgrund, F., Fischer, M., Janiesch, C., Winkelmann, A.: Approaching digitalization with business process management. In: Proceedings of the 26th Multikonferenz Wirtschaftsinformatik (MKWI, 2018), Ilmenau, Germany, pp. 1–12
43. Berger, S., Bitzer, M., Häckel, B., Voit, C.: Approaching digital transformation – Development of a multi-dimensional Maturity Model. In: Proceedings of the 28th European Conference on Information Systems (ECIS, 2020), Marrakech, Morocco, pp. 1–18
44. Eremina, Y., Lace, N., Bistrova, J.: Digital maturity and corporate performance: the case of the Baltic States. JOItmC. **5**(3), 54 (2019)
45. Venable, J., Pries-Heje, J., Baskerville, R.: FEDS: a framework for evaluation in design science research. Eur. J. Inf. Syst. **25**(1), 77–89 (2016)

The Evolution of IT Management Standards in Digital Transformation: Current Status and Research Implications

Gunnar Auth

Abstract For more than three decades professional standards have been popular as guidance and orientation to manage IT organizations. Although major standards like ITIL and COBIT have been updated with several versions to reflect changing requirements, their basic goals, concepts, and structures remained stable over time. In recent years this situation changed, when a number of new standards appeared to support new requirements for mastering digital transformation. This study explores the evolution of ITM standards during the last 20 years through analyzing a set of 60 formal, de facto, and emerging standards. Besides the rapid increase in number and update frequency starting in 2015, a shift of goals towards agility, lean management, and innovation was found. Finally, new problems and research questions raised by this evolution are presented.

Keywords IT management · Professional standard · Framework · Digital transformation

1 Introduction

In the ongoing societal phenomenon known as digital transformation or digitalization, many organizations are constantly in search of guidance and support for successfully managing their individual transformations [1–3]. Driven by digital technologies (DT) that emerge and spread with increasing speed these organizations face a growing innovation pressure to stay competitive in a networked environment characterized by volatility, uncertainty, complexity and ambiguity (VUCA) [4]. Using DT to create innovative digital solutions requires an organization to incorporate the respective capabilities and practices [5]. As DT builds on more conventional information technology (IT) [6], the IT function of an organization

G. Auth (✉)
University of Applied Sciences, Meißen, Germany
e-mail: gunnar.auth@hsf.sachsen.de

© The Author(s), under exclusive license to Springer Nature Switzerland AG 2021
S. Aier et al. (eds.), *Engineering the Transformation of the Enterprise*,
https://doi.org/10.1007/978-3-030-84655-8_19

consequently is involved in creating and implementing digital innovations. Hence, the discussion of the optimal role, alignment, governance, management, and organization of IT (including DT) and the respective department has received many new impulses and contributions during recent years (e.g., [6–8]).

Against this background, professional management standards appear as promising means expected to provide reliable orientation and systematic guidance for a relevant field of management. The International Organization for Standardization (ISO) defines the term standard as a "document, established by consensus and approved by a recognized body, that provides, for common and repeated use, rules, guidelines or characteristics for activities or for their results, aimed at achieving the optimum degree of order in a given context" [9]. Well-known examples of ISO standards for IT management (ITM) include ISO 20000 (IT service management), ISO 27000 (information security management), and ISO 38500 (IT governance). In contrast to the *formal standards* mandated by state-approved bodies, *de facto standards* arise from "unfettered market processes" [10]. These processes might be initiated by an originator with professional and/or commercial interest ("sponsored") [10]. One of the most popular de facto standards for ITM, ITIL [11], was originally created by the UK Government's Central Computer and Telecommunications Agency as a set of recommended practices and since 2013 is owned by the public-private joint venture AXELOS. While the consensus on de facto standards occurs from spreading popularity and practical use, a third category of *standard candidates* is still striving for the necessary spread to become an accepted standard. Nevertheless, the originator might promote its new candidate with the term "standard" right from the beginning. A recent example is provided by The Open Group (TOG) who published the first version of their ITM framework IT4IT as "standard" by declaration in 2015 [12, 13].

IT4IT is also an example for a new generation of ITM standards which explicitly addresses the changing role of the IT function in the course of the digital transformation [14]. Another one is VeriSM, which was introduced in 2017 as "a service management approach for the digital age" [15]. Around the same time SIAM emerged as an acronym for "Service Integration and Management" referring to a collection of practices for managing multiple external IT service providers ("multisourcing") [16]. Until 2019 the emergence of new ITM standard proposals focusing on digital transformation was also partly motivated by an aging ITIL, whose latest version then dated from 2011 and did not mention anything on Agile, DevOps and other new concepts that had become popular in the meantime. In 2019 ITIL4 was published, now including many of the missing new concepts and other changes. In addition, others of the more traditional ITM and related standards faced major updates with references to digital transformation, for instance COBIT (2018), TOGAF (2018), or the project management (PM) standards PRINCE2 (2017) and PMBoK (2017).

As a result of this development, the number of available ITM standards has increased significantly, giving rise to a confusing landscape. In this situation, it has become difficult to recognize which standards are competing and which are complementing one another. Companies in search of an ITM standard for supporting their individual digital transformation may choose from a growing number of alternatives requiring increasing effort for evaluation.

The objectives of this study are threefold:

1. to provide an overview of the developments during the last 20 years and the current state in the field of professional ITM standards,
2. to explore the evolution of ITM standards in digital transformation, and
3. to conclude on new research directions towards an improved understanding of adopting and utilizing ITM standards.

The remainder of this article is structured in five main sections. The first section summarizes conceptual foundations and gives a short overview of the related work. The methodology for collecting and reviewing the standards is described in Sect. 2. The third section presents the current state of professional ITM standards by listing the collected standards in four categories. Section 4 summarizes the findings drawn from a time-related and content-related analysis of the standards collection. Based on these findings the final section delineates future research directions related to the adaptation, implementation, and evaluation of ITM standards in digital transformation.

2 Conceptual Background and Related Work

Since the term standard is generally used in many different contexts, this section clarifies its meaning in the context of ITM. Its connections to other relevant concepts are illustrated to constitute a framework for the main investigation. Furthermore, a brief overview of related work is given.

2.1 Professional Standards and Related Concepts

From a design science perspective [17], a standard is an agreed upon artefact resulting from a design process and describing a to-be state of a domain in reality. Ahlemann et al. [18] regard standards as "socio-economic constructs reflecting a balance of perspective between stakeholders". The artefact intended to become a standard is often called a *framework*, similar to a conceptual or research framework. According to Jabareen [19], a conceptual framework is "a construct of interlinked concepts" [...] "in which each concept plays an integral role". In software engineering, a framework is considered as reusable design, consisting of components and patterns [20]. Design patterns describe "simple and elegant solutions to specific problems" [21]. This points further to *reference models* which are "abstract representations of domain knowledge [...] useful for capturing prescriptive and descriptive design knowledge for sociotechnical problems" [22]. In addition, they are intended to support "companies in the design of company-specific solutions"

[22]. While scientific reference models and professional standards share these general attributes, a difference lies in the character of the respective design process. Professional standards usually are designed by practitioners based on practical experience. Although theoretical knowledge and current research may be incorporated, a formalized description and scientific rigor are less important. Upon completion of a framework as standard candidate, the early adopters will select the framework depending on its value proposition which is considerably enabled by the expert level of its authors. The successful further dissemination of a standard can be explained by the network effect theory, indicating that "each additional stakeholder applying a standard makes it more useful for the rest of the community" [18]. This way, an increase of dissemination implies a positive evaluation through practical use. Hence, a professional standard can be regarded as a special type of informal reference model validated through practical use.

Another term closely related to professional standards is *method*. PM standards are often identified as *methodologies* comprising prescriptive descriptions of process models and techniques for PM (e.g., [23]). The term method can be found synonymously for methodology (e.g., [24, 25]) as well as for specific procedures being part of a PM methodology (e.g., earned value analysis [26]). The more comprehensive understanding of method (as with PM methodology) conforms to the concept of a *management method* based on situational method engineering (SME). Winter [27] describes a management method as a construct to "guide choices within the 'plan-act-control' solution space of an organization in order to achieve certain (management) goals". A relation between method and framework is shown by Winter and Fischer [28] when they describe method(s) for design and evolution as constituting components of an enterprise architecture framework.

Eventually, *best practice* is yet another term that frequently is used in the context of professional management standards. ITIL is a well-known example which explicitly identifies itself as "best practice method" [29]. The definition of best practice provided by AXELOS describes "a way of working that has been proven to be successful by multiple organizations" [30]. In management literature, best practice often is linked to improved performance of an organization [31]. Although being criticized for lacking evidence of cause and effect as well as generalization of results from individual case studies [31, 32], the concept is popular in both academia and practice until today (e.g., [33]). ISO prefers the term *good practice* [34] or (more recently) *recommended practice* [35] but then defines it as "the best way" of doing something [36]. In relation to methods, best practice can be understood as an attribute that motivates the prescriptive character of a method. Figure 1 illustrates the relationships between the terms in a conceptual model.

2.2   Related Work

Research on ITM standards can build on several decades of research in the wider context of general management frameworks and systems. In their literature review,

Fig. 1 Conceptual model of management standards and related concepts

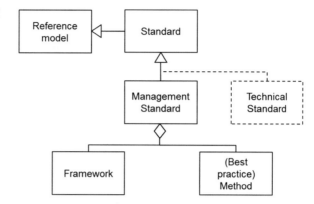

Yadav and Sagar [37] analyze trends in performance measurement and management frameworks from 1991 to 2011 and propose a categorization for 26 frameworks based on broad themes. With a focus on software process improvement, Paulk [38] diagnosed a "quagmire" of process models and standards and discussed strategies for organizations how to integrate multiple frameworks. Later he extended the scope to IT-related quality management and process improvement and proposed a taxonomy to support understanding and comparing diverse frameworks [39]. The idea of overcoming the quagmire through integrating the diverse framework drove the development of Enterprise SPICE (Software Process Improvement and Capability Determination), a domain independent integrated model for enterprise-wide assessment and improvement [40]. Enterprise SPICE was accepted by ISO/IEC[1] as international standard 33071 in 2016, but is rooting deeply in traditional quality management concepts developed prior to the digital era (e.g., [41]).

Existing research on ITM standards often concentrates on certain subareas of ITM like IT governance (e.g., [42]) and IT service management (e.g., [43]) or even single standards like COBIT (e.g., [44]) and ITIL (e.g., [45]). Several authors empirically analyzed the dissemination of standards (e.g., [11, 46]) often connected to questions for perceived and measured benefits after standard implementation (e.g., [45, 47]). When multiple standards are considered, the purpose is usually evaluation (e.g., [48, 49]) or integration (e.g., [50, 51]).

3 Research Method

In order to explore the evolution of ITM standards in digital transformation, a research process based on a systematic review was utilized. While the main review was targeted at exploring the standards, in the beginning relevant standards were identified through a preceding systematic literature review following the guidelines

---

[1] International Electrotechnical Commission.

and recommendations by vom Brocke et al. [52]. In this review, both peer-reviewed academic and professional literature like white papers, blog posts or commercial websites were included. Non-academic literature was included because academic literature on new standard versions or candidates is sparse or not existent. The conceptual model of management standards was used to create standard-related search words through combination with the terms "information technology", "IT", "information systems", and "IS". For retrieving literature, the databases of Google Scholar, Microsoft Academic Search, IEEE Xplorer and SpringerLink as well as Google Web Search and the ISO Standards Catalogue were searched. In addition to the focus on ITM standards, the search scope was limited to international, technology-independent standards (and candidates) for which official or recognized standard documents or framework descriptions are publicly available in English language. Because of the focus on professional standards, frameworks and methods proposed by scientists were excluded. Also excluded were frameworks exclusively developed by a single company like the Microsoft Operations Framework (MOF). Furthermore, standards explicitly targeted at software engineering (SE) were considered out of scope (e.g., ISO/IEC 12207 Software life cycle processes, ISO/IEC 15504 SPICE). Although, there are some close relations between SE and ITM, SE constitutes an autonomous topic. Relevant literature was selected from the original result set by checking title, key words, and abstract for references to ITM standards, before forward and backward search was performed. Eventually, the literature review revealed a total of 60 ITM standards and standard candidates which constituted the data set for the primary review.

In contrast to academic literature reviews, the primary review was performed on a data set consisting of the official or recognized standard documents and framework descriptions. As a first step towards an overview of the recent development and the current state of ITM standards a list was compiled, stating each standard with its main purpose (often reflected through the standard's name), the year of its first publication, and the year of the latest version or update. This list was used for a time-related analysis of ITM standard occurrences and revisions during a period of 20 years. Besides the time dimension, the standard contents were analyzed and categorized. Finally, the standards were compared regarding their central topics, investigating major similarities and differences. As a result of this process, a subject-based classification [53] was created.

4 The Current State of Professional IT Management Standards

Several authors have investigated the changing role of the IT function due to new requirements posed by digital transformation. Horlach et al. [54] describe and analyze the characteristics of a *digital IT* department compared to a traditional one. For the combination of the two operating models, Gartner coined the term *bimodal IT* in late 2013 [54], defining it as "the practice of managing two separate, coherent modes of IT delivery, one focused on stability and the other on agility. Mode 1 is traditional and sequential, emphasizing safety and accuracy. Mode 2 is exploratory and nonlinear, emphasizing agility and speed" [55]. According to Gartner, "both play an essential role in digital transformation" [55]. Haffke et al. add that digital transformation requires the IT function (especially in mode 2) to "become a driver of digital innovation" [56]. For the public sector, Ylinen and Pekkola [57] also highlight agility and additionally emphasize the importance of an adequate enterprise architecture to improve the agility of IT departments. Furthermore, they refer to the importance of a "strong" infrastructure and efficient collaboration between business and IT units, being clearly traditional requirements. Urbach et al. [8] stress that "IT functions are required to cooperate proactively and early on with business departments to be able to develop and implement [...] innovations jointly".

Obviously, the contemporary ITM standards could offer no guidance for responding to these new requirements. ITIL, as an example, had received a minor update in 2011 with only minimal content changes [58]. Furthermore, due to the consensual nature of standards, it takes time to evaluate and eventually integrate new ideas and concepts. Nevertheless, along with the rising pressure on the IT function to master the challenges of digital transformation, a growing demand for new guidance towards successful practices was stimulating the efforts of standardization bodies and professional organizations to enhance existing standards and create additional ones [59].

In the following, the collection of 60 current ITM standards as the result from the review of both academic and professional literature is presented. To reflect the reciprocal influences between digital transformation and ITM standards, each standard was assigned to one of four categories representing evolution stages in relation to digital transformation. Each category is represented with a separate table, listing the according standards. All four tables have a common structure, where each standard is listed with a short name (often an acronym), a long name (usually stating the main topic), year of publication, year of current version, availability of documentation, type of certification, and responsible body or organization. Publication year refers to the year of the first publication that describes a framework for professional use in ITM practice. Nevertheless, there might be earlier publications where foundations of the framework were published for a different purpose or audience. The origin of Scrum, as an example, is often attributed to Schwaber and Sutherland's presentation at the OOPSLA'95 workshop [60] although the term Scrum was already used in an article describing the basic approach for industrial product development by Takeuchi and Nonaka in 1986 [61]. Because of the focus on ITM in this study, the year 1995 is considered as publication year of Scrum. Current version indicates the year of the latest update or revision. Documentation (yes/no) refers to an official or commonly accepted description of the standard.[2] Certification

---

[2] Yes in parenthesis means literature is available but no standardized description.

(individual/organizational) indicates which type of certification is available. Finally, the organization is listed which provides the standard or has a leading reputation for it.[3]

4.1 Traditional IT Management Standards

The traditional ITM standards have become popular before the new phenomenon of digitalization or digital transformation has occurred. They focus on improving IT performance based on criteria like efficiency, effectivity, and service quality. According to several empirical studies, the service-focused and process-oriented ITIL is the most popular representative of this category. Including ITIL, Table 1 lists 20 standards assigned to this category.

4.2 ITM-Related Standards

This category comprises standards for professional management disciplines that exist independently from ITM but are also used in ITM. Starting with project management, this further includes quality, risk, organizational change, knowledge, and innovation management. Table 2 lists the 13 standards identified for this category.

4.3 Digital Technology Management Standards

The third category covers standards and frameworks that are either explicitly referring to digital transformation (e.g., VeriSM) or are dealing with concepts commonly referred to in characterizations of digital transformation (e.g., Agile and Lean). Since digital transformation is induced by digital technologies, this category is named digital technology management standards. The according 16 standards and frameworks are listed in Table 3.

4.4 Emerging Standards

Emerging standards are concepts, frameworks or practices that have become popular in ITM in the context of digital transformation without being standardized yet. A

---

[3]In parenthesis when no standard document is provided by this or any other organization.

Table 1 Traditional IT management standards

Short name	Long name/topic	Publ. year	Cur. year	Doc.	Cert.	Stand. org.
ASL2	Application Services Library	2000	2009	y	i	DID Fdn.[a]
BiSL	Business information Serv. Libr.	2002	2012	y	i	DID Fdn.
CMMI	Capability Maturity Model Integr.	2001	2018	y	i	CMMI Inst.
COBIT	Govern. of information & technol.	1996	2018	y	i	ISACA[b]
eTOM	Telco operations processes	2001	2017	y	i	TM Forum[c]
ITIL	IT service management	1989	2019	y	i	AXELOS
ISO16350	Application management	2015	2015	y	–	ISO/IEC
ISO19770	IT asset management	2012	2020	y	o	ISO/IEC
ISO20000	IT service management	2005	2020	y	o	ISO/IEC
ISO24760	Identity management	2011	2019	y	–	ISO/IEC
ISO250xy	System/software quality	2005	2019	y	–	ISO/IEC
ISO270xy	Information security	2009	2020	y	o	ISO/IEC
ISO29100	Information privacy	2011	2018	y	–	ISO/IEC
ISO29146	Access management	2016	2016	y	–	ISO/IEC
ISO33071	Process assessment for enterprise	2016	2016	y	–	ISO/IEC
ISO33074	Process assessment for (IT)SM	2020	2020	y	–	ISO/IEC
ISO3850x	IT governance	2008	2015	y	i	ISO/IEC
KCS	Knowledge-Centered Service	1996	2016	y	i	CfSI[d]
TOGAF	Enterprise architecture mgmt.	1995	2018	y	i	Open Group
ZeroOut	Zero Outage (IT)	2016	2020	y	i	ZOIS[e]
						Count: 20

[a]Digital Information Design Foundation
[b]Previously an acronym for Information Systems Audit and Control Association. Since 2016 the organization uses ISACA as name only
[c]Telemanagement Forum
[d]Consortium for Service Innovation
[e]Zero Outage Industry Standard Ltd

recent example is the DevOps concept for improving collaboration between IT development and operations teams based on agile principles [62]. Although there is plenty of literature on DevOps [63], no common accepted standard has occurred yet. Items in this category must not necessarily be new in general, but have been applied or adapted to ITM only recently (e.g., Kanban/Lean IT). Although classified as emerging standards in Table 4, their further development to formal standards is still uncertain.

Table 2 ITM-related standards

Short name	Long name/topic	Publ. year	Cur. year	Doc.	Cert.	Stand. org.
ACMP[a]	Change management	2014	2014	y	i	ACMP
BABoK	Business Analysis Body of Knowl.	2005	2015	y	i	IIBA[b]
ICB	IPMA[c] Competence Baseline	1998	2015	y	i	IPMA
ISO10006	Quality management in projects	1997	2017	y	–	ISO
ISO21500	Project management	2005	2020	y	–	ISO
ISO22301	Business continuity	2012	2019	y	o	ISO
ISO30401	Knowledge management	2018	2018	y	–	ISO
ISO31000	Risk management	2009	2018	y	–	ISO
ISO37500	Outsourcing	2014	2014	y	–	ISO
ISO56002	Innovation management	2019	2019	y	–	ISO
ISO900x	Quality management	1987	2018	y	o	ISO
PMBoK	Project Mgmt. Body of Knowl.	1996	2017	y	i	PMI[d]
PRINCE2	Project management	1989	2017	y	i	AXELOS
						Count: 13

[a]Association of Change Management Professionals
[b]International Institute of Business Analysis
[c]International Project Management Association
[d]Project Management Institute

5 Findings

The review of the collected ITM standards and candidates revealed several relevant aspects that characterize their evolution during the last two decades. The first feature appearing from a time-related consideration is a strong increase regarding the number of standards between the years 2000 and 2020. The bar diagram in Fig. 2 shows this trends for two data rows. The first one (light grey) shows the increase in number through publications of new standards per year (publ. year in Tables 1–4). Starting in 2000 with 12 existing standards, the number increases to 59 standards in 2020.[4] The second data row (dark grey) focuses on current versions of the standards (cur. year in Tables 1–4) to depict the current state of standard evolution. The diagram shows that the oldest standard version currently dates from 2009 (ASL2) while all other collected standards were published or updated during the following years.[5]

The bar diagram also shows that from the year 2015 the frequency of standard publications and updates increased significantly compared to the years before. Of the 56 standards published or updated since 2009 only 5 (8.9%) standards were

---

[4]ITR24586 not included because not published yet.
[5]DevOps, Design Thinking, Kanban and ITR24586 are not versioned, hence not included.

Table 3 Digital technology management standards

Short name	Long name/topic	Publ. year	Cur. year	Doc.	Cert.	Stand. org.
AgileSHIFT	Scaling Agile	2018	2018	y	i	AXELOS
Agile SM	Agile (IT) service management	2017	2017	y	i	(DevOps Inst.)
DA	Disciplined Agile (hybrid)	2015	2018	y	i	PMI
DPBoK	Digital Practitioner Body of Know.	2019	2019	y	i	Open Group
FitSM	Lean IT service management	2015	2015	y	i	ITEMO
IT4IT	IT reference architecture	2015	2017	y	i	Open Group
LeSS	Large-Scale Scrum	2013	2015	y	i	The Less Co.
Nexus	Scaling Scrum	2015	2018	y	i	Scrum.org
P2Agile	PRINCE2 Agile (hybrid)	2015	2015	y	i	AXELOS
Resilia	IT ("cyber") resilience	2015	2015	y	i	AXELOS
SAFe	Scaled Agile Framework	2011	2020	y	i	Scal. Ag., Inc.
Scrum	Agile product development	1995	2017	y	i	Scrum.org
Scrum@S	Scrum@Scale	2017	2020	y	i	Scrum Inc.
SIAM	Service Integration & Management	2017	2017	y	i	Scopism Ltd.
TBM	Technology Business Management	2016	2016	y	i	TBM Council
VeriSM	IT service management	2017	2017	y	i	IFDC[a]
						Count: 16

[a]International Foundation for Digital Competences

published or updated before the year 2015 while 51 (91.1%) appeared or were updated in or past 2015.

For a better understanding regarding the role of ITM standards in digital transformation, an additional content analysis was performed investigating the main topics and goals of the collected standards as stated in the standard documentations. The review of main topics allowed for a subject-based classification of the standards. The according subjects were created through identifying ITM subareas and related management areas that are essentially addressed by a standard (e.g., governance, service management, lean ITM). This resulted in 12 subjects with each standard assigned to exactly one subject via its primary topic. Figure 3 shows the full classification with all 60 standards and candidates assigned.

The subject-based classification shows that except for change management and business analysis several standards were found in each of the remaining ten management (sub)areas. While the content analysis showed that some of the members of the same class are competing (e.g., ITIL and VeriSM), others appear to be complementary (e.g., ITIL and SIAM). A detailed investigation of the relationships between the standards is necessary here, but was out of scope for this study.

Table 4 Emerging standards

Short name	Long name/topic	Publ. year	Cur. year	Doc.	Cert.	Stand. org.
BMC	Business Model Canvas	2005	2015	(y)	–	–
CyBoK	Cyber Security Body of Knowl.	2020	2020	y	–	Univ. of Bristol
DevOps	Development & operations	2009	n/a	(y)	i	(DevOps Inst.)
DesThink	Design Thinking	1991[a]	n/a	(y)	(i)	(d.school)
Flow	Flow Framework (IT value stream)	2018	2018	y	–	Tasktop
ISw	Intelligent Swarming	2019	2019	y	–	CfSI
ITR24586	Agile/DevOps	n/a	n/a	n	–	ISO/IEC
Kanban	Lean management	2003	n/a	(y)	–	–
Lean IT	Lean IT	2015	n/a	(y)	i	LITA[b]
Spotify	Scaling agile	2014	2014	(y)	–	Spotify
SRE	Site Reliability Engineering	2016	n/a	(y)	i	(DevOps Inst.)
						Count: 11

[a]First symposium on research in Design Thinking at Delft University, The Netherlands
[b]Lean IT Association

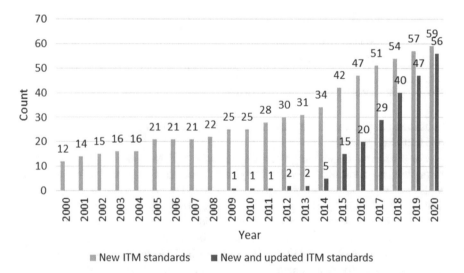

Fig. 2 Appearance of ITM standards and candidates from 2000 to 2020

A further finding from the content analysis is a shift of goals in support of digital transformation. Agile management principles [64] have clearly found their way from software development into ITM standards. This is obvious for the standard class of agile ITM standards (see Fig. 3). But also many traditional standards assigned to other classes have added agility to their established goals or reconciled their concepts

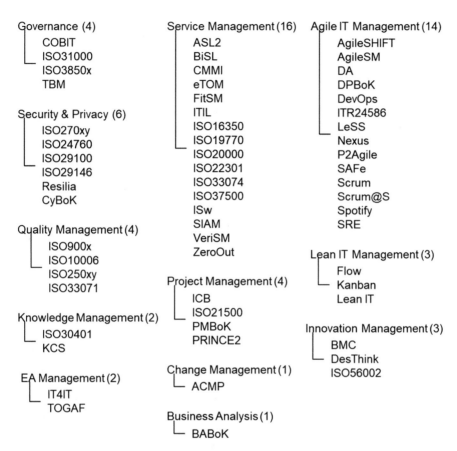

Fig. 3 Subject-based classification of current ITM standards

and practices accordingly with their latest updates (e.g., ITIL, COBIT, PMBoK). Closely connected to agility and also supporting digital transformation are the goals of lean management and innovation, each constituting a separate class in the standard classification. Together with the class of agile ITM standards, these three classes represent the evolution of ITM standards in support of digital transformation most prominently. But also all other new versions of ITM standards since the year 2015 clearly show adaptations induced by digital transformation. An interesting observation is, that these adaptions are not exclusively related to agile, lean, and innovation but also reflect the persistent importance of traditional ITM goals like availability, reliability, correctness, and security (e.g., in Resilia, SRE, ZeroOut).

6   Implications for Research

From the current state of the ITM standards evolution and the findings drawn, several interesting research problems arise. The quagmire of standards and frameworks observed by Paulk [38] in the first decade of the century still seems to exist, despite the development and publication of Enterprise SPICE. In the face of our VUCA world, an integration approach to combine multiple standards into one integrated super framework might not be able to meet the requirements of agility, lean management, and innovation. On the other hand, the standards quagmire might have transformed into a cornucopia, offering a rich choice of proven approaches and practices enabling individual responses to the new requirements of the digital era. This view on the ongoing evolution of ITM standards demands for a new approach of dealing with standards. IT organizations in search of support from ITM standards in the context of digital transformation need to find answers to the following questions:

1. *How should standards be selected to receive the best support for implementing a given strategy for digital transformation?*

Because of the rapidly growing number and the increasing update frequency of ITM standards, evaluation and selection require more and more time and effort. While IT service/solution providers working for external customers often situationally use the standards demanded by their customers, such reactive behavior is not appropriate for maximizing the potentials of standard use. New approaches for scouting, evaluating, and selecting standards could offer better results. A current example for a first response to the need for better orientation on available standards is the online compass for information security and data privacy, a website providing an overview on according standards jointly operated by the German Institute of Standardization (DIN) and the German IT industry association (Bitkom) [65].

2. *How can multiple standards be combined and tailored to increase their benefits and avoid conflicts?*

The growing number of standards also makes it more difficult to recognize which standards are competing and which are complementary or synergistic. Many standards explicitly require a tailoring to an organizations specific requirements (e.g., PRINCE2, VeriSM), some are recommended for concurrent use (e.g., ITIL and PRINCE2), and others are open for combination with further standards (e.g., Scrum). While the underlying flexibility is clearly an advantage for digital transformation, the process of tailoring, combining and maintaining a larger standards portfolio lacks methodological support.

3. *What standards are already known or in use in the organization?*

Depending on the size of an IT organization, it may not be trivial to create an accurate picture of what standards are currently in place in which parts of the corporation. Nevertheless, the information about the as-is standard portfolio is important to plan an appropriate to-be portfolio as well as a transformation strategy. Since staff training is a considerable part of implementing a standard, information on existing individual certifications among the workforce is also relevant here.

4. *How can value-in-use of standards be measured?*

Based on the findings regarding the evolution of ITM standards during the last 20 years, it can be expected that they will continue adapting ever faster to changing requirements. Hence, the effectiveness and efficiency of standards already implemented becomes more relevant for decisions on how to further improve the standard portfolio. According measures and methods will be required to identify, quantify, and monetize positive and negative effects of standards in use.

5. *How can standard-related data be used for standard-related decisions?*

As with many other activities in the digital era, the implementation and use of an ITM standard creates data. Many standards require the use of specific processes and practices or prescribe the use of specific information systems (e.g., ITIL's service management knowledge system or PMBoK's project management information system), information structures (e.g., COBIT control objectives and KPIs) and document types (e.g., PRINCE2 management products). If this data could be made available for processing and analysis, it would become a valuable resource for dealing with questions 1–4. Future research should investigate how approaches and methods from data warehousing, process mining, data sciences, and related fields could be transferred and adapted to constitute a digital standards management, where standard selection, adaptation and orchestration is supported by smart digital solutions.

References

1. Leimeister, J.M., Winter, R., Brenner, W., Jung, R.: Research Program "Digital Business & Transformation IWI-HSG". SSRN Electron. J. (2014). https://doi.org/10.2139/ssrn.2501345
2. Legner, C., Eymann, T., Hess, T., Matt, C., Böhmann, T., Drews, P., Mädche, A., Urbach, N., Ahlemann, F.: Digitalization: opportunity and challenge for the business and information systems engineering community. Bus. Inf. Syst. Eng. **59**, 301–308 (2017). https://doi.org/10.1007/s12599-017-0484-2
3. Ikegami, H., Iijima, J.: Unwrapping efforts and difficulties of enterprises for digital transformation. In: Agrifoglio, R., Lamboglia, R., Mancini, D., Ricciardi, F. (eds.) Digital Business Transformation, pp. 237–250. Springer, Cham (2020). https://doi.org/10.1007/978-3-030-47355-6_16
4. Klimenko, R., Winter, R., Rohner, P.: Designing capability maturity model for agile transformation excellence. In: The 13th Mediterranean Conference on Information Systems (MCIS'19), Naples, Italy. http://www.itais.org/ITAIS-MCIS2019_pub/ITAISandMCIS2019-pages/pdf/15.pdf (2019)
5. Ciriello, R.F., Richter, A., Schwabe, G.: Digital innovation. Bus. Inf. Syst. Eng. **60**, 563–569 (2018). https://doi.org/10.1007/s12599-018-0559-8
6. Betz, C.T.: Managing Digital: Concepts and Practices. The Open Group Press (2018)

7. Spremic, M.: Governing digital technology – how mature IT governance can help in digital transformation? Int. J. Econ. Manag. Syst. **2**, 214–223 (2017)
8. Urbach, N., Ahlemann, F., Böhmann, T., Drews, P., Brenner, W., Schaudel, F., Schütte, R.: The impact of digitalization on the IT department. Bus. Inf. Syst. Eng. **61**, 123–131 (2019). https://doi.org/10.1007/s12599-018-0570-0
9. ISO/IEC: ISO/IEC Guide 2:2004 – Standardization and related activities – General vocabulary (2004)
10. Belleflamme, P.: Coordination on formal vs. de facto standards: a dynamic approach. Eur. J. Polit. Econ. **18**, 153–176 (2002). https://doi.org/10.1016/S0176-2680(01)00073-8
11. Marrone, M., Gacenga, F., Cater-Steel, A., Kolbe, L.: IT service management: a cross-national study of ITIL adoption. Commun. Assoc. Inf. Syst. **34** (2014). https://doi.org/10.17705/1CAIS.03449
12. Tambo, T., Filtenborg, J.: Digital services governance: IT4ITTM for management of technology. J. Manuf. Technol. Manag. **30**, 1230–1249 (2019). https://doi.org/10.1108/JMTM-01-2018-0028
13. Hartmann, A., Auth, G.: Positioning IT4IT in the face of classic Enterprise Architecture Frameworks. In: Workshop (Agiles) Enterprise Architecture Management in Forschung und Praxis, INFORMATIK2020 (accepted), Karlsruhe, Germany (2020)
14. Akershoek, R.: IT4IT for Managing the Business of IT – A Management Guide. Van Haren Publishing (for The Open Group), Zaltbommel (2016)
15. Agutter, C., England, R., van Hove, S.D., Steinberg, R.: VeriSM(tm) – A Service Management Approach for the Digital Age. Van Haren Publishing, Zaltbommel (2017)
16. Nägele, D., Zander, R., Gräf, J., Auth, G.: Kritische Erfolgsfaktoren des IT-Multisourcings mit Service Integration and Management (SIAM). In: Multikonferenz Wirtschaftsinformatik 2018, Lüneburg, Germany, pp. 1777–1788 (2018)
17. vom Brocke, J., Winter, R., Hevner, A., Maedche, A.: Accumulation and evolution of design knowledge in design science research – a journey through time and space. J. Assoc. Inf. Syst. JAIS. (2020)
18. Ahlemann, F., Teuteberg, F., Vogelsang, K.: Project management standards – Diffusion and application in Germany and Switzerland. Int. J. Proj. Manag. **27**, 292–303 (2009). https://doi.org/10.1016/j.ijproman.2008.01.009
19. Jabareen, Y.: Building a conceptual framework: philosophy, definitions, and procedure. Int. J. Qual. Methods. **8**, 49–62 (2009). https://doi.org/10.1177/160940690900800406
20. Johnson, R.E.: Frameworks = (components + patterns). Commun. ACM. **40**, 39–42 (1997)
21. Gamma, E., Helm, R., Johnson, R., Vlissides, J.: Design Patterns: Elements of Reusable Object-Oriented Software. Addison-Wesley, Reading, MA (1995)
22. Legner, C., Pentek, T., Otto, B.: Accumulating design knowledge with reference models: insights from 12 years' research into data management. J. Assoc. Inf. Syst. **3**, 735–770 (2020). https://doi.org/10.17705/1jais.00618
23. Kerzner, H.: Project Management: A Systems Approach to Planning, Scheduling, and Controlling. Wiley, Hoboken, NJ (2013)
24. Wells, H.: How effective are project management methodologies? An explorative evaluation of their benefits in practice. Proj. Manag. J. **43**, 43–58 (2012). https://doi.org/10.1002/pmj.21302
25. Winter, R., Rohner, P., Kiselev, C.: Mission impossible? Exploring the limits of managing large IT projects and ways to cross the line. In: Proceedings of the 52nd Hawaii International Conference on System Sciences. pp. 6388–6397. Computer Society Press, Grand Wailea, HI (2019). https://doi.org/10.24251/HICSS.2019.768
26. Anbari, F.T.: Earned value project management method and extensions. Proj. Manag. J. **34**, 12–23 (2003). https://doi.org/10.1177/875697280303400403
27. Winter, R.: Construction of situational information systems management methods. Int. J. Inf. Syst. Model. Des. **3**, 67–85 (2012). https://doi.org/10.4018/jismd.2012100104
28. Winter, R., Fischer, R.: Essential layers, artifacts, and dependencies of enterprise architecture. J. Enterp. Archit., 1–12 (2007)

29. AXELOS: Global Best Practice Portfolio. https://www.axelos.com/best-practice-solutions, last accessed 2020/10/07
30. AXELOS: ITIL® Foundation – ITIL 4 edition – Glossary (2019)
31. Davies, A.J., Kochhar, A.K.: Manufacturing best practice and performance studies: a critique. Int. J. Oper. Prod. Manag. **22**, 289–305 (2002). https://doi.org/10.1108/01443570210417597
32. Bretschneider, S., Marc-Aurele, F., Wu, J.: "Best Practices" Research: A methodological guide for the perplexed. J. Public Adm. Res. Theory. **15**, 307–323 (2004). https://doi.org/10.1093/jopart/mui017
33. Ivančić, L., Vukšić, V., Spremić, M.: Mastering the digital transformation process: business practices and lessons learned. Technol. Innov. Manag. Rev. **9**, 36–50 (2019). https://doi.org/10.22215/timreview/1217
34. ISO/IEC: ISO/IEC Guide 59:1994 – Code of good practice for standardization (1994)
35. ISO/IEC: ISO/IEC Guide 59:2019 – ISO and IEC recommended practices for standardization by national bodies (2019)
36. ISO: A Guide to Good Practice. http://www.iso.org/iso/casco_guide.pdf (2012)
37. Yadav, N., Sagar, M.: Performance measurement and management frameworks: research trends of the last two decades. Bus. Process Manag. J. **19**, 947–971 (2013). https://doi.org/10.1108/BPMJ-01-2013-0003
38. Paulk, M.C.: Surviving the quagmire of process models, integrated models, and standards. In: Proceedings of the ASQ Annual Quality Congress, Carnegie Mellon University, Toronto, ON, Canada (2004). https://doi.org/10.1184/R1/6625949.V1
39. Paulk, M.C.: A taxonomy for improvement frameworks. In: Fourth World Congress for Software Quality (WCSQ), Bethesda, MD, pp. 15–18 (2008)
40. Ibrahim, L., Mitasiunas, A.: Enterprise SPICE: A Domain Independent Integrated Model for Enterprise-wide Assessment and Improvement. Presented at the Bonita Conference, Riga, Latvia (2011). https://issuu.com/smarterpublications/docs/bonitaconference
41. Ibrahim, L., Mitasiunas, A., Vickroy, R.: An enterprise SPICE capability profile for an ISO 9001:2015 compliant organization. In: Stamelos, I., O'Connor, R.V., Rout, T., Dorling, A. (eds.) Software Process Improvement and Capability Determination, pp. 329–336. Springer, Cham (2018). https://doi.org/10.1007/978-3-030-00623-5_23
42. Debreceny, R.S., Gray, G.L.: IT governance and process maturity: a multi-national field study. J. Inf. Syst. **27**, 157–188 (2013). https://doi.org/10.2308/isys-50418
43. Schmidt, M., Brenner, M., Schaaf, T.: IT service management frameworks compared – simplifying service portfolio management. In: IFIP/IEEE International Symposium on Integrated Network Management (IM2019), Washington, DC, pp. 421–427 (2019)
44. De Haes, S., Van Grembergen, W., Debreceny, R.S.: COBIT 5 and enterprise governance of information technology: building blocks and research opportunities. J. Inf. Syst. **27**, 307–324 (2013). https://doi.org/10.2308/isys-50422
45. Marrone, M., Kolbe, L.M.: Uncovering ITIL claims: IT executives' perception on benefits and Business-IT alignment. Inf. Syst. E-Bus. Manag. **9**, 363–380 (2011). https://doi.org/10.1007/s10257-010-0131-7
46. Disterer, G.: WHY FIRMS SEEK ISO 20000 CERTIFICATION – A STUDY OF ISO 20000 ADOPTION. In: ECIS 2012 Proceedings. 31. Barcelona, Spain (2012)
47. Cots, S., Casadesús, M., Marimon, F.: Benefits of ISO 20000 IT service management certification. Inf. Syst. E-Bus. Manag. **14**, 1–18 (2016). https://doi.org/10.1007/s10257-014-0271-2
48. Kumbakara, N.: Managed IT services: the role of IT standards. Inf. Manag. Comput. Secur. **16**, 336–359 (2008). https://doi.org/10.1108/09685220810908778
49. Năstase, P., Năstase, F., Ionescu, C.: Challenges generated by the implementation of the IT standards CobiT 4.1, ITIL v3 and ISO/IEC 27002 in enterprises. Econ. Comput. Econ. Cybern. Stud. Res. **43**, 1–16 (2009)
50. Bustamante, F., Fuertes, W., Diaz, P., Toulkeridis, T.: Integration of IT frameworks for the management of information security within industrial control systems providing metrics and indicators. In: 2017 IEEE XXIV International Conference on Electronics, Electrical

Engineering and Computing (INTERCON), pp. 1–4. IEEE, Cusco, Peru (2017). https://doi.org/10.1109/INTERCON.2017.8079672

51. Barafort, B., Mesquida, A.-L., Mas, A.: Integrating risk management in IT settings from ISO standards and management systems perspectives. Comput. Stand. Interfaces. **54**, 176–185 (2017). https://doi.org/10.1016/j.csi.2016.11.010

52. vom Brocke, J., Simons, A., Riemer, K., Niehaves, B., Plattfaut, R., Cleven, A.: Standing on the shoulders of giants: challenges and recommendations of literature search in information systems research. Commun. Assoc. Inf. Syst. **37**, (2015). https://doi.org/10.17705/1CAIS.03709

53. Garshol, L.M.: Metadata? Thesauri? Taxonomies? Topic Maps! Making sense of it all. J. Inf. Sci. **30**, 378–391 (2004). https://doi.org/10.1177/0165551504045856

54. Horlach, B., Drews, P., Schirmer, I.: Bimodal IT: Business-IT alignment in the age of digital transformation. In: Multikonferenz Wirtschaftsinformatik (MKWI) 2016, Ilmenau, Germany, pp. 1417–1428 (2016)

55. Gartner: Definition of Bimodal – Gartner Information Technology Glossary. https://www.gartner.com/en/information-technology/glossary/bimodal. Accessed 10 Oct 2020.

56. Haffke, I., Darmstadt, T., Kalgovas, B.: The transformative role of bimodal IT in an era of digital business. In: Proceedings of the 50th Hawaii International Conference on System Sciences, p. 5460. Computer Society Press, Waikoloa Village, HI (2017). https://doi.org/10.24251/HICSS.2017.660

57. Ylinen, M., Pekkola, S.: A process model for public sector it management to answer the needs of digital transformation. In: Proceedings of the 52nd Hawaii International Conference on System Sciences, pp. 6219–6228. Computer Society Press, Grand Wailea, HI (2019). https://doi.org/10.24251/HICSS.2019.748

58. Cabinet Office: ITIL 2011 Summary of Updates. http://www.escotal.com/ITIL_2011_Summary_of_Updates.pdf. Accessed 19 Oct 2020

59. Pomales, J.: It was never about ITIL. https://www.cio.com/article/3238671/it-was-never-about-itil.html. Accessed 19 Oct 2020

60. Schwaber, K.: SCRUM development process. In: Sutherland, J., Casanave, C., Miller, J., Patel, P., Hollowell, G. (eds.) Business Object Design and Implementation, pp. 117–134. Springer, London (1997). https://doi.org/10.1007/978-1-4471-0947-1_11

61. Takeuchi, H., Nonaka, I.: The new product development game. Harv. Bus. Rev. **64**, 137–146 (1986)

62. Alt, R., Auth, G., Kögler, C.: Continuous Innovation with DevOps: IT Management in the Age of Digitalization and Software-defined Business. Springer International Publishing, Cham (2021). https://doi.org/10.1007/978-3-030-72705-5

63. Leite, L., Rocha, C., Kon, F., Milojicic, D., Meirelles, P.: A survey of DevOps concepts and challenges. ACM Comput. Surv. **52**, 1–35 (2020). https://doi.org/10.1145/3359981

64. Beck, K. et al.: Principles behind the Agile Manifesto. http://agilemanifesto.org/principles.html. Accessed 19 Oct 2020

65. DIN/Bitkom: Kompass Informationssicherheit und Datenschutz | Kompass der IT-Sicherheitsstandards. https://kompass-sicherheitsstandards.de/. Accessed 19 Oct 2020

Towards Conscious Enterprises: The Role of Enterprise Engineering in Realizing Living Sciences Paradigms into Management Sciences

Antonio Fernandes and José Tribolet

Abstract In this paper, we address the challenge of endowing enterprises with a "nervous system," which enables its consciousness as a means to better deal with systemic aspects, the whole, of an organization. We propose using the Enterprise Engineering body of knowledge and expand that knowledge by using paradigms of life sciences as foundational bases for the continuous explanation of the whole and the emergence of organizational consciousness. Enterprise Engineering body of knowledge allows us to create artifacts to support the explicitness of its systemic aspects, dynamically continuously updated, which will help the parts, humans, and computers, to deal better, align themselves, and contribute to the whole. We present the Enterprise Operating System concept as a contribution to further research aiming to implement the proposed enterprise "nervous system" and realize the identified living science paradigms into governance and management systems.

Keywords Enterprise engineering · Organizational consciousness · Enterprise operating system · Socio-technical systems

1 Introduction

The need to deal with the systemic aspects, i.e., the whole of organizations, in our view, has been neglected or poorly addressed. We have now the deep conviction that is essential for any organization to equip itself with the adequate artifacts to control and configure its whole status and dynamics.

A. Fernandes
Instituto Superior Technico, University of Lisbon, Lisbon, Portugal

INESC-ID Lisbon, Lisbon, Portugal
e-mail: ajfernandes@dorisol.pt

J. Tribolet (✉)
INESC-ID Lisbon, Lisbon, Portugal
e-mail: jose.tribolet@inesc.pt

© The Author(s), under exclusive license to Springer Nature Switzerland AG 2021
S. Aier et al. (eds.), *Engineering the Transformation of the Enterprise*,
https://doi.org/10.1007/978-3-030-84655-8_20

To address this challenge, we propose using Enterprise Engineering body of knowledge and expand that knowledge by using paradigms of life sciences, namely of living organism's consciousness, as foundational bases for the continuous explanation of the whole and the emergence of organizational consciousness. And by doing that making an organization capable of being aware of its destiny and deliberately directing its future as a whole and autonomous entity.

We introduce the Enterprise Operating System concept, as the "neurophysiologic" enterprise system, enabling enterprises' sense of self, feelings, intentionality, and consciousness. These are ingredients we believe are essential to control and configure the enterprise's whole.

This paper is organized as follow: we begin by introducing the role of engineering and the emergent discipline of Enterprise Engineering discipline in addressing enterprise's change, construction and operations, through using engineering principles and methodologies; in Sects. 3 and 4, we present the need and challenge of addressing the whole of the organizations; in Sect. 5 we present the importance of organizational knowledge and organizational representation to build up from individual's actions higher levels of organizational consciousness, and by doing that reifying the whole; in Sect. 6 we present life science-based theories of consciousness and in Sect. 7 we finally introduce the Enterprise Operating System.

2 Background

Engineering results from man's constant search for adaptation and control of the environment through design, construction, operation, maintenance, and, eventually, dismantling of artifacts.

The conceptualization of organizations as systems led to the idea that they could be properly analyzed, designed, and managed using engineering principles and methodologies. And consequently, it led to the recent emergence of the Enterprise Engineering (EE) research field.

2.1 Enterprise Engineering

The Society of Enterprise Engineering (EE) defined EE as "a body of knowledge, principles, and practices having to do with the analysis, design, implementation, and operation of the enterprise" [1]. The EE world view stemming from this definition is that the enterprise is a complex and adaptive system of processes that can be engineered to accomplish specific organizational objectives. In other words, to apply to organizations the same engineering principles and practices used in dealing with other kinds of artifacts or systems.

From black-box thinking to white-box thinking

In management and organizational sciences, problems are traditionally addressed with knowledge concerning the function and the behavior of enterprises, i.e., black box thinking based knowledge. Although such knowledge is sufficient for managing an enterprise within the current range of control, it is inadequate for changing an enterprise. In order to change enterprises in a systematic and controlled way, white-box based knowledge is needed, i.e., knowledge concerning the construction and the operation of enterprises. Thus, to build and change a system, one needs to adopt the ontological system notion. It is about the construction and operation of a system, and therefore the dominant system notion in all engineering sciences. The relationship with function and behavior is that the behavior of a system is brought about by its construction and the operation; through this exhibiting of behavior, the function of the system is realized [2].

From an information-centered view to a communication-centered view

Information is one of the most critical and primordial notions in organizations. Therefore, there is a typical information-centered paradigm, in which communication is defined as an exchange of information. One of the problems with this paradigm is that the notion of action and the notion of the organization are quite disconnected from information and communication.

A community of researchers in information systems engineering, based on the Speech Act Theory [3, 4] and the Communicative Action Theory [5], proposed a paradigm shift [6]. Instead of information, it takes communication as the fundamental notion. Communication is defined as the sharing of thoughts between subjects (human beings) and information as the means of communication. Information thus becomes the vehicle for communication (and not the other way around). This communication-centered view leads to a more appropriate and more integrated understanding for all key notions: communication, information, action and organization. The essential core concepts in organizations became then communication, interaction patterns, and commitments among its actors.

In that sense, in [7] is said that the single assumption the enterprise ontology theory, Ψ-Theory, is founded is that the communication between human beings in organizations constitutes a necessary and sufficient basis for developing a theory of organizations, which provides an explanation of the construction and the operation of organizations.

Thus, the focus of organization design shift from processes and resources to transactions, i.e., interaction patterns and commitments among actors. Transactions became the essential building blocks of enterprises.

Moreover, those transactions appear to occur in generic recurrent patterns, the Elementary Ontological Transaction (see Fig. 1). The genericity of this pattern has turned out to be so omnipresent and persistent that it is considered a socioeconomic law.

An EOT is therefore structured of: 1) A human actor (A) who requests something; 2) A human actor (B) who promises (or decline), on behalf of an organization, to deliver what actor (A) has requested; 3) Human actor (B) activates his Organization

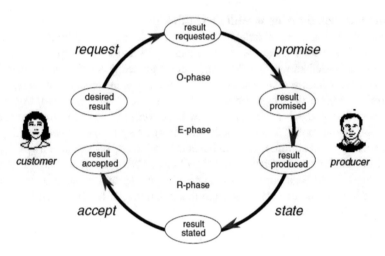

Fig. 1 Elementary Ontological Transaction pattern

so that "something" happens, objectify. This is called an "elementary act of production" and always corresponds to a "change of state of a resource."; 4) Human actor (B) presents the result of the "production act", the "something" intended by actor A, to human actor A. 5) Human Actor A accepts (or reject) the result, the "something" produced by the Organization of Actor B.

A simple state machine could model each EOT. The mathematical representation of any EOT is done using first-order Modal Logic, based on the symbolic mathematics of Computer Science. Thus, it is possible to analyze EOT chains and validate, at each moment, the state of coherence, completeness, and consistency of the execution of ongoing transactions. The organization's ontological modeling is thus invariant in relation to the technological instruments used in the organizations, just as it is invariant in relation to its organizational models and management methods used.

The ontological modeling of an organization captures the essentials of what it does and, therefore, what it is! Moreover, it is amenable to "real-time" analysis using ontological computing. Hence, the ontological modeling and computation of an organization, supported by Enterprise Engineering body of knowledge, could be an essential element to enable systemic control in real-time, contributing to the aim of providing an organization with the ability to experience and visualize its realities as a whole entity, in an integrated and quasi-real-time manner.

Moreover, the Enterprise Engineering body of knowledge, notably Enterprise Ontology and Ontological Modeling, is essential to our work as a means to represent and model the enterprise's complex reality in a holistic, intelligible, and manageable way.

2.2 Enterprises: A Coherent Whole or a Case of Schizophrenia?

An organization is a technical-social system whose particularity is to have human beings in its constitution, that is, agents endowed with intelligence, conscience, autonomy, and self-will.

This fact has led that, on the one hand, organizations as holistic entities, traditionally, have not been considered objects specific to science and engineering technologies. However, on the other hand, multiple aspects of organizational activities are the object of the most diverse sciences, from the "hardest" and "softest," providing precious contributions to the knowledge of organizations.

Unfortunately, this multiple knowledge is far from providing a common platform for, objectively, these different sciences to meet and validate themselves, in an effort to understand the holistic entity, that any real organization is. Thus, we do not yet have pragmatic tools and methodologies to apprehend and learn about the organizational whole.

In fact, what is observed in general is the simultaneity of multiple interventions in the most diverse aspects of the organizational reality, over time and space, without restrictions that guarantee a priori the coherence of the programmed interventions. Alike, it is not guaranteed, in real-time, the consistency of the different developments caused by these interventions, nor have the circuits for monitoring and controlling the preservation of the essential characteristics of the organizational whole, namely, the consistency of the personality of the holistic identity that each organization is.

Moreover, it is evident that people in organizations, while acting with a certain degree of autonomy, do not have the capacity to invoke information in real-time about the organizational whole since this information does not exist as such, explicitly!

Overall, it is a fact that we live in organizations with a greater or lesser degree of schizophrenic disorder.

3 Addressing the Whole: A Challenge of Enterprise Engineering

An enterprise or organization (we will use both terms interchangeable) could be defined as a label or "generic term to any kind of social entities of purposeful human endeavor, such as business, companies, firms, corporations, organizations and institution" [8].

From this definition, it is clear that an enterprise has purpose and intentionality. Thus, it pursues objectives and is structured and organized for its purpose and those objectives. Therefore, any organization has a design component. This design component goes from its initial conception to its construction and persists throughout its life cycle, along with its transformation processes.

In Enterprise Engineering, this design component is naturally addressed by the fact that Enterprise Engineering embraces the entire life cycle of the socio-technical object, which the enterprise is. And this cycle is a closed and continuous cycle, which goes from its conception to its construction and subsequent operation and transformation processes.

In the conceptions of an organization, in addition to the creation and operation of its parts, which performs the functional execution of activities, it is necessary to pay attention to the preservation of its systemic characteristics. Moreover, this preservation of the systemic characteristics, have to account that the enterprise object has to be dynamic, i.e., with the ability to transform itself over time while preserving its integrity.

What we have been exploring in our research is precisely how engineering deals with systemic aspects of the organization. What is the whole? What is the design, construction, operation and maintenance of the whole? How do we deal with the whole, and how do we endow it with a dynamic self-transformation capacity while preserving its identity, coherence, and integrity?

The need to deal with the systemic aspects, i.e., the whole of organizations, in our view, has been neglected or poorly addressed.

We believe that engineering, with concepts from General Systems Theory, Cybernetics and Dynamic Control Systems, as well as concepts from Enterprise Engineering, provides an important and robust body of knowledge to contribute to organizations that better deal with their systemic aspects.

In our investigation, we have identified some important and fundamental aspects to deal with this dimension of the organizational whole, like the representation or explanation of the whole, the organizational self-awareness and the organizational identity [9–13].

The question is, what contributions can engineering make to explore further these dimensions in relation to the enterprise "object"?

One of the contributions we can affirm is that GST, cybernetics and dynamic control systems give us the ability to understand better how to design, operate and manage the relationship between each part of the organization and the whole. It also gives us the understanding for the need to have always in its systemic mechanisms two major feedback loops: one that is stabilizing the system in its present environment (addressing the "here and now" of the organization), and one that is ensuring that this will also be possible in the future (addressing the "outside and. then" of the organization).

Concerning Enterprise Engineering body of knowledge, it gives us the opportunity to create artifacts to support the explanation of the whole, dynamically continuously updated, which will help the parts, humans and computers, to deal better, align themselves and contribute to the whole. One thing is sure: the more real-time information about the world and about itself an organization has access to, and make available to its elements, the more chances it will have to act and transform itself intelligently as a whole in order to preserve its future interests, namely its survival.

On the other hand, we realize that there are dimensions from patterns and paradigms of life sciences, which could be applied within the enterprise engineering context, to help us explore further important concepts to deal with the whole, namely the organizational self. Thus, we have been seeking those models and paradigms to help us instrument or reinforce the organization's self-awareness capacity. And by doing that, addressing the ultimate challenge: endowing enterprises with a high level of organizational consciousness. Why? Because these higher or reinforced levels of the organizational self and consciousness are important for managing the organization's present and future with purpose and intentionality, while preserving its integrity and identity.

We now have the deep conviction that it is essential for any organization to equip itself with the adequate artifacts in order to enable its ability to control and configure its whole status and dynamics.

For doing that we propose to use paradigms of life sciences as foundational bases for the continuous explanation of the whole and the emergence of an organizational consciousness, making an organization capable of being aware of its destiny and deliberately directing its future as a whole and autonomous entity.

4   From the Parts to the Whole and Back

4.1   *Organizational Knowledge*

Knowledge manifests itself in action! It is when an organizational agent, be it a human actor or a machine, does something determinedly, in a given context, that we see the knowledge he owns emerge (much of it is tacit). This area that of the manifestation of knowledge is well worked on in the social sciences.

In this way, and in a first approach, asking ourselves about Organizational Knowledge leads us to focus our attention on the way the actors act, in the way they dispose and invoke information, to enable them to make decisions and take action.

It is evident that people in organizations do not have the capacity to invoke information about the organizational whole since this information does not exist as such, explicitly!

The importance of communication and dialogue in organizations is evident. But to communicate and dialogue presupposes sharing the same semantic universe, synchronization, focusing on the same reality.

Synchronization between humans is a complex process facilitated by a whole collection of cultural codes and symbols, making it more efficient and expeditious in a given community or organization.

In a quasi-stationary context of slow changes in people's and organizations' lives, if we take the human life cycle as a unit of measure, the communication and representation technologies that we had were sufficient to synchronize human actors in their organizations. We talked, read, talked, slept on the subject, started to talk and read again and the communication was flowing, the synchronization of perceptions was happening. On the other hand, as each individual's action had a localized impact, except for senior managers, the universe of organizational knowledge relevant to potentiate each actor's action was more limited and involved the synchronization of much fewer actors. The articulation between the domains of local action was made based on explicit, slowly changing organizational rules.

However, in the context of today's world—locally globally and globally local—what prevails is the non-stationary nature of forms, in the search for the most appropriate practices, given the organization's objectives, and taking into account the dynamics of its environments, much more harsh, unpredictable and competitive. In this perspective, the forms of functional and hierarchical organization are no longer quasi-stationary, but gain a dynamic of adaptability, of intrinsic non-stationarity, necessary to sustain the life of the organization, either through the production processes of the products and services that it places as added value abroad, either through the production processes of products and services essential to its own self-sustained maintenance, as a Holistic Entity, live!

In this context, human actors no longer have their activities confined to a local and departmental scale but instead act in transversal processes to the entire organization and consequently have an intrinsically global impact.

For this reason, it becomes imperative to make organizational knowledge explicit, in semantically compatible ways with the mental universe of each human in the organization. Therefore, the human will be able to invoke the organization's holistic knowledge to better enable its decisions and actions. The human will thus act with greater awareness of its overall impact, on the whole of the organization. Furthermore, he will be increasingly able to critically analyze the whole and contribute to its adaptation and improvement.

4.2 Organizational Representation

For a non-trivial set of humans to be able to share the knowledge of an organization, namely the knowledge about itself—the Organizational "Self-Awareness"—it is necessary to explain it, with appropriate semantic representations for this set of humans.

At present, this explicit knowledge about organizations makes use of written language, making it clear to everyone that this form of representation is no longer adequate to current needs.

Interestingly, there are specific areas of organizational activities that use other instruments of representation, namely visual ones: in science, engineering, medicine, and in general in the fields of exact sciences, there are specific languages with primitive semantics and specific rules of composition, appropriate knowledge representation, and communication between the respective members of these initiatory communities of experts. The results are excellent, as is evident in the world today.

For example, an airplane is designed, produced, tested, operated, and maintained in its entirety over the life cycles of tens of years. The organization that sustains the processes throughout the entire life cycle is a very diverse socio-technical organization, multi-cultural, multi-lingual, regulated by the most diverse contracts, subject to the most diverse financial, commercial, legal, even atmospheric environments, and despite everything...the plane continues to fly! How is this possible, to maintain the holistic integrity of this system, in these non-stationary conditions, full of humans?

The key to the issue lies precisely in the fact that there is a representation of the whole throughout the entire life cycle of the airplane. This representation, which supports the most varied specialized views of its parts, whether functional or systemic, easily extended by the diverse communities of specialists that deal with them, is the key to the verification of the whole's consistency in the synthesis of the mutations of the parts. This holistic representation of each plane is always up to date after each intervention.

Thus, the existence of the holistic representation of the airplane—in addition to the specialized representations of each domain—supports the capacity of the entire organization responsible for the life cycle of the airplane—itself highly variable in time—to act locally with knowledge of the whole, preserving its holistic integrity at all times.

Enterprise Engineering allows us to develop and implement artifacts suitable for real-time Systemic Control. This capacity requires "Enterprise Cartography" always updated. This instrument should allow extracting multiple views of reality, in real-time, according to the contexts of action of specific actors and according to the respective missions. Fundamental in the construction and maintenance of this "organization mirror" is the coherence, completeness, and consistency of the representation. It must always "compile" without bugs"!

The simple process of "surveying" the realities of business execution and viewing them in real-time without "bugs", will allow detecting immediately essential non-conformities existing in the organization. Ontological modeling and computation, mentioned in Sect. 2, could significantly contribute for this aims.

The existence of a representation of the organization, always up to date, supports organizational "self-awareness" in relation to its ultimate purpose while performing its business processes, which is to maintain the organization's own integrity.

Organizational knowledge, therefore, implies the existence of an organizational representation, always up to date. A representation that results from the integration and the consistency of the different views on the same organization, by the different parts of the various specialized communities involved in it, is the keystone of the holistic capability we call Organizational Self Awareness.

This capability of an organization to be aware of itself at any point in time, is the equivalent to what we, single humans, do possess as most valuable to steer ourselves in life: our self-awareness, on top of which we build higher-order levels of self, such as conscience, values, and ethics [14].

4.3 Organizational Consciousness: The Reification of the Whole

A common, shared, coherent and explicit representation of the whole is essential for the ability of an enterprise, as a whole, to be aware of itself, of its situational "As Is" state.

However, suppose we want to endow enterprises with organizational self-will and intentionality and the ability to set their own purposes and goals. To achieve this goal, enterprises need higher levels of Self and Consciousness. For doing that, we will have to have means to represent in real-time the enterprises' internal states, its external world, and the interaction between both. We will need the means to represent organizational feelings and enable intentionality. We will need the means to enable the organization's awareness, self-awareness, information integration, goal-oriented behavior, and the ability to experience things.

In short words, we need to endow the enterprise system with Consciousness and with a sense of Self. And by doing that, we are somehow reifying the whole.

David Dennet, talking about his book "From Bacteria to Bach and Back" [15], proposed that Consciousness is an illusion. He argues it is maybe just a "user-friendly interface system" for the brain (as a user system), to use the brain (as an object system), to model, control and deal with the overwhelming complexity of itself and of its environment. Applying this idea for an enterprise, where the brain could be seen as its social-technical network of its autonomous agents, Organizational Consciousness could be characterized as a "user-friendly interface system" for the enterprise's actor-network to use itself to model, control and deal with its own internal and external complexity. Moreover, that "user-friendly interface system", the organizational consciousness, reifies the organization as a whole entity enabling the whole to, implicit or explicitly, communicate back to its parts, so that they could act in an orchestrated manner. This is important because we must always remember that what the whole does is just the result of what the parts are doing.

We should notice that we do not aim to anthropomorphize the enterprise. We are just saying that enterprise consciousness is an emergent systemic property in a highly complex and distributed social-technical system. In that sense, we make the proposition that all organizations could evolve to higher complexity levels, whereby at some point, "organizational consciousness" emerges as a reification, at a macro systemic level, of the social-technical network of its autonomous agents.

The different dimensions of organizational Consciousness
We are convinced that the concept of organizational Consciousness is essential in organizations and must support the "Doing" plan and the "Being" plan. The former concerns the immediate operational plan of the organization's activities and behaviors. The second aims to preserve the integrity of the organization's constituent parts and the complex webs of the relationship between them. Finally, we believe that the organizational Consciousness is also fundamental for the construction of the institutional "Becoming" plan, supporting the maintenance of the coherence of the whole

through time, explaining the mechanisms of preservation of the essential "glue" that defines the organization throughout the transformation phenomena and change processes. Therefore, we believe organizational Consciousness is essential for the dynamic control of both organization's operational and structural flows. The former is characterized by the organization's kinematic perspective (the different states of a stabilized form), the second by a dynamic perspective (the temporal evolution between the different forms of the object).

For this reason, the explanation of Organizational Consciousness must necessarily contain more complex representations than simply the static listing of the resources that compose it and the activities that are exercised in it for the execution of business processes in a given time.

5   Paradigms of Life Sciences: Theories of Consciousness

Progress in researching the phenomena of systems' consciousness, being biological, social, or artificial, will depend in the first place on our understanding of consciousness in humans. Although, there is no single, correct and undisputed theory of what it is and how works our consciousness, it is worth highlighting two relevant and promising consciousness theories: Tononi's Integration Information Theory of Consciousness [16–18] and Damasio's Theory of Consciousness [19–21]. We believe these theories could help us understanding better how we could develop the organizational self and organizational consciousness.

5.1   Integration Information Theory of Consciousness (IITC)

For many scholars consciousness is not a one-off thing, rather there could be different levels or grades of consciousness. Is there then a quantity that quantifies consciousness? According to the Italian neuroscientist Giulio Tononi, there is one such quantity, which he calls the "integrated information" [22].

According to IITC, consciousness corresponds to the ability of a system to integrate information. This statement is motivated by two essential phenomenological properties of consciousness: 1) differentiation—the ability to discriminate a specific conscious experience within a large number of other possible systemic states or conscious experiences; and 2) integration—the unity of each of them. In other words, the fact that only when the information about an organism's systemic state is interpreted by its "modeler" in a unified and holistic way, the meaning of such a state, at a given time and context, is revealed.

Thus, a physical system will be able to generate consciousness to the extent that it has, at a given time and context, a large repertoire of available internal states (information), which cannot be simply interpreted aa a collection of autonomous and independent subsystems, but rather can be composed in a complete, consistent and coherent way, as a full system (integration).

Tononi's IITC approach to the problem of consciousness takes the phenomenology of consciousness as primary and then addresses its implementation by physical mechanisms [16–18].

IITC provides a way to analyze physical systems' mechanisms and determine if they are adequately structured and organized to give rise to consciousness. Moreover, IITC presents a mathematical framework for evaluating the quality and quantity of consciousness, thus informing how much and of what kind of consciousness could be enabled by a specific physical system.

Regarding our research interest, IITC supports the proposition that organizational consciousness could emerge with varying degrees in the enterprise's actor-network due to the characteristics related to both the topology of the network and the transactional attributes practiced in that network between the actors.

In this enterprise actor-network context, IITC states that there is a set of postulates that should be kept in mind to account for the emergence of organizational consciousness. These postulates concern the following five aspects:

1. Existence—that the elements of the network exist at each moment in a particular state, and actively interact in the network;
2. Composition—that the network is structured, i.e., it is a composite entity that combines and forms higher-order combinations of several aspects of the phenomenology of the activities of that network;
3. Information—that the network intrinsically generates specific and unique information, which is linked to a specific occurrence of interactions within the actor-network;
4. Integration—that the information generated by the actor-network results from the integration of a set of activities and only makes sense in its integrated combination;
5. Exclusion—that the integrated information generated by the actor-network is exclusive within a given space-time granularity.

In summary: the IITC approach tell us that consciousness is quantitatively and qualitatively measurable, and that it should be possible to build organizational artifacts to create the conditions for the emergence of various degrees of consciousness in an enterprise actor-network.

However, as with any theory of consciousness, IITC is not immune to controversy. One of the main controversial aspects is whether information integration ability is a necessary and sufficient condition for consciousness (as IITC claims), or is just a necessary but not a sufficient condition. Antonio Damasio, whose theories on consciousness are addressed below, is one of the scholars that claim integration information is a necessary but not sufficient condition for consciousness.

5.2   Damasio's Theory of Consciousness

According to Damasio, the existence of a mind with the capacity to create images that integrate all information about experiences is not enough for the emergence of consciousness [21]. It also requires a physical substrate, a body, and the emergence of feelings.

It all started with the emergence and complexification of the nervous system over millions of years of evolution of various forms of life. With the emergence of more complex nervous systems capable of mapping structures, creating detailed sensory maps and images, feelings arise. Feelings incorporate facts about the state of the organism's interior in a continuous mental flow and value them according to their contribution to the overall system's purpose. Thus, Feelings are not limited to represent an organism's internal state; they qualify and value such a state.

Feelings are characterized by images of the interior, which dynamically detail changes in the organism's internal configurations, and images about the continuous and intimate interaction process between its neural mapping sensors and their body sources, reflecting how the body "feels" those same internal changes. As Damasio argues, by doing so, feelings "naturally reveal that the maps are created within the organism they represent, that the organism owns the mind. Thus, it surges the sense that everything that occurs in the mind—maps of the interior and maps of other objects that exist in the surrounding exterior—is constituted from the organism's perspective."

Damasio calls the sensation of self that emerges from this process the Nuclear Self, and argues that it appears when the maps of the organism's internal configuration change as the result of the interactions with an object. The Nuclear Self is the first stage of consciousness and coincides precisely with the knowledge of feeling something.

The emergence of the Nuclear Self, jointly with the ability to memorize, enables conscious organisms to maintain a history of their lives, their interactions with others, and their environment. Hence, surges the ability to maintain a history of each individual life in the perspective of each individual organism. It connects the sense of self, not only to a specific present moment but also to past and perceived future events in an autobiographical narration. In this way arises the autobiographical self! [21].

We should notice that in this process of the autobiographical self, both the past, which has been experienced, and the future are essential: "memories of our desires and of the outcomes we expect generate pressure in each moment on our self" [20].

Hence, the formation of the self, enabled by feelings, can be then characterized as a process to recruit and organize the brain's information about the past and perceived future of the body to which it belongs.

The role of informing and value the state of the organism is a primary function of feelings. However, it is not the only role of feelings. Feelings also encourage the mind to react according to the organism's state information and its valuation. Feelings give us the will and incentive to act according to the information and valuation they provide and do what is most appropriate for each context in which we find ourselves. Thus, through feelings, intentionality arises!

So far, we saw the importance of feelings as precursors of consciousness and its critical role for the rise of the self and intentionality. However, how does Damasio explains the consciousness phenomena?

According to Damasio: "a human organism is said to be conscious when its mind, its mental state, represents objects and events in relation to itself, that is when the representation of objects and events is accompanied by the sense that the organism is the perceiving agent" [20]. Thus, consciousness emerges when the brain generates: 1) neural patterns and images about objects; 2) neural patterns and images about changes those objects cause in the internal state of the organism; 3) second-order neural patterns that interrelate a) and b) [21]. This second-order neural patterns describing the relationship between the organism and the object is the neural basis of subjectivity, for it portrays the organism as the protagonist to which objects are referred. In doing so, it establishes a core consciousness.

Moreover, Damasio explains that images in our mind originate in two fundamental universes: 1) the external world around us—images of objects, actions, and relationships present in the environment we occupy and which we continuously analyze with our sensors; 2) the inner world inside us—images of objects, actions, and relationships, but within the organism. However, instead of being limited to representing the shapes of internal objects, the images of this inner world universe, this second type of images represent the states of those objects in relation to their function, i.e., they qualify and value the state of the internal objects. This internal universe's processes work in a continuous interaction between "real" objects and the images that represent. It is a hybrid process, being both "body" and "mind", allowing images on the mental side to be updated whenever a new change occurs on the body side, and at same time valuate and "feel" that change.

Overall, it is never too much to emphasize the central role that feelings play in consciousness. Although most authors link consciousness to cognition and thinking, Damasio also links consciousness primarily to feelings. Damasio's motto could be: "I feel, therefore I am". Damasio says that feelings are among the first examples of mental phenomena; they are the first precursors of consciousness [19]. Besides, according to Damasio, feelings guarantee a strong bond between body and mind, overcoming the classic gap that typically separates the physical body from mental phenomena.

5.3 Lessons from Life Sciences Based Theories of Consciousness

The above-discussed consciousness theories gave us some crucial insights regarding our challenge to explore higher levels of enterprise self and organizational consciousness.

IITC will guide us on the needed topology and attributes of the enterprise's actor-network (the enterprise physical substrate), in order to respect the IITC's postulates, which specifies which conditions physical mechanisms must satisfy to account for the phenomenology of consciousness. IIT will also be essential to give us a means, a method, to measure the quantity of an enterprise's consciousness and assess its quality.

Damasio's theory of consciousness will be relevant to frame our model with the need for: a vigilant state (need for external and internal observability); a mind (need for the ability to model/mapping the internal and external reality); and a self (need for build a sense of enterprise self, induced by the emergence of enterprise's feelings, and a biographical memory). Moreover, the critical role of feelings in Damasio's theory will give relevant insights to the need for defining means to represent and evaluate enterprise feelings, which we call organizational feelings. We believe organizational feelings are key to endow enterprises with a "value system" and intentionality.

In other words, we learn with Damasio's Theory that in order for conscience to emerge, we need a body/being, a mind, and a self, and to connect all we need feelings. We need a nervous system, integrated and embedded in the body, enabling the organism to map structures and build images. We need sensory systems that sweep the outside. We need a simulator to imagine the perceived future and a memory to memorize the relevant history and the imagined future.

Our research is now focused on integrating the discussed theories of consciousness into the same universe of Engineering and Enterprise Engineering discourse, notably into more hard concepts and dynamic models from General Systems Theory, Cybernetics, and Enterprise Ontology. It is a working progress process, whose results we will be published later. We should also notice that in our view nothing in these reviewed conscious theories conflicts with the concepts and models that we have been developing within the enterprise engineering research area. Rather the contrary, they validate and enrich the body of knowledge of enterprise engineering.

6   The Enterprise Operating System Concept

As we have seen, the emergence of consciousness in organisms was preceded by the emergence of the first nervous systems: control and coordination devices, which came to help the first basic mechanisms of governance and life management—homeostasis. These nervous systems paved the way for map structures, followed by image production, thus giving rise to the mind.

Likewise, suppose we want to empower an organization with a sense of self and consciousness to manage better and govern its life. In that case, we must start by providing it with an adequate "neurophysiological" system.

This enterprise's neurophysiologic systems, i.e., its self-governing and managing system, is what we have been calling the Enterprise Operating System (EOS). We use the term EOS as a metaphor of the essential role of the operating system in computing devices, in assuring that the computer is "alive" as a whole coordinated and integrated system [23].

General Systems Theory, Cybernetics and Dynamic Control Systems give us the understanding for the need to have always in any system systemic mechanisms two major feedback loops. One that is stabilizing the system in its present environment (addressing the "here and now" of the organization). The other is ensuring that this will also be possible in the future (addressing the "outside and then" of the organization) [24, 25]. Thus, we need to endow the EOS with a broadly distributed and holistic, dynamic control concept which integrates management (the cinematic perspective—"run the mill") and governance (the dynamic perspective—"change the mill").

Piaget [26] refers to this broadly control concept as the equilibration process, consisting of overcoming and stabilizing, inseparably. In other words, bringing together constructions and compensations. He argues that only by behaving alike can the system's whole preserve the parts and vice versa. Le Moigne [25] points out that Piaget's equilibration concept, the process for forming a better equilibrium, should be interpreted in relation to the system's projects and purposes. Hence, any system defines its ideal of equilibrium not by the invariance of its structure but by its projects' permanent satisfaction. The teleological hypothesis, on which the systemic paradigm is based, is thus unambiguously explained here. A system's performance can thus be measured by the distance in relation to its final stability, i.e., to its potential forms that permit achieving its ultimate goals: stay viable now and in the perceived future.

Therefore, we will need constructs to provide an organization with the capacity to be aware of itself and of its environment, of its history and perceived future, and all this in relation to its own goals and projects.

6.1   The Enterprise Operating System (EOS)

We propose the existence within each enterprise of a self-governing and managing system (or decision and information system) aiming to preserve the whole, its identity, and integrity. From GST and cybernetics, particularly the Viable System Model [24] and the Nine Level Model [25], we learn the need for such a system to have mechanisms for regulating and stabilizing its internal milieu. These mechanisms are responsible for controlling and monitoring the enterprise's activities, for coordinating its subsystems activities, for imagining, projecting and planning its future; and finally, for giving closure and enabling the emergence of consciousness, values, and intentionality, in order to be able to define its own purposes and projects of intervention [23–25].

Any Organization, as a System, has its own Operating System (its EOS), its "neurophysiologic system". The EOS uses Organizational Governance instruments at a systemic and holistic level and permeates, uses and intervenes at all organization levels!

The Organization's Governance requires the ability to mapping structures, the existence of its representation maps, its "World Atlas", continuously fed by instruments to capture and understand the reality of what it is, that is, what it does.

The views extracted from the Organization's "Atlas", allow at the Governance level, the alignment of the specialized languages of each of its members, facilitating the communication and objectivity of the interactions.

The use of the Organization's simulators, based on its "Atlas", allows the Governance level to visualize the systemic effects of the proposed actions or expected events and anticipate the perceived future, thus supporting better decision-making by Organization's executive bodies.

The Organization's "Atlas" is a "core" artifact of its Enterprise Operating System and should support the enterprise's feelings, consciousness and autobiographical self.

Notice that from life sciences theories of consciousness, we learn the need to map, share, and integrate information, as well as the importance of feelings, in enabling the consciousness phenomena. Feelings, instead of being limited to representing the shapes of internal objects, the images of our inner world, represent the states of these objects in relation to their function, i.e., they qualify and value the state of the system's interior objects. Moreover, feelings are extremely important not only to inform about a system's internal overall state, but also to encourage that system to react in accordance with the information it provides.

In that sense, although today's "digital twin enterprise" concept could represent and map the inner state of an organization's operations in real-time, it cannot make the collective "feel" what that state means. For that, our EOS must be placed and fused with the enterprise's body (its actor-network) and deal with its member's feelings to collective value and qualify its internal state. In that sense, we could think of a homeostatic equilibrium mechanism between all its members' feelings, emerging in that process an organizational and collective feeling. Thus, EOS should also enable the enterprise to deal, at an organizational level, with one of the most important and always present dimensions of its human members: their individual feelings.

6.2   The Metaphor

In order to extrapolate consciousness theories to a social-technical context, we propose to use a metaphor where EOS works as the enterprise's "neurophysiologic system". Its autonomous agents' network, its actor-network, represents its body, and a subnetwork of this actor-network represents its nervous system inside its body. Actors represent the neurons, whilst potential transactions between them represent the synapses and activated/enacted transactions the actual communication/information flows.

Thus, this metaphor is coherent with Damasio's claim for the need for a strong bond between the mind and the body to arise consciousness. This bond, powered by the emergence of feelings, is realized by the fact that the mind is generated by the nervous system which is placed inside the organism and imbricated with it, giving the sense that the organism is the perceiving agent of its own representative images.

Using this kind of metaphor, we intend to extrapolate to social-technical contexts the relevant fundamental concepts, processes, and properties from consciousness theories.

6.3 Modeling and Representational Languages

As we already noticed, we have more formal and concise languages in sciences and engineering, particularly in Enterprise Engineering, which contribute to making the organization's complexity intellectually manageable and have a holistic perspective.

Enterprise Engineering body of knowledge developed ontological theories like the PSI theory, the DELTA theory and the OMEGA Theory [27]. It also developed modeling methodologies such as DEMO or PRISMANETS [27]. They are all instruments that help us designing and capture the essence of the enterprise's constructions and operations.

Regarding the capture and eventual memorization of experiences or moments that represent the pulse of organizational consciousness, we must develop the capacity to map structures and build images. We suggest using graphs or matrices that can project a pictographic image of the choreography of transactions between enterprises' actors, which occurs on a given space-time scale.

A matrix or graph, providing an image of the shape of the system as a whole, can also support the evolution process, i.e., its dynamic flow of transformations. The evolution could be represented by the sequence of the graph's/matrix's shapes, which the organization takes in each transformation cycle. In each one of these transformations, elements and relations of the graphs, could be added or removed according to possible alternative viable forms that can be generated. In addition, we also plan to explore the potential of images, of the shapes of objects, as a potential for representing memories, impulses of consciousness and feelings.

By manipulating these forms and using distance or similarity measures between forms, we could have a means of measuring the alignment between the representations of individual actors and the whole, measuring the performance of the organization or assessing the viability of certain forms for the whole. Moreover, concerning the dynamics of organizations, we could see it as a ceaseless creation, evolution, and destruction of forms.

René Thom has developed an abstract, purely geometrical theory of morphogenesis, independent of the substrate of forms and the nature of the forces that create them [28]. We also intend to explore its application to capture the dynamic flow, that is, the transformation process in the various forms that an organization takes, identifying the points of catastrophe or disruption as well as the points of attraction and consequent creation of new possible viable forms, after that. Simultaneously, we can measure the distance of an organization's specific form in relation to the possible forms that it could take to realize its objectives better.

Finally, from the moment an organization as a whole has the capacity to represent and create images, it can always through the manipulation and simulation of symbols, create new images, thus enabling the system's creativity and imagination.

7 Conclusion

We have been researching within the enterprise Engineering body of knowledge concepts as organizational representation, organizational knowledge, organizational self-awareness and organizational identity, as a means to address the challenge of mastering the whole of organizations. To explore further those concepts, we propose to explore theories of consciousness, as foundational bases for the continuous explanation of the whole and the emergence of organizational Consciousness. We learned the importance of endowing an organization with a "nervous system", enabling an organization to map structures and integrate information in images, to "feel", and ultimately to emerge its Consciousness. In that sense, we introduce the Enterprise Operating System (EOS) concept, as the enterprise's "neurophysiologic system". We also propose a metaphor and some representation and modeling possibilities to address the challenge of designing such an EOS.

In today's technological world, where computers and humans are fused in bionic organizations, more than ever, engineering sciences and management sciences should collaborate in addressing enterprise's ultimate challenge: enabling its consciousness and transforming organizations in conscious super minds. Super minds where human minds will be connected to each other in new ways and at unprecedented scales, and people and computers together will do things that were never possible before, becoming increasingly smarter and conscious bionic socio-technical systems.

References

1. Liles, D.H., Presley, A.: Enterprise modeling within an enterprise engineering framework. In: 96 Winter Simulation Conference, San Diego, CA (1996)
2. Dietz, J.L.G., Hoogervorst, J.A.P.: Enterprise ontology in enterprise engineering. In: Proceedings of the ACM Symposium on Applied Computing (2008). https://doi.org/10.1145/1363686.1363824
3. Austin, J.L.: How to Do Things with Words. Harvard University Press, Cambridge (1962)
4. Searle, J.R.: Speech Acts: An Essay in the Philosophy of Language. Cambridge University Press, London (1969)
5. Habermas, J.: The Theory of Communicative Action. Polity Press, Cambridge (1986)
6. Weigand, H.: Two decades of the language-action perspective. Commun. ACM. **49**(4), 44–46 (2006)

7. Dietz, J.: The atoms, molecules and fibers of organizations. Data Knowl. Eng. **47**, 301–325 (2010)
8. Hoogervorst, J.: Foundations of Enterprise Governance and Enterprise Engineering, 1st edn. Springer, The Netherlands (2017)
9. Aveiro, D., Silva, A.R., Tribolet, J.: Towards a G.O.D. organization for organizational self-awareness. In: Albani, A., Dietz, J.L.G. (eds.) Advances in Enterprise Engineering IV, pp. 16–30. Springer, Berlin (2010)
10. Magalhães, R., Sousa, P., Tribolet, J.: The role of business processes and enterprise architectures in the development of organizational self-awareness. Polytechn. Stud. Rev. **6**(9) (2008)
11. Páscoa, C., Aveiro, D., Tribolet, J.: Organizational configuration actor role modeling using DEMO. In: Practice-Driven Research on Enterprise Transformation – 4th Working Conference, pp. 18–47. Springer (2012)
12. Tribolet, J., Sousa, P., Caetano, A.: The role of enterprise governance and cartography in enterprise engineering. Enterprise Model. Inf. Syst. Architect. J. (2014)
13. Zacarias, M., Magalhães, R., Caetano, A., Pinto, S., Tribolet, J.: Towards organizational self-awareness: an architecture and ontology framework. In: Rittgen, P. (ed.) Handbook of Ontologies for Business Interaction. IRM Press, Hershey (2007)
14. Magalhães, R., Tribolet, J.: Engenharia Organizacional: das partes ao todo e do todo às partes na dialéctica entre pessoas e sistemas, Cap. do livro 'Ventos de Mudança'. Editora Fundo de Cultura, Brasil (2007)
15. Dennett, D.C.: From Bacteria to Bach and Back: The Evolution of Minds. W.W. Norton, New York (2017)
16. Oizumi, M., Albantakis, L., Tononi, G.: From the phenomenology to the mechanisms of consciousness: integrated information theory 3.0. PLoS Comput. Biol. **10**(5) (2014)
17. Tononi, G., Boly, M., Massimini, M., Koch, C.: Integrated information theory: from consciousness to its physical substrate. In: Nature Reviews Neuroscience, vol. 17, issue 7, pp. 450–461. Nature Publishing Group (2016). https://doi.org/10.1038/nrn.2016.44
18. Tononi, G.: An information integration theory of consciousness. BMC Neurosci. **5** (2004). https://doi.org/10.1186/1471-202-5-42
19. Damasio, A.R.: The Feeling of What Happens: Body and Emotion in the Making of Consciousness. Harcourt Brace, New York (1999)
20. Damasio, A., Meyer, K.: Consciousness: an overview of the phenomenon and of its possible neural basis 1. In: Laureys, S., Tononi, G. (eds.) The Neurology of Consciousness: Cognitive Neuroscience and Neuropathology. Academic Press (2008)
21. Damasio, A.R.: Self Comes to Mind: Constructing the Conscious Brain. Pantheon, New York (2010)
22. Massimini, M., Tononi, G.: Sizing Up Consciousness: Towards an Objective Measure of the Capacity for Experience. Oxford University Press, New York, NY (2018)
23. Fernandes, A., Tribolet, J.: Enterprise operating system: the enterprise (self) governing system. Proc. Comput. Sci. **164**, 149–158 (2019)
24. Beer, S.: The Hearth of Enterprise. Wiley, Chichester (1979)
25. Le Moigne, J.-L.: La Théorie du Systéme General- Théorie de la modélisation, 2nd edn. Presses Universitaires de France, Paris (1983)
26. Piaget, J.: Léquilibration des structures cognitives, problémes central du development. Presses Universitaires de France, Paris (1975)
27. Dietz, J.L.G., Mulder, H.B.F.: Enterprise Ontology: A Human-Centric Approach to Understanding the Essence of Organisation. Springer Nature Switzerland AG, Cham (2020). https://doi.org/10.1007/978-3-030-38854-6
28. Thom, R.: Structural Stability and Morphogenesis: Outline of a General Theory of Models. CRC Press, Taylor & Francis Group LLC. Kindle Edition (2018)

Digital Resilience to Normal Accidents in High-Reliability Organizations

Paolo Spagnoletti 🆔 and Stefano Za 🆔

Abstract Digital technologies play a dual role on organizational resilience. On one side, digital systems introduce new technological risks. On the other side, digital systems increase the performances in response to hazardous accidents. Normal Accident Theory (NAT) and High-Reliability Organization (HRO) provide useful ground to explain the dynamics of digital resilience. However, the two theories have been either used as alternatives or with one theory dominating the other. We posit that to fully understand digital resilience we need to integrate NAT and HRO concepts instead of using them in isolation. We conduct a bibliometric analysis to identify major themes and application domains characterizing HRO and NAT research. We look at similarities and differences between the two streams and we build an integrated framework for the analysis of digital resilience. With our systematic analysis of the NAT and HRO discourses we advance the current understanding on resilience in digitally enabled operations.

Keywords Digital resilience · Reliability · Accident · Crisis management · Complex socio-technical system

1 Introduction

The COVID19 pandemic has affected the operations of public and private companies at a global level [1]. The effects of the pandemic on organizational performances are contingent to the nature of operations and their level of digitalization. Purely

P. Spagnoletti (✉)
Luiss University, Rome, Italy

University of Agder, Kristiansand, Norway
e-mail: pspagnoletti@luiss.it

S. Za
G. D'Annunzio University, Pescara, Italy
e-mail: stefano.za@unich.it

© The Author(s), under exclusive license to Springer Nature Switzerland AG 2021
S. Aier et al. (eds.), *Engineering the Transformation of the Enterprise*,
https://doi.org/10.1007/978-3-030-84655-8_21

digital operations have demanded more bandwidth, devices and computational power and resulted in failures when such infrastructural resources where missing. Human-based operations have been switched into alternative modes of working to preserve the safety which resulted in low performances or even failures and breakdowns. Some organizations have also experienced positive outcomes by relying on a mix of digital and human-based operations for managing demand peaks of products and services.

In several industries, operations are increasingly supported by digital technologies with their automating and informating functionalities [2]. Digital technologies enable mindless automation by replacing human activities to reduce costs, improve efficiency and increase accuracy. Moreover, digital technologies enable mindful action by informating human decisions with explicit knowledge on the underlying processes and hence enhance improvement and learning in organizations [3]. Such combination of mindless algorithms and mindful human actions can have contrasting impacts on technological risk and resilience of digitally enabled operations.

On one hand, mindless automation may increase the unpredictability and unreliability of the technological system. Physical operations and work practices are controlled by a huge number of software components that are integrated with the underlying infrastructures made by shared data bases, supply chain's systems and work practices. In such complex socio-technical systems, small failures can potentially escalate into high-consequence events by propagating through tightly coupled organizational processes, practices and technological systems [4]. On the other hand, digital technologies may contribute to the achievement of digital resilience by supporting decision making, cooperation and coordination. Digital resilience refer to the design, deployment, and use of information systems to quickly recover from or adjust to major disruptions and exogenous shocks [5]. Information-sharing is a prerequisite for learning in high-reliability organizations and build feedback loops in crisis management and resilient operations [6].

Resilience is the generalized capacity to learn and act without knowing in advance the situation or event that needs to be acted upon. Two major theories have addressed the problem of resilience in complex socio-technical systems. Charles Perrow's Normal Accident Theory (NAT) focus on high-risk technologies. NAT posits that complex technological systems are never completely safe since they are characterized by tightly coupled components and interactive complexity. Risk is inherent to the existence of complex interactions in tightly coupled systems that make impossible to gain a complete and updated knowledge about operations in all circumstances. On the contrary, the theory of High Reliability Organization (HRO) posits that operations can be error-free when organizations develop a collective mindfulness capability defined as 'a pattern of heedful interrelations of actions in a social system' [7]. HROs such as air traffic control and healthcare systems are characterized by an active search for reliability through information processes, heedful action and mindful attention.

The NAT and HRO perspectives provide analytical frameworks for understanding accidents and to design controls for early detection and prevention [8]. In the renowned debate between NAT and HRO, the two theories have attracted either criticisms or support (e.g. [9]) but few attempts have been made to move beyond and integrate them into a comprehensive framework aimed at seeking digital resilience in complex socio-technical systems [10]. Therefore, given the role of digital technologies in the operational processes of high-reliability organizations, we argue that is time to revitalize the NAT and HRO debate to understand the phenomenon of digital resilience in digitally enabled HROs. In this paper we conduct a bibliometric analysis to identify major themes and application domains characterizing NAT and HRO research. We look at similarities and differences between the two streams and we build an integrated framework for the analysis of digital resilience. With our systematic analysis of the NAT and HRO discourses we advance the current understanding on resilience in digitally enabled operations.

2 Resilience in Digitally Enabled Operations

Resilience refers to the organizational ability to quickly respond to external threats, faster recover and safely operate under adverse conditions [6]. The resilience concept has been widely used in business and management research with fragmented and sometimes divergent views that put emphasis on various aspects such as organizational responses, reliability, adaptation and supply chain disruptions [11]. Theories on resilience and crisis management explain how organizations prepare for, respond to, and overcome various forms of crises [6]. However, far too little attention has been paid to the problem of resilience in digitally enabled operations.

We use the term digital resilience to refer to design, deployment, and use of information systems to recover from or adjust to major disruptions in complex organizations. Digital resilience is fueled by digital technologies that support organizational learning and coordination processes in crisis management operations. For instance, digital twins can simulate the behavior of complex systems and foster "intelligent failure" through large-scale experimentations [12]. Moreover, digital platforms support fragmented coordination in emergency and crisis management [13, 14] by fostering information sharing, collaboration and collective action [15].

Research on resilience suffers from its highly fragmented conceptualization. Resilience has been conceptualized and operationalized in different ways, meaning that the different research streams have developed their own definitions, theories and understandings of resilience [11]. Conceptual similarities and differences among these streams have seldom been explored resulting in the lack of generalizable principles for developing resilience in digitally enabled operations. Furthermore, resilience research has been highly context-dependent, and little is known about the transferability of insights across different contexts. Seminal works on resilience were focused on detecting and attributing the causes of large-scale accidents and disasters. NAT proposed that high-risk technological systems are vulnerable to failure because they are becoming increasingly complex and difficult for personnel to operate. On a different stance, HRO studies proposed a view of resilience focused on collective mindfulness, the capacity of organizational units to learn and act without knowing in advance the situation.

The reliability-seeking view on resilience prevailed over time and HRO became the dominant theory in the last two decades. Research on resilience in digitally enabled operations have addressed specific problems in different sectors such as healthcare [16], transport [17], energy [18], manufacturing [19] and the public sector [20]. In some cases the proposed solutions are cross industry such as in the case of cybersecurity operations [21, 22]. However, the two theories have been either used as alternatives or with one theory dominating the other. An explanation is that only few exceptions assume a dynamic relationship between risk and control in digital infrastructures. An exception is given by Baskerville, Spagnoletti, & Kim [23] who claim that organizations must balance the search for reliability (i.e. NAT) and validity (i.e. HRO) in their cybersecurity strategies. We attempt to generalize this finding to advance the understanding of digital resilience by integrating the NAT and HRO approaches instead of using them in isolation. We aim at building an integrated framework for the analysis of digital resilience. With our systematic analysis of the NAT and HRO discourses we advance the current understanding on resilience in digitally enabled operations.

3 Research Design

This paper adopts a bibliometric approach in order to explore the academic discourse concerning NAT and HRO [24]. Bibliometric analysis employs a quantitative approach for the description, evaluation and monitoring of published research [25]. This method has the potential to introduce a systematic, transparent and reproducible review process and thus improve the quality of reviews [26]. Bibliometric methods are a useful aid in literature reviews even before reading begins by guiding the researcher to the most influential works and mapping the research field without subjective bias [27]. Bibliometric methods have two main uses: performance analysis and science mapping [28]. The former investigates the research and publication performance of individuals and institutions. The latter seeks to discover the structures and dynamics of the scientific field under investigation [27].

We performed a co-word analysis in order to provide a complete picture of the current body of research, a precise and objective conceptual structure of the discipline, and help to discover key clusters [29].

Co-word analysis is based on the assumption that keywords represent a meaningful description of an article's content [30] and they can be used to understand the conceptual structure of the research field. Co-word analysis allows us to discover the main concepts treated by the field and it is a powerful technique for discovering and describing the interactions between different fields in scientific research [28]. This type of analysis involves the use of co-occurrence of a pair of items in a set of

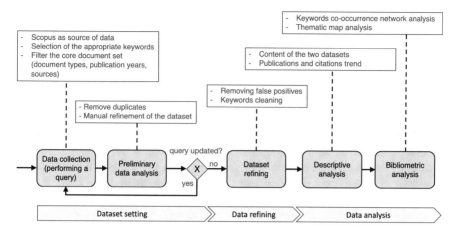

Fig. 1 The research protocol, adapted from [33]—© 2017 Springer International Publishing; reprinted with permission

articles. Focusing on the process of co-word analysis, the co-occurrences of two words in the same article is an indicator of how these two concepts are related to each other [31, 32]. The co-word analysis is the only method to use the actual content of documents to construct a similarity measure while others relate documents indirectly based on citations or co-authorships [27].

For bibliometric studies, the literature selection is a key aspect to ensure validity and consistency. To select the literature and analyze the results, we delineate a three-step procedure as shown in Fig. 1. First, we needed to select the database that contains bibliometric data and filter the core document set. Since we need to explore the discourse on NAT and HRO separately before to compare the results, we identify two different datasets composed by 64 and 450 papers respectively. For identifying the contributions for each dataset, we looked into abstract, title and authors' keywords the item "Normal Accident Theory" for the first dataset and "High-Reliability Organization*" OR "High-Reliability Organisation*" for the second one.

Once the datasets were identified the data refining phase was performed for each one, cleaning and standardizing the content of some fields in the corpus. We work mainly on the authors' keywords used by the authors in their contributions. We replaced all the authors' keywords indicating the same topic with a unique one (e.g. all the "NAT" alternatives were replaced with "Normal Accident Theory", as well as all the "HRO" occurrences with "High Reliability Organizations").

Once the dataset is refined, the next phase concerns the data analysis, composed by two steps:

- the analysis of descriptive performance indicators (descriptive analysis);
- the analysis of the conceptual structure of the dataset, exploring the main themes discussed in the corpus, through co-word analysis adopting SNA tools (bibliometric analysis).

The bibliometric analysis was carried out using R and the Bibliometrix package [34, 35].

4 Descriptive Analysis

The refined datasets include 64 (NAT) and 450 (HRO) contributions, last updated in late July 2020. In the next paragraphs, we provide a general overview of the whole dataset by summarizing the main information presented in Table 1. Afterwards, we briefly describe the trend of publications comparing the trend of the two datasets (see Fig. 2). Then, we report the most productive journals (Table 2).

Exploring the datasets, we observe that the publication year of the oldest paper in the HRO dataset is 1986 while papers in the NAT dataset start 10 years later, as shown in Fig. 2, notwithstanding the first edition of Charles Perrow's book was published in 1984. In both datasets, the majority of papers has been published in recent years, depicting an increasing interest of the scientific community in both topics. Based on the publication trends, more than 60% of the papers was published in the last decade for both datasets.

Table 2 shows the list of the most productive journals for both datasets. The journals with at least eight publications considering the sum of HRO and NAT papers are the following: *Safety science, Journal of contingencies and crisis management, Health services research*, and *Cognition technology and work*. Those journals publish both HRO and NAT papers. Looking at the scope of these journals, it is confirmed that the main fields in which HRO and NAT are discussed concern Safety, Crisis Management and Healthcare.

In order to explore more in depth, the key topics addressed in each corpus, we conduct a bibliometric analysis on the co-occurrences of authors' keywords. The resulting graphs and thematic maps are then compared to address the research question.

Table 1 Main information

	HRO dataset	NAT dataset
Timespan	1986:2020	1997:2020
Sources (Journals, Books, etc)	271	46
Documents	450	64
Average years from publication	8.45	8.88
Average citations per documents	35.08	36.44
Average citations per year per doc	2.65	3.711
Author's Keywords	802	111
Authors	1066	120
Authors of single-authored documents	112	21
Authors of multi-authored documents	954	99

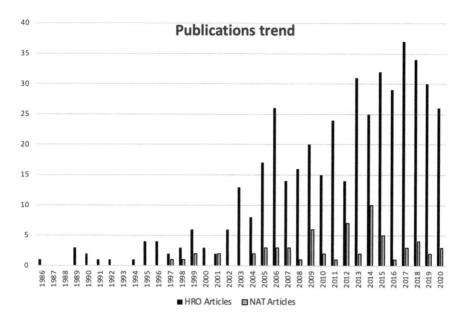

Fig. 2 Publication trends for both dataset

Table 2 Source of publications

Journals	HRO dataset	NAT dataset	Total
Safety science	26	7	33
Journal of contingencies and crisis management	16	7	23
Health services research	10	1	11
Cognition technology and work	7	1	8
Quality and safety in health care	7	0	7
Risk analysis	7	0	7
Journal of healthcare management	5	1	6
Management communication quarterly	6	0	6
Human relations	2	3	5
Journal of applied communication research	5	0	5
Journal of healthcare risk management	5	0	5
Journal of organizational change management	5	0	5
Academic emergency medicine	4	0	4
Joint commission journal on quality and patient safety	4	0	4
Journal of advanced nursing	4	0	4
Journal of business research	4	0	4
Journal of patient safety	4	0	4
Journal of safety research	4	0	4
Military medicine	4	0	4
Pediatric clinics of North America	4	0	4
Surgical clinics of North America	3	1	4

5   Bibliometric Analysis

The analysis of the keywords provides insights on the content and the main issues of HRO and NAT papers addressed by the authors of the 450 and 64 contributions respectively. The keywords analysis provides an overview of research trends, since keywords reflect the focus of individual articles. We identify the most popular keywords in use and create a graph based on their co-occurrences for each dataset (Figs. 3 and 4). In the network, nodes represent keywords and ties link keywords that are listed together in the same publication (co-occurrence); the thickness indicates the number of papers in which the pair appears.

Figure 3 shows the 49 most frequent keywords used in the HRO dataset, where "high reliability organizations" is the most frequent with 178 occurrences, followed by "healthcare" with more than 100 occurrences, and "safety", "culture" and "reliability" with more than 30 occurrences (62, 41 and 34 respectively). The size of each node (and its label) represents the number of occurrences of a keyword in the dataset (how many papers use it). Overall, analyzing the graph, it is possible to identify five clusters. The first cluster (in red) focuses on the main topic that is strongly linked with healthcare, safety and human-related keywords such as collective mindfulness, training, teams, human factor and communication. The second cluster (in green) includes the keyword Normal Accident Theory. The third cluster (in blue) includes only nuclear power. The fourth cluster (in purple on the right side of the graph) includes accidents and errors. Finally, the fifth cluster (in turquoise at the bottom of the graph) includes information systems and simulation.

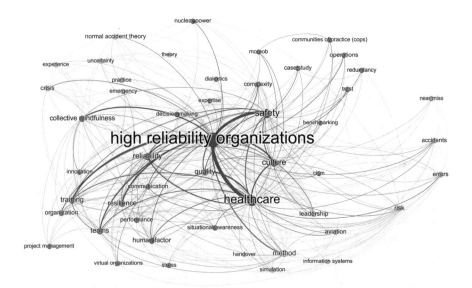

Fig. 3 Keywords co-occurrence graph of the HRO dataset

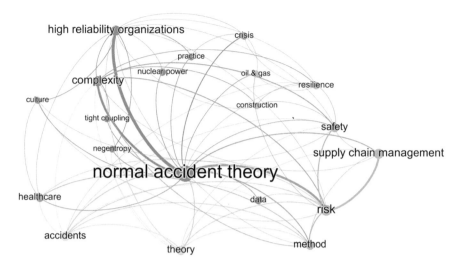

Fig. 4 Keywords co-occurrence graph of the NAT dataset

Figure 4 shows the 20 most occurred keywords in the NAT dataset, where "normal accident theory" is the most used component with 30 occurrences, followed by "risk" with more 13 occurrences, and "supply chain management", "complexity" and "high reliability organizations" each with more than 11 occurrences. Overall, analyzing the resulting graph, it is possible to recognize also in this case five main clusters. The first cluster (in purple) is focused on the main topic that is strongly linked with high reliability organizations and complexity. The second cluster (in green) includes the remaining most recurring keyworks, "supply chain management" and "risk". The third cluster (in yellow) includes accidents and theory. The fourth cluster (in turquoise) includes resilience. Finally, the fifth cluster (in orange) is related to healthcare (identified only by one keyword).

In order to further investigate the topics discussed in the dataset, we elaborate the thematic map, as suggested by [28]. The thematic map shows clusters (research themes) of keywords and their interconnections. The clusters are identified by an algorithm taking into consideration the keyword co-occurrence in the dataset. Once the clusters (a collection of keywords) are identified, two parameters are calculated. The "density" is based on the strength of internal ties among all keywords in the same cluster (recognizing the "theme's development"). The "centrality" identifies the strength of the external connections from a cluster to the others (the relevance of the research theme for the specific field of study).

The combination of high and low values for both parameters allows to define a diagram based on four quadrants, distributing the research themes in four groups [28], as shown in Figs. 5 and 6.

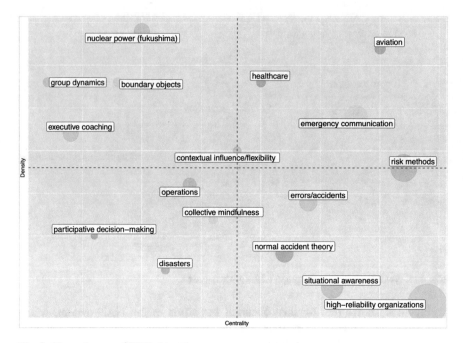

Fig. 5 Thematic map of HRO dataset

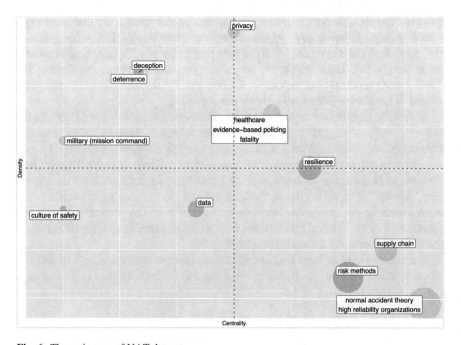

Fig. 6 Thematic map of NAT dataset

6 Discussion

The thematic maps of HRO and NAT studies, allow to compare the two theories and to identify differences and commonalities in their approaches and applications (Table 3).

The themes positioned in the high centrality—low density quadrant represent basic and transversal themes. The map shows that both HRO and NAT studies focus on methods to manage risk in complex settings. The two theories are seldom used in isolation, being NAT mentioned in HRO studies and vice-versa. Therefore, the two theories provide a common ground for scholars working on various aspects of risk in complex sociotechnical systems. While HRO studies focus on situational awareness and cognitive aspects, NAT studies concentrate more on structural aspects such as supply chain issues. These basic and transversal themes characterize the two datasets and show the general orientation of HRO and NAT on agency and structural aspects respectively. From a methodological perspective, the two streams offer an interesting application domain to simulation studies aimed at both predicting empirical observations for mitigating operational risk and theory building through the experimental study of emergent phenomena through experimental theory [36].

The low centrality—high density quadrant contains "motor-themes" that provide well established and relevant concepts for the theoretical development of an integrated framework of digital resilience. Motor-themes in HRO studies are related to flexibility and communication in emergency management situations. These studies investigate processes and capabilities to respond to adverse events by adapting to adverse contextual conditions. Flexible decision-making is needed to effectively manage available resources when unexpected events make difficult to oversee the situation. Flexibility requires agile coordination and communication among frontline operators to support situational understanding. The relation between flexibility

Table 3 Key concepts for building an integrated framework of digital resilience

	HRO	NAT
Basic and transversal themes	- Risk methods - HRO and NAT - Situational awareness	- Risk methods - HRO and NAT - Supply chain
Motor-themes	- Flexibility - Emergency communication - Healthcare and aviation - Contextual influence	- Resilience - Evidence-based policing - Healthcare - Fatality
Highly developed and isolated themes	- Group dynamics - Boundary objects - Executive coaching - Nuclear power (Fukushima)	- Deterrence - Deception - Privacy - Military (Mission command)
Emerging or declining themes	- Disasters - Collective mindfulness - Participative decision-making - Operations	- Culture of safety - Data

and communication in emergency management has been applied to the domains of healthcare and aviation, two contexts characterized by the need of situational awareness whenever unexpected events put at risk the safety of patients and passengers. In HRO studies contextual influences play a fundamental role in achieving flexibility through effective communication and are also externally related to themes positioned in other quadrants.

Motor-themes in NAT studies are related to resilience and evidence-based policing. While both NAT and HRO theories provide a rational for resilience [37], the NAT approach privileges the structural determinants of continuity and recovery. Resilience is concerned with how organizations anticipate and circumvent threats to their continued existence. Resilience is the outcome of a complex process involving both operational and decision-making responsibility, as well as the constitutional rules and policies that define appropriate actions [38]. The effectiveness of rules and policies can be improved through foresight, the ability to plan and think systematically about future scenarios. Our data reflect the interest of NAT studies in control mechanisms to mitigate risk. Evidence-based policing can improve the effectiveness of foresight through simulations and empirically tested models. Healthcare represents a central domain of interest also for NAT studies that are concerned with the safety of patients. In fact, fatalities are another major theme that is externally related also to safety in other domains such as military operations and construction. NAT studies focus on control mechanisms to mitigate the risk of fatalities in complex socio-technical systems.

The concepts reported in the low-centrality and high-density quadrant, represent themes that are highly developed but isolated themes with few external ties and so are still of only marginal importance for the field. In the HRO dataset, these themes are group dynamics, boundary objects and executive coaching. These themes confirm the focus on communication and cognitive aspects of HRO studies. In the NAT dataset, the focus on deterrence, privacy and deception confirms the emphasis of these studies on risk avoidance and prevention. Some concepts are also related to accidents in specific domains, such as nuclear power plants (e.g. Fukushima) for HRO studies and military operations in NAT. Interestingly, concepts belonging to the domain of military organizations (e.g. Mission command), which are normally considered HROs, are present as well developed but isolated themes in NAT studies [39].

Finally, in the low-centrality and low-density quadrant, we find both emerging and declining themes that are considered marginal and weakly established. Our data shows that, disasters, collective mindfulness, participative decision-making and operations are positioned in this quadrant. Given the focus on collective mindfulness in major disasters of the seminal works on HRO, the first two themes can be considered as declining. Instead, emerging themes are participative decision making in normal operations, possibly supported by digital technologies. The NAT studies in this quadrant refer to safety culture and data. The first theme can be considered declining since human factor has been traditionally considered as a cause of accidents in many NAT studies. Instead, the presence of data in this quadrant, confirms the interest on data-centered systems as an emerging theme in digital resilience [40, 41].

7 Conclusion

Digital resilience is an emerging concept that attract the interest of scholars and practitioners in technology management and engineering fields. In this study, we argue that digital resilience needs to be reconceptualized to take into account the duality of digital technologies in complex operations and crisis management. We challenge the way in which digital resilience has been conceived by identifying commonalities and divergences between NAT and HRO perspectives. An integration between the two theories is envisaged as a way to move beyond the limits of resilience theories in addressing the issues of digitalization. Our findings answer the following questions: which technical and managerial problems of digital resilience can be addressed with an integrated view of NAT and HRO? How can NAT and HRO advance the current understanding of digital resilience? Which architectural and governance model can promote digital resilience in modern organizations? How can industry specific methods be extended across industries to advance knowledge on digital resilience? Future works can address these questions to advance research on digital resilience and contribute to the practice of managing digitally enabled HRO.

Although supported by the background literature, the selected concepts represent only a first attempt to pave the road for a new wave of impactful studies on digital resilience. In particular, our understanding and interpretation of the declining and emerging themes must be carefully reviewed with an in-depth analysis of the most influential NAT and HRO contributions. Future studies can address this issue by further developing a conceptual framework of digital resilience that integrates the NAT and HRO perspective into a new theory of operational resilience.

References

1. Muzio, D., Doh, J.: COVID-19 and the future of management studies. Insights from leading scholars. J. Manag. Stud. (2021). https://doi.org/10.1111/joms.12689
2. Burton-Jones, A.: What have we learned from the Smart Machine? Inf. Organ. 24(2), 71–105 (2014). https://doi.org/10.1016/j.infoandorg.2014.03.001
3. Surendra, N.C., Nazir, S.: Creating "informating" systems using Agile development practices: an action research study. Eur. J. Inf. Syst. 28(5), 549–565 (2019). https://doi.org/10.1080/0960085X.2019.1620649
4. Hanseth, O., Ciborra, C.: Risk, Complexity and ICT. Edward Elgar, Cheltenham (2007)
5. Rai, A.: Editor's Comments: The COVID-19 pandemic: building resilience with IS research. MIS Q. 44(2), iii–vii (2021)
6. Williams, T.A., Gruber, D.A., Sutcliffe, K.M., Shepherd, D.A., Zhao, E.Y.: Organizational response to adversity: fusing crisis management and resilience research streams. Acad. Manag. Ann. 11(2), 733–769 (2017). https://doi.org/10.5465/annals.2015.0134
7. Weick, K.E., Roberts, K.H.: Collective mind in organizations: heedful interrelating on flight decks. Adm. Sci. Q. 38(3), 357–381 (1993)

8. Rijpma, J.A.: From deadlock to dead end: the normal accidents-high reliability debate revisited. J. Conting. Crisis Manag. **11**(1), 37–45 (2003). https://doi.org/10.1111/1468-5973. 1101007

9. Leveson, N., Dulac, N., Marais, K., Carroll, J.: Moving beyond normal accidents and high reliability organizations: a systems approach to safety in complex systems. Organ. Stud. **30** (2–3), 227–249 (2009). https://doi.org/10.1177/0170840608101478

10. Salovaara, A., Lyytinen, K., Penttinen, E.: High reliability in digital organizing: Mindlessness, the frame problem, and digital operations. MIS Q. Manag. Inf. Syst. **43**(2), 555–578 (2019). https://doi.org/10.25300/MISQ/2019/14577

11. Linnenluecke, M.K.: Resilience in business and management research: a review of influential publications and a research agenda. Int. J. Manag. Rev. **19**(1), 4–30 (2017). https://doi.org/10. 1111/ijmr.12076

12. Za, S., Spagnoletti, P., Winter, R., Mettler, T.: Exploring foundations for using simulations in IS research. Commun. Assoc. Inf. Syst. **42**(1), 268–300 (2018). https://doi.org/10.17705/1CAIS. 04210

13. Noori, N.S., Wolbers, J., Boersma, K., Cardona, X.V.: A dynamic perspective of emerging coordination clusters in crisis response networks. In: Proceedings of the International ISCRAM Conference (2016)

14. Wolbers, J., Boersma, K., Groenewegen, P.: Introducing a fragmentation perspective on coordination in crisis management. Organ. Stud. **39**(11), 1521–1546 (2018). https://doi.org/ 10.1177/0170840617717095

15. Spagnoletti, P., Resca, A., Lee, G.: A design theory for digital platforms supporting online communities: a multiple case study. J. Inf. Technol. (Palgrave Macmillan). **30**(4), 364–380 (2015). https://doi.org/10.1057/jit.2014.37

16. Rubbio, I., Bruccoleri, M., Pietrosi, A., Ragonese, B.: Digital health technology enhances resilient behaviour: evidence from the ward. Int. J. Oper. Prod. Manag. **39**(2), 260–293 (2019). https://doi.org/10.1108/IJOPM-02-2018-0057

17. Roth, E.M., Multer, J., Raslear, T.: Shared situation awareness as a contributor to high reliability performance in railroad operations. Organ. Stud. **27**(7), 967–987 (2006). https://doi.org/10. 1177/0170840606065705

18. O'Dwyer, E., Pan, I., Charlesworth, R., Butler, S., Shah, N.: Integration of an energy management tool and digital twin for coordination and control of multi-vector smart energy systems. Sustain. Cities Soc. **62**(July), 102412 (2020). https://doi.org/10.1016/j.scs.2020.102412

19. Scholz, R.W., Czichos, R., Parycek, P., Lampoltshammer, T.J.: Organizational vulnerability of digital threats: a first validation of an assessment method. Eur. J. Oper. Res. **282**(2), 627–643 (2020). https://doi.org/10.1016/j.ejor.2019.09.020

20. Zamora, D., Barahona, J.C., Palaco, I.: Case: Digital Governance Office. J. Bus. Res. **69**(10), 4484–4488 (2016). https://doi.org/10.1016/j.jbusres.2016.03.013

21. Gajek, S., Lees, M., Jansen, C.: IIoT and cyber-resilience: could blockchain have thwarted the Stuxnet attack? AI Society. (0123456789) (2020). https://doi.org/10.1007/s00146-020-01023-w

22. Parri, J., Patara, F., Sampietro, S., Vicario, E.: A framework for Model-Driven Engineering of resilient software-controlled systems. Computing. (2020). https://doi.org/10.1007/s00607-020-00841-6

23. Baskerville, R., Spagnoletti, P., Kim, J.: Incident-centered information security: managing a strategic balance between prevention and response. Inf. Manag. **51**(1) (2014). https://doi.org/10. 1016/j.im.2013.11.004

24. Castriotta, M., Loi, M., Marku, E., Naitana, L.: What's in a name? Exploring the conceptual structure of emerging organizations. Scientometrics. (2019). https://doi.org/10.1007/s11192-018-2977-2

25. Scornavacca, E., Paolone, F., Za, S., Martiniello, L.: Investigating the entrepreneurial perspective in smart city studies. Int. Entrepreneur. Manag. J. (2020). https://doi.org/10.1007/s11365-019-00630-4

26. Cram, W.A., Templier, M., Paré, G.: (Re)considering the concept of literature review reproducibility. J. Assoc. Inf. Syst. **21**(5), 1103–1114 (2020). https://doi.org/10.17705/1jais. 00630
27. Zupic, I., Čater, T.: Bibliometric methods in management and organization. Organ. Res. Methods. **18**(3), 429–472 (2015). https://doi.org/10.1177/1094428114562629
28. Cobo, M.J., López-Herrera, A.G., Herrera-Viedma, E., Herrera, F.: An approach for detecting, quantifying, and visualizing the evolution of a research field: a practical application to the Fuzzy Sets Theory field. J. Inform. **5**(1), 146–166 (2011). https://doi.org/10.1016/j.joi.2010.10.002
29. Za, S., Pallud, J., Agrifoglio, R., Metallo, C.: Value co-creation in online communities: a preliminary literature analysis. In: Exploring Digital Ecosystems, LNISO, vol. 33, pp. 33–46. (2020). https://doi.org/10.1007/978-3-030-23665-6_4
30. Callon, M., Courtial, J.-P., Turner, W.A., Bauin, S.: From translations to problematic networks: an introduction to co-word analysis. Soc. Sci. Inf. **22**(2), 191–235 (1983). https://doi.org/10. 1177/053901883022002003
31. Cambrosio, A., Limoges, C., Courtial, J.P., Laville, F.: Historical scientometrics? Mapping over 70 years of biological safety research with coword analysis. Scientometrics. **27**(2), 119–143 (1993). https://doi.org/10.1007/BF02016546
32. Lamboglia, R., Lavorato, D., Scornavacca, E., Za, S.: Exploring the relationship between audit and technology. A bibliometric analysis. Meditari Account. Res. (2020). https://doi.org/10. 1108/MEDAR-03-2020-0836
33. Za, S., Braccini, A.M.: Tracing the roots of the organizational benefits of IT services. In: Za, S., Drăgoicea, M., Cavallari M. (eds.) LNBIP – Exploring Services Science, pp. 3–11. (2017). https://doi.org/10.1007/978-3-319-56925-3_1
34. Aria, M., Cuccurullo, C.: Bibliometrix: an R-tool for comprehensive science mapping analysis. J. Inform. **11**(4), 959–975 (2017). https://doi.org/10.1016/j.joi.2017.08.007
35. Cuccurullo, C., Aria, M., Sarto, F.: Foundations and trends in performance management. A twenty-five years bibliometric analysis in business and public administration domains. Scientometrics. **108**(2), 595–611 (2016). https://doi.org/10.1007/s11192-016-1948-8
36. Beese, J., Haki, M.K., Aier, S., Winter, R.: Simulation-based research in information systems: epistemic implications and a review of the status quo. Bus. Inf. Syst. Eng. **61**(4), 503–521 (2019). https://doi.org/10.1007/s12599-018-0529-1
37. Heeks, R., Ospina, A.V.: Conceptualising the link between information systems and resilience: a developing country field study. Inf. Syst. J. **29**(1), 70–96 (2019). https://doi.org/10.1111/isj. 12177
38. Constantinides, P.: The failure of foresight in crisis management: a secondary analysis of the mari disaster. Technol. Forecast. Soc. Chang. **80**(9), 1657–1673 (2013). https://doi.org/10. 1016/j.techfore.2012.10.017
39. Fraher, A.L., Branicki, L.J., Grint, K.: Mindfulness in action: discovering how U.S. Navy seals build capacity for mindfulness in high-reliability organizations (HROs). Acad. Manag. Discov. **3**(3), 239–261 (2017). https://doi.org/10.5465/amd.2014.0146
40. Spagnoletti, P., Salvi, A.: Digital systems in High-Reliability Organizations: balancing mindfulness and mindlessness. In: Proceedings of the 6th International Workshop on Socio-Technical Perspective in IS Development (STPIS 2020), June 8–9, 2020. CEUR Workshop Proceedings (CEUR-WS.org) (2020)
41. Spagnoletti, P., Salvi, A.: Digitalization in mission command and control: fragmenting coordination in military operations. In: Lucarelli, S., Marrone, A., Moro, F.N. (eds.) NATO Decision-Making in the Age of Big Data and Artificial Intelligence, pp. 28–37. (2021)

Mind the Gap: Why There Is a Gap Between Information Systems Research and Practice, and How to Manage It

Ralf Abraham, Stefan Bischoff, Johannes Epple, Nils Labusch, and Simon Weiss

Abstract In this paper, we investigate the gap between information systems (IS) research and IS practice; why it exists and how it can be managed. In a qualitative study, we interview experts from both sides of the gap: IS researchers and IS practitioners. We identify different incentive systems, abstraction levels, and time frames as the main factors for the gap between IS research and practice. First, accepting and actually embracing the differences between research and practice is crucial. Building on mutual acceptance and shared understanding, we then draw on the notion of "boundary spanners" as a potential way to manage the IS research/ practice gap via human agents that are considered legitimate and knowledgeable in both worlds. Eventually, we provide a set of specific recommendations for both IS research and IS practice to facilitate collaboration and improve mutual understanding, and some avenues for further research.

Keywords IS research · IS practice · Knowledge boundary · Shared understanding · Boundary spanner

1 Introduction

In order to create value, information systems (IS) research results need to be applied in practice [1]. IS researchers have studied the transfer from rigor to relevance from various theoretical perspectives [2–5]. "As an applied field, IS should improve the practice of information systems" [6]. From a practitioner's perspective, the transfer from scholarly results into real-world application is still limited and often does not create impact and real value. Having spent our PhD life in the IS research world and being in practice for several years now, we observe that the vast majority of IS managers do not consider IS research as a source for action but much more often

R. Abraham · S. Bischoff (✉) · J. Epple · N. Labusch · S. Weiss
HSG Alumni, University of St. Gallen, St. Gallen, Switzerland
e-mail: ralf.abraham@hsgalumni.ch; stefan.bischoff@hsgalumni.ch;
johannes.epple@hsgalumni.ch; nils.labusch@hsgalumni.ch; simon.weiss@hsgalumni.ch

© The Author(s), under exclusive license to Springer Nature Switzerland AG 2021
S. Aier et al. (eds.), *Engineering the Transformation of the Enterprise*,
https://doi.org/10.1007/978-3-030-84655-8_22

glossy magazines written by consultants or other practitioners. Therefore, the real-world application, which is a prerequisite for value creation [1] and actual relevance of the research, is not accomplished.

From a practical perspective, it is essential that the artifacts delivered by IS research are not only fancy constructs from a theoretical perspective but deliver immediate impact that is measurable. Practitioners hardly have the budget and time for longitudinal studies or complex translation of scientific results into understandable terminology. Additionally, in practice there is typically no room for a "trial and error" working approach and it is often not acceptable to implement a totally new artifact using the design, implement, evaluate and iterate approach. Managers need to deliver value in short cycles and need to rely on practically established methods and solutions that can be applied out of the box.

Knowing both worlds—science and practice—and also recognizing the virtues of IS research, it seems that IS research is not always able to transport its qualities to practice and unfold its qualities to full potential. Furthermore, practitioners often do not know what to expect from science and confuse relevant scientific work with consulting input. The reason for this confusion is that they are oftentimes not used to scientific work and its value proposition. They either do not have enough time or experience to search, obtain, interpret and adopt scientific results towards their real-world problems.

The academic world strives for high-ranked publications and the reputations of researchers is being built upon them. Tenure-track and chair candidates are evaluated based on research quality (publication ranking) and not the practical value of their research results. Furthermore, researchers do not get paid according to the relevance of their research results. Consequently, researchers first fulfill the academic requirements of A(+)-level publications and consider real practical applicability only as a side-effect. PhD students, for example, need to deliver research contributions of high rigor in a limited amount of time, a true application in practice comes second, and they lack practical experience because most of them come fresh from universities. Currently, researchers have to deal with conflicting goals between rigor and relevance.

For bridging the gap between rigorous scientific work and practical application, i.e. utility or value creation [1], both disciplines need to work together more closely and understand each other. Therefore, we aim at contributing insights from both worlds that help practice and science to benefit from each other. Consequently, we ask the following research question:

What are challenges and success factors for bridging the gap between IS practice and IS research?

2 Conceptual Foundations

Following the aforementioned aspiration of practical relevance, this paper is conceptionally based on design science research. In contrast to the behavioral science which intends to explain or predict human or organizational behavior, design science seeks to create new artifacts with practical utility [4]. As such, the parameters, needs and concerns of the environment, i.e. the real-life business application domains, are of particular interest. This interchange between design science research and it's practical applicability is commonly referred to as "relevance cycle" as in Hevner's [7] three cycle view of design science research.

Improving the relevance cycle requires input from both practitioners and researchers. Bringing both perspectives together allows to increase mutual understanding, acknowledgement of respective objectives, concerns and value propositions and to eventually increase the utility provided to each other. Former research studied this topic in various flavors. Otto and Österle [8, 9], for example, investigated the approach of Consortium Research to arrive at more relevant design science artifacts. They propose a research method that facilitates knowledge transfer and multilateral collaboration of researchers and practitioners [10]. Of course, further approaches exist to facilitate a fruitful exchange between multiple interest groups in general, and research and practice in particular. Respective approaches include conferences (e.g., [11]), co-creation approaches such as living labs [12] and the concept of boundary spanners between communities of practice [13].

In this work, we contribute to a mediation between both worlds by throwing a spotlight on researchers' and practitioners' opinions through an interviewing approach as outlined in the following.

3 Research Method

The objective of this research is not only to understand why there is a gap between IS research and IS practice, but also to make a contribution towards reducing this gap. As indicated in the previous chapter, we are not primarily concerned with understanding a phenomenon as in behavioral research, but rather with constructing artifacts that will eventually influence the phenomenon towards a desired state as in design science research (e.g. [3, 4, 14, 15]).

We therefore choose a pragmatic epistemological approach, which is considered well-suited for constructing knowledge that can be practically applied in a useful fashion [16, 17]. At the center of this approach is the repeated, mutual exchange between actions and interventions: actions are purposefully employed to influence selected aspects of reality [18].

We opt for a qualitative research design since we want to gather a deep understanding of the problem domain [19]. In this research, we primarily aim at developing an understanding why there is a gap between IS research and IS practice, not at testing some already existing hypotheses. We therefore use a theoretical sampling approach, i.e., we purposefully select a number of experts to illuminate the phenomenon under investigation from multiple and diverse perspectives [20].

In total, we interviewed eight experts. We approached (1) academics as in the literal sense of the word: those currently working in academia (i.e., professors) and (2) practitioners (i.e., employees of private sector organizations). The distribution in our sample was three researchers and five practitioners. A great number of our interview partners graduated from Prof. Winter's chair at the University of St. Gallen. To keep the focus on the IS domain, we selected experts occupying IS-related positions such as enterprise architects who are distributed across industries such as software providers, healthcare providers, construction, or technology consulting. The organizations are roughly evenly distributed between Germany and Switzerland. We conducted semi-structured interviews via telephone. This type of interview allows to focus on the main problem while at the same time remaining open for new and unexpected ideas [21, 22]. Interviews were conducted one-on-one between an author and an expert. Each interview took around 60 min, with the option of exceeding this timeframe if circumstances proved favorable.

We first asked for some statistical information in order to understand the participants' biography and background. To investigate the research topic itself, we asked open-ended questions. We wrapped up each interview with a completely open-ended, final question, thus permitting the interviewees to contribute additional themes to the results [23].

Data collection stopped when theoretical saturation had been reached [23], i.e., after we did not gain any additional insight from further inquiry.

In a first step, we analyzed our data using open, axial and selective coding techniques [24]. The main statements and themes were then consolidated and grouped in a process of reflection and abstraction, with the purpose of investigating how certain material properties lead to a specific outcome in a given setting [25].

4 Results

4.1 The Researchers' Perspective

Taking the perspective of the group of researchers (Ri), different topics can be experienced in practice. Our interview partners especially considered topics around privacy and trust, IT project management and maturity models, technology acceptance (R1), enterprise architecture, digital platforms, and digital nudging (R3) as relevant in practice. Such research is oftentimes driven by cooperation with practice. R1, for example, received calls from companies around the world that asked for advice in the design of maturity models. Since we are predominantly interested in understanding the current gap between research and practice, we asked for *challenges* from the scientist's point of view. The most important ones seem to be abstraction, communication and different speeds.

For starters, R1 highlighted that "Science should solve generic problems; you could even quote Robert on this". Thus, while research searches for patterns and solutions on a certain level of abstraction, particular solutions in practice require specific adaption of scientific findings. According to R1, this is the key challenge, and many practitioners are either not able or not willing to abstract their particular problem at hand in order to leverage scientific findings on a more generic level.

All researchers see the way they communicate results of research as very critical when it comes to challenges concerning the gap between research and practice. Communication can be differentiated in "where" and "how". R1 and R2 are both convinced that no practitioner "will ever read" (R2) high-ranked IS journals such as ISR or MISQ. In regard to terminology, the different language of both worlds is seen as a challenge by R3. Further, he also stressed semantic differences when applying existing terminologies. Researchers are typically cautious prior to using certain terms. In contrast, practice uses the same terms in a common sense and "without thinking about how the terms are defined in the scientific world" (R3).

The necessity of speed concerning the presentation of results is seen as a third major challenge. The speed of and urgency for change in practice, especially in IT, is seen as tremendous by R3. Keeping up with the speed of change while, at the same time, selecting the right research topics is key to success in the eyes of R3. Long review cycles of—sometimes—several years in top journals, would absolutely not fit to the speed of change in the world of corporate practice. In order to not get outpaced by practice, research would need to stay close to practice and up to date with what is going on outside of their "ivory tower". However, the difficulty for researchers when they are close to practice is not to jump on every ephemeral hype topic in order to be fashionable. This dilemma of long-term orientation in research versus short-term perspectives in practice is seen as the biggest challenge to be tackled to bridge the gap between the two worlds.

The group of researchers also brings up some *success factors* for bridging the gap between research and practice—some refer to their own behavior, some to the behavior of corporate practice.

Concerning the problem of abstraction, R1 wishes more openness from practitioners even if the relation between problem and solution is not clear right from the beginning. Further, R1 asks practice for fair expectations and increased abstraction: "one cannot solve the problems of the last 10 years with one external researcher", but also "researchers should communicate in a pragmatic manner; practitioners should start thinking more abstract". In a similar vein, R2 confirms this by highlighting that short-term, consulting-like engagements between research and practice would be "worthless". Both sides can get to know each other, discover what the values of the other party are, how the goal system looks like, which specific skill all participants have. Researchers might also realize that there is quite some publication potential of longitudinal case studies.

R2 experiences that another critical success factor for bridging the gap between science and practice is to thoroughly understand both target systems and motivations in order to adapt the project setup accordingly. For practitioners, it is crucial to understand that practical impact is not part of the academic target systems and neither delivers citations nor high quality journal papers. Researchers also need to understand the practitioner's goal system, which usually is more short-term result-oriented, and specific (one time) problems need to be solved accordingly.

When it comes to communication, R1 experienced that a simple message that everyone catches, a specific use case to catch publicity and finally different output formats apart from MISQ-papers (e.g., hackathons, TV, Twitter) help a lot to get noticed and be useful for corporate practice. R1 experienced that "today an image that everyone can share has more impact than a long paper". R2 also suggests that researchers should include practitioner outlets in their publication strategy. Journals like HMD, MISQE, HBR, MIT Sloan Management Review, and California Management Review are more likely to be read by practitioners because authors speak their language, and the papers focus on topics that help practitioners to make decisions or introduce best practices. R3 shares the position and encourages research to "not being more catholic than the Pope". According to R3, if research obtains interesting results, they should (also) be shared as soon as possible and not undergo multi-year and complex review cycles.

Communication could also be fostered by switching careers between research and practice. From R1's perspective, it is very positive that in IS research many people know both worlds, which is not the case in many other disciplines. However, R1 criticizes that some professors have never been working in a private company and are just running after papers, which may hinder practice-oriented translation. R3 directs the appeal to practitioners to come back to research from time to time to spend support. Further, practice should not be too picky about spending money for research—even if they do not have an immediate benefit for themselves.

4.2 The Practitioners' Perspective

The group of practitioners (Pi) that we conducted interviews with is experienced in working with research institutions and consultancies. Topics the practitioners experienced in their working lives cover a wide range of the IS discipline, including business process management (and related concepts, e.g., Lean Management, Kaizen, Kanban, iterative process prototyping, etc.), project management models, and statistical methods (e.g. for simulations, machine learning algorithms, nearest neighbor, etc.) (P2, P4), maturity models, theory based KPI model, business intelligence (P3), architectures of analytical information systems, and agile as well as classical project management concepts (P4), software development, solution architecting and enterprise architecture (P5).

We discussed *challenges* concerning the gap between research and practice. The first challenge is related to abstraction and adaptability. Companies need people who are able to understand, transfer and convince other people in the own company that abstract approaches are transferable (P1). Thus, according to P3, in order to be able to transfer generic inputs into their context, companies and managers need to be intellectually mature. Close context with research and a profound academic education of important stakeholders is required. Otherwise, academic work is hardly understood or cannot be applied to practitioners' specific problems.

Relevance is another challenge that the practitioners identify. IS research results and research questions are relevant for practice and in particular add overall economic value and use for practice (P1, P2). IS research results are considered a source of inspiration and orientation for practice, but finding the relevant results in the "heaps and heaps of irrelevant research" appears to be difficult (P2, P5). According to P5, the gap arises from different thematic orientations: Cutting-edge research in academia vs. good-practice proven solutions in practice. For this reason, the interviewees generally prefer to read practitioner-oriented publications instead of highly ranked scientific journals.

Joint projects—oftentimes considered a good way of cooperation between research and practice—induce challenges of their own. Our interviews show that practitioners had bad experiences for different reasons. First, many researchers were lacking relevant practical experience, industry experience, knowledge about specific processes or trends in the industry (P2). Second, upskilling unexperienced researchers is very tedious for a busy practitioner (P2). Third, researchers follow their own agenda (e.g., their next publication or PhD thesis) rather than providing applicable results for practice—practice seems to be a kind of playground for researchers. Fourth, the limited time of researchers—which is constrained by their own agenda—may be detrimental to the success of the projects. P4 experienced that in contrast to researchers, consultants are interested in delivering results and have a higher work standard and better work attitude. P3 also experienced that universities try to compete with consulting companies, which according to P3 is not a good idea. Science needs to differentiate itself and built up a USP for delivering practical value. P3 uses consultants for short term projects that urgently need to deliver results. In P3's point of view, consultants are capable of motivating mangers, have charisma and engage people. However, when working with researchers, P1 feels positive that they are less driven by the idea of selling a long-term consulting contract. If the flight-level of abstraction fits, working with researchers from his point of view is more fruitful since "you less get the feeling of having to buy a washing machine in addition".

This being said, P5 questions whether immediate application of IS research results in practice is actually a problem given that nowadays sufficient software producers, start-ups, consultancies and mainstream-providers offer high-end solutions that would completely overexert the very most organizations. According to P5, this was very different 30 years ago where practice-oriented research was at the forefront of building innovative IT solutions.

The group of practitioners also stated some *success factors* concerning the cooperation with researchers.

First, communication and especially the presentation of results is very important. Less quantitative and more qualitative research would make research results more applicable in practice (P2). The communication style needs to be adapted to the target group. According to P3, managers and important stakeholders follow certain intrinsic motivational factors (e.g., influence, power, connections,). These need to be taken into account by researchers whenever they deal with practitioners and want to communicate their results. Additionally, this perspective should be included in theoretical models. Further, researchers should keep in mind that even the best idea is only considered in practice if it is presented by the right people (accepted experts) at the right time. You need to get charisma and be able to engage people; dry presentations of research results are not valued in practice. Even worse, oftentimes trivial and well-known knowledge is packed into complex forms to impress other researchers (P4). Thus, P4 recommends taking practical relevance (i.e., practical impact) into consideration in the evaluation and ranking of research results.

Some of the practitioners gained the feeling that practice is seen as a playing field by researchers. Thus, they call for more devotion to the project and more experience from a researcher they would work with in future (P2). P4 reminds of the economic value that all practice activities need to deliver. Otherwise, P2 states, practice would rather prefer to hire experienced consultants.

However, if the right mode of working is identified and mutual expectations are clarified, discussions with researchers are considered fruitful "because it helps to look beyond one's own nose" (P1). Living in two completely different worlds, having different mindsets, and different quality criteria is the biggest threat to the success of a joint project, said P1. To overcome this challenge, P4 and P5 recommend to have a clear alignment of expectations and be honest from the beginning of a collaboration. For the very start, this includes clear stakeholder-awareness and who you do a project for: An in-house IT looking for proven practices and support, or a software provider interested in integrating latest findings and ideas from young researchers? Further, the presentation of results should be clear, and a focus on the discussion of implications and consequences instead of intellectual „smart ass" discussions. P3 states that "universities should never try to compete with consultants, but to deliver different values". According to P5, such a value (or utility) could be method contributions or method education—especially in the areas of managing people and processes, given the technology itself is rarely the problem. Further, academia can provide well-educated graduates to facilitate innovation inflow and fresh thinking.

With respect to scientific work, P3 appreciates it whenever he needs a long-term view and an objective perspective or insight into the latest trends that have not been used in practice before (i.e. there is no best practice view from a consulting company available). In contrast, P5 is most interested in experience report, i.e., in concrete experiences of what worked well and what did not. To that end, research could indeed contribute—be it with short- or long-term case work.

Concerning collaboration, P3 characterizes a suitable setup as follows: Practitioners should enable and allow scientists to think forward and be open to revolutionary ideas. Researchers need to be able to translate their results and ideas into the language of practitioners and be able to derive the specific meaning for an individual company's context. For P3, generic results are worthless. Joint projects need to have regular adjustment stops. In addition, the right people need to be selected for a joint project because "only the right people deliver good work" (P3).

In general, it is considered important to ensure that the gap between research and practice does not become too large (P1). It is a good approach to have joint groups that work together on specific topics. Exchanging positions is important, in the best case across universities and enterprises. P2 pointed out that the research topics as well as the results shall have a certain maturity and not just deal with current hype topics.

5   Discussion

Summarizing the results above, we can identify success factors and challenges in the cooperation of research and practice. Figure 1 illustrates these findings.

During the interviews, we repeatedly stumbled upon fundamental differences between the worlds of IS research and IS practice. The core differences that we identified are the underlying incentive systems, levels of abstraction, and time frames.

Regarding the incentive systems, IS researchers are nowadays rewarded for publications in highly ranked outlets. These outlets tend to value scientific rigour over practical relevance. IS practitioners, on the other hand, are rewarded for achievements typically found in project management contexts in large organizations, such as finishing a project on time, on budget, and achieving a predefined quality metric. Luckily and important to note though, is that design science research and certain research groups in particular showcase nicely that practice-oriented research with clear practical implications is possible—also as part of top IS journals (c.f. [26, 27]).

Regarding the level of abstraction, IS research is interested in patterns, i.e. generic solutions that are applicable to a group of comparable problems, whereas IS practice is interested in instances, a specific solution to the concrete project or problem at hand [28].

Regarding the time frames, IS researchers' primary concern is long-term scientific progress, with the predominant metric being publications in highly-ranked journals [29, 30]. Notably, rigorous research does consume a lot of time. In addition, the publication process, particularly in journals, often takes several years to advance from a submitted manuscript through the peer-review process to eventual publication. IS practitioners, on the other hand, are more often than not under considerable time pressure in their respective organizations, with time-critical projects being the norm rather than the exception. A circumstance that is in no way exclusive to IS projects, with practitioners rightfully pointing out that there is no long run without a short run.

These differences may look daunting or even irreconcilable at the first glance. The most important requirement for a successful and mutually beneficial collaboration between IS research and IS practice is therefore understanding, accepting, and ideally embracing these differences—from both sides, that is. Imagine if IS research and IS practice were identical. Then there would be no point in collaboration, since

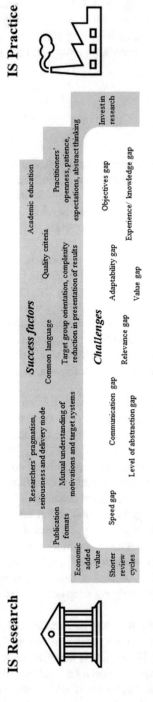

Fig. 1 Summary of challenges and success factors to bridge the IS research and practice gap

the two domains would be indistinguishable. However, cooperation and innovation are fostered by differences, and a diverse environment is a fertile ground for an exchange of ideas, methods and patterns and ultimately beneficial for project success.

The key to not letting the differences between IS research and IS practice become insurmountable is to develop some form of shared understanding. To achieve this, both sides should know about and understand the other's incentive systems, motivation, and strengths and weaknesses. In a highly cited paper on IS strategic alignment, Preston and Karahanna [31] identify shared domain knowledge as a highly significant factor contributing to a shared understanding. Shared domain knowledge, in their setting, is defined as the CIO's knowledge of business and the top managers' knowledge of IS. Transferring these findings to the communities of IS researchers and practitioners, we can expect mutual knowledge about the other's domain to increase shared understanding and thereby the chances for a successful collaboration.

The different incentive systems lead to different interests and hence to a 'pragmatic knowledge boundary' [32] between IS researchers and IS practitioners. In addition to different terminology (syntactic knowledge boundary), unclear dependencies and different interpretations of concepts (semantic knowledge boundary), a pragmatic or political knowledge boundary may also cause actors to adamantly stick to their own world views for fear of losing knowledge or paying too high a price for adaptation (path dependency).

To overcome a pragmatic knowledge boundary, a combination of 'boundary objects' and 'boundary spanners' can be used [13]. Boundary objects can take a variety of forms, from sketches over models to physical prototypes. They are malleable enough to be jointly understood and edited by both parties, thus helping to uncover and resolve differences. Boundary spanners are human actors, who are either nominated to empower collaboration between two different communities, and/or who collaborate in practice themselves [33]. Boundary spanners should have knowledge of both domains, as well as some form of legitimacy [33]. They should be respected by both parties and trusted to negotiate and represent each side's interests in a fair and sustainable way.

In the case of spanning a pragmatic knowledge boundary between IS research and IS practice, these criteria may fit former PhD students from IS programmes, i.e., those who (like the majority in IS programmes) have left the academic world after receiving their PhD and have then joined corporate practice. They have demonstrated their ability to work scientifically (which is, after all, the definition of a PhD), while at the same time, they are employed in a practitioner's organization and can thus be regarded a legitimate representative of that domain. Obviously, factors like personal abilities and individual motivation play a decisive role in whether someone is accepted and successful as a boundary spanner or not. Having completed a PhD does not automatically qualify someone to succeed in such an assignment, just like not having a PhD does not lead to automatic disqualification as boundary spanner. Still, the group of former IS (PhD) students is a promising pool from which to draw potential boundary spanners.

Eventually, we arrive at the following recommendations for those involved in a joint IS research/practice project to maximize the odds of success.

1. Understand and embrace the differences between IS research and IS practice before entering a closer collaboration. Communicate expectations clearly and at the beginning. Pose the right questions to the right collaboration partner.
2. Prefer long-term collaboration over short-term engagements, but with clear milestones and intermediate goals to accommodate both sides' timeframes.
3. Put people with knowledge about the other side on the project team, so they can act as boundary spanners and knowledge amplifiers. On the practitioner side, former PhD student may be well suited for this task (contingent on individual abilities and project setting).
4. Manage expectations regularly during the project and re-adjust quality criteria and deliverables when needed. Bear in mind that research is particularly strong when it comes to 'conceptual relevance', i.e., coining names for new phenomena ('linguistic constructs'), methodological inputs and uncovering dependencies between abstract concepts [34].
5. Have fun! Enjoy the joint projects, and value the opportunity to observe things outside the scope of your own peer group. Embrace fresh and alternative perspectives. For researchers, observe how your assumptions and theories work out in practice and experience the day-to-day problems of operations. For practitioners, discover patterns from other contexts that apply to your setting as well, and engage in new (and hopefully unconventional) ways of thinking.

6   Conclusion

In this paper, we have analyzed the gap between IS research and IS practice, the reasons for its existence and how this gap can be handled or bridged. From a series of expert interviews with both IS researchers and IS practitioners, we have learned that different incentive systems, a focus on generic solutions for problem classes vs. specific solutions for problem instances, and different time frames are the major contributing factors to the IS research/practice gap.

Our contribution is an explanation on why this gap exists and why it should be managed (bridged) rather than levelled (closed). We then draw on the concepts of knowledge boundaries and boundary spanners to propose former PhD students from IS programs as potential boundary spanners.

No research is free of limitations, and this paper is no different. Our sample included a limited number of experts from academia and practice and none of them is currently engaged in a boundary spanning function. Further, we only probed into their experiences in a general fashion, but not for one specific (and joint!) project in depth.

Further research should investigate which qualities and contingency factors, apart from personal abilities, enable boundary spanning between IS research and IS practice. Regarding research designs, a longitudinal study of IS research/practice collaboration might be particularly insightful.

On a more practical note, we provide a set of actionable recommendations to participants in IS research and practice collaborations to make joint engagements or projects more successful (and hopefully more fun, too).

Acknowledgement We like to thank all interviewees for their valuable input. The authors and the interviewees like to send their best wishes and a happy birthday to Robert Winter.

References

1. Benbasat, I., Zmud, R.W.: The identity crisis within the IS discipline: defining and communi-cating the discipline's core properties. MIS Q. **27**, 183–194 (2003) https://doi.org/Article
2. Aier, S., Fischer, C.: Criteria of progress for information systems design theories. Inf. Syst. E-Bus. Manag. **9**, 133–172 (2011)
3. Gregor, S., Hevner, A.R.: Positioning and presenting design science research for maximum impact. MIS Q. **37**, 337–355 (2013). https://doi.org/10.25300/MISQ/2013/37.2.01
4. Hevner, A.R., March, S.T., Park, J., Ram, S.: Design science in information systems research. MIS Q. **28**, 75–105 (2004). https://doi.org/10.2307/25148625
5. Peffers, K., Tuunanen, T., Rothenberger, M.A., Chatterjee, S.: A design science research methodology for information systems research. J. Manag. Inf. Syst. **24**, 45–77 (2007). https://doi.org/10.2753/MIS0742-1222240302
6. Te'Eni, D., Seidel, S., Vom Brocke, J.: Stimulating dialog between information systems research and practice. (2017). https://doi.org/10.1057/s41303-017-0067-9
7. Hevner, A.R.: A three cycle view of design science research. Scand. J. Inf. Syst. **19**, 87–92 (2007) http://aisel.aisnet.org/sjis/vol19/iss2/4
8. Otto, B., Österle, H.: Relevance through consortium research? A case study. In: 18th European Conference on Information Systems, ECIS 2010 (2010)
9. Otto, B., Österle, H.: Relevance through consortium research? Findings from an expert inter-view study. In: Lecture Notes in Computer Science (including subseries Lecture Notes in Artificial Intelligence and Lecture Notes in Bioinformatics), pp. 16–30 (2010). https://doi.org/10.1007/978-3-642-13335-0_2
10. Österle, H., Otto, B.: Konsortialforschung: Eine Methode für die Zusammenarbeit von Forschung und Praxis in der gestaltungsorientierten Wirtschaftsinformatikforschung. Bus. Inf. Syst. Eng. **52**, 273–285 (2010). https://doi.org/10.1007/s11576-010-0238-y
11. Aier, S., Winter, R.: St.Galler Anwenderforum. https://awf.iwi.unisg.ch/. Accessed 04 Oct 2020
12. Følstad, A.: Living labs for innovation and development of information and communication technology: a literature review. Electron. J. Virtual Organ. Netw. **10**, 99–129 (2008)
13. Abraham, R., Aier, S., Winter, R.: Crossing the line: overcoming knowledge boundaries in enterprise transformation. Bus. Inf. Syst. Eng. **57**, 3–13 (2015). https://doi.org/10.1007/s12599-014-0361-1
14. Winter, R.: Design science research in Europe. Eur. J. Inf. Syst. **17**, 470–475 (2008). https://doi.org/10.1057/ejis.2008.44
15. Vom Brocke, J., Winter, R., Hevner, A., Maedche, A.: Accumulation and evolution of design knowledge in design science research – a journey through time and space. J. Assoc. Inf. Syst. **21**, 520–544 (2020). https://doi.org/10.17705/1jais.00611
16. Goldkuhl, G.: Pragmatism vs interpretivism in qualitative information systems research. Eur. J. Inf. Syst. **21**, 135–146 (2012). https://doi.org/10.1057/ejis.2011.54

17. Wicks, A.C., Freeman, R.E.: Organization studies and the new pragmatism: positivism, anti-positivism, and the search for ethics. Organ. Sci. **9**, 123–140 (1998). https://doi.org/10.1287/orsc.9.2.123
18. Blumer, H.: Symbolic Interactionism: Perspective and Method. University of California Press, Berkeley, CA (1969)
19. Paré, G.: Investigating information systems with positivist case research. Commun. Assoc. Inf. Syst. **13**, 233–264 (2004). https://doi.org/10.17705/1cais.01318
20. Eisenhardt, K.M., Graebner, M.E.: Theory building from cases: opportunities and challenges. Acad. Manag. J. **50**, 25–32 (2007). https://doi.org/10.5465/AMJ.2007.24160888
21. Ghauri, P., Grønhaug, K., Strange, R.: Research Methods in Business Studies. Cambridge University Press, Cambridge (2020). https://doi.org/10.1017/9781108762427
22. Flick, U.: An Introduction to Qualitative Research. Sage, Thousand Oaks, CA (2014)
23. Eisenhardt, K.M.: Building theories from case study research. Acad. Manag. Rev. **14**, 532–550 (1989). https://doi.org/10.5465/AMR.1989.4308385
24. Urquhart, C., Lehmann, H., Myers, M.D.: Putting the "theory" back into grounded theory: guidelines for grounded theory studies in information systems. Inf. Syst. J. **20**, 357–381 (2010). https://doi.org/10.1111/j.1365-2575.2009.00328.x
25. Gregor, S., Müller, O., Seidel, S.: Reflection, abstraction, and theorizing in design and development research. In: ECIS 2013 – Proceedings of the 21st European Conference on Information Systems. Paper 74 (2013)
26. vom Brocke, J., Hevner, A., Maedche, A. (eds.): Design Science Research. Cases. Springer International, Cham (2020). https://doi.org/10.1007/978-3-030-46781-4
27. Haki, K., Beese, J., Aier, S., Winter, R.: The evolution of information systems architecture: an agent-based simulation model. MIS Q. Manag. Inf. Syst. **44**, 155–184 (2020). https://doi.org/10.25300/MISQ/2020/14494
28. Winter, R.: Construction of situational information systems management methods. Int. J. Inf. Syst. Model. Des. **3**, 67–85 (2012). https://doi.org/10.4018/jismd.2012100104
29. Frey, B.S.: Publishing as prostitution? – Choosing between one's own ideas and academic success. Public Choice. **116**, 205–223 (2003)
30. Mertens, P.: Zufriedenheit ist die Feindin des Fortschritts – ein Blick auf das Fach Wirtschaftsinformatik. In: Arbeitspapier Nr. 4/2004. Universität Erlangen-Nürnberg, Bereich Wirtschaftsinformatik I, Nürnberg (2004)
31. Preston, D.S., Karahanna, E.: Antecedents of IS strategic alignment: a nomological network. Inf. Syst. Res. **20**, 159–179 (2009). https://doi.org/10.1287/isre.1070.0159
32. Carlile, P.R.: Transferring, translating, and transforming: an integrative framework for managing knowledge across boundaries. Organ. Sci. **15**, 555–568 (2004). https://doi.org/10.1287/orsc.1040.0094
33. Levina, N., Vaast, E.: The emergence of boundary spanning competence in practice: implications for implementation and use of information systems. MIS Q. **29**, 335–363 (2005). https://doi.org/10.2307/25148682
34. Nicolai, A., Seidl, D.: That's relevant! Different forms of practical relevance in management science. Organ. Stud. **31**, 1257–1285 (2010). https://doi.org/10.1177/0170840610374401

The Connection Between Winter and Information Systems

Reima Suomi

Abstract The article documents a systematic literature review on the impacts of the season of winter on Information Systems. The search delivered 43 articles, of which 36 ended up to content analysis. On the contrary to the original research idea, winter seems to have no whatsoever impact on information systems, at least according to our sample. On the contrary, information systems are used to support key society activities in winter conditions. According to the findings the most important areas are road and airport maintenance and management in winter conditions, and increasing of wheat crops in winter time.

Keywords Winter · Information systems · Impact · Effect · Interaction

1 Introduction

The original research idea of this paper was to study the impact of Professor Robert Winter on information systems and their research. After some preliminary investigations it was however concluded that the season "winter" might however have some more impact on those than the professor Robert Winter, whose impact by any means however is not marginal.

Also, the study is on the impact of the season winter on information systems, and how it is reflected in academic research. Again, after some initial analysis, it turned out that winter seems not much to be impacting information systems, but—on the other way around—information systems might impact winter conditions in offering support to understand, control and manage them.

R. Suomi (✉)
University of Turku, Turku, Finland
e-mail: reima.suomi@utu.fi

© The Author(s), under exclusive license to Springer Nature Switzerland AG 2021
S. Aier et al. (eds.), *Engineering the Transformation of the Enterprise*,
https://doi.org/10.1007/978-3-030-84655-8_23

369

2 Methodology

A systematic literature review was performed following the guidance of leading
guidance in literature [1, 2]. For the sake of simplicity and free access to resources
search was limited to the tool of Google Scholar.

In the search the option in which both words "winter" and "information system"
had to be in the title of the entry included was used. The time frame of the entries was
limited to this millennium, also to entries made in year 2000 or later. The search
returned 43 entries.

To make some sensitivity analysis, similar search with terms. Combination
"summer" and "information system" was not more popular than winter, 40 entries
were found. To rise the abstraction level neither helped, the combination "season"
and "information system" delivered just 30 entries. Search terms "winter" and "IS"
were not successful, as the results made no difference between the acronym IS for
information systems and the English verb "is". Turning to German language neither
helped, the search on terms "winter" and "informationssystem" delivered one entry,
on gamekeeping. As a final test, the Finnish language was tried (in Nordic countries
there is anyway hard winter). However, the search combination "talvi" and
"tietojärjestelmä" provided zero findings on Google Scholar (Table 1).

After reading the material provided by Google Scholar and some extra searches
on Google and Google Scholar, seven articles were dropped out of the analysis.
Three articles were dropped as "winter" in their data refereed to the issue of the
journal, not to the title. One article was dropped out because it was a newspaper
article. Of two potentially interesting articles no further trace was found. One article
without further track would have been from Switzerland with an interesting topic:
avalanche management. Sadly, the original article was not found. One article was
dropped out of analysis as it seemed to be in Chinese, just the title was in English.
Total of 36 articles were included in further analysis, these articles are in Appendix.
The entries of the references are in the form that Google Scholar automatically
exported to EndNote library, unfortunately all not very structured or neat.

Table 1 Alternative literature searches

Key terms	Entries found
winter IS	2300
winter information	690
winter data	2030
summer information system	40
season information system	31
winter, informationssystem	1
sommer informationssystem	0

3 Results

One central area of interaction between winter and information systems emerged as dominant in the content analysis. Logistic, and especially road maintenance and management. A total of 20 articles in this group was found, publications both in conferences and similar forums, and in academic journal. To the area of logistics also belonged airport management, again in challenges during the winter season in freezing countries at that season, with four articles found. One of these previous articles was discussing both airport and road management.

Another area of academic discussion was that of agriculture, and more exactly the increase of crops in winter time, especially for wheat. A total of six articles was found in this category. Also oat got its attention in one article.

Two articles were deemed to be in the area of biology. One was on systems support for browse use of trees and shrubs (by birds mainly) and one on the winter birth population in river and lake areas in Turkey.

Tourism was represented with one article on Geographic Information System support for winter tourism. One article was to support with Information Systems elderly people's housing. One article discussed also logistics, but this time waterway management (Caspian Sea in winter). One article aimed to support winter sports arrangement (Harbin 24th winter universiade). One article was on geosciences, more exactly on an information system support for evapotranspiration calculation (Table 2).

4 Discussion

It seems that we have built information systems as an artefact that is not impacted at all by seasons, not even the hard winter. On the contrary, information systems seem to be used to help in the control and management of winter conditions, especially for the management of road and airport infrastructures.

Another area of interest is related to nature, both from agriculture and biology point of view. Crop management for winter wheat seems to be an import topic, as well as the ornithological aspect of bird winter behavior. The later also seems to have

Table 2 Content analysis of the articles

Area	Topic	Entries found
Logistics	Road management	19
Logistics	Airport management	3
Logistics	Airport and road management	1
Agriculture	Crop management (mainly wheat)	6
Biology	Wild birds and their and other species nurturing	2
Others		5

R. Suomi

some connections. With tourism, that has its special characteristics in winter, as discussed in one article.

The literature review was started with the idea that articles on how winter (or maybe seasons in general) affect information systems. Topics like electricity use and heat production and use on computing machinery were expected to be encountered. Likewise research on topics such as sensitivity of hardware on cold was anticipated, as well as how cold affects different telecommunication media. On the software side, one could for example how one models and displays snow in computer games and similar visual environments. A big area of research could be how electronic commerce, social media use, and healthcare IS solutions—just to take up a few key area examples—adjust to seasonal variations. However, all this was absent in the sample. Somehow the search neither caught any material from meteorology, a scientific area that surely must take seasons to its agenda. True, using just the term "information system" to represent information and communication technology in its various forms was of course limiting findings.

In total, seasons in general and winter in particular seem not to be important topics in IS research. Admittedly, our sample and analysis was rather modest, but it surely gives some basic understanding of the topic area. The positive finding was that the area in every case keeps up activity: articles were also found from the most recent years.

The topic is not without its merits. Worldwide, seasons affect the whole function of the society, and information systems surely get their share of these effects. Seasons are very different in different regions of the world, and seasonal variations in different activities can vary from non-existing to very strong. The topic surely deserves more attention in the future.

The study has of course its limitations. Using just database platform (Google Scholar) to find studies is a very much limiting factor. The search terms were also just kept simple and plain. Having more than one researcher analyzing the material could also have brought up new ideas to discussion.

5 Conclusions

It turns that the original research idea of studying the impact of Professor Robert Winter on information systems and their research would have been more lucrative: Alone Google Scholar returned 3,420,000 entries with the search term "Robert Winter". Also the season winter beaten with ample marginal in this setting! I want to congratulate Professor Robert Winter for this achievement and for the occasion of his 60th birthday, also as a colleague born in the same year.

As an epilogue, even though absolutely so already before, after this article professor Robert Winter can be considered as seasoned.

Appendix: The Entries Accepted for Content Analysis (n = 36)

	Article	Forum	Area	Topic
1	Abdi, A., Lind, H., & Birgisson, B. (2012). Use of Road Weather Information System (RWIS) as assistive tool for effective winter road maintenance: Technical and contractual interactions'. *International journal of engineering and technology, 2*(12), 2002–2012.	Journal	Logistics	Road maintenance
2	Burkheimer, D. (2000). Iowa DOT weather information system to support winter maintenance operations. MID-CONTINENT TRANSPORTATION SYMPOSIUM PROCEEDINGS	Conference paper	Logistics	Road maintenance
3	Çelik, A. D. E. Determination Of Ornithological Richness Of Erçek Lake, Dönemeç And Bendimahi Deltas (Van/Turkey) In Winter Season And Mapping With Geographic Information System. INTERNATIONAL JOURNAL OF SCIENTIFIC & TECHNOLOGY RESEARCH VOLUME 6, ISSUE 04, APRIL 2017	Journal	Biology	Ornitology
4	Harbaugh, C. R., & Norville, J. M. (2020). *Winter Severity Index: Using Road Weather Information System Data to Improve Preparedness for the Pennsylvania Department of Transportation.* Paper presented at the 100th American Meteorological Society Annual Meeting.	Conference paper	Logistics	Road maintenance
5	Hu, J., Wang, Q., Sadek, A. W., & Wang, Z. (2013). *Transportation System Performance Under Inclement Winter Weather: Perspectives from Weather-Induced Multiple Hazard Situations and Traveler Information.* Transportation Research Board 92nd Annual Meeting	Conference paper	Logistics	Road maintenance
6	Kochumman, G., & Nixon, W. (2003). A Prototype System to Extract Winter Weather Information for Road Users. *International journal of the computer, the internet and management, 11*(1), 42–50.	Journal	Logistics	Road maintenance
7	Kramberger, T. (2015). A Contribution to Better Organized Winter Road Maintenance by Integrating the Model in a Geographic Information System. In	Book	Logistics	Road maintenance

(continued)

Article	Forum	Area	Topic
Encyclopedia of Information Science and Technology, Third Edition (pp. 5431–5441): IGI Global.			
8 Kurihara, T., Takebayashi, Y., & Oka, T. (2001). Field Test of Residential Remote-care System for Elderly People-Measuremental Study on Housing Indoor Environment and the Information Feedback in Winter. *TRANSACTIONS-SOCIETY OF HEATING AIR CONDITIONING AND SANITARY ENGINEERS OF JAPAN*, 77–88.	Journal	Housing	Indoor environment
9 Kwon, T. J., Fu, L., & Melles, S. J. (2017). Location optimization of road weather information system (RWIS) network considering the needs of winter road maintenance and the traveling public. *Computer-Aided Civil and Infrastructure Engineering, 32*(1), 57–71.	Journal	Logistics	Road maintenance
10 Köck, K., Paulitsch, H., Randeu, W., Teschl, R., & Perschl, G. (2006). *WIIS-Weather Image Information System: A new weather information and early warning system for winter road maintenance.* Paper presented at the World Road Association AIPCR, XII International Winter Road Congress.	Conference paper	Logistics	Road maintenance
11 LIANG, L., CHEN, Y.-q., GAO, W.-s., SUI, P., & CHEN, D.-d. (2009). 2, ZHANG Wei1 (1. Circular Agriculture Research Center, China Agricultural University, Beijing 100193, China; 2. Agricultural Information Institute, Chinese Academy of Agricultural Sciences, Beijing 100081, China); Life Cycle Environmental Impact Assessment in Winter Wheat-Summer Maize System in North China Plain [J]. *Journal of Agro-Environment Science, 8.*	Journal	Agriculture	Crops management
12 Mahoney, W. (2001). *An Advanced Weather Information Decision Support System for winter Road Maintenance.* Paper presented at the 8th World Congress on Intelligent Transport SystemsITS America, ITS Australia, ERTICO (Intelligent Transport Systems and Services-Europe).	Conference paper	Logistics	Road maintenance

(continued)

	Article	Forum	Area	Topic
13	Mahoney, W., & Myers, W. (2003). The Winter Road Maintenance Decision Support System (MDSS) Project Update and Future Plans, Preprints, 19th Conf. on Interactive Information and Processing Systems, Long Beach, CA. *Amer. Meteor. Soc, 10.*	Conference paper	Logistics	Road maintenance
14	Matsuzawa, M., Kajiya, Y., & Yamagiwa, Y. (2005). *Survey on the Effectiveness of Snowstorm Information Provision in the Winter Road Mainte-nance Decision Support System.* Paper presented at the 12th World Congress on Intelligent Transport SystemsITS AmericaITS JapanERTICO.	Conference paper	Logistics	Road maintenance
15	MINBASHI, M. M., RAHIMIAN, M. H., BAGHESTANI, M., ALI, Z. M., KHEIRKHAH, M., NAZER, K. S., & DIEHJI, A. (2013). DETERMINATION THE PHENOLOGY AND USING GEOGRAPHIC INFORMATION SYS-TEM (GIS) FOR MANAGEMENT WINTER WILD OAT (AVENA LUDOVICIANA) IN WHEAT FIELDS.	Journal	Agriculture	Crops management
16	Mohammed, S., Alsafadi, K., Ali, H., Mousavi, S. M. N., Kiwan, S., Hennawi, S., . . . Ali, R. (2020). Assessment of land suitability potentials for winter wheat cultivation by using a multi criteria decision Support-Geographic information system (MCDS-GIS) approach in Al-Yarmouk Basin (S syria). *Geocarto International*, 1–19.	Journal	Agriculture	Crops management
17	Motoda, Y., Fujishima, K., & Ogata, Y. (2000). *Road surface condition information system for the winter sea-son.* Paper presented at the 7th World Congress on Intelligent Transport Systems.	Conference paper	Logistics	Road maintenance
18	Nagata, Y., Hagiwara, T., Araki, K., Kaneda, Y., & Sasaki, H. (2008). Application of road visibility informa-tion system to winter maintenance. *Transportation Research Record, 2055* (1), 128–138.	Journal	Logistics	Road maintenance
19	Nelson, R. J. (2009). Information Flow System for Winter Service. *Routes/ Roads, 342.*	Journal	Logistics	Road maintenance

(continued)

	Article	Forum	Area	Topic
20	Ohiro, T., Takakura, K., Maruyama, T., & Morinaga, H. (2014). *EFFICIENT WINTER ROAD MANAGEMENT USING A CONTACT AREA INFOR- MATION SENSING (CAIS)-BASED ROAD SURFACE CONDITION JUDG- MENT SYSTEM. PIARC.* Paper presented at the XIV INTERNA- TIONAL WINTER ROAD CON- GRESS, Session T5-5.	Conference paper	Logistics	Road maintenance
21	Oshima, J. (2000). Outline of a mobile collection system of winter road surface information. *Journal of Snow Engineer- ing of Japan, 16*(2), 109–110.	Journal	Logistics	Road maintenance
22	Pasero, E., Moniaci, W., & Raimondo, G. (2008). AWIS: An airport winter information system. *Proceedings of the XIV Standing International Road Weather Commission (SIRWEC), Prague, Czech Republic*, 14–16.	Conference paper	Logistics	Airport management
23	Paulitsch, H., & Perschl, G. (2005). *An automatic Weather Information System for Airport Winter Operation.* Paper presented at the SWIFT 2005.	Conference paper	Logistics	Airport management
24	Paulitsch, H., Perschl, G., & Randeu, W. (2008). *WIIS–A versatile weather information and warning system for the winter service on roads and airports, for traffic control and air safety improve- ment.* Paper presented at the Proceedings of The Lakeside Conference-Safety in Mobility 2008.	Conference paper	Logistics	Airport manage- ment Road maintenance
25	Rea, R. V., Svendsen, J. D., & Massicotte, H. B. (2017). Combining photography and a geographic informa- tion system to measure winter browse use. *Alces: A Journal Devoted to the Biology and Management of Moose, 52*, 67–72.	Journal	Biology	Browse use of trees and shrubs
26	Sha, S., Zhang, M., Wang, W., Zhong, Z., Hong, S., & Li, M. (2014). *A remote monitoring system for winter jujube environment and growth information.* Paper presented at the 2014 Montreal, Quebec Canada July 13–July 16, 2014.	Conference paper	Agriculture	Crops management
27	Sukuvaara, T., Mäenpää, K., Stepanova, D., & Karsisto, V. (2020). Vehicular Networking Road Weather Information System Tailored for Arctic Winter Con- ditions. *International Journal of Com- munication Networks and Information Security, 12*(2), 281–288.	Journal	Logistics	Road maintenance

(continued)

	Article	Forum	Area	Topic
28	Sukuvaara, T., Mäenpää, K., Ylitalo, R., Konttaniemi, H., Petäjäjärvi, J., Veskoniemi, J., & Autioniemi, M. (2015). Vehicular networking road weather information system tailored for arctic winter conditions. *International Journal of Communication Networks and Information Security, 7*(1), 60.	Journal	Logistics	Road maintenance
29	Šváb, P., Korba, P., Albert, M., & Kolesár, J. (2019). *Information system to support the management of winter airport maintenance.* Paper presented at the 2019 New Trends in Aviation Development (NTAD).	Journal	Logistics	Airport management
30	Wei, Y. (2007). 2, Wang Xiu1, Ma Wei1, Li Min-zan2 (1. National Engineering Research Center for Information Technology in Agriculture, Beijing 100097, China; 2. Key Laboratory of Modern Precision Agriculture System Integration Research, Ministry of Education, China Agricultural University, Beijing 100083, China); Variable-rate fertilizing for winter wheat based on canopy spectral reflectance [J]. *Journal of Jilin University (Engineering and Technology Edition), 6.*	Journal	Agriculture	Crops management
31	WU, Q.-w., XING, W., MA, L.-h., & XU, Q.-h. (2010). The research and establishment of sports event information system model for Harbin 24th winter universiade. *Journal of Qiqihar University (Natural Science Edition)*(1), 20.	Journal	Sport	Event management
32	Xing, Q., Wu, B., Zhu, W., & Lu, S. (2013). *The improvement of et calculation in winter by introducing radar-based aerodynamic roughness information into ETWatch system.* Paper presented at the 2013 IEEE International Geoscience and Remote Sensing Symposium-IGARSS.	Conference paper	Geoscience	evapotranspiration (ET) calculation
33	Yaitskaya, N., Lychagina, Y., & Berdnikov, S. (2014). The ice conditions study of the Caspian Sea during the winter periods 2008–2010 using satellite monitoring data and geographical information system. *Fresenius Environmental Bulletin, 23*(11), 2771–2777.	Journal	Logistics	Waterway management

(continued)

	Article	Forum	Area	Topic
34	Yansheng, D. (2012). 1, Chen Hongping 2, Wang Huifang 1, 3, Gu Xiaohe 1, Wang Jihua 1 (1. Beijing Research Center for Information Technology in Agriculture, Beijing 100097, China; 2. Key Laboratory of Regional Climate-Environment Research for Temperate East Asia, Institute of Atmospheric Physics, Chinese Academy of Sciences, Beijing 100029, China; 3. Institute of Agricultural Remote Sensing and Information System Application, Zhejiang University, Hangzhou 310029, China); Assessing freeze injury to winter wheat with multi-temporal HJ-1 satellite imagery [J]. *Transactions of the Chinese Society of Agricultural Engineering, 20*	Journal	Agriculture	Crops management
35	Yoon, G.-Y., Kim, N.-H., Choi, H.-K., Jung, D.-Y., Choi, S.-H., & Kim, G.-T. (2011). A winter road weather information system using ubiquitous sensor network. *Journal of Korea Multimedia Society, 14*(3), 392–402.	Journal	Logistics	Road maintenance
36	ÖCAL, S., & USUL, N. (2006). DEVELOPING A GEOGRAPHIC INFORMATION SYSTEM FOR SARIKAMIŞ WINTER TOURISM CENTER.	Conference paper	Tourism	Winter tourism support

References

1. Okoli, C., Schabram, K.: A guide to conducting a systematic literature review of information systems research. Sprouts: Working Papers on Information Systems, pp. 10–26 (2010)
2. Vom Brocke, J., et al.: Standing on the shoulders of giants: challenges and recommendations of literature search in information systems research. Commun. Assoc. Inf. Syst. 37(1), 9 (2015)